Invaluable source material for professional theatre directors and for students of English dramatic literature is provided by this detailed examination of playhouse procedures for Shakespeare's own acting company. In careful analysis, T. J. King reveals how the size and composition of the casts of characters for Shakespeare's plays were determined by common theatrical practices at London playhouses between 1590 and 1642. King closely examines manuscripts, contemporary playbooks, and authoritative texts of Shakespeare to determine the numbers of actors required and the procedures for actors doubling roles. The volume contains numerous illustrations of playhouse documents as well as tables and lists of actors, plays, and roles.

Casting Shakespeare's plays

Casting Shakespeare's plays

London actors and their roles,

1590 – 1642

T. J. KING

Professor of English
The City College of the
City University of New York

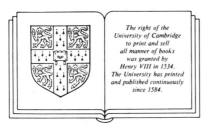

The right of the
University of Cambridge
to print and sell
all manner of books
was granted by
Henry VIII in 1534.
The University has printed
and published continuously
since 1584.

CAMBRIDGE UNIVERSITY PRESS

Cambridge   New York   Port Chester
Melbourne   Sydney

Published by the Press Syndicate of the University of Cambridge
The Pitt Building, Trumpington Street, Cambridge CB2 1RP
40 West 20th Street, New York, NY 10011-4211, USA
10 Stamford Road, Oakleigh, Victoria 3166, Australia

First published 1992

Printed in Great Britain at the University Press, Cambridge

Cataloguing in publication records for this book
are available from the British Library

Library of Congress cataloguing in publication data
King, T. J. (Thomas James), 1925–
    Casting Shakespeare's plays: London actors and their roles, 1590–1642/T. J. King.
        p.   cm.
Includes bibliographical references and index.
ISBN 0 521 32785 7
1. Shakespeare, William, 1564–1616 – Stage history – To 1625.
2. Shakespeare, William, 1564–1616 – Stage history – 1625–1800.
3. Shakespeare, William, 1564–1616 – Stage history – England – London.
4. Theater – England – London – Casting – History – 17th century.
5. Theater – England – London – Casting – History – 16th century.
6. Actors – England – London.   I. Title.
PR3095.K5   1991 792'.028'0942109031–dc20 90–26180 CIP

ISBN 0 521 32785 7 hardback

For Emily

Contents

Illustrations

Acknowledgements

I hope my notes clearly indicate my extensive debt to earlier scholarship. Here it is a pleasure to give thanks to those who have helped my work in a more personal way. I am especially grateful to Sean Magee, who encouraged me in our lengthy correspondence during the early stages of this inquiry, and to G. R. Hibbard, who invited me to speak at the Ninth International Conference on Elizabethan Theatre held at the University of Waterloo in July 1981. My paper, 'The King's Men on Stage: Actors and Their Parts, 1611–1632', appears in *The Elizabethan Theatre IX*, ed. G. R. Hibbard (Port Credit, Ontario 1986), and I am grateful for permission to reprint parts of it here. Thanks are also due to several persons who have offered helpful questions and criticism at later stages of my investigation: Linda Anderson, John H. Astington, Bernard Beckerman, Thomas L. Berger, Herbert Berry, David Bevington, Judith Brugger, S. P. Cerasano, Margaret Emory, Andrew Gurr, Trevor Howard-Hill, Robert G. Hunter, Michael Jamieson, Scott McMillin, Arthur H. Scouten, Ann Pasternak Slater, and Leslie Thomson.

The authorities of the British Library, the Folger Shakespeare Library, the Henry E. Huntington Library, the P. G. Wodehouse Library at Dulwich College, and the Library of the Victoria and Albert Museum have all given prompt and considerate help in allowing me to examine and to obtain photographic copies of the primary documents for this study. The staffs of the City College of New York Library, Columbia University Library, and New City, New York, Library have also given unfailing and courteous help. My research was aided by two travel grants from the City University of New York Research Foundation.

Thanks are also given to the following for permission to reproduce illustrations: the Henry E. Huntington Library (for Nos. 1, 2, 3, 13, 14, 15, 16, 19, 20, 21, 22, 23, 24, 25, 26, 27); the British Library (4, 5, 6, 7, 10, 11, 12, 18); the Victoria and Albert Museum Library (8, 9); the County Record Office, Trowbridge, Wiltshire (17).

Finally, I owe the most to my wife, Joan, for her love and encouragement and to our daughter, Emily, who has helped this work in many ways.

Abbreviations

1 Shakespeare's plays

Ado	*Much Ado about Nothing*
Ant.	*Antony and Cleopatra*
AWW	*All's Well that Ends Well*
AYLI	*As You Like It*
Cor.	*Coriolanus*
Cym.	*Cymbeline*
Err.	*The Comedy of Errors*
Ham.	*Hamlet*
1H4	*The First Part of King Henry the Fourth*
2H4	*The Second Part of King Henry the Fourth*
H5	*King Henry the Fifth*
1H6	*The First Part of King Henry the Sixth*
2H6	*The Second Part of King Henry the Sixth*
3H6	*The Third Part of King Henry the Sixth*
H8	*King Henry the Eighth*
JC	*Julius Caesar*
John	*King John*
LLL	*Love's Labour's Lost*
Lear	*King Lear*
Mac.	*Macbeth*
MM	*Measure for Measure*
MND	*A Midsummer Night's Dream*
MV	*The Merchant of Venice*
Oth.	*Othello*
Per.	*Pericles*
R2	*King Richard the Second*
R3	*King Richard the Third*
Rom.	*Romeo and Juliet*
Shr.	*The Taming of the Shrew*
Temp.	*The Tempest*
TGV	*The Two Gentlemen of Verona*
Tim.	*Timon of Athens*
Tit.	*Titus Andronicus*
TN	*Twelfth Night*

TNK	*The Two Noble Kinsmen*
Tro.	*Troilus and Cressida*
Wiv.	*The Merry Wives of Windsor*
WT	*The Winter's Tale*

2 Other plays

BA	*The Battle of Alcazar* (Plot and Q-1594)
Barn.	*Sir John van Olden Barnavelt* (MS.)
BAYL	*Believe as you List* (MS.)
DF	*The Deserving Favorite* (1629)
DM	*The Duchess of Malfi* (1623)
DMF	*The Dead Man's Fortune* (Plot)
1FMW	*The First Part of the Fair Maid of the West* (1631)
2FMW	*The Second Part of the Fair Maid of the West* (1631)
Fred.	*Frederick and Basilea* (Plot)
Han.	*Hannibal and Scipio* (1637)
HL	*Holland's Leaguer* (1632)
HMF	*The Honest Man's Fortune* (MS.)
2HR	*The Second Part of Henry Richmond* (Plot)
KJM	*King John and Matilda* (1655)
Mess.	*The Tragedy of Messalina* (1640)
Pict.	*The Picture* (1630)
RA	*The Roman Actor* (1629)
Ren.	*The Renegado* (1630)
SMT	*The Second Maiden's Tragedy* (MS.)
2SDS	*The Second Part of the Seven Deadly Sins* (Plot)
SC	*The Soddered Citizen* (MS.)
Swis.	*The Swisser* (MS.)
1TC	*The First Part of Tamar Cam* (Plot)
Wed.	*The Wedding* (1629)
WGC	*The Wild Goose Chase* (1652)

3 Other abbreviations and short titles

Bentley	Gerald Eades Bentley, *The Profession of Player in Shakespeare's Time* (Princeton 1984)
C	Chorus
DS	Dumbshow
Diary	R. A. Foakes and R. T. Rickert (eds.), *Henslowe's Diary* (Cambridge 1961)
Documents	W. W. Greg (ed.), *Dramatic Documents from the Elizabethan Playhouses* (2 vols., Oxford 1931). Volume I contains commentary, volume II reproductions and transcripts.

E	Epilogue
ES	E. K. Chambers, *The Elizabethan Stage* (4 vols., Oxford 1923)
F	Folio
Folio	W. W. Greg, *The Shakespeare First Folio* (Oxford 1955)
Herbert	J. Q. Adams (ed.), *The Dramatic Records of Sir Henry Herbert* (New Haven 1917)
HLQ	*Huntington Library Quarterly*
Ind.	Induction
JCS	G. E. Bentley, *The Jacobean and Caroline Stage* (7 vols., Oxford 1941–68)
Meres	Francis Meres, *Palladis Tamia: Wits Treasury* (1598), as cited by *WS* II, 193–4
MP	*Modern Philology*
MRDE	*Medieval and Renaissance Drama in England*
MSC	*Malone Society Collections*
MSR	*Malone Society Reprints*
N&Q	*Notes and Queries*
Nungezer	E. Nungezer, *A Dictionary of Actors and of Other Persons Associated with the Public Representation of Plays in England before 1642* (New Haven 1929)
O	Octavo
OED	*Oxford English Dictionary*
P	Prologue
Papers	W. W. Greg (ed.), *The Henslowe Papers* (London 1907)
PBSA	*Papers of the Bibliographical Society of America*
Pr	Presenter
Q	Quarto
RES	*Review of English Studies*
SB	*Studies in Bibliography*
SP	*Studies in Philology*
SQ	*Shakespeare Quarterly*
SR	Edward Arber (ed.), *A Transcript of the Registers of the Company of Stationers of London: 1554–1640 A.D.* (5 vols., London and Birmingham 1875–94)
ShS	*Shakespeare Survey*
WS	E. K. Chambers, *William Shakespeare* (2 vols., Oxford 1930)
W&T	Stanley Wells and Gary Taylor with John Jowett and William Montgomery, *William Shakespeare: A Textual Companion* (Oxford 1987)

NOTES ON CONVENTIONS

All citations to Shakespeare's plays are to *The First Folio of Shakespeare*, the Norton facsimile, prepared by Charlton Hinman (New York 1968) – referred to in my text as

F – or to M. J. B. Allen and K. Muir (eds.), *Shakespeare's Plays in Quarto* (Berkeley 1981). The abbreviated titles of Shakespeare's plays have been modified from those used in the *Harvard Concordance to Shakespeare*. All act, scene, and line references to his plays are to the New Arden editions.

Citations to other early texts are to microfilm copies of manuscript playbooks and early printed plays, and to Greg's transcriptions of the playhouse plots, which my Appendix A reprints from *Documents*. In early documents, some dates are entered according to the Old Style calendar, in which the year ended on 25 March. I have silently emended these dates to conform with the modern calendar. I have retained original spellings in quotations except that I have silently emended the Elizabethan typographical conventions of i for j, initial v and medial u to conform with modern usage. In my tables of parts, the spellings of actors' names are retained as they first appear in the original documents, but in my text the spellings of actors' names are standardized according to the first listing in Nungezer.

## CHAPTER ONE

Introduction and tables 1–3

In recent years, scholars have offered many valuable studies of the Globe and other playhouses where the plays of Shakespeare and his contemporaries were first acted. As yet, however, there has been little systematic investigation of important questions about casting procedures for the Lord Chamberlain's Men, later known as the King's Men, the repertory company for which Shakespeare wrote his plays. For example: how many men and boys are required as actors for the earliest text of each play by Shakespeare? How many actors are required for the variant texts of these same plays? Which actors in Shakespeare's company usually play the principal male roles, and which play the principal female roles? Which actors play minor parts and mute supernumeraries? Which of these actors double in two or more roles? When actors double, how much time is usually allowed for each change of costume? To answer these and other questions about casting for Shakespeare's company, the present study closely examines eight manuscripts from performances at Elizabethan playhouses, fifteen pre-Restoration plays that identify the men and boys who play principal roles, and authoritative texts of all thirty-eight plays ascribed wholly or in part to Shakespeare. This evidence shows for the first time how the size and composition of Shakespeare's casts of characters were determined by common theatrical practices at London playhouses between 1590, about the time that the author began his work as a playwright, and 1642, when the theatres were closed by order of Parliament.[1] These findings will interest producers and directors of Shakespeare as well as theatre historians.

Although there is a wide range in the number of actors required in minor parts and as mute supernumeraries in the plays of Shakespeare and his contemporaries, the number of actors required in principal roles remains fairly constant: an average of ten men in principal male roles – defined empirically as those who speak twenty-five or more lines – and four boys in principal female roles – those who speak ten or more lines. My use of the term 'principal' to designate the actors who play leading roles follows Ben Jonson, who in his *Workes* (1616) lists Shakespeare as one of ten 'principall Comœdians' with the Lord Chamberlain's Men when they acted *Every Man in his Humour* in 1598 (Illustration 1) and as one of eight 'principall Tragœdians' with the King's Men when they acted *Sejanus* in 1603 (Illustration 2). The significance of the term 'principal' is also evident in the front matter of the Shakespeare First Folio (F), where the author and twenty-five other men are listed as 'the Principall Actors in all these Playes' (Illustration 3). Here it should be noted that in Elizabethan acting companies the sharers – the men who jointly own the assets of

(72)

This Comoedie was first
Acted, in the yeere
1 5 9 8.

By the then L. CHAMBERLAYNE
his Seruants.

The principall Comœdians were.

WILL SHAKESPEARE.	RIC. BVRBADGE.	
AVG. PHILIPS.	IOH. HEMINGS.	
HEN. CONDEL.	THO. POPE.	
WILL. SLYE.	CHR. BEESTON.	
WILL. KEMPE.	IOH. DVKE.	

With the allowance of the Master of REVELLS.

---

1 Ben Jonson, *Workes* (1616), p. 72, lists ten 'principall Comœdians' when the Lord Chamberlain's Men acted *Every Man in his Humour* in 1598.

(438)

This Tragœdie vvas firſt
acted, in the yeere
1603.

By the Kings *Maieſties*
SERVANTS.

The principall Tragœdians were,

RIC. BVRBADGE.   WILL. SHAKE-SPEARE.
AVG. PHILIPS.   IOH. HEMINGS.
WILL. SLY.   HEN. CONDEL.
IOH. LOWIN.   ALEX. COOKE.

With the allowance of the Maſter of REVELLS.

2 Ben Jonson, *Workes* (1616), p. 438, lists eight 'principall Tragœdians' when the King's Men
acted *Sejanus* in 1603.

the company and who share in its profits – usually play the principal roles. However, as will be shown, not all actors in principal roles are sharers, nor do all the available sharers appear in each of the plays that the company performs. My analysis of casting requirements therefore describes the leading actors as 'principals' rather than as 'sharers'.[2]

G. E. Bentley, *The Profession of Player in Shakespeare's Time* (Princeton 1984) provides a comprehensive study of customary playhouse practice, and he describes the documents that identify actors in principal roles. However, Bentley does not from this evidence draw inferences about the casting requirements for Shakespeare's plays. Instead, he cites a valuable introduction to this subject by William Ringler, Jr, 'The Number of Actors in Shakespeare's Early Plays', in *The Seventeenth Century Stage*, ed. G. E. Bentley (Chicago and London 1968), pp. 110–34. In his review of previous scholarship, Ringler cites T. W. Baldwin, *The Organization and Personnel of the Shakespearean Company* (Princeton 1927), who attempts to describe the personal characteristics that define the 'line of parts' played by each principal actor in Shakespeare's company. Baldwin then assigns one of these actors to each role in Shakespeare's plays when they were first performed.[3] However, as Ringler points out, Baldwin's theories do not take into account the wide variety of roles the actors in Shakespeare's company are known to have played. For example, Baldwin suggests that Richard Robinson is 'nearly always' one of the minor principal players who 'ranks as about first dignified handyman, of good presence and oratorical ability'.[4] But, as the present study observes, Robinson is identified in two decidedly dissimilar roles: in 1611 as a boy actor he plays the leading female role in *The Second Maiden's Tragedy* (*SMT*), the Lady who kills herself rather than yield to the lustful Tyrant; about 1619 in *The Duchess of Malfi* (*DM*), Robinson plays the evil Cardinal who murders his mistress, Julia, by having her kiss a poisoned Bible. Each of these roles differs significantly from what Baldwin describes as 'first dignified handyman'.

Furthermore, as Ringler observes, Baldwin does not take into account the well-established practice of doubling. For example, Baldwin observes that in *Believe as you List* (*BAYL*) William Penn plays the Jailer, whom Baldwin describes as 'both sympathetic and a bit whimsically humorous, though not broadly comic'.[5] However, Baldwin evidently overlooks the fact that in *BAYL*, Penn not only plays the Jailer (30 lines), he also doubles as the nondescript 2 Merchant (49 lines). Ringler notes an important exploratory article, W. J. Lawrence, 'The Practice of Doubling and its Influence on Early Dramaturgy', in *Pre-Restoration Stage Studies* (Cambridge, Mass. 1927), pp. 43–78 and a significant study by David M. Bevington, *From Mankind to Marlowe* (Cambridge, Mass. 1962), who shows 'the effect of troupe structure upon the creation and development of a popular dramatic structure'.[6]

Although Bevington does not extend his study to include the plays of Shakespeare, my own investigation owes much to his analysis of a group of approximately twenty plays dating from the 1530s through the 1570s, which are 'offered for acting', that is printed with casting lists to indicate how many actors are required to perform the play. For example, *Like Will to Like* (1568), a moral interlude by Ulpian Fulwell, shows how five actors 'may easily play' sixteen roles.[7] *Horestes* (1567), a moral interlude by John Pickering, shows how six actors can play twenty-seven roles. Here Bevington notes that in this play for the first time 'an author distinguishes between "bit" parts assigned to a trained player and those relegated to the extras'.[8] For *Clyomon and Clamydes* (1570), an heroical romance perhaps by Thomas Preston, six actors can play twenty-one roles. However, in this play the number of available supernumeraries is evidently variable: '*Enter King Alexander the Great, as valiantly set forth as may be, and as many souldiers as can.*'[9] My estimates about the casting requirements for Shakespeare's plays correspond closely to Bevington's estimates about the requirements for Marlowe's plays: *Tamburlaine the Great, Part One* (1587) 'could be performed easily by eleven men and four boys';[10] *Tamburlaine the Great, Part Two* (1588) 'could be handled easily by thirteen players, together with one or two boys';[11] *The Jew of Malta* (1589) 'requires at least seven experienced actors and three boys';[12] *Edward II* (1592) requires 'ten or so company members, additional hired actors, and two to four boys';[13] *Doctor Faustus* (1604 edition) 'could be performed by nine actors, one or two boys . . . and seven extras'.[14]

Ringler also observes that J. Englelen, 'Die Schauspieler-Ökonomie in Shakespeares Dramen', in *Shakespeare Jahrbuch* 62 (1926), 36–97 and 63 (1927), 75–158 and M. Sack, *Darstellerzahl und Rollenverteilung bei Shakespeare* (Leipzig 1928), have made preliminary studies of doubling in Shakespeare's plays, but Ringler finds 'their results are inconclusive because they concentrate on the major speaking parts and pay inadequate attention to the entire company, which must also include the mutes'.[15] However, Ringler does not take into account a brief but valuable study by Arthur Colby Sprague, *The Doubling of Parts in Shakespeare's Plays* (London 1966), who examines evidence about doubling in performance records of English professional acting companies. For example, Sprague lists fifty-five performances of *Hamlet* between 20 April 1730 (Goodman's Fields) and 30 April 1914 (Stratford-upon-Avon) in which the actor who plays Polonius doubles as First Gravedigger.[16]

Ringler defines the purpose of his own study: 'I do not wish at this time to guess which actors played what parts. I wish to ask only one question: "how many actors were available to Shakespeare for his earlier plays?"'.[17] Ringler lists the ten 'principall Comœdians' who acted Ben Jonson's *Every Man in his Humour* in 1598: William Shakespeare, Augustine Phillips, Henry Condell, William Sly, William Kempe, Richard Burbage, John Heminges, Thomas Pope, Christopher Beeston, and John Duke (see Illustration 1). Ringler notes: 'The first eight of these ten names reappear either as shareholders in the Globe lease of 21 February 1599 or as members of the company when it received its patent as the King's Men in 1603.'[18] Ringler further asserts: 'Beeston and Duke were probably hirelings, and the other hirelings in 1598 were probably Richard Cowley . . . and John Sinklo (or Sincler) . . . These were the twelve adult actors of the company in 1598.' His analysis then equates these twelve men with the number of adult actors required to perform the plays. However, as already suggested here, all the principal actors of the company – most of whom are named in the royal patents and in livery lists – do not appear together in any one of the King's Men plays that identify actors in principal parts. For example, the royal patent dated 24 June 1625 names thirteen King's Men,[19] but only eight of these are identified in the cast of seventeen men required for *The Roman Actor* (*RA*), licensed for performance on 11 October 1626.[20] Presumably the other nine male roles are played by unidentified hired men or playhouse attendants. Thus the number of principal actors available does not necessarily determine the number of actors who perform any given play.[21]

Nevertheless, Ringler contends: 'Between 1594 and 1599, Shakespeare *never* wrote a play for more than 16 actors including mutes, [and] the composition of his company during that period appears to have remained stable with 12 adults and 4 boys.'[22] He illustrates his argument with a Doubling Chart (Figure 4) for *A Midsummer Night's Dream* (*MND*) showing how it is possible for twelve men and four boys to act this play, but some of his suggestions about doubling are questionable. For example, Ringler's chart suggests that the actor who plays Theseus, the largest male role (218 lines in Q1), doubles as the Faerie (25 lines) who speaks with Puck in 2.1. However, in the King's Men plays that identify actors in principal parts, the actors who play the largest roles do *not* double. Furthermore, Ringler's chart suggests that the actors who play the adult male roles of Flute, Starveling, Snout, and Snug double as Peaseblossom, Cobweb, Moth, and Mustardseed, roles that most scholars assign to boy actors of the period.[23] However, evidence from eight Elizabethan playhouse documents shows that the boy actors with these companies do *not* play adult male roles, nor do adult actors play female roles. It is hoped that the present study – based on evidence from these documents and fifteen other pre-Restoration texts that identify actors and the roles they play – will provide reliable answers to some important questions that Ringler and other scholars have raised about the casting requirements for Shakespeare's plays.

As will be shown, authors of the period carefully planned the number of actors required for each play in a plot or outline listing the characters who appear in each scene, and this plot was submitted to the acting company for its approval before the author wrote dialogue for a given play. In most of the plays considered here, including those of Shakespeare, the men and boys who play the principal characters speak over 90% of the lines. This large share of lines spoken by principal roles makes it possible for the leading actors to rehearse the play without the supporting cast until shortly before the first public performance, at which time the company can enlist the hired men, playhouse attendants, and boys needed for minor parts. This procedure is indicated in seven playhouse manuscripts of the period – and in seven early texts of Shakespeare – where almost every actor's name entered in the margin or in a stage direction is that of a hired man who plays a minor part and who probably joined the cast late in the rehearsal period (see Appendix B). Flexibility in the number of mute supernumeraries is shown in *Titus Andronicus* (*Tit.* Q1-1594) where the direction for the triumphal entrance of Titus with Tamora, the Queen of the Goths, calls for '*others as many as can be*' (1.1.69).

My second chapter considers the casting requirements for eight playhouse documents used to regulate rehearsals and performances: four prompt books from the repertory of Shakespeare's company, the King's Men, and four playhouse plots – scene-by-scene outlines posted backstage to remind the actors about which parts they play – from the repertories of Lord Strange's Men and the Lord Admiral's Men. As will be shown, the actors who first performed Shakespeare's plays probably followed casting procedures similar to those followed by the other London companies of his day. Some actors moved from one company to another just as acting companies moved from one playhouse to another, so it seems likely that the theatrical practices and stage equipment used by these companies did not differ significantly.

Valuable evidence about Elizabethan theatrical practice is found in the records of Philip Henslowe, the financial manager and money-lender for several Elizabethan and Jacobean acting companies. This evidence is assembled in Henslowe's *Diary* and a collection known as the *Henslowe Papers*. In order to show the theatrical significance of these playhouse documents, it may be helpful here to review seven important steps taken when actors who worked with Henslowe acquired plays and prepared them for performance.

I. Henslowe – at the request of one or more of the actors – advanced 'earnest' money to an author or authors after the acting company had given its approval of a 'plot' that the author had prepared showing the outline of his proposed new play. The plot indicates the scene-by-scene order in which characters enter, and in this way the author shows the actors that the casting requirements for his new play are suitable for their company. Henslowe paid the author in instalments as he wrote the play, and Henslowe paid him in full when he delivered 'fair copy' of the 'book of the play'. When and if the play was performed, the actors repaid Henslowe from playhouse receipts.[24]

In two entries of his *Diary*, Henslowe mentions a plot or plots that Ben Jonson showed to the Admiral's Men:

> lent unto Bengemen Johnson the 3 of desembr 1597 ⎫
> upon a boocke wch he showed the plotte unto the   ⎪
> company wch he promysed to dd unto the company   ⎬ xxs
> at cryssmas next the some of . . .[25]   ⎭

There is no record of Jonson having completed this unidentified play, but almost a year later Henslowe notes payment to Robert Shaw and Edward Juby for two acts of what may be another play based on a plot by Jonson:

> Lent unto Robart shawe & Jewbey the 23 of octobr ⎫
> 1598 to lend unto mr Chapmane one his playe   ⎪
> boocke & ii ectes of A tragedie of bengemens plotte ⎬ xxx li
> the some of . . .[26]   ⎭

'Bengemens plotte' was probably a list of scenes with the characters appearing in each, such as we find in the fragment of a plot for the now lost *The Second Part of Henry Richmond* (*2HR*) by the actor-author Robert Wilson. This list of the characters, but not the actors, who appear in each of the first five scenes is in the hand of Shaw, who served as negotiator between the author and Henslowe:

> 1. Sce. Wm Wor: & Ansell & to them ye plowghmen
>   Q.& Eliza:
> 2. Sce: Richard ⎩ Catesbie, Lovell, Rice ap Tho: Blunt, Banester

   3. Sce: Ansell Davye Denys Hen: Oxf: Courtney Bou'chier & Grace to them Rice ap Tho:
     & his Soldiors
   4. Sce: Mitton Ban: his wyfe & children
   5. Sce: King Rich: Catesb: Lovell. Norf: Northumb: Percye[27]

This fragment is probably a scrap from a plot that Shaw had prepared with Wilson's assistance when Wilson first proposed the play. When Wilson wrote the play, he probably followed this plot – or a copy of it – as his plan for the sequence of scenes. On the back is a note, also in Shaw's hand, dated 8 November 1599 requesting that Henslowe pay Wilson for the completed book:

> mr Henshlowe we have heard their booke and lyke yt
> their pryce is eight pounds, wch I pray pay now to mr
> wilson according to our promysse . . .
>   yours Robt Shaa[28]

Also on 8 November 1599, Henslowe's *Diary* records a note from Wilson acknowledging receipt of eight pounds as payment in full:

> Receeaved of mr. Ph: Hinchlow by a note
> under the hand of mr Rob: Shaw in full
> payment for the second pt of Henrye
> Richmond sold to him & his Companye   } viii li
> the some of eight powndss Current moneye
> the viiit daye of November 1599
>   By me R Wilson[29]

Two other authors mention plots in their notes to Henslowe, and in each case the author refers to the plot as a necessary guide for writing the play. The first author is John Day, who with William Haughton received forty shillings as 'earnest' money for *The Conquest of the West Indies*:

> Lent unto John daye & wm hawghton the 4 of
> aprell 1601 in earnest of playe called the conqueste   } xxxx s
> of the weste enges at the apoyntment of
> Samwell Rowlye the some of . . .[30]

Day, or Haughton, or both, received subsequent payments for this play, and in Day's note to Henslowe, which Greg dates 4 June 1601 (?), Day refers to having absent-mindedly left with Henslowe the plot that he had prepared for this play, on which he was apparently still at work:

> I have occasion to be absent about the plott of the
> Indyes therfre pray delyver it to will Hamton sadler
>   by me John Daye[31]

Henslowe made further payments to the authors for this play, and what was probably the last partial payment was made on 1 September:

> Lent unto the company the 1 of september to
> Lend John daye in pt of payment of   } x s
> A Boocke called the weaste enges the some of . . .[32]

The company may have begun rehearsals shortly after this last recorded payment to the author and given the first performance of the play about a month later, or shortly after 31 September [*sic*], when Henslowe lent ten pounds and ten shillings to the company 'to bye divers thinges and sewttes & stockenes for the playe of the weaste inges'.[33] However, as will be shown, some other plays probably had shorter rehearsal periods.

A plot for another play (not identified) is described in a note to Henslowe from the actor-author Nathan Field; Greg suggests a date at the end of June 1613, at which time Field was one of the leading actors for Lady Elizabeth's Men:

> Mr. Hinchlow
> Mr. Dawborne and I have spent a great deale of time in conference about this plott, wch will make as beneficiall a play as hath Come these seaven years. It is out of his love he detaines it for us, onely [ten pounds] is desir'd in hand, for wch wee will be bound to bring you in the play finish'd upon the first day of August . . . Pray let us know when wee shall speake wth you; Till when and Ever I rest Yor loving and obedient Son: Nat: Field[34]

2. After the company approved the plot and the players made initial payment, the author or authors wrote the dialogue for the play, which followed the sequence of scenes that one or more authors had outlined in the plot. The anonymous *The Dead Man's Fortune* (*DMF*, see Appendix A) is an example of a plot that lists the names of the characters who appear in each scene, but not the names of the actors who play the principal roles. The only actors identified – Burbage, Robert Lee, Darlowe and a boy (?) called Sam – are assigned to minor parts, and in some cases it is uncertain which part each actor plays.[35] The plot also indicates that a 'tyre man' plays an Attendant. One possible explanation for the state of *DMF* is that the actors used it at rehearsal when they assigned minor roles. Presumably, before the actors performed the play publicly, the playhouse scribe prepared another, complete plot that identified each of the actors and the part or parts he played. Four playhouse plots that identify most of the actors are discussed below and transcribed in Appendix A.

3. As noted, before the acting company or Henslowe made final payment, they expected to receive 'fair copy', that is, a text free from the tangles and confusions usually associated with 'foul papers'. For example, on 17 April 1613, Henslowe agrees to pay Daborne twenty pounds for a tragedy, *Machiavel and the Devil*. In the next few weeks, Henslowe makes partial payments to Daborne as he sends to the players sheets 'fayr written'. On 25 June, Daborne writes: 'I have took extraordynary payns with the end & altered one other scean in the third act which they have now in parts.'[36] Here the playhouse scribe apparently began to prepare the actors' parts even before the author had finished writing the play.

4. The only extant Elizabethan actor's part is the one a playhouse scribe prepared for the title role of Robert Greene's *Orlando Furioso*. This was probably performed at the Rose on 21 or 22 February 1592 by Edward Alleyn, an Admiral's Man, who was then acting with Lord Strange's Men.[37] Although the part is mutilated and defective in many places, it preserves about 530 lines of cues and speeches for Orlando written on strips of paper six inches wide and varying from ten to sixteen inches in length. When Alleyn used this part, the strips were pasted together to form a long roll (hence

the French *rôle*). These strips have now been separated and bound as leaves in a volume preserved among Alleyn's papers at Dulwich College where it now forms MS. 1, Item 138. The cues for Orlando usually consist of two or three words to the right of a line drawn across the strip. For example, on strip 5 the phrase 'on his neck' is the cue for Orlando, who 'enters with a mans legg' and says:

> villayns provide me straight a lions skyne
> for I thou seest/ I am mighty Hercules
> see whers my massy clubb upon my neck
> I must to hell to fight with Cerberus.[38]

Most of the part is in a secretary hand, that of the playhouse scribe. He was apparently unable to read all of the text from which he copied the part, and he leaves blank spaces into which the actor can insert the appropriate words at rehearsal. For example, towards the bottom of strip 8 the scribe leaves a space into which another hand, which Greg identifies as Alleyn's, inserts an entire line of iambic pentameter probably derived from the prompt book: 'Inconstant base injurious & untrue'.[39]

   5. At rehearsals, a very important member of the company was the book-keeper, a term defined by John Higgens, *Nomenclator* (1585), as 'he that telleth the players their part when they are out and have forgotten, the prompter or book-holder'.[40] Thus in Elizabethan usage the terms 'book-keeper', 'book-holder', and 'prompter' are virtually synonymous, and hereafter I refer to this person as the book-keeper. Rehearsals were usually held in the morning with a public performance of another play in the afternoon. This work schedule is indicated by articles of agreement drawn up between Robert Dawes, an actor, and Philip Henslowe and Jacob Meade, dated 7 April 1614. They require that Dawes

> will and at all tymes during the said terme [of three years] duly attend all suche rehearsall
> which shall the night before the rehearsal be given publickly out . . . and [on] every daie
> whereon any play is or ought to be played be ready apparrelled to begin the play at the hower
> of three of the clock in the afternoon.[41]

The four manuscript prompt books examined here are prepared for performance by the King's Men: *SMT* probably by Thomas Middleton (1611), *Sir John van Olden Barnavelt* (*Barn.*) probably by John Fletcher and Philip Massinger (1619), *The Honest Man's Fortune* (*HMF*) by Nathan Field probably with help from Fletcher and Massinger (1625), and *BAYL* in the autograph of Massinger (1631). In each of these manuscripts, the book-keeper notes changes in the text, adds the names of a few minor actors, and adds cues for some, but not all, of the required properties and effects. Added at the end of *BAYL* is a list of properties that identifies indirectly the principal roles played by six leading actors of the company (Illustration 11). This list is in the hand of Edward Knight, book-keeper for the King's Men, who is also the scribe for the manuscript prompt book for *HMF* and the manuscript of *The Soddered Citizen* (*SC*). Knight's name appears first in the list of 'musicians and other necessary attendants' whom Sir Henry Herbert, Master of the Revels, protects from arrest 'during the Time of the Revels' in his order of 27 December 1624 (see Appendix C).

For each of these prompt books – and for each of the other plays that identify actors in principal roles – I prepare a table that tallies the number of lines spoken by each character and ranks them accordingly. These totals are significant because in *BAYL*, for example, we find that Joseph Taylor plays King Antiochus, the largest role (680 lines) and John Lowin plays Flaminius, the second largest role (597 lines). These men are also identified as the leading actors of the company in the *Diary of Thomas Crosfield* for 18 July 1634, who notes that for the Kings Men at Blackfriars, the masters or chief players were Taylor and Lowin.[42]

The prompt book for *Barn.* does not identify the actors who play the three largest principal roles, Barnavelt (790 lines), the Prince of Orange (387 lines), and Leidenberch (221 lines), and, given the length of these roles, it is unlikely that the actors in these roles double. However, two actors who are identified in lesser principal roles double in smaller parts, and each actor is off-stage for a full scene for each change of costume. Early in the play, John Rice is identified as 1 Captain [English] (207 lines), and he is off-stage for 4.5 before he doubles as an important Servant (49 lines) in 5.1; he is then off-stage for 5.2 before he returns as 1 Captain in 5.3. Early in the play, Richard Robinson is identified as 1 Captain [Dutch] (45 lines), and he is off-stage for 4.4 and 4.5 before he doubles as Ambassador Boisise (40 lines) in 5.1; he is then off-stage for 5.2 before he returns as 1 Captain in 5.3. Both Rice and Robinson are included in the list of 'Principall Actors' in F (Illustration 3).

Most of the other actors' names added to the texts of the prompt books – and the early texts of Shakespeare – are those of hired men who play minor parts. For example, in *BAYL* William Pattrick, Nicholas Underhill, and William Mago are identified as Attendants, Guards and Officers in marginal notes added by Edward Knight, the book-keeper; these three men are also included on the list of 'musicians and other necessary attendants' who Sir Henry Herbert, Master of the Revels, protects from arrest 'during the Time of the Revels' in his order of 27 December 1624 (see Appendix C). Thomas Tawyer, another hired man on this list, is also named in the text of *MND* (F), where the direction '*Tawyer with a Trumpet before them*' precedes '*Enter Pyramus and Thisby, Wall, Moon-shine and Lyon*' (5.1.126). Also named on this list of hired men is Thomas Tuckfeild, who is identified as a mute with Theseus in *The Two Noble Kinsmen* (*TNK*), and John Rhodes, who is identified as 2 Creditor (6 lines) in *HMF*. This evidence suggests that there were two classes of adult actors: men named in the royal patents and livery lists who also played most of the principal roles, and hired men like Patrick, Underhill, Mago, Tawyer, Tuckfeild, and Rhodes, who could probably be ready to play minor parts with very little rehearsal. A principal actor might occasionally double in a minor part, but, as we shall see, very seldom did a hireling act a principal role.

The Admiral's Men probably observed similar distinctions between principal players and hired men. For example, on 8 December 1597 a note signed by Edward Alleyn records an agreement with William Kendall for the latter to be a 'Covenant servant' for two years with wages of ten shillings a week when playing in London and five shillings a week in the country.[43] Kendall is also identified in the plot for *The*

The Workes of William Shakespeare,

containing all his Comedies, Histories, and
Tragedies: Truely set forth, according to their first
ORIGINALL.

The Names of the Principall Actors
in all these Playes.

illiam Shakespeare.

Richard Burbadge.

John Hemmings.

Augustine Phillips.

William Kempt.

Thomas Poope.

George Bryan.

Henry Condell.

William Slye.

Richard Cowly.

John Lowine.

Samuell Crosse.

Alexander Cooke.

Samuel Gilburne.

Robert Armin.

William Ostler.

Nathan Field.

John Underwood.

Nicholas Tooley.

William Ecclestone.

Joseph Taylor.

Robert Benfield.

Robert Goughe.

Richard Robinson.

Iohn Shancke.

Iohn Rice.

3 William Shakespeare, *Comedies, Histories & Tragedies* (1623), sig. B2, lists twenty-
six 'Principall Actors in all these Playes'.

Battle of Alcazar (*BA*) – probably performed at the Rose some time between 1 December 1598 and 1 March 1599 – where he plays three mute parts and Hercules, a minor part (23 lines in Q-1594) (see Appendix A).

It should be emphasized that these seventeenth-century manuscripts differ from the prompt books prepared for present-day theatrical productions. A modern prompt book provides the complete text and stage directions for a given play, along with detailed information about the cues for lights, music, sounds, and scene changes, but the Elizabethan book-keeper did not enter all of this information in his prompt book. Instead, as noted, he prepared a plot, or scene-by-scene outline based on the plot that the author first submitted to the company. After an actor's name had been added for each of the characters, this plot was hung in the tiring house as a reminder for actors and stage-keepers. Thus when at rehearsals the book-keeper jotted in the book some actors' names and some of the properties and effects needed, he was probably taking notes that he later transferred to the plot. Seven other theatrical manuscripts, although not officially approved prompt books, may have been used for prompting at rehearsals because they include the names of actors who play minor parts and who probably joined the cast late in the rehearsal period. Two of these manuscripts specify that stage-keepers play Guards and Soldiers (see Appendix B). William Gascoyne, the stage-keeper who opens the trap door for Taylor in *BAYL*, is included in the list of 'necessary attendants' protected from arrest by the Master of the Revels (see Appendix C).

In my tables of parts for the prompt books and for other texts that identify actors and the roles they play, I underscore the names of these actors and their roles. For example, Table 9 shows that in *SMT* the boy actor Richard Robinson is identified as the Spirit of the Lady (22 lines) and presumably her person (136 lines). My tables also indicate possibilities for doubling, but I do not underscore the names of the roles unless the actors who play them are identified. For example, in *SMT* it is possible for the actor who plays the seventh largest male role, Sophonirus (72 lines) who is killed in 3.1, to double in the eighth largest role, the important 1 Soldier (46 lines) who first appears in 4.2. This possibility for doubling is consistent with evidence in other playhouse documents where an actor who doubles in lesser principal roles usually has an interval of one scene off-stage for each change of costume.

In the four prompt books for the King's Men, the number of principal actors ranges from seven for *SMT* to fourteen for *Barn.*, or an average of 10.5 actors who play the principal male roles. In principal female roles, prompt books require an average of 3.5 boys per play. The men and boys in principal roles speak an average of 95.5% of the lines. In *SMT*, the largest minor male role is Memphonius (24 lines), and a marginal note by the prompter identifies 'Mr Gough' as the actor who plays this minor part (Illustration 5). As a practical matter, an actor can learn a minor part of twenty-five lines or less with about an hour of study and rehearsal. This is consistent with the fact that most of the actors identified in the King's Men prompt books – except those named in the property list for *BAYL* – speak less than twenty-five lines. As noted, these parts need very little rehearsal, and these actors probably joined the cast late in the rehearsal period. The actor who doubles in minor parts usually, but not always, has an interval of one scene off-stage for each change of costume. For example, in *Barn.* the book-keeper makes notes in the text that identify an actor known only as 'R. T.' in four minor parts: Messenger (3 lines in 2.2 and 5 lines in 2.5), Officer (2 lines in 3.2), Servant (2 lines in 3.6), 2 Huntsman (8 lines in 4.1), and Servant again (3 lines in 4.3). Given these identifications, my table suggests that 'R. T.' also plays the Officer (mute in 1.2 and 14 lines in 4.5). It is also possible for 'R. T.' to play the Executioner from Harlem (14 lines) who appears in 5.1. only.

Evidence about the length of rehearsal time is not so clear as we could wish. Although, as we have seen, Henslowe's *Diary* shows that in the case of *The Conquest of the West Indies* the time elapsed between last recorded payment to the author or authors and the first public performance was probably about a month, a shorter interval is evident in the history of *The Madman's Morris*. On 31 June [*sic*] 1598 Henslowe's *Diary* notes that he paid three pounds 'in erneste of a boocke called the made manes mores';[44] on 9 July he paid another pound for the same play, and on 10 July he paid two more pounds 'in fulle payment' for the play.[45] On 25 July, Henslowe lent four pounds, thirteen shillings, and four pence to the actor William Bourne (or Bird) – no relation to Theophilus Bird (or Bourne) – 'to by a sewte of satten for the playe of made manes moris'.[46] If the tailor was paid on delivery of the costume, and if the first performance was given a day or so later, then the company rehearsed this play for about two weeks.

6. When parts were assigned to actors, the book-keeper or playhouse scribe took the plot the author had prepared when he first offered the play, and to it the book-keeper added the name of the actor who played each part. As noted, my study examines four plots that list the characters who appear in each scene and identify the actor who plays each part: *The platt of The secound parte of the Seven Deadlie Sinns* (*2SDS*), probably prepared for a performance by an amalgamation of Lord Strange's Men and the Lord Admiral's Men at the Curtain about 1590;[47] *The plott of ffrederick & Basilea* (*Fred.*), probably prepared for performance by the Lord Admiral's Men at the Rose on 3 June 1597; *The plot of The Battell of Alcazar* (*BA*), probably prepared for a revival at the Rose some time between 1 December 1598 and 1 March 1599;[49] *The plott of The First parte of Tamar Cam* (*1TC*), probably prepared for performance by the Lord Admiral's Men at the Fortune in 1602.[50]

The separate functions of the book and the plot are indicated at the play-within-the-play scene in *The Spanish Tragedy* (1592):

> *King* Heere brother, you shall be the booke-keeper
> There is the argument of what they shew.
> *He giveth him a booke*
> . . . .
> Heere comes Lorenzo, looke upon the plot
> And tell me, brother, what part plaies he?   (K3-3v)

For each revival of a given play, the cast of actors, especially those in minor parts, probably differed from the cast at the first performance. It would therefore be necessary for the book-keeper to draw up a new plot and to record there the names of the actors in the revival.

For each of the plots, I prepare a table of parts similar to those for the prompt books. Although the plots include no spoken lines, the distinction between principal parts and minor parts is clear. For example, Burbage plays two principal male roles in *2SDS*: Gorboduc in the first sequence (about Envy) and Tereus in the third sequence (about Lechery). Four boys are identified in seven principal female roles, with Saunder doubling as Queen in the first episode and Progne in the third episode; 'R. Go', who plays Aspatia in the second episode, is off-stage for two scenes before he doubles as Philomele in the third episode. Eight men are identified in thirty-eight minor parts. For example, R. Cowley plays six parts, five of which are identified by function: Lieutenant, Soldier, Lord, Captain, and Musician. Cowley's only part with a name, Giraldus, appears in only one scene. In *Fred.* ten leading actors of the company are identified in ten principal roles without doubling; four boys play four principal female roles without doubling. Two hired men play ten minor parts, and five playhouse attendants and gatherers play Lords, Guards, Confederates, and Soldiers.

BA is the only Elizabethan play that survives in both a plot and an early printed text (Q-1594).[51] In order to show the relative sizes of the roles in this play, a tally is made of the number of lines spoken by each character in Q, and this tally is included with the table of parts for the plot of *BA*. Edward Alleyn, the leading actor of the Lord Admiral's Men, plays the largest role, Muly Mahamet (213 lines). The actor who plays Sebastian, the second largest role (196 lines) is not identified, and Richard Alleyn (no relation to Edward) plays the Portingall-Presenter (156 lines) and the Governor of Lisbon (23 lines), which may be variant names for the same role. Thomes Towne plays Stukely (135 lines), Humphrey Jeffes plays Xeque (82 lines), and Anthony Jeffes (no relation to Humphrey) plays Young Mahamet (60 lines). Four other men who play the lesser principal parts double in minor parts, and in each case the actor is off-stage for at least one scene for each change of costume. For example, Charles Massey plays Zareo (57 lines) in scenes 1 and 3, and the Duke of Barcelis (mute) in scene 6. He is off-stage during the Third Dumbshow, and plays an Ambassador of Spain (20 lines) in scene 7. Two boys are required in female roles. Jeames plays Ruben in scenes 1 and 3, and he is off-stage for scenes 4 and 5 before he doubles as a Page in scenes 6 and 7. Seven men are identified in twenty-one minor parts.

In *1TC*, the three principal actors of the company play the title role and two other large parts without doubling; five other leading actors play principal roles and double in minor parts, but each actor is off-stage for an interval of at least one scene for each change of costume. Two boys play two principal female roles without doubling. Six hired men play forty-seven minor parts; two leading members of the company – and eight men who are probably playhouse attendants – appear in exotic costumes for the final procession only.

The playhouse documents usually identify three actors in groups of mute supernumeraries such as Attendants, Soldiers, and Lords. Therefore, in my estimates of the number of mutes required for other plays, including those by Shakespeare, my tables of parts indicate that Attendants, Soldiers, and Lords are three in number. However, there was probably a variety in the number of actors who served as mutes; as we have seen, a stage direction in *Tit.* calls for '*others as many as can be*'.

7. After the actors had rehearsed the play and were about ready for the first public performance, they sent the book to the Master of the Revels who, for a fee, read the play, deleted those passages he considered objectionable, and affixed his licence at the end of the text. *SMT* carries a licence signed by Sir George Buc, Master of the Revels, dated 31 October 1611 (Illustration 4); *Barn.* was censored by Buc who includes a note of reprimand in the right margin (Illustration 6), but the Revels licence, if any, does not survive. *HMF* carries the remnants of a licence for a revival dated 8 February 1625 in the hand of Sir Henry Herbert, who succeeded Buc as Master of the Revels (Illustration 8); *BAYL* carries a licence signed by Herbert, dated 6 May 1631 (Illustration 10).

In his study of Herbert's office-book, J. Q. Adams points to two episodes that indicate the actors submitted a play for censorship late in the rehearsal period. First, Herbert licensed Shirley's *The Ball* on 16 November 1632; two days later on 18 November Herbert saw a performance and discovered that 'ther were divers personated so naturally, both of the lords and others of the court that I took it ill, and would have forbidden the play, but that [Christopher Beeston, the manager] promiste many things which I found faulte withall should be left out'.[52] Second, on the morning of 18 October 1633, the King's Men submitted to Herbert the book of *The Tamer Tamed*, which they planned to act that afternoon. However, Herbert found the play offensive, and he records a warrant to the King's Men: 'These are to will and require you to forebeare the actinge of your play called *The Tamer Tamed* ... this afternoon, or any more till you have leave from mee: and this at your perill.' Herbert also notes that the company 'acted *The Scornful Lady* instead of it'.[53]

Adams notes that Buc, who served as Master of the Revels from 1597 to 1622, charged one pound per play, and this was at first the regular charge made by Herbert, who served from 1623 to 1642. However, if the censorship was unusually heavy and therefore required a second reading, Herbert's fee was two pounds. After about 1632, Herbert regularly charged two pounds for a new play and one pound for a revival.[54]

Chapter 3 describes the casting requirements for fifteen plays of the period that identify all the men and boys who act the principal roles in each play. Seven of these plays were first acted by Shakespeare's company, the King's Men, between 1613 and 1636: *The Duchess of Malfi* (*DM*) by John Webster, *The Roman Actor* (*RA*) by Philip Massinger, *The Deserving Favorite* (*DF*) by Lodowick Carlell, *The Picture* (*Pict.*) by Massinger, *The Soddered Citizen* (*SC*) by John Clavell, *The Swisser* (*Swis.*) by Arthur Wilson, and *The Wild Goose Chase* (*WGC*) by John Fletcher. Six plays were first acted by Queen Henrietta's Men between 1626 and 1635: *The Wedding* (*Wed.*) by James Shirley, *The Renegado* (*Ren.*) by Massinger, *The First Part of the Fair Maid of the West* (*1FMW*) and *The Second Part of the Fair Maid of the West* (*2FMW*) by Thomas Heywood, *King John and Matilda* (*KJM*) by Robert Davenport, and *Hannibal and Scipio* (*Han.*) by Thomas Nabbes. Two plays were first acted by other London companies: *Holland's Leaguer* (*HL*) by Shakerly Marmion, acted by Prince

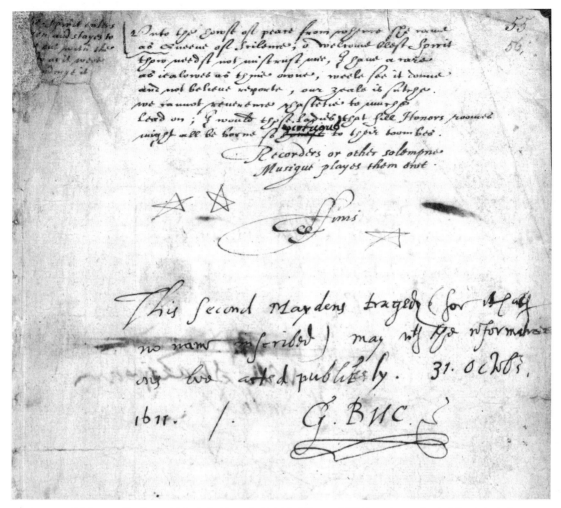

4 Thomas Middleton, *The Second Maiden's Tragedy*, British Library, MS. Lansdowne 807b, fol. 56, includes a licence signed by Sir George Buc, Master of the Revels.

Charles's (II) Men in 1631, and *Messalina* (*Mess.*) by Nathanael Richards, acted by the King's Revels company in 1634.

For each of these fifteen plays, I give a brief stage history, and I prepare a tally of spoken lines with a table of parts according to the same procedures followed for the prompt books and the playhouse plots. As noted, *The Diary of Thomas Crosfield* for 18 July 1634 identifies Taylor and Lowin as the masters or chief players with the King's Men at Blackfriars.[55] These two men act the largest roles in every play in which the parts they perform are identified, and each man plays a variety of parts. Taylor replaces Burbage as Duke Ferdinand, the evil twin brother of the Duchess of Malfi. Taylor also plays: Paris, the Roman actor; the Duke who wins Clarinda in *DF*; Mathias, a faithful husband in *Pict.*; Arioldus, a gentleman who leaves retirement to become a successful general in *Swis.*; Antiochus, the deposed and ageing King of

Syria, in *BAYL*; and Mirabell, a young Benedick who finally succumbs to love and marriage, in *WGC*. Lowin is apparently skilful as villains and tyrants, but he also plays sympathetic roles. He plays Bosola, the villain who spies on the Duchess of Malfi and who supervises her execution; Caesar Domitian in *RA* is a tyrant, and Jacomo in *DF* is a villain, but Eubulus in *Pict.* is an old windbag courtier reminiscent of Polonius. Undermyne in *SC* is an unscrupulous citizen, but Andrucho in *Swis.* is the sympathetic Count Aribert in disguise; Flaminius in *BAYL* is a tyrannical Roman consul, but Belleur in *WGC* is the companion of Mirabell and the bashful lover of Rosalura.

For Queen Henrietta's Men at the Phoenix or Cockpit in Drury Lane, Crosfield's *Diary* names 'Their master Mr [Christopher] Beeston Mr Boyer' and three other actors.[56] Beeston, who in 1598 acted with Shakespeare in *Every Man in his Humour* (Illustration 1), was manager of Queen Henrietta's Men, and Michael Bowyer plays the leading role in five of the six casts in which his roles are identified: Vitelli in *Ren.*, Beauford in *Wed.*, Spencer in *1* and *2FMW*, and King John in *KJM*. In the sixth play, Bowyer plays Scipio, the second largest male role in *Han.* Crosfield names 'Mr Cane' as one of the chief actors with Prince Charles's (II) company at the Red Bull and Christopher Goad as one of the nine chief actors with the King's Revels company at Salisbury Court.[57] Andrew Cane plays Trimalchio, the largest male role in *HL*, and Goad plays Silius, the largest male role in *Mess.* There should be no need to multiply examples. Further analysis shows that each of the principal actors of this period played a wide variety of roles. Here it should be emphasized that the most important consideration in casting a given part was not the type of role to be acted but the *length* of that role. It should come as no surprise that the principal actors of the King's Men and other London companies almost invariably play the largest parts, a practice that continues in the theatre of our own day.[58]

In these fifteen plays, the number of men required in principal male roles ranges from six in *DF* to twelve in *KJM*, or an average of 9.3 actors who play principal male roles. In principal female roles, these plays require an average of 3.7 boys. The men and boys in principal roles speak an average of 97.2% of the lines. Most of the actors identified in the largest principal male roles do not double, but as we have seen in the prompt book for *BAYL*, actors who play the lesser principal roles double in minor parts. For example, in *DM* John Underwood plays Delio (185 lines), the good friend and confidant of Antonio, the steward secretly married to the Duchess; Underwood doubles as a Madman (8 lines) who torments the sleep of the Duchess when the eight Madmen 'sing and daunce, And act their gambols to the full o' th' moone'. If an actor in a principal part doubles, he usually has a full scene off-stage for each change of costume. For example, Underwood plays Delio in seven scenes, and he is off-stage for three scenes before he plays a Madman in 4.2. He is then off-stage for 246 lines before he enters again as Delio at the start of 5.1.

The principal actors play minor parts in only a few plays in this group. In *DM*, Nicholas Tooley, who is named in the royal patent of 27 March 1619,[59] plays three roles: the cowardly Count Malateste (18 lines), Forobosco, a comic servant (9 lines), and a Madman (10 lines). Other minor parts are usually played by hired men. For example, in *RA* William Pattrick, who is identified as Palphurius (19 lines in 5 scenes), probably does not double; George Vernon is identified as 1 Lictor (5 lines) and 2 Tribune (4 lines); it is also possible for him to play a mute prisoner and a mute hangman. Patrick and Vernon are named in the list of hired men whom the Master of the Revels protects from arrest 'during the Time of the Revels' on 27 December 1624 (see Appendix C). For those plays that do not identify actors in minor parts, my tables of parts suggest possibilities for doubling that are consistent with the evidence about casting in the prompt books and the playhouse plots.

Boy actors play all the principal female roles and the usually small roles of boys and pages. Baptismal records survive for three boy actors with the King's Men, and this evidence indicates the ages at which these boys play female roles and the ages at which these same boys first act adult male roles. For example, John Honyman was baptized on 7 February 1613; he plays Domitilla (113 lines) in *RA*, licensed on 11 October 1626; he plays Sophia (484 lines) in *Pict.*, licensed on 8 June 1629; he plays Clarinda (499 lines) in *DF* (1629?). Thereafter, Honyman plays adult male roles: Sly, a tricky servant (98 lines), in *SC* (1630?); 1 Merchant (46 lines) in *BAYL*, licensed on 6 May 1631; Young Factor (42 lines) in a 1632 revival of *WGC*. On 15 April 1633, Honyman was sworn in as 'A Groome of ye Chamber . . . to attend in ye quality of a Player'.[60]

Chapter 4 describes the casting requirements for all thirty-eight plays attributed wholly or in part to Shakespeare. It may be helpful here to illustrate my procedures by describing the casting requirements for two decidedly different works: *Titus Andronicus* (*Tit.* Q1-1594), a tragedy probably first acted by the Earl of Sussex's Men on 23 January 1594 and revived by an amalgamation of 'my Lord Admeralle men & my Lorde chamberlen men' at Newington Butts on 5 June 1594,[61] and *The Tempest* (*Temp.* F), a late romance acted by the King's Men at court on 1 November 1611.[62] All of my estimates about casting for Shakespeare's plays are based on evidence in the eight playhouse documents described in chapter 2 and the fifteen pre-Restoration plays that identify the actors who play principal roles described in chapter 3.

As Table 1 indicates, *Tit.* (Q1) requires ten men who can play thirteen principal male roles – those who speak twenty-five or more lines – and four boys who play the four principal female roles – those who speak ten or more lines. As Table 2 indicates, *Temp.* requires ten men who play ten principal male roles and four boys who play four principal female roles. Thus Shakespeare's earliest tragedy (1594) and a late romance (1611) have the same basic plan for casting. As the present study shows, this plan for casting Shakespeare's plays is derived from common theatrical practice at London playhouses of this period.

Although the requirements for minor parts and mute supernumeraries differ slightly in *Tit.* and *Temp.*, in each play the men and boys in principal roles speak over 98% of the lines. In the thirty-eight plays attributed wholly or in part to Shakespeare, an average of ten men and four boys are required in principal roles, and these actors speak an average of 95% of the lines. As noted, this large share of lines spoken by principal roles makes it possible for the leading actors to rehearse the play without the supporting cast until shortly before the first public performance, at which time the company can enlist the hired men, playhouse attendants, and boys needed for minor parts. As the playhouse documents show, the leading actor of the company almost invariably plays the largest role. The title role of *Tit.* (641 lines) is much the largest, and if, as Henslowe's *Diary* indicates, the play was acted by an amalgamation of the Admiral's Men and the Lord Chamberlain's Men, then Titus was played either by Edward Alleyn, the leading actor with the former company, or by Burbage, the leading actor with the latter company. Burbage, who in 1611 was the leading actor for the King's Men, probably played Prospero, the largest male role (653 lines) in *Temp.*[63]

In recent years, several studies have offered imaginative conjectures about possibilities for doubling in Shakespeare's plays, but none of these studies has taken into account the evidence about casting readily available in the extant Elizabethan playhouse documents.[64] The suggestions for doubling offered in the present study are consistent with the casting for the playhouse plots, where the actors who play the largest principal parts do not double. However, in some cases an actor doubles in a lesser principal role and a small part, and, if so, he usually has an interval of one scene off-stage for each change of costume.

In *Tit.* the actors who play the six largest male roles probably do not double, but Bassanius (the seventh largest male role, 65 lines), Martius (the ninth largest male role, 33 lines), and Quintus (the tenth largest male role, 25 lines) die early in the play, and the actors in these three parts are free to play a Roman Lord (26 lines), a Goth (25 lines), and the Clown (25 lines) respectively. There are many other possibilities for doubling in these minor parts, and it should be emphasized that we cannot be certain whether the actor who plays Bassanius doubles as a Roman Lord, or as a Goth, or as the Clown, but it is highly probable that he doubles in one or another of these roles. My tables of parts suggest *only one set of possibilities* for doubling for each play, not hard-and-fast rules. What *is* certain about the casting for *Tit.* is that all the principal roles can be played by ten men and four boys.

Tit. has five small parts who speak a total of forty-four lines. Mutes are also required as Followers for Bassanius, Followers for Saturninus, the Army of Goths, and Others with Titus. As we have seen, the playhouse documents usually identify three actors in each group of Lords, Attendants, and Soldiers, and so my tables assign three actors to each group of mutes in Shakespeare's plays. However, this is only an estimate because the number of available mutes was probably flexible, as is shown by a stage direction in *Tit.* that calls for '*others as many as can be*' (1.1.69). It should also be noted that the Followers of Bassanius leave the stage at 1.1.55, and the Followers of Saturninus leave at 1.1.59. With quick changes of costume – like those sometimes required for minor parts in the playhouse plots – it is possible for these same actors to return about ten lines later as '*others as many as can be*'. My table of parts therefore estimates a total of thirteen men in twenty-nine minor parts.[65]

Temp. has only five small speaking parts with a total of thirty-one lines (songs are not included in the tally of spoken lines). My table includes two Mariners and two Others with the Court Party as mutes in 1.1, and three Reapers played by men who dance with three Nymphs played by boys at 4.1.138. These six actors can double as 'divers Shapes of Dogs and Hounds' at 4.1.254. My Table 2 therefore includes a total of five men and four boys in twenty-two minor parts.

There are two substantive texts of *Tit.*: Q1-1594, which Greg and other scholars suggest was printed from Shakespeare's foul papers, and F, which was printed from a copy of Q3 that had been annotated by comparison with another source, possibly the prompt book.[66] This may have been the source for the added stage direction '*He kils him*' when Titus slays Mutius (1.1.291). Evidence about the probable sources of printer's copy is subject to a wide diversity of scholarly interpretation, and the present study makes no claim to settle what are often hotly debated bibliographical and textual problems.[67] Nevertheless, if my study shows significant differences in the casting requirements for variant texts of a given play, it is hoped that these differences will interest scholars who attempt to determine the source of printer's copy for these variant texts. For example, my Table 3 shows that *Tit.* (F) adds an important 85-line scene (3.2), and F assigns to a Goth a speech that Q1 assigns to a Roman Lord (5.3.73–95). The substitution of a Goth for the Roman Lord reduces the number of principal parts, and it allows the actor who plays Quintus to double in the small part of Nuntius-Emillius (14 lines). This casting change is apparently a matter of theatrical expediency, and this evidence lends support to the hypothesis that a prompt book was consulted for the copy from which F is printed. It is hoped that further study of problems about casting for Shakespeare's plays will provide new perspectives about the author and his fellow actors at work.

Table 1
Titus Andronicus (Q1-1594)

	1	2				3	4				5			
	1	1	2	3	4	1	1	2	3	4	1	2	3	Totals
Principal Parts														
Men														
#1 Titus Andronicus	138	–	15	9	–	189	56	–	73	–	–	132	29	641
#2 Aron	0	88	–	37	–	19	–	110	–	–	86	–	10	350
#3 Marcus	75	–	3	–	47	48	47	–	19	–	–	1	45	285
#4 Saturninus	106	–	2	35	–	–	–	–	–	55	–	–	10	208
#5 Lucius	30	–	0	0	–	39	–	–	–	–	40	–	69	178
#6 Demetrius	10	34	2	14	6	–	–	27	–	0	–	2	–	95
#7 Bassanius	48	–	1	16	–	–	–	–	–	–	–	–	–	65
Roman Lord	–	–	–	–	–	–	–	–	–	–	–	–	26	26
#8 Chiron	1	20	0	10	4	–	–	12	–	0	–	4	–	51
#9 Martius	4	–	0	29	–	0	–	–	–	–	–	–	–	33
Goth	–	–	–	–	–	–	–	–	–	–	24	–	1	25
#10 Quintus	1	–	0	24	–	0	–	–	–	–	–	–	–	25
Clowne	–	–	–	–	–	–	–	–	19	6	–	–	–	25
Boys														
#1 Tamora	69	–	0	84	–	–	–	–	–	43	–	61	2	259
#2 Lavinia	10	–	4	45	0	0	0	–	–	–	–	0	0	59
#3 Lucius Sonne-Puer	–	–	–	–	–	–	26	3	0	–	–	–	4	33
#4 Nurse	–	–	–	–	–	–	–	17	–	–	–	–	–	17

Total Lines Principal Parts 2,372

Minor Parts
Men

	1	2				3	4				5			
	1	1	2	3	4	1	1	2	3	4	1	2	3	Totals
#1 Mutius	4	–	–	–	–	–	–	–	–	–	–	–	–	4
Messenger	–	–	–	–	–	7	–	–	–	–	–	–	–	7
#2 Captaine	6	–	–	–	–	–	–	–	–	–	–	–	–	6
Emilius	–	–	–	–	–	–	–	–	–	8	6	–	4	18
#3 Alarbus	0	–	–	–	–	–	–	–	–	–	–	–	–	0
Publius	–	–	–	–	–	–	–	4	–	–	5	–	–	9
#4 Tribune	0	–	–	–	–	–	–	–	–	–	–	0		0
Judge	–	–	–	–	–	0	–	–	–	–	–	–	–	0
#5 Tribune	0	–	–	–	–	–	–	–	–	–	–	0		0
Judge	–	–	–	–	–	0	–	–	–	–	–	–	–	0
#6 Senator	0	–	–	–	–	0	–	–	–	–	–	–	–	0
Another	–	–	–	–	–	–	–	0	0	–	–	–	–	0

Table 2   23

Table 1 (*cont.*)

```
#7
Senator          0  -  -  -  -  0  -  -  -  -  -  -  -     0
Gentleman        -  -  -  -  -  -  -  -  0  -  -  -  -     0
#8
Follower[Bass.]  0  -  -  -  -  -  -  -  -  -  -  -  -     0
Man[Titus]       0  -  -  -  -  -  -  -  -  -  -  -  -     0
Army[Goths]      -  -  -  -  -  -  -  -  -  -  0  -  -     0
#9
Follower[Bass.]  0  -  -  -  -  -  -  -  -  -  -  -  -     0
Man[Titus]       0  -  -  -  -  -  -  -  -  -  -  -  -     0
Army[Goths]      -  -  -  -  -  -  -  -  -  -  0  -  -     0
#10
Follower[Bass.]  0  -  -  -  -  -  -  -  -  -  -  -  -     0
Other[Titus]     0  -  -  -  -  -  -  -  -  -  -  -  -     0
Army[Goths]      -  -  -  -  -  -  -  -  -  -  0  -  -     0
#11
Follower[Saturn.] 0 -  0  -  -  -  -  -  -  -  -  -  0     0
Other[Titus]     0  -  -  -  -  -  -  -  -  -  -  -       0
#12
Follower[Saturn.] 0 -  0  -  -  -  -  -  -  -  -  -  0     0
Other[Titus]     0  -  -  -  -  -  -  -  -  -  -  -       0
#13
Follower[Saturn.] 0 -  0  -  -  -  -  -  -  -  -  -  0     0
Other[Titus]     0  -  -  -  -  -  -  -  -  -  -  -       0
```

Total Lines Minor Parts $\overline{44}$ = 2%
Principal Parts $\underline{2,372}$ = 98%
$\overline{2,416}$

Table 2
The Tempest (F)

	1	1	2	2	3	3	3	4	5	E	Totals
	1	2	1	2	1	2	3	1	1		
					Principal Parts						
					Men						
#1 Prospero	-	329	-	-	10	-	15	97	182	20	653
#2 Gonzalo	21	-	88	-	-	-	28	-	36	-	173
#3 Caliban	-	30	-	46	-	64	-	20	8	-	168
#4 Stephano	-	-	-	70	-	59	-	23	5	-	157
#5 Anthonio	7	-	123	-	-	-	13	-	2	-	145
#6 Ferdinando	0	44	-	-	59	-	-	23	13	-	139
#7 Sebastian	4	-	95	-	-	-	11	-	9	-	119
#8 Trinculo	-	-	-	55	-	31	-	16	5	-	107
#9 Alonso	2	-	25	-	-	-	26	-	46	-	99
#10 Boteswaine	28	-	-	-	-	-	-	-	17	-	45

Table 2 (*cont.*)

Boys

#1											
Ariel	-	70	5	-	-	4	30	28	22	-	159
#2											
Miranda	-	98	-	-	45	-	-	2	7	-	152
#3											
Iris	-	-	-	-	-	-	-	41	-	-	41
#4											
Ceres	-	-	-	-	-	-	-	16	-	-	16

Total Lines Principal Parts 2,173

Minor Parts
Men

#1											
Other	0	-	-	-	-	-	-	-	-	-	0
Adrian	-	-	11	-	-	-	1	-	0	-	12
#2											
Other	0	-	-	-	-	-	-	-	-	-	0
Francisco	-	-	10	-	-	-	1	-	0	-	11
#3											
Ship-master	4	-	-	-	-	-	-	-	0	-	4
Other	-	-	0	-	-	-	-	-	-	-	0
Shape	-	-	-	-	-	-	-	0	-	-	0
Reaper	-	-	-	-	-	-	-	0	-	-	0
#4											
Mariner	1	-	-	-	-	-	-	-	-	-	1
Other	-	-	0	-	-	-	-	-	-	-	0
Shape	-	-	-	-	-	-	-	0	-	-	0
Reaper	-	-	-	-	-	-	-	0	-	-	0
#5											
Mariner	0	-	-	-	-	-	-	-	-	-	0
Reaper	-	-	-	-	-	-	-	0	-	-	0
Shape	-	-	-	-	-	-	-	0	-	-	0

Boys

#1											
Juno	-	-	-	-	-	-	-	3	-	-	3
#2											
Nimph	-	-	-	-	-	-	-	0	-	-	0
Shape	-	-	-	-	-	-	-	0	-	-	0
#3											
Nimph	-	-	-	-	-	-	-	0	-	-	0
Shape	-	-	-	-	-	-	-	0	-	-	0
#4											
Nimph	-	-	-	-	-	-	-	0	-	-	0
Shape	-	-	-	-	-	-	-	0	-	-	0

Total Lines Minor Parts 31= 1%

Principal Parts 2,173=99%

2,204

Table 3   25

Table 3
Titus Andronicus (F)

	1	2				3		4				5			
	1	1	2	3	4	1	2	1	2	3	4	1	2	3	Totals

Principal Parts
Men

	1.1	2.1	2.2	2.3	2.4	3.1	3.2	4.1	4.2	4.3	4.4	5.1	5.2	5.3	Totals
#1 Titus Andronicus	140	-	15	11	-	192	73	59	-	75	-	-	132	30	727
#2 Aron	0	88	-	41	-	19	-	-	110	-	-	87	-	10	355
#3 Marcus	75	-	3	-	47	50	11	46	-	19	-	-	1	40	292
#4 Saturninus	110	-	5	35	-	-	-	-	-	-	56	-	-	12	218
#5 Lucius	29	-	0	0	-	40	-	-	-	-	-	43	-	78	190
#6 Demetrius	10	34	2	15	6	-	-	-	38	-	0	-	2	-	107
#7 Bassanius	49	-	1	15	-	-	-	-	-	-	-	-	-	-	65
Goth	-	-	-	-	-	-	-	-	-	-	-	32	-	24	56
#8 Chiron	1	21	0	14	5	-	-	-	12	-	0	-	4	-	57
#9 Martius	4	-	0	30	-	0	-	-	-	-	-	-	-	-	34
Clown	-	-	-	-	-	-	-	-	-	16	6	-	-	-	22
#10 Quintus	1	-	0	26	-	0	-	-	-	-	-	-	-	-	27
Nuntius-Emillius	-	-	-	-	-	-	-	-	-	-	8	6	-	-	14

Boys

	1.1	2.1	2.2	2.3	2.4	3.1	3.2	4.1	4.2	4.3	4.4	5.1	5.2	5.3	Totals
#1 Tamora	69	-	0	88	-	-	-	-	-	-	42	-	62	2	263
#2 Lavinia	10	-	2	50	0	0	0	0	-	-	-	-	0	0	62
#3 Young Lucius-Boy	-	-	-	-	-	-	2	24	3	0	-	-	-	4	33
#4 Nurse	-	-	-	-	-	-	-	-	19	-	-	-	-	-	19

Total Lines Principal Parts 2,541

Minor Parts
Men

	1.1	2.1	2.2	2.3	2.4	3.1	3.2	4.1	4.2	4.3	4.4	5.1	5.2	5.3	Totals
#1 Mutius	4	-	-	-	-	-	-	-	-	-	-	-	-	-	4
Publius	-	-	-	-	-	-	-	-	-	9	-	-	6	-	15
#2 Captaine	6	-	-	-	-	-	-	-	-	-	-	-	-	-	6
Roman	-	-	-	-	-	-	-	-	-	-	-	-	-	3	3
#3 Alarbus	0	-	-	-	-	-	-	-	-	-	-	-	-	-	0
Messenger	-	-	-	-	-	7	-	-	-	-	-	-	-	-	7
#4 Tribune	3	-	-	-	-	-	-	-	-	-	-	-	-	0	3
Judge	-	-	-	-	-	0	-	-	-	-	-	-	-	-	0
#5 Tribune	0	-	-	-	-	-	-	-	-	-	-	-	-	0	0
Judge	-	-	-	-	-	0	-	-	-	-	-	-	-	-	0

Table 3 (*cont.*)

	1	2	3	4	5	6	7	8	9	10	11	12	13	14	Total
#6															
Senator	0	-	-	-	-	0	-	-	-	-	-	-	-	-	0
Another	-	-	-	-	-	-	-	-	0	0	-	-	-	-	0
#7															
Senator	0	-	-	-	-	0	-	-	-	-	-	-	-	-	0
Gentleman	-	-	-	-	-	-	-	-	-	0	-	-	-	-	0
#8															
Follower[Bass.]	0	-	-	-	-	-	-	-	-	-	-	-	-	-	0
Man[Titus]	0	-	-	-	-	-	-	-	-	-	-	-	-	-	0
Army[Goths]	-	-	-	-	-	-	-	-	-	-	-	0	-	0	0
#9															
Follower[Bass.]	0	-	-	-	-	-	-	-	-	-	-	-	-	-	0
Man[Titus]	0	-	-	-	-	-	-	-	-	-	-	-	-	-	0
Army[Goths]	-	-	-	-	-	-	-	-	-	-	-	0	-	0	0
#10															
Follower[Bass.]	0	-	-	-	-	-	-	-	-	-	-	-	-	-	0
Other[Titus]	0	-	-	-	-	-	-	-	-	-	-	-	-	-	0
Army[Goths]	-	-	-	-	-	-	-	-	-	-	-	0	-	0	0
#11															
Follower[Saturn.]	0	-	0	-	-	-	-	-	-	-	-	-	-	-	0
Other[Titus]	0	-	-	-	-	-	-	-	-	-	-	-	-	-	0
Other[Saturn.]	-	-	-	-	-	-	-	-	-	-	-	-	-	0	0
#12															
Follower[Saturn.]	0	-	0	-	-	-	-	-	-	-	-	-	-	-	0
Other[Titus]	0	-	-	-	-	-	-	-	-	-	-	-	-	-	0
Other[Saturn.]	-	-	-	-	-	-	-	-	-	-	-	-	-	0	0
#13															
Follower[Saturn.]	0	-	0	-	-	-	-	-	-	-	-	-	-	-	0
Other[Titus]	0	-	-	-	-	-	-	-	-	-	-	-	-	-	0
Other[Saturn.]	-	-	-	-	-	-	-	-	-	-	-	-	-	0	0

Total Lines Minor Parts $\overline{38}$ = 1%

Principal Parts   2,541 = 99%

2,579

## CHAPTER TWO

Eight playhouse documents

These documents provide valuable evidence about actual playing conditions, and this chapter offers a systematic analysis of the way roles were assigned to actors in four plots from the repertories of Lord Strange's Men and the Lord Admiral's Men, and in four prompt books from the repertory of the King's Men.

PLOTS

Four plots used to regulate performances of Elizabethan plays are well enough preserved to identify most of the actors and the parts they play; a fifth plot identifies actors, but only in a few small parts.[1] Appendix A reprints Transcripts I, II, III, VIA, and VII in Greg, *Documents*. Each plot is divided into scenes by rules drawn across its columns, and my transcript adds an arabic numeral to identify each scene in each plot. Each scene begins with '*Enter*' followed by the names of one or more characters. The actor playing each role is usually identified at his first entrance in that role, but not necessarily at subsequent entrances in that role. When one or more characters join others already on stage, this entrance is usually indicated by '*to them*', '*to him*', or '*to her*'. In my tables of parts, each actor is listed on a row, with the part or parts he plays listed below his name; the names of the actors and the parts in which they are identified are underscored, and the initials of each actor identified in a part are entered in the appropriate row and column. If an actor is named for a scene but the role he plays is not identified, an 'x' is entered in the table; if a role is named for a scene but the actor who plays it is not identified, a 'y' is entered in the table.

As noted, *BA* is the only Elizabethan play that survives in both a plot and an early printed text (Q-1594).[2] In order to show the relative sizes of the roles in this play, a tally is made of the number of lines spoken by each character in Q, and this tally is included in the table of parts for the plot of *BA*. In this quarto, the men and boys who play principal characters – male roles who speak twenty-five or more lines and female roles who speak ten or more lines – speak 96% of the lines. As we shall see, this ratio corresponds closely to the distribution of lines in the extant prompt books acted by the King's Men and in fifteen other pre-Restoration plays that identify actors in principal parts.

Although there are no printed texts of the other plays for which plots survive, the distinction between principal parts and minor parts is evident nevertheless. As noted, in *2SDS* Richard Burbage plays two principal roles, Gorboduc in the first sequence (about Envy) and Tereus in the third sequence (about Lechery), while

Richard Cowley plays six minor parts, five of which are identified by function: Lieutenant, Soldier, Lord, Captain, and Musician. Cowley's only part with a name, Giraldus, appears in only one scene. Several of the actors with Lord Strange's Men joined the newly organized Lord Chamberlain's Men in 1594,[3] and ten of the actors identified in parts for *2SDS* are also listed as 'Principall Actors' in the front matter of F (Illustration 3): Burbage, Cowley, Augustine Phillips, Thomas Pope, George Bryan, Henry Condell, William Sly, Alexander Cooke, Nicholas Tooley, and Robert Goughe. Cowley is identified in *Much Ado about Nothing* (*Ado* Q1) as the actor who plays Verges (4.2). Other actors identified in *2SDS* played minor parts in Shakespeare's plays. John Sincler (or Sincklo) plays four small parts in *2SDS*, and in the Induction to *The Taming of the Shrew* (*Shr.* F), 'Sincklo' heads a speech by one of the visiting players; in *The Second Part of King Henry the Fourth* (*2H4* Q1), 'Sincklo' plays a Beadle (5.4); *The Third Part of King Henry the Sixth* (*3H6* F) has the direction '*Enter Sinklo, and Humfrey, with Crosse-bowes in their hands*' (3.1). *2SDS* identifies John Holland in four small parts, and *The Second Part of King Henry the Sixth* (*2H6* F) identifies him as one of Cade's rebels: '*Enter Bevis, and John Holland*' (4.2).[4] These actors in minor parts had few, if any, lines to learn and, as noted, they probably joined the cast late in the rehearsal period.

As will be seen in the plots for *Fred.*, *BA*, and *1TC* – all plays performed by the Admiral's Men between June 1597 and 1602 – almost all the principal male roles are played by the leading actors of the company who are named in one or more of the six lists described below from Henslowe's *Diary*. When these lists were made, the men named apparently had collective financial responsibility to Henslowe, and Greg therefore suggests that they were at the time 'sharers' who jointly owned the company and divided the profits. Greg also observes that most of the actors included in the lists are given the honorific 'Mr' in the plots, and he infers that these men had sharer status.[5] However, Foakes and Rickert cast serious doubts on the assumptions that only sharers are named in the lists and that 'Mr' in the plot is used only for sharers.[6] Furthermore, a recent study by S. P. Cerasano argues convincingly that 'Mr' was an abbreviation for 'Master', a title bestowed on players of high capability, and that this was not necessarily an indication of sharer status.[7] These six lists are summarized in Table 4: 1. Eight names without caption or date, listed between entries for 14 December 1594 and 14 January 1595: Edward Alleyn, John Singer, Richard Jones, Thomas Towne, Martin Slater, Edward Juby, Thomas Downton, and James Tunstall;[8] 2. Henslowe's note for 14 October 1596 for money he lent to Edward Alleyn, Slater, James Tunstall and Edward Juby;[9] 3. A list of 'my lord admerelles players' dated 11 October 1597: William Bourne (or Bird), Gabriel Spencer, Robert Shaw, Jones, Downton, Edward Juby, Towne, Singer, Anthony Jeffes, and Humphrey Jeffes;[10] 4. A reckoning dated some time between 8 and 13 March 1598, in which ten actors acknowledge their debt to Henslowe: Singer, Downton, Bourne (or Bird), Charles Massey, Shaw, Jones, Rowley, Spencer, Towne, and Humphrey Jeffes;[11] 5. A reckoning dated 10 July 1600, in which eleven actors acknowledge their debt of three hundred pounds to Henslowe: Singer, Shaw, Downton, Towne, Bourne (or Bird), Humphrey Jeffes, Edward Juby, Anthony

Jeffes, Jones, Massey, and Rowley;[12] 6. A reckoning made on the occasion of the retirement of Jones and Shaw some time between 7 and 13 February 1602: Singer, Downton, Bourne (or Bird), Edward Juby, Towne, Humphrey Jeffes, Anthony Jeffes, Rowley, and Massey.[13]

The platt of the secound parte of the Seven Deadlie Sinns, (Dulwich College, MS. XIX)

This plot, preserved with the papers of Edward Alleyn, is apparently derived from a performance by an amalgamation of Lord Strange's Men and the Admiral's Men at the Theatre about 1590.[14] Horizontal lines divide the plot into twenty-three scenes, including interludes of commentary by King Henry VI and Lydgate, plus two dumbshows (Table 5).

The introductory scene (1) establishes the framework in which King Henry, asleep in his tent, awakens (2) and apparently tells Lydgate of his dreams about the Deadly Sins. The first sequence of scenes (3–8) shows the effect of Envy in the story of Ferrex and Porrex, sons of Gorboduc. In the first interlude (9), King Henry and Lydgate apparently speak as choral commentators. The second sequence (10–16) shows the effect of Sloth in the story of Sardanapalus, described in Thomas Cooper's *Thesaurus* (1565) as 'An Emperour of Assyria, so exceedingly given to effeminate wantonnesse and follie, as he may seeme to have chaunged his sexe or kinde'.[15] In the second interlude (17), King Henry and Lydgate speak again. The third sequence (18–21) shows the effect of Lechery in the legend of Tereus and Philomela. In conclusion, King Henry awakens (22), and Lydgate delivers the Epilogue (23).

Eight men play twelve principal roles, but no actors are identified in the leading roles of King Henry and Lydgate. The names of the actors who play these parts may have been omitted because these characters remain on stage throughout the play and these actors would have no reason to consult the plot, which was hung in the tiring house. Since the plot is preserved in the papers of Edward Alleyn, it seems likely that he played one of these leading roles. Phillips and Pope play one role each; Bryan, Burbage, Sly, and Harry (probably Henry Condell) play two roles each. Four boys play seven principal female roles: Ned (not further identified) plays one part; Saunder (probably Alexander Cooke), Nick (probably Nicholas Tooley, an apprentice to Burbage) and Robert Goughe (possibly an apprentice to Pope) each play two parts. Each actor who doubles in principle parts is off-stage for an interval of at least one full scene between roles. For example, Burbage plays Gorboduc in 1DS, 4, and 6; he doubles as Tereus in 18, 20, 21, and 2DS.

In minor parts, eight men play thirty-eight parts, and two boys play six parts. These actors are required to make a total of thirty-two costume changes. For twenty-four of these changes, the actor is off-stage for one full scene, but some quick changes are required. For example, Duke, Pallant, Holland, and Kit (probably Christopher Beeston) appear as four Attendants to Queen Videna at the start of 1DS. Presumably they leave the stage before the end of that scene because at the start of 3 Duke and Kit enter as soldiers of Ferrex, while Pallant and Holland enter as soldiers of Porrex. The shortest time allowed for changes of costume is when Cowley and Sincler, who play Captains at the start of 13, enter as Musicians later in the same scene. The actors who play the Seven Deadly Sins and Mercury are not identified, and the table of parts indicates how these parts can be played by men and boys who double in other minor parts. All Seven Deadly Sins appear briefly in 1; Envy appears in 2, Sloth in 9, Lechery in 17, and Mercury in 2DS. The following abbreviations of actors' names are used in the table of parts: AC = Alexander Cooke; AP = Augustine Phillips; CB = Christopher Beeston; GB = George Bryan; HC = Henry Condell; JD = John Duke; JH = John Holland; JS = John Sincler (or Sincklo); N = Ned; NT = Nicholas Tooley; RB = Richard Burbage; RC = Richard Cowley; RG = Robert Goughe; RP = Robert Pallant; TB = T. Belt; TG = Thomas Goodale; TP = Thomas Pope; V = Vincent; W = Will; WS = William Sly.

The plott of ffrederick & Basilea (British Library MS. Add. 10449, fol. 2)

This plot of an anonymous play was probably prepared for its first performance by the Lord Admiral's Men at the Rose on 3 June 1597; three other performances that year are recorded, the last on 4 July.[16] Horizontal lines divide the plot into eighteen scenes plus a Prologue and an Epilogue (Table 6). Alleyn, the leading actor of the company, who as Henslowe's son-in-law probably had special financial status with the company, plays Sebastian, the leading role, and that role only. Six of the other men who play principal roles – Juby, Slater, Towne, Tunstall, Massey, and Rowley – are included in one or more of the six lists of leading actors with the Admiral's Men already cited. Other actors in principal parts were Richard Alleyn – no relation to Edward – who on 25 March 1598 signed a contract binding him for two years as a 'hired servant' to Henslowe.[17] Edward Dutton and Robert Ledbetter, who also play principal parts, were probably hired men, as were Thomas Hunt and Black Dick, who play minor parts only. Four boys play one principal female role each: Dick (possibly Dutton's apprentice), Griffen, Will, and Pigg (possibly Edward Alleyn's apprentice). Hunt and Black Dick play five minor parts each, and these two actors are required to make thirteen changes of costume. For six of these changes, the actor is off-stage for an interval of at least one full scene for each change, but some quick changes are required. Hunt plays a Messenger in 5, and he probably doubles as one of the Soldiers who enter with Myronhamec later in that same scene; Black Dick enters as a Messenger at the start of 18, and he probably doubles as a Soldier later in that same scene. In mute parts, attendants (probably backstage helpers) play Lords in 8; gatherers (collectors of admission money) play Guards in 9, Confederates in 10, Guards in 11, and Soldiers in 18. The tables of parts list three attendants and two gatherers to make the number of actors in mute parts consistent with the number of actors identified in mute parts in the other plots. The following abbreviations of actors' names are used in the table of parts: A = Attendant; BD = Black Dick; CM = Charles Massey, D = Dick; EA = Edward Alleyn; ED = Edward Dutton; EJ = Edward Juby; G = Gatherer; Gr = Griffen; JD = James Tunstall; MS =

Martin Slater; P = Pigg; RA = Richard Alleyn; RL = Robert Ledbetter; TH = Thomas Hunt; TT = Thomas Towne; W = Will.

The plott of The Battell of Alcazar (British Library MS. Add. 10449, fol. 3)

As noted, this is the only Elizabethan play for which both a complete printed text (Q-1594) and a plot have been preserved. It was probably written by George Peele about 1589,[18] and Henslowe's *Diary* shows that between 20 February 1502 and 20 January 1593 an amalgamation of Lord Strange's Men and the Lord Admiral's Men acted this play twelve times with the variant title *Muly Mollocco*.[19] The anonymous title page of Q states that the play is 'as it was sundrie times plaid by the Lord high Admirall his servants'. The plot, probably prepared for a revival at the Rose some time between 1 December 1598 and 1 March 1599, is mutilated, parts of it are lost, and it corresponds with only the first four acts of Q; Greg suggests that the last scenes of the plot probably continued on its now lost back sheet.[20] Horizontal lines divide what remains of this plot into thirteen scenes, four of which are dumbshows (Table 7). Edward Alleyn plays Muly Mahamet, the largest role, and that role only, but the actor who plays Sebastian, the second largest role, is not identified; this may have been played by Singer or by Bird (or Bourne), both of whom are included on one or more of the six lists of principal actors with the Admiral's Men already cited, as are six of the other men who played principal roles – Downton, Towne, Humphrey Jeffes, Massey, Anthony Jeffes, and Edward Juby. Massey plays Zareo, the eighth largest part (57 lines in Q), and he doubles as an Ambassador of Spain (20 lines) and the mute Duke of Barcelis; Juby plays Calcepis Bassa (41 lines), and he doubles as the Duke of Avero (9 lines); Shaw plays the Irish Bishop (24 lines), and he doubles as the Governor of Tangier (29 lines); Jones plays the mute Luis de Silva, and he doubles as an Ambassador of Spain (27 lines). In each case where an actor in principal parts doubles, he is off-stage for at least one full scene for each change of costume. The plot also identifies Richard Alleyn, who, as noted, was probably a hired man, as Portingall-Presenter and the Governor of Lisbon, but these may be different names for the same role. In principal female roles, James plays Ruben Arches in 1 and 3, and he plays a Page in 6 and 7; the boy who plays Calipolis is not identified. In minor parts, seven men play twenty-one parts, and six boys play seven parts. Jones, Rowley, and Shaw are included in one or more of the six lists of Admiral's Men already cited, while William Kendall, Dick Juby, Robert Tailor, Thomas Hunt, William Cartwright, and George Somersett are probably hired men. Actors who play minor parts are required to make twenty-two changes of costume. For twelve of these changes, the actor is off-stage for at least one full scene for each change, but some quick changes are required. For example, Kendall enters as Abdelmenen towards the end of 1DS, and at the start of 1 he enters as an Attendant to Calcepius Bassa.

The plot's scene division is consistent with the scene division in the first four acts of Q, except that a scene of thirty-five lines between Abdelmelec and Zareo (D3-D3v) is apparently cut from the version on which the plot is based.[21] Q is the longer of the two versions, and a tally of the lines spoken by each character in Q is included with the table of parts to indicate the relative sizes of the parts. The eleven men and two boys in principal roles speak 96% of the lines. The following abbreviations of actors' names are used in the tables of parts: AB = Alleyn's Boy; AJ = Anthony Jeffes; CM = Charles Massey; D = Dab; DJ = Dick Juby; EA = Edward Alleyn; EJ = Edward Juby; GS = George Somersett; H = Harry; HF = Humphrey Jeffes; J = James; RA = Richard Alleyn; RJ = Richard Jones; RS = Robert Shaa (or Shaw); RT = Robert Tailor; SR = Samuel Rowley; TD = Thomas Downton; TDr = Thomas Drom; TH = Thomas Hunt; TP = Thomas Parsons; TT = Thomas Towne; WC = William Cartwright, Sr.

The plott of The First parte of Tamar Cam: transcript of a plot from Steevens's 'Variorum' Shakespeare 1803

This anonymous play is lost, but a transcript of the plot by George Steevens was printed by Isaac Reed in the 1803 'Variorum' Shakespeare. Greg observes that the First Part of the play was apparently written some time before 28 April 1592, when the Second Part was acted by Lord Strange's Men at the Rose as a new play, and that the plot probably belongs to a revival by the Admiral's company some time in 1602.[22] Horizontal lines divide the plot into nineteen scenes plus five entrances for the Chorus (Table 8). Edward Alleyn plays the leading role, Tamar Cam, and that role only. Seven other men who play principal roles – Humphrey Jeffes, Singer, Rowley, Downton, Massey, Bird (or Bourne), and Towne – are included in one or more of the six lists of Admiral's Men already cited. Jeffes and Singer each play one principal role and that role only. The five other actors in principal parts double in small parts, and when each of these actors doubles he is off-stage for at least one full scene for each change of costume. Two unidentified boys play the principal female roles of Tarmia and Palmeda, and apparently these actors do not double.

In minor parts, fourteen men can play fifty-eight parts, and five boys play nine parts. Anthony Jeffes and Edward Juby, both of whom are included in one or more of the six lists of Admiral's Men already cited, each play two minor parts, probably mute: Satyrs in 18 and Moores in the final procession. The six actors who play forty-seven other minor parts were probably hired men: Dick Juby, Cartwright, Thomas Marbeck, William Parr, Thomas Parsons, and Somersett. Actors in minor parts are required to make sixty-five changes of costume. For twenty-six of these changes the actor is off-stage for one full scene for each change, but some quick changes are required. For example, in 16 Parsons plays three small parts: the Nurse for Tarmia's children, a Guard, and a Persian Attendant. Six men and five boys who are probably backstage helpers such as stage-keepers and tiremen are in the final procession only. The following abbreviations of actors' names are used in the tables of parts: AJ = Anthony Jeffes; CM = Charles Massey; DB = Downton's Boy; DJ = Dick Juby; EA = Edward Alleyn; EJ = Edward Juby; GB = Gil's Boy; GE = Gedion; GI = Gibbs; GS = George Somersett; HJ = Humphrey Jeffes; J = Jeames; JG = Jack Gregory; JS = John Singer; LW = Little Will Barne; NB = Ned Browne;

RE = Rester; RF = Red Faced Fellow; SR = Samuel Rowley; TD = Thomas Downton; TM = Thomas Marbeck; TP = Thomas Parsons; TR = Thomas Rowley; TT = Thomas Towne; WB = William Bird (or Bourne); WC = William Cartwright, Sr; WP = William Parr.

PROMPT BOOKS

Evidence about casting for these documents – and for the plays of Shakespeare and other authors considered in later chapters – is summarized in tables of parts showing the number of men and boys required to perform each play, the number of lines spoken by each actor in each scene, and the total number of lines spoken by each part. Tables of parts are prepared according to the following procedures.

1. For each play, each character named in speech-prefixes and each mute part described in stage directions or in scene headings is listed on a row. Each scene in the play is listed in a column where the number of lines spoken by each character in that scene is recorded. The tables of parts preserve the spellings of the names of actors and parts as they first appear in the early texts, but my commentary follows the standardized spellings of actors' names in Nungezer. If a given character is assigned more than one name, the names are joined by a hyphen. For example, in *MND* (F) Bottom the Weaver (1.2.1) is also designated Clowne (3.1.1) and Pyramus (5.1.89); the table of parts therefore lists this character as Bottom-Clowne-Pyramus.

2. If a single line of verse is set on two typographical lines, it is counted as two lines. For example, *MND* (F) has:

> *Dem.* Quick, come.
> *Her. Lysander*, whereto tends all this? (3.2.256)

The table of parts tallies this as one line spoken by Demetrius and one line spoken by Hermia. Songs are not included in the tally of spoken lines, nor are lines by 'Both' and 'All'.

3. Principal parts are ranked – in separate tables for men and boys – according to the number of lines spoken by each part. This distinction between principal parts and minor parts observes an Elizabethan theatrical convention. As noted, in the present study a principal adult male role is defined as one who speaks twenty-five or more lines; a principal female role is one who speaks ten or more lines.

4. If a text identifies the actor who plays a given part, the names of the actor and the part he plays are underscored, as in the table of parts for *SMT*, which identifies Richard Robinson as the Spirit of the Lady. Also, the initials of each actor identified in a part are added in the appropriate row and column in the table of parts; for example, the initials RR are shown for 4.4., in which Robinson is identified as the Lady. The tables also indicate possibilities for doubling – without underscoring for actors' names or parts – that are consistent with the practice of doubling shown in the four Elizabethan stage plots that identify the part or parts played by each actor. In these plays, adult actors in the largest principal parts usually do not double, but actors in lesser principal parts double, sometimes in one or two minor roles. As noted, in *BA*

Charles Massey, who plays the principal role of Zareo in scenes 1 and 3, doubles in the small parts of the Duke of Barcelis in scene 6 and a Spanish Ambassador in scene 8. My tables of parts suggest possibilities for doubling that allow a principal actor who doubles to be off-stage for at least one full scene for each change of costume, a procedure followed in all four plots.

5. As noted, the early printed texts of Shakespeare include the names of several actors, but most of these are hired men in minor parts that need very little rehearsal.

6. Minor parts are ranked – in separate tables for men and boys – according to the number of lines each character speaks. If speech prefixes include numbers to differentiate between minor parts, these numbers are included in the table of parts. For example, speech prefixes in *DM* assign a number to each of four Madmen who speak, but a stage direction reads: *Daunce consisting of 8 Mad-men, with musicke* (sig. K). The table of parts therefore records the number of lines spoken by each of four Madmen and assigns numbers to the four other Madmen who are mute. However, most of the minor characters in the texts examined here are not so numbered. Unless a stage direction or scene heading specifies the number of mute parts required in a given scene, the table follows the casting procedures in the four stage plots, where Soldiers, Nobles, and Attendants are usually three in number. For example, *1TC* scene 1 identifies Edward Alleyn, the leading actor for the Admiral's Men, in the title role, and scene 4 has the direction: 'To him Tamor Cam [and] Otanes: 3 nobles W. Cart[wright]: Tho. Marbeck: & W.Parr.' Cartwright, Marbeck, and Parr are hired men, and in the course of this play each of these actors plays at least six minor parts. Where necessary, the table of parts adds in brackets the name of the principal characters whom a minor character serves. For example, in *BAYL* Francis Balls (FB) plays an Attendant [Prusias] in 3.2 and an Attendant [Marcellus] in 5.1.

The Second Maiden's Tragedy (1611, British Library MS. Lansdowne 807–2)

This anonymous play, probably by Thomas Middleton, is preserved in a volume containing three manuscripts that remain of the collection of John Warburton (1682–1759).[23] After the final stage direction and *ffinis*, Sir George Buc, Master of the Revels, affixes his licence and signature:

> This second Maydens tragedy (for it hath
> no name inscribed) may with the reformati-
> ons bee acted publikely   31. octbr
>   1611   G.Buc.   (Illustration 4)

The text is divided into five acts numbered in Latin, but individual scenes are not numbered; in the table of parts, scene numbers follow Lancashire's edition. My tally of spoken lines includes fifty-eight lines added by the playhouse scribe, but not 155 lines cut for reasons of censorship or of theatrical expediency. In principal parts, six men play one role each, and a seventh, the actor who plays Sophonirus (72 lines), can double as the important 1 Soldier (43 lines). Two boys play one principal role each, and a third, Richard Robinson, who in 1611 was probably an apprentice to Richard Burbage, plays the Lady who kills herself rather than yield to the lustful Tyrant.[24] When the hero, Govianus, visits the tomb of the Lady, her Spirit appears and speaks to him. In 4.4, the book-keeper notes '*Enter Lady Richard Robinson*', probably as a reminder that Robinson plays both the Lady and her Spirit and that this information should be entered in the plot. The seven men and three boys in principal parts speak 95% of the lines (Table 9).

In minor parts, eight men can play twelve small speaking parts and two mutes; one boy can play a Page (1 line) and the mute body of the Lady in 4.4. The playhouse scribe, probably at rehearsal, adds to the prompt book a slip of paper with an eleven-line speech for Memphonius, a minor part (24 lines). In the left margin of the prompt book, the book-keeper adds 'Enter mr Goughe' (Illustration 5), probably as a reminder that this new entrance for Memphonius should be added to the plot and that his new lines should be added to Goughe's part. Robinson and Robert Goughe are listed as 'Principall Actors' in F (Illustration 3). The following abbreviations of actors' names are used in the table of parts: RG = Robert Goughe; RR = Richard Robinson.

Sir John van Olden Barnavelt (1619, British Library MS. Add. 18653)

This anonymous play, probably by Fletcher and Massinger, deals with the unsuccessful struggle of Barnavelt, the great Dutch patriot, to assert the sovereignty of the provincial estates against the claims of Maurice, Prince of Orange. Barnavelt was executed on 13 May 1619, and an approximate date of the play's first performance, presumably at the second Globe, is indicated by two letters, dated 14 and 27 August 1619, from Thomas Locke to Sir Dudley Carleton, English Ambassador to the Hague (1616–21). The first letter notes that this play had recently been suppressed: 'The Players heere were bringing of Barnavelt upon the stage, and had bestowed a great deale of money to prepare all things for the purpose, but at th' instant were prohibited by my Lo: of London.' Nevertheless, the play was performed some time before 27 August, when Locke's second letter describes the play's popularity: 'Our players have fownd the meanes to goe through with the play of Barnavelt, and it hath had many spectators and receaved applause.'[25]

Most of the text is in the hand of Ralph Crane, the scribe who prepared four other extant manuscripts from the repertory of the King's Men.[26] The Master of the Revels, Sir George Buc, has censored the text extensively, and he has signed his initials to a note of reprimand: 'I like not this: neither do I think yt the pr.[ince] was thus disgracefully used. besides he is to much presented. G.B' (see upper right margin, Illustration 6). No Revels licence is affixed to this play, but in his edition Howard-Hill notes: 'The evidence of damage which brought about loss of part of the manuscript at the end leaves the question of the licence open.'[27] In a more recent study, he observes 'many inconsistencies, obscurities, and errors', and he concludes that 'the manuscript did not give a prompter all the information he would have

5 Thomas Middleton, *The Second Maiden's Tragedy*, British Library, MS. Lansdowne
807b, fol. 48, has notes in the left margin to mark the entrance of 'mr. Goughe'.

6 John Fletcher and Philip Massinger, *Sir John van Olden Barnavelt*, British Library, MS. Add. 18653, fol. 5v, has a note in the upper right margin with a reprimand by Sir George Buc, Master of the Revels.

required to guide performances'. Howard-Hill therefore suggests that *Barn*. is 'not a prompt book proper', but it is a leading example of 'a topical play adjusted initially to prevailing political interests and then, but only in part, to the practical requirements of the theatre'.[28] The manuscript is divided into acts and scenes numbered in Latin. My tally of spoken lines includes fifty-four lines added by the book-keeper, but not 131 lines deleted for reasons of censorship or of theatrical expediency.

In principal parts, seven men play one role each, four men can play two roles each, two men can play three roles each, and one man plays one principal role and three small parts. Three of these actors who play principal roles are identified in the manuscript playbook by a hand other than Crane's, presumably that of the book-keeper at rehearsals. As noted, John Rice and Richard Robinson (both listed as 'Principall Actors' in F, see Illustration 3) play two principal roles each. Rice plays the fourth largest part (207 lines), 1 Captain of English mercenaries who appears in 1.1 (identified as 'Jo:R' in the right margin, see Illustration 7), 1.3, 2.1, 2.3, 2.4, 3.2, 3.3, 4.1, and 4.4; he is off-stage for 4.5, and he doubles as an important Servant (49 lines) in 5.1; he returns as Captain in 5.3. Rice is named in the livery lists for the King's Men on 7 April 1621.[29] Robinson, who in 1611 played the Lady in *SMT*, is listed in the patent for the King's Men on 27 March 1619.[30] In *Barn*. he plays the eighth largest part, a Dutch Captain of the Guard (45 lines) in 1.3, 2.1, 2.4, 3.3, 4.2, and 4.3. He is then off-stage for two scenes before he doubles as Ambassador Boisise (40 lines) in 5.1; he returns as the Captain in 5.3. 'Migh[el]' (not otherwise identified) plays 2 Captain of English mercenaries (39 lines) in 1.1 (see Illustration 7), 1.3, 2.6, and 3.2; an English Soldier in 2.3 and 5.3; a Dutch Captain in 3.3 and 5.3; and 1 Huntsman in 4.1.

Four boys are required in principal roles as three Dutch Women and an English Gentlewoman. Three of these boys can each play one other female role, and a fourth can play Leidenberch's son. The book-keeper identifies 'G. Lowen' as Barnavelt's Wife and 'Nick' (possibly Nicholas Underhill) as Barnavelt's Daughter. Underhill, a boy actor in this play in 1619, is named in a list of men with the King's Men whom Sir Henry Herbert exempted from arrest on 27 December 1624 (see Appendix C). The fourteen men and four boys in principal roles speak 95% of the lines (Table 10).

Seven men can play sixteen small speaking parts and twelve mutes. The book-keeper identifies three of these actors by names or initials, and in almost every case an actor who doubles in these minor parts is off-stage for an interval of at least one full scene for each change of costume. 'R. T.' (not otherwise identified) plays an Officer in 1.2, 3.2, and 4.5, and Messenger in 2.2 and 2.5. He plays a Servant in 3.4, and he is off-stage for fifty-five lines before he enters as 2 Huntsman in 4.1; he is off-stage for 4.2 and re-enters as a Servant in 4.4. 'Tp' (Thomas Pollard) plays Holderus in 2.2 and 2.5, and he doubles as a Servant in 4.2. 'Mr Bir.' (George Birch) is identified as a Servant in 5.1, and can also play 2 Officer in 1.2, a Colonel in 1.3 and 3.3, and 2 Lord in 5.3. In minor female roles, 'T:Holc' (probably Thomas Holcombe) plays the Provost's Wife (1 line), and he can double as 4 Dutch Woman (4 lines). The following abbreviations of actors' names are used in the table of parts: GB = George Birch; GL = G. Lowin; JR = John Rice; M = Migh; NU = Nicholas Underhill; RR =

7 John Fletcher and Philip Massinger, *Sir John van Olden Barnavelt*, British Library, MS. Add. 18653, fol. 3, has notes in the right margin to mark the entrance of '2 Captains' played by 'Jo: R[ice]' and 'migh[el]'.

Richard Robinson; RT is unidentified; TH = Thomas Holcombe; TP = Thomas Pollard.

The Honest Man's Fortune (1625, Victoria and Albert Museum Library, MS. Dyce 9)

According to a note on the fly-leaf, this was 'Plaide in the year 1613', and although the work is credited to Fletcher in the Beaumont and Fletcher Folio of 1647, it was probably written by Nathan Field – with help from Fletcher and Massinger – in 1613, when Field was the leading actor for Lady Elizabeth's Men.[31] On what remains of the last leaf of the playbook, there are five lines of a Revels licence in the hand of Sir Henry Herbert. A modern hand has added 'Taylor' in ink to the left of the licence:

> This play being an olde one
> and the original lost was
> reallowed by mee This : 8 of Febru.
> Taylor   [1625]
> Att the Intreaty of Mr. . . .   (Illustration 8)

This is corroborated by a note in Herbert's office-book: 'For the King's company. An olde play called *The Honest Man's Fortune*, the original being lost, was re-allowed by mee at Mr Taylor's entreaty, and on condition to give me a booke this 8 February [1625].'[32] The text on which this manuscript is based was probably a prompt book that came to the King's Men by way of Field, who joined the company after the death of Shakespeare in 1616, or by way of Taylor, who joined the King's Men after the death of Burbage of 1619. Chambers cites the Beaumont and Fletcher Folio of 1679, which lists six men as principal actors in *HMF* – Nathan Field, Joseph Taylor, Robert Benfield, William Ecclestone, Emanuel Reade, and Thomas Basse – all of whom were at one time with Lady Elizabeth's Men.[33] Field, Taylor, Benfield, and Ecclestone are also listed as 'Principall Actors' in F (Illustration 3). According to J. Gerritsen, most of the manuscript is in the secretary hand of Edward Knight, the book-keeper for the King's Men, who also makes revisions in the prompt book for *BAYL*.[34] *HMF* is divided into five acts numbered in Latin, but only the first scene in each act is numbered. In the table of parts, scene numbers follow Gerritsen's edition. The tally of spoken lines does not include 147 lines deleted for reasons of censorship or theatrical expediency. The manuscript omits 5.3, which is included in the Beaumont and Fletcher Folio of 1647. Nine men play nine principal roles, and four boys play four principal female roles; the thirteen actors in principal roles speak 98% of the lines (Table 11). In 1.1, at the first entrance of the 1 Creditor (46 lines) and 2 Creditor (6 lines), Knight adds 'G. Ver.' and 'J. Rho.' in the left margin (Illustration 9). George Vernon is included in the list of King's Men who took part in the funeral procession for King James on 7 May 1625;[35] John Rhodes is included in a list of hired men whom the Master of the Revels exempted from arrest on 27 December 1624 (see Appendix C). Five men can play eight small speaking parts and nine mutes; one boy plays a mute Page. In addition to the actors' initials already noted, Knight adds 'G. Rick' to identify George Rickner as a mute Servant in 1.2; Rickner's name is included

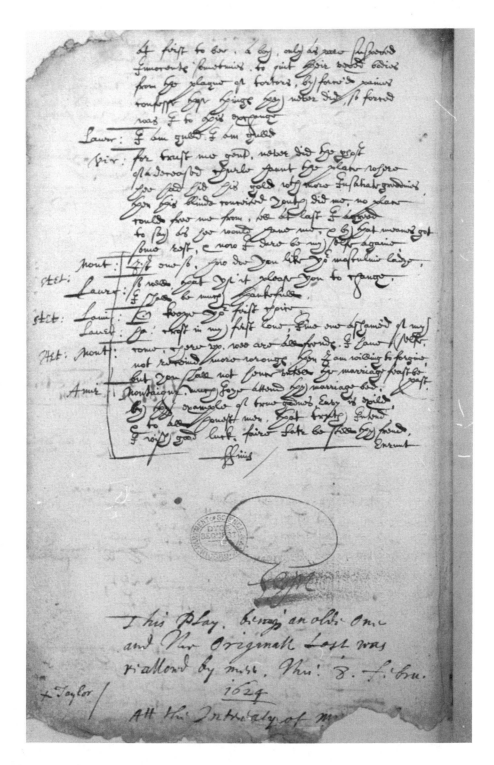

8 Nathan Field, with John Fletcher and Philip Massinger, *The Honest Man's Fortune*, Victoria and Albert Museum Library, MS. Dyce 9, fol. 34v, has the remains of a licence in the hand of Sir Henry Herbert, Master of the Revels.

9 Nathan Field, with John Fletcher and Philip Massinger, *The Honest Man's Fortune*, Victoria and Albert Museum Library, MS. Dyce 9, fol. 5, has initials in the left margin to identify 'G[eorge] Ver[non]' and J[ohn] Rho[des]' as the actors who play two Creditors.

with, but then deleted from, the same list that names Rhodes as one of the hired men whom the Master of the Revels exempted from arrest on 27 December 1624. The following abbreviations for actors' names are used in the table of parts: GR = George Rickner; GV = George Vernon; JR = John Rhodes.

Believe as you List (1631, British Library MS. Egerton 2828)

This prompt book in the autograph of Philip Massinger is a revision of an earlier draft for which Sir Henry Herbert refused a licence, as he notes in his office-book for 11 January 1631:

> I did refuse to allow of a play of Messinger's because itt did contain dangerous matter, as the deposing of Sebastian king of Portugal, by Philip the [Second] and ther being a peace sworen twixte the kings of England and Spayne. I had my fee notwithstandinge, which belongs to me for reading itt over, and ought to be brought always with the booke.[36]

In order to make the play acceptable, Massinger revised the text, and for the story of Sebastian, deposed by Spain, the author substituted the story of Antiochus, a Syrian king deposed by Rome in 192 BC.[37] The revised play met with Sir Henry's approval, and at the end of the text he adds his licence and signature:

> This Play, called Believe
> as you list may be acted this
> 6 of May 1631.
> > Henry Herbert   (Illustration 10)

   Massinger divides the text into acts and scenes appropriately numbered in Latin. On the last leaf of the manuscript, the book-keeper, Edward Knight, adds a list of six properties with the names of the six actors who need them (Illustration 11); the roles these actors play are identified indirectly because these properties correspond to those needed by six characters named in the stage directions or identified in speech-prefixes: 1. '*writing out of the booke wth a small peece of Silver for Mr Swantton*' corresponds to '*a writing [&] pen[y]*' needed by Chrysalus in 1.1; 2. '*3 notes for Mr Pollard*' corresponds to '*Ent: Berecinthius: (with 3 papers)*' (1.2); 3. '*Act:2: A writing for Mr Taylor*' corresponds to the '*scrowle writ with my royall hand*' that Antiochus mentions in 2.2; 4. '*Act:3: A letter for Mr Robinson*' corresponds to '*Ent: Lentulus: mr Rob: (wth a letter)*' (3.1); 5. '*2 letters for Mr Lowin*' corresponds to '*Ent: flaminius wth 2 letters*' (3.1); 6. '*Act:5 A letter for Mr Benfield*' corresponds to '*Ent Marcellus wth a letter*' (5.1). All six actors named on the property list are among the fourteen King's Men named in the livery list of 6 May 1629.[38] *The Diary of Thomas Crosfield* for 18 July 1634 notes that among the five companies of players in London is the King's Men at Blackfriars, for which company the masters or chief players were Taylor and Lowin.[39] As is customary, these leading actors play the leading roles: Taylor plays Antiochus, the largest part, and Lowin plays Flaminius, the second largest part.

   In preparing the text for performance, Knight cancels or writes over many of Massinger's stage directions. In addition to the property list, Knight adds to the text notes that identify seven actors who play principal roles: Taylor as Antiochus (4.1);

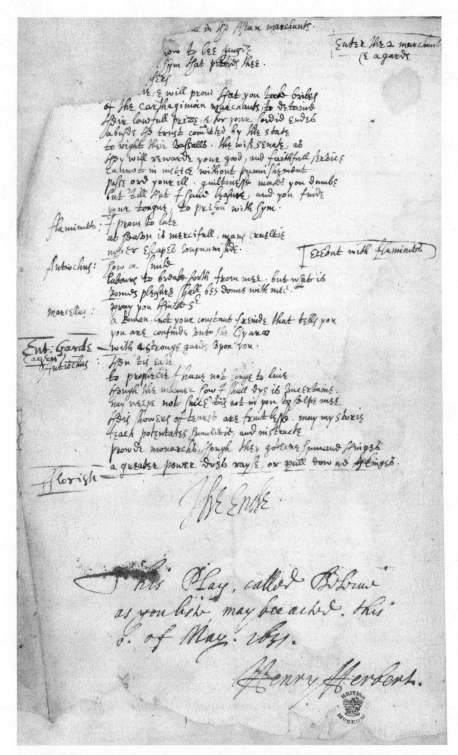

10 Philip Massinger, *Believe as you List*, British Library, MS. Egerton 2828, fol. 27v, has a
licence in the hand of Sir Henry Herbert, Master of the Revels.

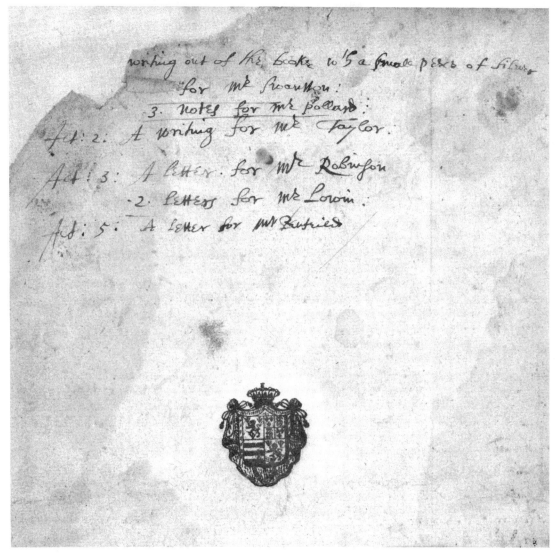

11 Philip Massinger, *Believe as you List*, British Library, MS. Egerton 2828, fol. 29v, has a list of properties and the six actors who require them.

Robinson as Lentulus (3.1); Honyman as 1 Merchant (4.3); Penn as Jailer (4.2) and 2 Merchant (5.1); Greville as 3 Merchant (5.2); Rowland Dowle as mute 1 Officer (2.2), Philoxenus (3.2), mute Other (4.2), and mute Servant (5.2); it is possible for Richard Baxter to exit as the Carthaginian Carthalo (24 lines) at line 1,176 (2.2), and at line 1,258 (3.1) to enter as Titus (27 lines), a role in which he is identified. As noted, Taylor, Robinson, and Penn received livery allowances on 6 May 1629; Honyman, Greville, Dowle, and Baxter were probably hired men in 1631.[40]

The most elaborate of Knight's additions are warnings for two stage-keepers and Taylor to be ready for an important entrance: 'Gascoine & Hubert below ready to open the trap door for Mr Taylor' (Illustration 12). William Gascoyne is named in a list of musicians and 'other necessary attendants' with the King's Men whom Sir Henry Herbert protected from arrest on 27 December 1624 (see Appendix C); Hubert is not otherwise identified. About fifty lines later, Knight adds another warning: 'Antiochus ready under the stage', and Antiochus speaks from 'below' before he emerges from his 'dungeon' (4.2). Taylor, Lowin, and Pollard are on stage frequently in the three largest roles and these actors probably do not double. However, it is possible for the actors in lesser principal roles to double. Swanston, who plays Chrysalus in 1.1 and 2.1, can play Sempronius in 4.1, 4.2, and 4.4; Robinson, who plays Lentulus in 3.1, can play the Stoic in 1.1 and Metellus in 4.1, 4.2, and 4.4; Benfield, who plays Marcellus in 5.1 and 5.2, can play Amilcar in 2.2 and King Prusias in 3.2 and 3.3. The three unidentified boys in principal female roles probably do not double; the twelve men and three boys in principal roles speak 96% of the lines (Table 12).

In minor parts, seven men can play seven speaking parts and thirteen mutes; three boys can play one speaking part and four mutes. Knight identifies five of the actors who play minor parts: Thomas Hobbes is named in the livery list of 6 May 1629, but he was never a prominent member of the company;[41] William Pattrick, Nicholas Underhill, and William Mago are named in the list of hired men already noted; Francis Balls was probably a hired man.[42] Knight's notes for casting show inconsistencies and contradictions in the assignment of roles. For example, the small part of Demetrius, who speaks a total of six lines, is assigned to three actors: Patrick in 2.1, Dowle in 2.2 and 3.1, and Baxter in 3.2, 3.3, and 5.1. Although it was common practice for actors to double in two or more minor roles, it is highly unlikely that the company would hire three actors to play the same small role at any one performance.[43] One explanation for these apparent inconsistencies is that Knight made these notes at rehearsals when the company was trying out various hired men in various parts and was testing the possibilities for doubling. When the casting of these parts was finally decided, the names of the actors and the parts they played were presumably entered in the plot; then the inconsistent notes that Knight had entered in the prompt book could be ignored. Another explanation for these inconsistencies may be that the company performed the play two or more times with different casting in minor parts. Knight identifies three minor actors as Attendants to each of two principal roles; Balls, Mago, and Underhill are Attendants to King Prusias in 3.2 and 3.3; Balls, Rowland, and Underhill are Attendants to Marcellus in 5.2. This casting is consistent with evidence in the playhouse plots, where Attendants are usually three in number.

Knight adds a Prologue (19 lines) and an Epilogue (14 lines) after the Revels licence, but these lines are not included in the table of parts because the text does not identify the actor or the character who speaks them. The following abbreviations of actors' names are used in the table of parts: BX = Richard Baxter; CG = Curtis Greville; ES = Elliard Swanston; FB = Francis Balls; JH = John Honyman; JL = John Lowin; JT = Joseph Taylor; NU = Nicholas Underhill; RB = Robert Benfield; RD = Rowland Dowle; RR = Richard Robinson; TH = Thomas Hobbes;

12 Philip Massinger, *Believe as you List*, British Library, MS. Egerton 2828, fol. 18v, has a note in the left margin 'Gascoine & Hubert below ready to open the trap doore for Mr. Taylor'.

TP = Thomas Pollard; PT = William Pattrick; WM = William Mago; WP = William Penn.

SUMMARY

Table 13 summarizes the casting requirements for eight playhouse documents: an average of 9.9 men in principal male roles and 3.3 boys in principal female roles. In *BA* (Q-1594) – and in the four extant prompt books from the repertory of the King's Men – the actors in the principal roles speak over 95% of the lines. As noted, this large share of lines spoken by the principals enables them to rehearse the play as long as necessary before enlisting hired men and boys in minor parts and as mute supernumeraries. For example, *Fred.* specifies that gatherers and attendants – in addition to their other playhouse duties – play supernumerary Lords, Guards, Confederates, and Soldiers. Thus the size of the acting company is not limited to the principal actors and the men hired as actors primarily. The following conventions are observed in casting:

1. One of the leading actors of the company plays one of the largest male roles and that role only. As noted, Crosfield's *Diary* for 18 July 1634 identifies Taylor and Lowin as the leading actors with the King's Men at Blackfriars. In *BAYL* (1631) Taylor plays Antiochus, the largest role; Lowin plays Flaminius, the second largest role. Edward Alleyn, the leading actor of the Admiral's Men, plays Muly Mahamet, the role with the most lines in *BA* (Q-1594); Alleyn also plays the leading roles of Sebastian in *Fred.* and Tamar Cam, the title role in *1TC*.

2. Other leading actors of the company play most of the lesser principal male roles, but every member of the company did not act in every play. A property list for *BAYL* (1631) identifies six men in principal male roles, and all six are among the fourteen King's Men named in the livery list of 6 May 1629. However, the other eight men on this list probably did not act in *BAYL*. In *Fred.*, *BA*, and *1TC*, each of the principal male roles is played by one of the following: Edward Juby, Slater, Towne, Tunstall, Dutton, Massey, Rowley, Downton, Humphrey Jeffes, Anthony Jeffes, Singer, and Bird (or Bourne). Each of these actors is also included in one or more of the six lists of Admiral's Men in Henslowe's *Diary* already cited.

3. Leading actors who play principal roles sometimes also play two or more minor parts. For example, in *BA* Massey plays Zareo, the seventh largest role (57 lines), and he doubles as an Ambassador of Spain (20 lines) and the mute Duke of Barcelis. For each of his changes of costume, Massey is off-stage for at least one full scene. Occasionally, leading actors play minor parts only. For example, in *1TC* Anthony Jeffes, Edward Juby, and Rowley make brief appearances as mutes in exotic costumes for the final procession.

4. Boy actors, some of whom are apprentices to the leading actors, play all of the principal adult female roles, but not until these same boys become young men do they act adult male roles. As noted, Richard Robinson, who as a boy was probably an apprentice to Richard Burbage, plays the Lady who kills herself rather than yield to the lustful Tyrant in *SMT* (1611). About eight years later, as an adult, Robinson

replaces Henry Condell as the evil Cardinal who murders his mistress by having her kiss a poisoned Bible in *DM*.

5. As noted, most minor parts are played by hired men or playhouse attendants, and most of these men double in two or more parts each. In the prompt books, most of the actors identified in minor parts are hired men who were probably cast late in the rehearsal period. In the plots, where almost all the actors and their roles are identified, there is a wide range in the number of actors required in minor parts. *Fred.* requires seven men for nineteen parts, while *1 TC* requires fourteen men for fifty-eight parts. However, as we have seen, not all of these supernumeraries are necessarily trained actors.

As will be shown in the chapter that follows, the casting requirements for fifteen pre-Restoration plays that identify actors in principal parts correspond closely to the casting requirements for these eight playhouse documents.

## CHAPTER THREE

Fifteen plays that identify actors in principal roles

Two manuscript playbooks and thirteen early printed texts identify the men and boys who act the principal roles in each play. Seven of these plays were first performed by Shakespeare's company, the King's Men, between 1619 and 1631, and eight were first acted by other London companies between 1625 and 1636. Tables of parts for these plays are prepared according to the same procedures as those followed for the prompt books examined in the previous chapter. As noted, the leading actors play most of the principal roles in any given play, but in no instance do all the leading actors of the company perform in any one play. As we have seen in the playhouse plots, hired men paid weekly wages by the company play some of the lesser principal roles and almost all the minor parts. Thus the size of the cast employed in a given play does not correspond exactly to the number of men named in the livery lists and royal patents.

KING'S MEN PLAYS

Table 14 summarizes ten documents from the years 1603–35 that identify the leading actors for the King's Men. 1. On 19 May 1603, King James issued a licence to Lawrence Fletcher, William Shakespeare, Richard Burbage, Augustine Phillips, John Heminges, Henry Condell, William Sly, Robert Armin, Richard Cowley,

> and the rest of theire Associates freely to use and exercise the Arte and faculty of playinge Comedies, Tragedies, histories, Enterludes, morralls, [and] pastoralls . . . for the recreation of our lovinge Subjects, as for our Solace and pleasure . . . as well within theire noew usual howse called the Globe within our County of Surrey as alsoe within anie towne halls or Moute halls or other coveniente places within anie other Cittie, universitie, towne, or Boroughe whatsoever within our saide Realmes or domynions.[1]

2. For the Proceedings of King James through London on 15 March 1604, the Master of the Great Wardrobe furnished each of nine King's Men with four and a half yards of red cloth: Shakespeare, Phillips, Fletcher, Heminges, Burbage, Sly, Armin, Condell, and Cowley.[2] 3. On 17 March 1619, King James issued another patent that names twelve men as his 'well beloved servants': Heminges, Burbage, Condell, John Lowin, Nicholas Tooley, John Underwood, Nathan Field, Robert Benfield, Robert Goughe, William Ecclestone, Richard Robinson and John Shank (Chambers notes that Burbage died on 13 March, probably while the patent was being prepared).[3] 4. On 19 May 1619 the Earl of Pembroke signed an order for liveries for the King's Men, and the twelve actors named are the same as those named in the licence of 17 March, except that Joseph Taylor replaces Burbage.[4] 5. On 7

April 1621 a livery allowance was granted, and the twelve actors named are the same
as the 1619 list, except that John Rice replaces Field, who died some time before
August 1620.[5] 6. On 20 December 1624, eleven King's Men signed an apology to the
Master of the Revels for performing *The Spanish Viceroy* without first obtaining the
required Revels licence: Taylor, Robinson, Elliard Swanston, Thomas Pollard,
Benfield, George Birch, Lowin, Shank, Rice, William Rowley, and Richard Sharp.[6]
7. A livery allowance for the funeral procession of King James on 7 May 1625 was
granted to fifteen men: Heminges, Condell, Richard Perkins, Birch, Sharp,
Robinson, George Vernon, Shank, Swanston, Taylor, Benfield, Rice, James Horn,
Pollard, and Lowin.[7] 8. On 24 June 1625 a royal patent was granted by King Charles
to thirteen men: Heminges, Condell, Lowin, Taylor, Robinson, Benfield, Shank, W.
Rowley, Rice, Swanston, Birch, Sharp, and Pollard.[8] 9. On 6 May 1629 a livery
allowance was granted to fourteen men: Heminges, Lowin, Taylor, Robinson,
Shank, Benfield, Sharp, Swanston, Pollard, Anthony Smith, Thomas Hobbes,
William Penn, Vernon, and Horn.[9] 10. The so-called 'Sharers Papers', a series of
petitions filed in 1635 by actors Benfield, Swanston, and Pollard, requested the Lord
Chamberlain to force the housekeepers for the Globe and Blackfriars playhouses –
Cuthbert Burbage, Mrs (Burbage) Robinson, Mrs Condell, Shank, Taylor, Lowin,
and the heirs of the actor John Underwood – to sell part of their shares to the
petitioners.[10]

The Duchess of Malfi, John Webster (Q-1623)

Its title page states that this play was 'presented privatly, at the Black-Friers; and
publiquely at the Globe, By the Kings Majesties Servants', and Chambers suggests
that it was first performed in the season of 1613–14.[11] The title page also states that Q
is 'the perfect and exact Coppy, with diverse things Printed, that the length of the
play would not beare in the Presentment'. Q is divided into acts and scenes identified
by roman numerals, and each scene heading lists all the major characters who appear
in that scene. For example, 1.1 is headed 'Antonio and Delio, Bosola, Cardinal', but
Antonio and Delio start the scene and Bosola and the Cardinal enter twenty-eight
lines later. On title page verso, a list of 'The Actors Names (Illustration 13) identifies
seven of the eight actors who play principal male roles and three boys who each play
one principal female role; the eleven actors in principal roles speak 90% of the lines
(Table 15).

Two casts are listed: 1. from before the death of Ostler on 16 December 1614 and
2. from after the death of Burbage on 13 March 1619, but before that of Tooley in
June 1623. In both cases Lowin plays Bosola, the largest role; Burbage, who in the
earlier cast plays Ferdinand, the second largest role, is replaced by Taylor; Ostler,
who in the earlier cast plays Antonio, the third largest role, is replaced by Benfield;
Condell, who in the earlier cast plays the Cardinal, the fourth largest role, is replaced
by Robinson. The men in the four largest roles do not double, but Underwood and
Rice who play the fifth and sixth largest male roles, and Robert Pallant, Jr, who in the
second cast plays the Doctor, the seventh largest role, each double as a Madman. All

The Actors Names.

Bosola, *I. Lowin.*
Ferdinand, 1 *R. Burbidge.* 2 *I. Taylor.*
Cardinall, 1 *H. Cundaile.* 2 *R. Robinson.*
Antonio, 1 *W. Ostler.* 2 *R. Benfeild.*
Delio, *I. Vnderwood.*
Forobosco, *N. Towley.*
Malateste.
The Marquesse of Pescara, *I. Rice.*
Siluio, *T. Pollard.*
The seuerall mad men, *N. Towley. I. Vnderwood, &c.*
The Dutchesse, *R. Sharpe.*
The Cardinals Mis. *I. Tomson.*
The Doctor,
Cariola,   } *R. Pallant.*
Court Officers.
Three young Children.
Two Pilgrimes.

13 John Webster, *The Duchess of Malfi* (1623), title page verso, has a list of 'The Actors Names' that identifies two casts: one before December 1614, the other some time between March 1619 and June 1623.

of the men who play the largest roles – Burbage, Taylor, Ostler, Benfield, Condell, Robinson, Underwood, and Rice – are included in the list of 'Principall Actors' in F (Illustration 3). In the principal female roles, Sharp plays the title role, and Thompson plays Julia, the Cardinal's mistress. Bentley suggests that Robert Pallant, Jr, who was baptized on 28 September 1605, could have played Cariola when he was about nine in 1613–14 and doubled as the Doctor, the Officer, and a Madman in 1623.[12]

Two other men on the list of 'Actors Names' play minor parts. Tooley, who is named in the patent of 17 March 1619, plays three minor parts in both casts: Forobosco, a comic servant, the cowardly Count Malateste, and a Madman. Pollard, one of the actors who signed the apology to the Master of the Revels on 20 December 1624, plays Silvio and doubles as a Madman in both casts. Six other men are needed to play nine other small speaking parts and eight mutes. Three boys are needed to play one small speaking part and three mutes. The actors identified in more than one role have ample time for changes of costume. For example, Underwood, who plays Delio in seven scenes, is off-stage for three scenes before he plays a Madman in 4.2. He is then off-stage for 246 lines before he enters as Delio again at the start of 5.1. Rice, who plays Pescara in 3.3 and a Madman in 4.2, is off-stage for 263 lines before he enters again as Pescara in 5.1.

The Roman Actor, Philip Massinger (Q-1629)

Its title page states that this play was 'with good allowance Acted at the private Play-house in the Black-Friers by the Kings Majesties servants', and Sir Henry Herbert, Master of the Revels, licensed it for the King's Men on 11 October 1626.[13] Q is divided into acts with roman numerals and into scenes with arabic numerals. On title page verso, lists of 'The persons presented' and 'The Principall Actors' identify the parts played by twelve men and four boys (Illustration 14). Nine men can play eleven principal male roles, and five boys play four principal female roles and a boy player. The fourteen actors in principal roles speak 98% of the lines (Table 16).

Lowin plays Domitianus Caesar, the largest role, and Taylor plays Paris, the Roman actor, the second largest role. Of the nine actors in principal roles, eight men – Lowin, Taylor, Sharp, Pollard, Benfield, Swanston, Robinson, and Smith – are among the thirteen King's Men named in the royal patent of 24 June 1625.[14] Greville, probably a hired man, is identified in the role of Latinus (32 lines), and he can double as 1 Tribune (83 lines). In principal female roles, Thompson plays Domitia, Honyman plays Domitilla, Trigg plays Julia, Alexander Goughe plays Canis, and an unidentified boy plays a boy actor.

In minor parts, eight men can play nine small speaking parts and sixteen mutes. Three men are identified in minor parts: Horn, who received a livery allowance for the funeral procession of King James on 7 May 1625,[15] plays 2 Lictor (5 lines) and 3 Tribune (3 lines), and he is free to play a Prisoner and a Hangman. Pattrick, who plays Palphurius (19 lines in 5 scenes), probably does not double; Vernon plays 1 Lictor (5 lines) and 2 Tribune (4 lines), and he can play a Prisoner and a Hangman.

The persons presented.	The principall Actors.
Domitianus Cæsar.	IOHN LOVVIN.
Paris the Tragædian.	IOSEPH TAYLOR.
Parthenius a free-man of *Cæsars.*	RICHARD SHARPE.
Ælius, Lamia, and *Stephanos.*	THOMAS POLLARD.
Iunius Rusticus.	ROBERT BENFIELD.
Aretinus Clemens, Cæsars spie.	EYLLARDT SVVANSTONE.
Æsopus a Player.	RICHARD ROBINSON.
Philargus a rich Miser.	ANTHONY SMITH.
Palphurius Sura, a Senator	WILLIAM PATTRICKE.
Latinus a Player.	GVRTISE GREVILL.
3. Tribunes.	
2. Lictors.	GEORGE VERNON.
	IAMES HORNE.
Domitia the wife of *Ælius Lamia.*	IOHN TOMPSON.
Domitilla cousin germane to *Cæsar.*	IOHN HVNNIEMAN.
Iulia Titus Daughter.	WILLIAM TRIGGE.
Canis, Vespatians Concubine.	ALEXANDER GOVGH.

14 Philip Massinger, *The Roman Actor* (1629), title page verso, has lists of 'The persons presented' and 'The principall Actors'.

Patrick and Vernon are on the list of hired men protected from arrest on 27 December 1624 (see Appendix C), and Vernon is named on the livery list for the funeral procession of King James on 7 May 1625.[16] Actors identified in more than one role have ample time for changes of costume. Pollard plays Aelius Lamia in 1.1, 1.3, 1.4, and 2.1; there is an interval of 241 lines between his exit as Lamia and his entrance as Stephanos in 3.1. Greville plays Latinus in 1.1, 1.3, 1.4, 3.2, and 4.2; there is an interval of 201 lines between his exit as Latinus and his entrance as 1 Tribune in 5.1.

The Deserving Favorite, Lodowick Carlell (Q-1629)

Its title page states that this play was acted 'first before the Kings Majestie, and since publikely at the Black-Friers by his Majesties Servants'. Evidence about the date of first performance is inconclusive, and Bentley suggests that the play may have been written as early as 1622.[17] Q is divided into five acts numbered in Latin, but scenes are not numbered. In the table of parts, scene numbers are assigned according to the convention that a scene begins when one or more characters enter a clear stage, and a scene ends when an *exeunt* clears the stage. On A3v, a list of 'The Names of the Actors' identifies the parts played by seven men and three boys (Illustration 15). Six men play six principal male roles, and three boys play three principal female roles; the nine actors in principal roles speak 97% of the lines (Table 17).

Sharp plays Lysander, the largest male role, and Taylor plays the Duke, the second largest male role. All six men identified in principal male roles – Sharp, Taylor, Benfield, Lowin, Swanston, and Robinson – are among the fifteen King's Men named in the livery list of 6 May 1629, as is Anthony Smith, who plays Gerard, a minor part.[18] In principal female roles, Honyman plays Clarinda, Thompson plays Cleonarda, and Horton plays Mariana. In minor parts, Smith and nine other men can play ten small speaking parts and eight mutes.

The Picture, Philip Massinger (Q-1630)

Its title page states that this play was 'often presented with good allowance, at the Globe, and Blacke-Friers Play-houses, by the Kings Majesties servants', and Sir Henry Herbert, the Master of the Revels, licensed it for the King's Men on 8 June 1629.[19] Acts and scenes are numbered appropriately in Latin. On title page verso, lists of 'Dramatis personæ' and 'The Actors names' identify the principal parts played by eight men and four boys (Illustration 16); the twelve actors in principal roles speak 99% of the lines (Table 18).

Taylor plays Mathias, the largest male role, and Lowin plays Eubulus, the second largest male role; other principal male roles are played by Pollard, Swanston, Shank, Benfield, Penn, and Sharp. All eight men in principal roles are among the fourteen actors named in the livery list of 6 May 1629.[20] In principal female roles, Thompson plays Queen Honoria, Alexander Goughe plays Acanthe, Honyman plays Sophia, and Trigg plays Corsica. In minor parts, six men can play eight small speaking parts and eleven mutes; three boys play three mutes. The list of 'The Actors names'

THE NAMES OF THE ACTORS.

Mᵣ. *Benfield, the King.*

Mᵣ. *Taylor, the Duke.*

Mᵣ. *Lewin, Iacomo.*

Mᵣ. *Sharpe, Lyſander.*

Mᵣ. *Swanſtone, the Count
Vtrante.*

Mᵣ. *Robinſon, Count Orſi-
nio, and Hermite.*

Mᵣ. *Smith, Gerard.*

Women.

Iohn Honiman, Clarinda.

Iohn Tomſon, Cleonarda.

Edward Horton, Mariana.

*Iaſpero, Bernardo, Seruants,
Huntſmen, &c.*

THE

A 3

15 Lodowick Carlell, *The Deserving Favorite* (1629), sig. A3, has a list of 'The Names of the Actors'.

Dramatis perſonæ.	The Actors names.
Ladiſlaus King of Hun-garie.	*Robert Benfield.*
Eubulus an old Counſay-lor.	*Iohn Lewin,*
Ferdinand Generall of the army.	*Richard Sharpe.*
Mathias a knight of *Bo-hemia.*	*Ioſeph Taylor.*
Vbaldo, *Ricardo,* 2. wild courtiers.	*Thomas Pollard.* *Eylardt Swanſtone.*
Hilario, ſeruant to *Sophia.*	*Iohn Shanucke.*
Iulio Baptiſta a great ſcholler.	*William Pen.*
Honoria the Queene.	*John Tomſon.*
Acanthe a maid of honor.	*Alexander Goffe.*
Sophia wife to *Mathias.*	*Iohn Hunnieman.*
Coriſca, Sophias woman.	*William Trigge.*

6.   Maſquers.
6. ſeruants to the Queene
Attendants.

16 Philip Massinger, *The Picture* (1630), title page verso, has lists of 'Dramatis personæ' and 'The Actors names'.

specifies '6 Masquers' and '6 servants to the Queene', but masquers are not mentioned in the text and Queen Honoria has only two servants, Acanthe and Silvia.

The Soddered Citizen, John Clavell (c. 1630, MS. private collection)

Bentley suggests a production date of about 1629 or 1630 for this 'confused and contradictory [play] that must have caused the company some embarrassment'.[21] The plot concerns the way in which an unscrupulous citizen, Undermyne, is mended or soldered by Dr Makewell. There is no record of a Revels licence, and the text shows no signs of censorship such as are found in the prompt books. It is therefore possible that the actors began rehearsals but abandoned the play before they applied for a licence. Pafford notes that the manuscript is in the hand of a professional scribe and that a theatrical reviser – whom Gerritsen identifies as Edward Knight, the book-keeper for the King's Men prompt books of *BAYL* and *HMF* – has added a number of notes and directions.[22] There are alterations in other hands that suggest revisions of a literary nature. The tally of spoken lines includes twenty-five lines added by the playhouse scribe, probably at rehearsal, but does not include 167 lines marked for deletion, probably for reasons of theatrical expediency.

The text is divided into acts and scenes numbered in Latin, and a new scene is indicated whenever a new character or group of characters enters. For example, 'Actus Primi [*sic*] Scaena Prima' begins with the direction '*Enter Undermyne, Sly (Halfe drunke)*'; these characters speak 64 lines and are still on stage when 'Scaena Secunda' begins with '*Enter Ffewtricks*'. Because the action of scenes 1.1 and 1.2 is continuous, the table of parts lists this as 1.1; other scenes are also re-numbered according to the convention that a scene begins when one or more characters enter a clear stage and a scene ends when an *exeunt* clears the stage.

On fol. 3v, lists of 'The Persons (And) Actours' (Illustration 17) identify the parts played by nine men and four boys. Eight men play eight principal male roles, and four boys play three principal female roles and a boy. These twelve actors in principal roles speak 96% of the lines (Table 19). Lowin plays Undermyne, the largest male role, and of the eight men identified in principal roles, six men – Lowin, Benfield, Sharp, Pollard, Smith, and Shank – are among the fourteen actors named in the livery list of 6 May 1629.[23] Greville and Honyman, who also play principal parts, are probably hired men. Richard Sharp speaks the Prologue and Epilogue, but the latter is missing from the text. In principal female roles, Thompson plays Miniona, Trigg plays Modestina, and 'John Shank's Boy' plays a Maid to Miniona. Alexander Goughe plays Fewtricks, a boy.

In minor parts, eleven men can play fifteen small speaking parts and seven mutes. Underhill, who is identified in the minor part of Shackle, is included in a list of hired men whom the Master of the Revels protected from arrest on 27 December 1624 (see Appendix C). Two boys can play three mutes; in addition, the list of 'Persons' includes 'A Maide-Serv. to Modestina' played by a 'Mute', but this character is omitted from the text.

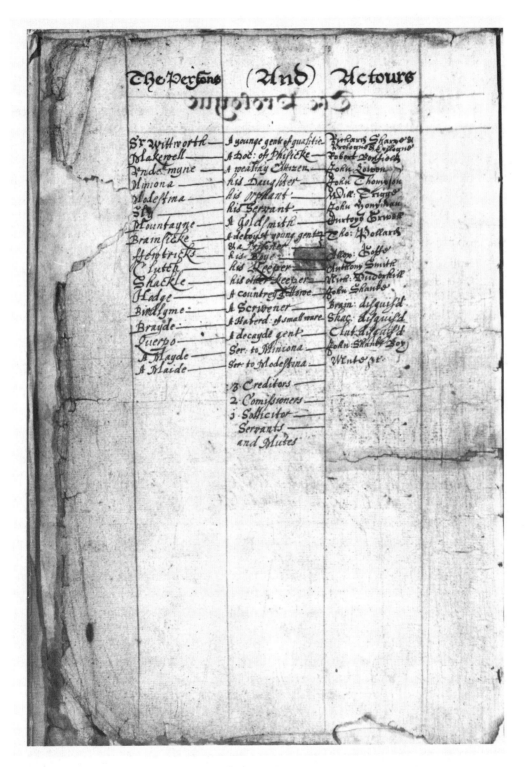

17 John Clavell, *The Soddered Citizen*, MS. private collection, fol. 3v, has lists of 'The Persons (And) Actours'.

The Swisser, Arthur Wilson (1631, British Library MS. Add. 36759)

The text is a careful calligraphic copy in the autograph of Arthur Wilson, and the title page states: 'Acted At the Blackfriers 1631'. Greg notes that there are normal speech rules but no trace of playhouse use in the manuscript, which may possibly have been prepared for the press.[24] The text is divided into acts and scenes numbered in Latin. On fol. 2a, lists of 'Persons' and 'Actors' identify the nine men who play nine principal male roles, and three boys who play three principal female roles (Illustration 18). The twelve actors in principal roles speak 99% of the lines (Table 20).

Taylor plays Arioldus, the largest male role, and Sharp plays the King of the Lombards, the second largest male role. Of the nine actors in principal roles, eight men – Taylor, Sharp, Lowin, Pollard, Benfield, Penn, Swanston, and Smith – are among the fourteen actors in the company named in the livery list of 6 May 1629.[25] Greville, who plays Iseas, the ninth largest male role, is probably a hired man.[26] In principal female roles, Alexander Goughe plays Eurinia, Trigg plays Selina, and Thompson plays Panopia. In minor parts, six men can play seven small speaking parts and eight mutes; one boy can play a small speaking part and a mute. The manuscript includes a Prologue and an Epilogue, but the speaker of neither is identified.

The Wild Goose Chase, John Fletcher (F-1652)

Its title page states that the play was 'Acted with singular Applause at the *Blacke-Friers*'; it was also acted at court by the King's Men in the Christmas season of 1621 and revived, probably at Blackfriars, in November 1632.[27] F is divided into acts and scenes numbered in Latin. In the front matter, a list headed 'Drammatis Personæ' – probably from the 1632 revival – identifies nine men who play nine principle male roles, and three boys who play three principal female roles (Illustration 19). A fourth boy is required as Footboy (11 lines) and a Boy (4 lines). The thirteen actors in principal roles speak 99% of the lines (Table 21).

Taylor plays Mirabell, the largest male role, and Lowin plays Belleur, the second largest male role. Of the nine adult actors identified, eight men – Taylor, Lowin, Pollard, Benfield, Swanston, Robinson, Penn, and Shank – are among the fourteen actors named in the livery list of 6 May 1629.[28] Honyman, who plays the Young Factor, the ninth largest male role, is probably a hired man. In principal female roles, 'Sander' Goughe plays Lillia-Bianca, Trigg plays Rosalura, and Hammerton plays Oriana. Three men can play four small speaking parts and four mutes; seven boys can play five small speaking parts and seven mutes.

QUEEN HENRIETTA'S MEN PLAYS

Six documents from the period 1629–41 identify a few of the leading actors of this company. 1. On 19 June 1629, a livery allowance is granted to Christopher Beeston

2

The Scene.

Lombardie.

Actor

Persons.

The King of the Lombards. —————————, Sharpe

Arioldus. A nobleman, retird. 2 —————————, Taylor

Andrucho A Swisser of Count. ⎫ —————————, Lowe
Count Aribert banisht ⎭ 3

Timentes. A fearfull Generall 2 —————————, Pollard

Antharis ⎫ Two old noble men ⎫ —————————, Benfeild
Clephis ⎭ Mortall Enemies ⎭ —————————, Penn

Alcidonus. Sonne to Antharis 2 —————————, Swan

Asprandus ⎫ Two gentlemen ⎰ —————————, Smith
Aeros ⎭ ⎱ ——————— Greuill

Panopia. The kings sister. 2 ————————— Toms

Eurinia. A Captiue 2 ————————— Goffe

Selina. Daughter to Clephis 2 ——————— Trigg

1 Gentleman . 4 Souldiers
1 Gentlewoman . 2 Seruants.

Gaurd.

18 Arthur Wilson, *The Swisser*, British Library, MS. Add. 36759, fol. 2a, has lists of 'Persons' and 'Actors'.

DRAMMATIS PERSONÆ.

DE-GARD, A Noble stayd Gentleman that ⎫ Acted by Mr.
being newly lighted from his Travells, af- ⎬ Robert Benfield.
sists his sister *Oriana* in her chase of *Mira-* ⎩
bell the *Wild-Goose.*

LA-CASTRE, the Indulgent Father to *Mi-* ⎫ Acted by Mr.
rabell.   ⎬ *Richard Robinson.*

MIRABELL, the *Wild-Goose*, a Travayl'd ⎫
Monsieur, and great defyer of all Ladies ⎪ Incomparably
in the way of Marriage, otherwise their ⎬ Acted by Mr.
much loose servant, at last caught by the ⎪ *Joseph Taylor.*
despis'd *Oriana.*   ⎩

PINAC, his fellow Traveller, of a lively spi- ⎫ Admirably well
rit, and servant to the no lesse sprightly ⎬ Acted by Mr.
Lillia-Bianca.   ⎩ *Thomas Pollard.*

BELLEUR, Companion to both, of a stout ⎫ Most naturally
blunt humor, in love with *Rosalura.*   ⎬ Acted by
                                         ⎩ Mr. *John Lowin.*

NANTOLET, Father to *Rosalura* and *Lil-* ⎫ Acted by Mr.
lia-Bianca.   ⎬ *William Penn.*

LUGIER, the rough and confident Tutor to ⎫
the Ladies, and chiefe Engine to intrap ⎬ Acted by Mr.
the *Wild-Goose.*   ⎩ *Hilliard Swanston.*

ORIANA, the faire betroth'd of *Mirabell,* ⎫ Acted by Mr.
and wittie follower of the *Chase.*   ⎬ *Steph. Hammerton.*

ROSALURA ⎫ the Aërie Daughters of ⎧ *William Trigg.*
LILLIA-BIANCA ⎭ *Nantolet.*   ⎩ *sander Gough.*

PETELLA, their waiting-woman.   Their Servant Mr *Shanck.*

MARIANA, an English Courtezan.

A young FACTOR. by Mr. *John Hony-man.*

PAGE.

SERVANTS.

SINGING-BOY

TWO MERCHANTS.

PRIEST.

FOURE WOMEN.

THE SCENE PARIS.

19 John Fletcher, *The Wild Goose Chase* (1652), sig. Av, has a list of 'Drammatis Personæ'.

'& thirteene others his fellowes'.[29] 2. On 20 November 1630, a livery allowance is granted to William Allen '& thirteene others his fellowes the Queenes Players'.[30] 3. Crosfield's *Diary* for 18 July 1634 notes that among the five 'severall Companies of Players in London' are 'The Queens servants at ye Phoenix in Drury Lane. Their master Mr Beeston, Mr Boyer, Shirly Robinson, Clarke.' Bentley notes that Christopher Beeston is undoubtedly the 'master', and he suggests that 'Shirley' stands for 'Sherlock' and 'Robinson' for 'Robins'.[31] 4. On 16 December 1634, a livery allowance is granted to Christopher Beeston '& 13 others his fellows'.[32] 5. On 20 December 1638, a livery allowance is granted to Richard Perkins '& 13 of his fellows'.[33] 6. On 8 January 1641, a livery allowance is granted to Richard Perkins and Anthony Turner '& twelve of their fellows'.[34]

The Wedding, James Shirley (Q-1629)

Its title page states that the play was 'lately Acted by her Majesties Servants at the Phenix in Drury Lane', and Bentley suggests 1626 as a probable date of composition.[35] Q is divided into five acts numbered in Latin, but scenes are not numbered. For the table of parts, scenes are numbered according to the convention that a scene begins when one or more characters enter a clear stage and it ends when an *exeunt* clears the stage. On title page verso, a list of 'The Actors names' identifies the ten men who play ten principal male roles and the four boys who play four principal female roles (Illustration 20). An eleventh actor can double as a Surgeon (9 lines) and a Physician (29 lines); these fifteen actors speak 98% of the lines (Table 22).

Michael Bowyer plays Beauford, the largest male role, and William Allen plays Captain Landby, the second largest male role. Of the ten men identified in principal male roles, Bowyer, William Sherlock, and William Robins are identified as leading actors for Queen Henrietta's Men by Crosfield's *Diary* for 18 July 1634, as is Hugh Clark, who in 1626 plays Gratiana, a principal female role in this play.[36] In other principal female roles, Edward Rogers plays Milliscent, John Page plays Jane, and Timothy Read plays Cardona. Five men can play three small speaking parts and two mutes. Robins, as Rawbone, speaks the Epilogue, but no Prologue survives.

The Renegado, Philip Massinger (Q-1630)

Its title page states that the play was 'often acted by the Queenes Majesties servants, at the private Play-house in Drurye-Lane', and Herbert notes in his office-book for 17 April 1624: 'For the Cockpit; *The Renegado, or the Gentleman of Venice*, Written by Messenger'.[37] The title is entered in *SR* on 22 March 1630; Q is divided into acts and scenes numbered in Latin. On title page verso, lists of 'Dramatis Personæ' and 'The Actors names' identify seven men who play seven of the nine principal male roles, and two boys who play two of the three principal female roles (Illustration 21). The twelve actors in principal roles speak 98% of the lines (Table 23).

Bowyer plays Vitelli, the largest male role, and John Blaney plays Asambeg, the

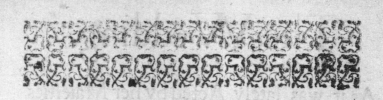

The Actors names.

Sir *Iohn Belfare*.	*Richard Perkins*.
Beauford, a paſſionate louer of *Gratiana*.	*Michael Bowyer*.
Marwood friend to *Beauford*.	*Iohn Sumpner*.
Rawbone a thin Citizen.	*William Robins*.
Lodam a fat Gentle man.	*William Sherlocke*.
Iuſtice *Landby*.	*Anthony Turner*.
Captaine *Landby*.	*William Allin*.
Iſaac, Sir *Iohns* man.	*William Wilbraham*.
Hauer a yong Gentle-man, louer of Miſtreſſe *Iane*.	*Iohn Yong*.
Cameleon, *Rawbones* man.	*Iohn Dobſon*.
Phyſition. Surgeon.	
Keeper. Seruants.	

Gratiana, Sir *Iohns* Daughter.	*Hugh Clarke*.
Iane, Iuſtice *Landbys* daughter.	*Iohn Page*.
Miliſent, *Cardonaes* daughter.	*Edward Rogers*.
Cardona.	*Tymothy Read*.

TO

Dramatis Personæ.	The Actors names.

ASAMBEG, *Viceroy of* Tunis.	Iohn Blanye.
MVSTAPHA, *Basha of* Aleppo.	Iohn Sumner.
VITELLI, *A Gentelman of* Venice *disguis'd.*	Michael Bowier.
FRANCISCO, *A Jesuite.*	William Reignalds.
ANTHONIO GRIMALDI *the* Renegado.	William Allen.
CARAZIE *an Eunuch.*	William Robins.
GAZET *servant to* Vitelli.	Edward Shakerley.
AGA.	
CAPIAGA.	
MASTER.	
BOTESVVAINE.	
SAYLORS.	
IAILOR.	
3. TVRKES.	
DONVSA, *neece to* AMVRATH.	Edward Rogers.
PAVLINA, *Sister to* Vitelli.	Theo. Bourne.
MANTO, *servant to* Donusa.	

Philip Massinger, *The Renegado* (1630), title page verso, has lists of 'Dramatis Personæ' and 'The Actors names'.

second largest male role. Of the seven men identified in principal male roles, Bowyer and Robins are identified as leading actors for Queen Henrietta's Men in Crosfield's *Diary* for 18 July 1634.[38] In principal female roles, Rogers plays Donusa, Theophilus Bird (or Bourne) plays Paulina, and an unidentified boy plays Manto. In minor parts, seven men can play six small speaking parts and seven mutes.

The First Part of the Fair Maid of the West, Thomas Heywood (Q-1631)

Bentley suggests that Part One was written about 1603; it was first published, together with Part Two, in 1631 with one Prologue and one Epilogue for both plays, which were probably acted at Hampton Court by Queen Henrietta's Men some time between 30 October 1630 and 20 February 1631.[39] The title page of Part One states that it 'was lately acted before the King and Queen with approved liking. By the Queens Majesties Comedians.' Q is divided into acts numbered in Latin, but scenes are not numbered. For the tables of parts, scenes are numbered according to the convention that a scene begins when one or more characters enter a clear stage, and it ends when an *exeunt* clears the stage.

On A4v, a list headed 'Dramatis personæ' (Illustration 22) identifies Bowyer, Perkins, William Robins, and Sherlock as the actors who play the four largest roles and Hugh Clark as the boy who plays Bess Bridges, the only principal female role. Bowyer, Sherlock, Robins, and Clark are also identified as leading actors with Queen Henrietta's Men by Crosfield's *Diary* for 18 July 1634.[40] In addition, the 'Dramatis personæ' specifies that William Allen plays Mullisheg, King of Fesse, a principal role (144 lines), who first enters late in the play, and earlier Allen can double as 1 Captain (35 lines). Christopher Goad is identified as Mr Forset (46 lines), and as a Spanish Captain (17 lines); Wilbraham is identified in the minor role of Bashaw Alcade and he can also play the Mayor (36 lines) and Mr Carol (17 lines); Robert Axen is identified as the English Merchant (15 lines), who first enters late in the play, and earlier Axen can double as 2 Captain (28 lines). The nine actors in principal roles speak 92% of the lines (Table 24).

Eight men can play thirteen small speaking parts and ten mutes. The cast list identifies Anthony Turner – who plays the principal role of Justice Landby (206 lines) in *Wed.* – in the small comic part of the Kitchen Maid (5 lines); he can double as Bashaw Joffer (5 lines). The 'Dramatis personæ' specifies 'Two Vintners boyes', and speech-prefixes identify them as 1 and 2 Drawer. The speaker of the Prologue (12 lines) is not identified.

The Second Part of the Fair Maid of the West, Thomas Heywood (Q-1631)

Bentley suggests that Part Two was probably written about 1630; as noted, Parts One and Two were issued together in 1631 with one Prologue and one Epilogue for both plays, which were probably acted at Hampton Court by Queen Henrietta's Men

Dramatis personæ.

Two Sea Captains.
M^r. Caroll, *a Gentlemã*.
Mr. Spencer.   By M^r.
Michael Bowyer.
Captain Goodlack, Spencers *friend*; *by* M^r. Rich. Perkins.
Two Vintners boyes.
Beſſe Bridges, *The fair Maid of the weſt*; *by* Hugh Clark.
M^r. Forſet, *a Gentleman*; *by* Chriſtoph. Goad.
M^r. Ruffman, *a ſwaggering Gentleman*; *by* William Shearlock.
Clem, *a drawer of wine under* Beſſe Bridges; *by* M^r. William Robinſon.
Three Saylers. A Surgeon.

A kitching Maid; *by* M^r. Anthony Furner.
The Maior of Foy, *an Alderman, and a ſervant.*
A Spaniſh Cap. by C. Goad
An Engliſh Merchant; *by* Rob. Axell.
Mulliſheg, K. of Feſſe, *by* M^r. Will. Allen.
Baſhaw Alcade; *by* M^r. Wilbraham.
Baſhaw Ioffer.
Two Spaniſh Captains.
A French Merchant.
An Italian Merchant.
A Chorus.
The Earl of Eſſex *going to* Cales: *the Maior of* Plimoth, *with Petitioners, Mutes, perſonated.*

Prologue.

Amongſt the Grecians there were annuall feaſts,
To which none were invited as chief gueſts,
Save Princes and their Wives. Amongſt the men,
There was no argument diſputed then,
But who beſt govern'd: And (as't did appeare)
He was eſteem'd ſole Soveraigne for that yeare.
   The Queens and Ladies argued at that time,
For Vertue and for beauty which was prime,
And ſhe had the high honour. Two here be,
For Beauty one, the other Majeſty,
Moſt worthy (did that cuſtome ſtill perſever)
Not for one yeare, but to be Soveraignes ever.

THE

22 Thomas Heywood, *The First Part of the Fair Maid of the West* (1631), sig. A4v, has a list of 'Dramatis personæ'.

some time between 30 October 1630 and 20 February 1631.[41] The title page of part Two is identical with that of Part One, except for the words 'second' and 'first' in their respective titles. The text of Part Two is divided into acts numbered in Latin, but scenes are not numbered. For the table of parts, scenes are numbered according to the convention that a scene begins when one or more characters enter a clear stage, and it ends when an *exeunt* clears the stage. On A4v, a list headed 'Dramatis Personæ' (Illustration 23) lists six principal parts for which five men and a boy are identified in Part One: Spencer, Goodlack, Ruffman, Clem, Mullisheg, and Bess. Presumably the same six actors play these same roles in Part Two. As noted, Bowyer, Sherlock, Robins, and Clark are identified as leading actors in Queen Henrietta's Men by Crosfield's *Diary* for 18 July 1634.[42]

Other role assignments are changed, however. In Part One, Wilbraham, a minor actor, plays Bashaw Alcade (18 lines); in Part Two this role is larger (70 lines), and Anthony Turner takes this part. Turner can also double as the English Merchant. Another leading actor, John Sumner, does not appear in Part One, but in Part Two he plays the Duke of Florence, the second largest part (295 lines). An unidentified actor plays the principal part of Bashaw Joffer (119 lines). Theophilus Bourne (or Bird) plays Toota, Queen of Fesse, the second largest female role in Part Two. The ten men and two boys who play principal parts speak 97% of the lines (Table 25). In minor parts, Christopher Goad, who in Part One is identified in the parts of Forset (46 lines) and the Spanish Captain (17 lines), is identified in Part Two as the Duke of Ferrara (39 lines). Robert Axall (or Axen) is identified as the Duke of Mantua (28 lines), and he can double as a Porter (8 lines). However, Axall cannot double as the English Merchant – the part for which he is identified in Part One – because the Merchant and the Duke of Mantua are on stage at the same time in 5.5. In addition, five men can play six small speaking parts and eleven mutes. The speaker of the Epilogue (19 lines) is not identified.

King John and Matilda, Robert Davenport (Q-1655)

Its title page states that this play 'was Acted with great Applause by her Majesties Servants at the Cock-pit in Drury-lane'. Bentley suggests a date of first performance some time after 1630, when Hugh Clark – who acts Hubert, the seventh largest male role in *KJM* – played Bessie in *1* and *2FMW*, but before 1634 when John Young and Christopher Goad – who act Leicester and Oxford in *KJM* – had left the Queen's Men for the King's Revels company.[43] Q is divided into five acts numbered in Latin, but scenes are not numbered. For the table of parts, scenes are numbered according to the convention that a scene begins when one or more actors enter a clear stage, and it ends when an *exeunt* clears the stage. On title page verso, a list headed 'The Names of the Persons in the Play, And of the Actors that first Acted it on the Stage, and often before their Majesties' identifies ten of the twelve actors who play principal male roles; four boys not identified play five principal female roles (Illustration 24). These sixteen actors in principal roles speak 99% of the lines (Table 26).

Bowyer plays King John, the largest male role, and Richard Perkins plays

Dramatis Personæ.

Toota, *Queen of* Fesse, *and wife of* Mullisheg. *By* Theophilus Bourne
Bashaw Ioffer.
Ruffman.
Clem, *the Clown.*
Mullisheg, *King of* Fesse.
Bashaw Alcade. *By* M^r. Antonie Turner.
M^r. Spencer.
Capt. Goodlacke.
Forset.
Besse Bridges.
A Porter of the kings gate.
A Lieutenant of the Moors.

A Guard.
A Negro.
A Chorus.
A Captain of the Bandetti.
The D. of Florence, *with followers. By* M^r. Ioh. Somner.
The Duke of Mantua. By Rob. Axall.
The D. of Farara. By Christoph. Goad.
An English Merchant.
Two Florentine lords.
Pedro Venturo, Generall at Sea for the D. of Florence.

23 Thomas Heywood, *The Second Part of the Fair Maid of the West* (1631), sig. A4v, has a list of 'Dramatis Personæ'.

The Names of the Persons in the Play,
And of the Actors that first Acted it on the
Stage, and often before their *Majesties*.

King *John*,   M. *Bowyer*.
   Fitzwater,   M *Perkins* } Whose action gave Grace to the Play.
Old Lord *Bruce*,   M. *Turner*.
Young *Bruce*,   M. *Sumner*.
Chester,   M. *Iackson*.
Oxford,   M. *Goat*.
Leister,   M. *Young*.
Hubert,   M. *Clarke*.
Pandolph,   M. *Allen*.
Brand,   M. *Shirelock*, who
                        performed excellently well.

Other Lords and Gentlemen,
   Attendants on the *King*.

   Queen *Isabel*.
Matilda.
   Ladies of honour.
   Lady *Abbesse*.

24 Robert Davenport, *King John and Matilda* (1655), title page verso, has a list of 'The
Names of the Persons in the Play, And of the Actors that first Acted it on the Stage, and
often before their Majesties'.

Fitzwater, the second largest male role. Of the ten actors identified in principal male roles, Bowyer, Sherlock, and Clark are also identified as leading actors for Queen Henrietta's Men by Crosfield's *Diary* for 18 July 1634.[44] William Allen, who on 20 November 1630 is granted a livery allowance with 'thirteene others his fellowes the Queenes Players',[45] is identified as Pandulph (31 lines). Five men are required for one small part and thirteen mutes; three boys are needed as three mutes.

Hannibal and Scipio, Thomas Nabbes (Q-1637)

Its title page states that this play was 'Acted in the yeare 1635 by the Queenes Majesties Servants, at their Private house in Drury Lane'. The text is divided into five acts with an argument preceding each. A new scene is indicated whenever a new character or characters enter, and each act continues from the first entrance until an *exeunt* at the end of the act clears the stage. The table of parts therefore lists each act in a single column.

On A4, a list of 'The speaking persons' identifies the parts played by eleven men and one boy (Illustration 25). Eleven men play fourteen principal male roles and four minor parts; four boys play four principal female roles; these fifteen actors speak 99% of the lines (Table 27). William Allen, who is named as the leading actor of the company in the livery list of 20 November 1630,[46] plays Hannibal, the largest male role; Bowyer, Clark, and Sherlock, who are named as leading actors for this company in Crosfield's *Diary* for 18 July 1634,[47] also play principal roles. Bowyer, who plays Scipio, the second largest male role, speaks the Epilogue and presumably the Prologue as well. Clark doubles as Syphax, the third largest male role, and as an important Nuntius. Sherlock doubles in the principal parts of Maharball and Prusias; Bird (or Bourne), Sumner, Perkins, and Page play one principal role each. George Stutfield is identified as a Soldier and Bostar, and Robert Axen as Bomilcar and Giscon; Anthony Turner plays Piston, and he can also play Flaminius. The actors who are identified in more than one principal role all have ample time for changes of costume. For example, Sherlock is off-stage for Acts 3 and 4 while he changes from Maharball to Prusias. Clark has an interval of 58 lines between his exit as Nuntius in Act 1 and his entrance as Syphax in Act 2; he has an interval of 340 lines between his exit as Syphax in Act 3 and his re-entrance as Nuntius in Act 4.

Ezekiel Fenn, a boy, plays Sophonisba, the largest female role; three other unidentified boys are required in three other principal female roles, and they can double as attendants to Sophonisba. Eight men are required in three small speaking parts and as eighteen mutes.

PLAYS OF OTHER LONDON COMPANIES

Holland's Leaguer, Shakerly Marmion (Q-1632)

Its title page states that this play was 'often Acted with great applause, by the high and mighty Prince Charles his Servants, at the private house in Salisbury Court'.

The speaking persons.

Maharball.	By *William Shurlock.*
Himulco.	By *Iohn Sumner.*
Souldier.	By *George Stutfield.*
A Lady.	
Hannibal.	By *William Allen.*
2. other Ladies.	
Nuntius.	By *Hugh Clerke.*
Bomilcar.	By *Robert Axen.*
Syphax	By *Hugh Clerke.*
Piston.	By *Anthony Turner.*
Crates.	
Messenger.	
Scipio.	By *Michael Bowyer.*
Lelius	By *Iohn Page.*
Sophonisba.	By *Ezekiel Fenn.*
Massanissa.	By *Theophilus Bird.*
Hanno.	By *Richard Perkins.*
Gisgon.	By *Robert Axen.*
Bostar.	By *George Stutfield.*
Lucius.	
A young Lady.	
Prusias.	By *William Shurlock.*

Mutes.

Ladies.   Souldiers.
Attendants.   Senators.

I desire thee Reader to take notice that some escapes have past the
Presse ; As Tuning for Tunny ; dimacing for dimning : meane for
meere ; stand for share, &c. which notwithstanding are corrected
in divers of the copies : where they are not, let thine owne judge-
ment rectifie them, before thy rashnesse condemne me. Farewell.

25 Thomas Nabbes, *Hannibal and Scipio* (1637), sig. A4, has a list of 'The speaking persons'.

Herbert notes in his office-book that the play was 'acted six days successively at Salisbury Court in December, 1631',[48] and the title is entered in *SR* on 26 January 1632. Q is divided into acts and scenes, but there are inconsistencies in the numbering of scenes. For the table of parts, scenes have been re-numbered according to the convention that a scene begins when one or more characters enter a clear stage, and it ends when an *exeunt* clears the stage.

On A4v, a list of 'Dramatis Personæ' identifies Andrew Cane as Trimalchio, the largest male role, Matthew Smith as Aguertes, the second largest role, and Ellis Worth as Ardelio, the third largest role (Illustration 26). Crosfield's *Diary* for 18 July 1634 names 'Mr Cane, Mr Worth, and Mr Smith' as the leading actors with Prince Charles's (II) company at the Red Bull.[49] Seven other men are identified in one principal role each; six boys are identified in one principal female role each, and a seventh boy is needed as 1 Whore (17 lines). The seventeen actors who play principal roles speak 99% of the lines (Table 28). In minor parts, two men are required for one speaking part and two mutes; one boy can play two small parts.

The Tragedy of Messalina, Nathanael Richards (O-1640)

Its title page states that this play was 'Acted With generall applause divers times, by the Company of his Majesties Revells'. Bentley suggests that it was probably first acted by the King's Revels company some time after the Crosfield's *Diary* entry for 18 July 1634 and before 12 May 1636, when the theatres were closed because of the plague.[50] O is divided into acts numbered in arabic, but scenes are not numbered. For the table of parts, scenes are numbered according to the convention that a scene begins when one or more characters enter a clear stage, and it ends when an *exeunt* clears the stage.

On B, a list of 'The Actors Names' identifies six of the eleven men who play principal male roles and three of the five boys who play principal female roles (Illustration 27); the sixteen actors in principal roles speak 96% of the lines (Table 29). As noted, Crosfield's *Diary* identifies nine men who were the 'chief' actors at Salisbury Court,[51] and four of these men are also identified in principal male roles for *Mess.*: Goad plays Silius, the largest male role; John Robinson plays Sausellus, the second largest male role; Sam Tomson and William Cartwright, Sr play the fourth and sixth largest male roles respectively. In principal female roles, John Barret plays the title role, Thomas Jordan plays Lepida, and Mathias Morris plays Sylana. Nine men are needed to play nine small speaking parts and seven mutes; eleven boys are needed to play five small speaking parts and twenty mutes. A Prologue and an Epilogue are included, but the speaker of neither is identified.

Bentley observes: 'Besides the roles cast, there are over thirty other characters (most of whom speak), dances, processions and spectacles, including Messalina and Silius appearing aloft in a cloud and then descending as in a masque.' He therefore suggests that even with extensive doubling it would be 'next to impossible to stage this play in its present form'.[52] The most elaborate casting requirements are for '*Eight Furies dance and Anticke and depart*' (2.2) and for an '*Antimasque consisting of*

Dramatis Personæ.

Philautus, a Lord inamor'd of himselfe.	William Browne.
Ardelio, his parasite.	Ellis Worth.
Trimalchio, a humorous gallant.	Andrew Keyne.
Agurtes, an Impostor.	Mathew Smith.
Autolicus, his disciple.	Iames Sneller.
Capritio, a young Novice.	Henry Gradwell.
Miscellanio, his Tutor.	Thomas Bond.
Snarle, *Fidelio.* } *friends to Philautus.*	Richard Fowler. Edward May.
Ieffery, tenant to Philautus	Robert Huyt.
Triphæna, wife to Philautus.	Robert Stratford.
Faustina, sister to Philautus.	Richard Godwin.
Millescent, daughter to Agurtes.	Iohn Wright.
Margery her maid.	Richard Fouch.
Quartilla, Gentlewoman to Triphæna.	Arthur Savill.
Bawd.	Samuell Mannery.
2 Whores. Pander. Officers.	

26 Shakerly Marmion, *Holland's Leaguer* (1632), sig. A4, has a list of 'Dramatis Personæ'.

The Actors Names,

Claudius Emperour —— Will. Cartwright Sen.
Silius chiefe Favorite } Christopher Goad.
  to the Empresse.
Saufellus chiefe of Counsell } Iohn Robinson.
  to Silius and Messallina
Valens } Of the same faction and favorites.
Proculus
Menester an actor and Favorite }
  compel'd by the Empresse. } Sam. Tomson.
Montanus a Knight in Rome } Rich. Iohnson.
  defence vertuously inclined.
Mela Seneca's Brother —— Will. Hall.
Virgilianus and } Senators of Messallinas Faction.
Calphurnianus
Sulpitius of the same Faction.
Narcissus }
Pallas } Minnions to the Emperour of his faction
Calistus }
Evodius a Souldier.

Messallina Empresse —— Iohn Barret.
Lepida mother to Messallina —— Tho. Iordan.
Sylana wife to Silius —— Mathias Morris.
Vibidia matron of the Vestalls.
Calphurnia a Curtizan.
Hem and Stitch, two Panders.
Three murdered Roman Dames.
Manutius and Folio, Seryants to Lepida.
Three Spirits.
Two severall Antimasques of Spirits and Bachinalls.
B

27 Nathanael Richards, *The Tragedy of Messalina* (1640), sig. B, has a list of 'The Actors Names'.

eight Bachinalians' (5.1). In the plot for *BA*, Thomas Parsons, a boy, plays a Fury, which suggests the Furies and the Bachinalians in *Mess.* are played by boys. After the Bachinalians leave the stage, there is solemn music and eighteen lines are spoken before '*three courtesans in the habit of Queens enter*'; presumably three of the Bachinalians can double as the three Courtesans. My estimate of twenty men required for *Mess.* does not differ significantly from the twenty-two men in the plot for *1TC*. However, the requirement for thirteen boys in *Mess.* is unusually high.

SUMMARY

Table 30 summarizes the casting requirements for fifteen plays that identify actors in principal roles. An average of 9.3 men are required in principal male roles and 3.7 boys in principal female roles, and on average the men and boys in principal roles speak over 97% of the lines. These requirements correspond closely to the requirements for the eight playhouse documents examined earlier. The following conventions are observed in casting:

1. One of the leading actors of the company plays the largest male role and that role only. As noted, Crosfield's *Diary* for 18 July 1634 identifies the leading actors with the King's company at Blackfriars as 'Mr Taylor [and] Mr Lowen'.[53] Taylor plays the largest male role in three of the plays considered here: Mathias in *Pict.*, Arioldus in *Swiss.*, and Mirabell in *WGC*; he plays the second largest male role in three plays: Ferdinand in *DM*, Paris in *RA*, and the Duke in *DF*. Lowin plays the largest male role in three plays: Bosola in *DM* (both casts), Domitianus Caesar in *RA*, and Undermyne in *SC*; he plays the second largest male role in two plays: Eubulus in *Pict.* and Belleur in *WGC*.

Crosfield names Michael Bowyer as one of four leading actors with Queen Henrietta's Men at the Phoenix or Cockpit in Drury Lane,[54] and Bowyer plays the largest male role in five of the six casts in which he is identified: Vitelli in *Ren.*, Beauford in *Wed.*, Spencer in *1* and *2FMW*, and King John in *KJM*; Bowyer also plays Scipio, the second largest male role in *Han.* Hannibal, the largest male role, is played by William Allen, who is named as the leading actor for Queen Henrietta's Men in a livery allowance on 20 November 1630.[55] Crosfield names 'Mr Cane' as one of the chief actors with Prince Charles's (II) company at the Red Bull,[56] and Andrew Cane plays Trimalchio, the largest male role in *HL*. Crosfield names Christopher Goad as one of the nine chief actors with the King's Revels company at Salisbury Court, and Goad plays Silius, the largest male role in *Mess.*

2. Other leading actors of the company play most of the lesser principal male roles, but every member of the company does not act in every play. As noted, on 6 May 1629 a livery list for the King's Men names fourteen actors, but only eight of these men are identified in the principal male roles in *Pict.* (Q-1630), which Herbert licensed for the King's Men on 8 June 1629.[57]

3. Some of the leading actors play two or more smaller roles. For example, in *DM* three actors who play principal roles double in minor parts: Underwood, who plays Delio (the fifth largest male role, 185 lines), doubles as a Madman (8 lines); Rice, who

plays Pescara (the sixth largest male role, 70 lines), doubles as a Madman (7 lines); Robert Pallant, Jr, who plays a Doctor (the seventh largest male role, 42 lines), doubles as an Officer (4 lines) and as a Madman (10 lines). The shortest time allowed for any of these changes in *DM* is the 246 lines that elapse between Underwood's exit as a Madman in 4.2 and his re-entrance as Delio in 5.1.

4. Boy actors, some of whom are apprentices to the leading actors, play all the principal female roles, and when some of these boys become young men they act adult male roles. For example, John Honyman was baptized on 7 February 1613,[58] and he plays Domitilla in *RA* (1626) Clarinda in *DF* (1629?), and Sophia in *Pict.* (1629). About 1630 Honyman changes to principal male roles when he plays Sly, a tricky servant in *SC*; in 1632, he plays the Young Factor in *WGC*.

5. Hired men and playhouse attendants usually play most of the minor parts, and most of these men play two or more parts each. For example, Pollard plays Silvio (21 lines) and doubles as a Madman (10 lines) in *DM*; Vernon plays 1 Lictor (5 lines) and doubles as 2 Tribune (4 lines) in *RA*; Horn plays 2 Lictor (5 lines) and 3 Tribune (3 lines) in *RA*.

The next chapter shows how the casting requirements for thirty-eight plays usually attributed to Shakespeare correspond closely to the requirements for these fifteen pre-Restoration plays that identify actors in principal roles.

## CHAPTER FOUR

Thirty-eight plays by Shakespeare

The casting requirements for the thirty-six plays printed in the Shakespeare First Folio (1623) – hereafter referred to as F – are described in the order of composition proposed by Chambers.[1] Also studied are *Pericles* (*Per.* Q1-1609) and *The Two Noble Kinsmen* (*TNK* Q-1634), which are not included in F but are attributed wholly or in part to Shakespeare. F provides the only authoritative text for eighteen plays, but eighteen others survive in at least one earlier quarto. F reprints five of these quartos without significant change, and for these plays I describe the requirements for Q only. For thirteen other plays there are significant differences between F and earlier quartos, and for these plays I describe the requirements of F, as well as one or more variant quartos. For each of these texts, the date of entry in the *Stationers' Register* is given, as well as the dates and places of performance, if any, before 1642. Tables of parts are prepared according to the same procedures as those followed for the fifteen plays that identify actors in principal roles.

PLAYS OF THE FIRST FOLIO

The Second Part of King Henry the Sixth (Q1-1594 and F)

Q1 title page identifies this as 'The First Part of the Contention betwixt the two famous Houses of Yorke and Lancaster, with the death of the good Duke Humphrey: And the banishment and death of the Duke of Suffolke, and the tragicall end of the proud Cardinall of Winchester, with the notable Rebellion of Jacke Cade; and the Duke of Yorkes first claime unto the Crowne'. On 12 March 1594, Thomas Millington entered in *SR* 'a booke' with essentially the same title.

   Q1 is not divided into acts and scenes, and it has 1,932 spoken lines. Nine men can play eleven principal and five minor male roles; two boys play two principal female roles. These eleven actors speak 85% of the lines (Table 31). In addition, fifteen men are needed to play forty small speaking parts and thirty-nine mutes; three boys are needed for six minor parts.

   F is not divided into acts and scenes, and it has 3,109 spoken lines. Ten men can play eighteen principal and two minor male roles; two boys play two principal female roles. These twelve actors speak 90% of the lines (Table 32). In addition, fourteen men can play thirty-nine small speaking parts and thirty-five mutes. Three boys can play five minor parts. Thus while Q1 has fewer spoken lines, both texts require about the same number of actors, and this suggests that Q is not necessarily a text abridged for a smaller company touring the provinces.[2] In F, the scene heading for 4.2 is 'Enter

Bevis, and John Holland', and speech-prefixes for these characters are '*Bevis*' and '*Hol*' (in Q1 they are Rebels named *Nick* and *George*). Bevis is not otherwise identified; he can double in two other minor parts. John Holland is also identified in the plot for *2SDS* – probably acted by an amalgamation of Lord Strange's Men and the Lord Admiral's Men about 1590 – as an Attendant, a Soldier, a Captain, and a Warder; in F, Holland can double in at least one other minor part.

The Third Part of King Henry the Sixth (O-1595 and F)

Octavo title page identifies this as 'The True Tragedie of Richard Duke of Yorke, and the death of good King Henrie the Sixt, with the whole contention betweene the two Houses Lancaster and Yorke, as it was sundrie times acted by the Right Honourable the Earle of Pembrooke his servants.'

O is not divided into acts and scenes, and it has 2,163 spoken lines. O omits 4.3 – as numbered in modern editions – and the five subsequent scenes are transposed as 4.5, 4.4, 4.7, 4.6, and 4.8 – as numbered in modern editions. Eight men can play ten principal male roles and two minor parts; four boys can play two principal female roles and two boys. The twelve actors in principal parts speak 92% of the lines (Table 33). In addition, fourteen men are needed for twenty-one small speaking parts and fifty mutes. One boy can play two small parts. .

The title is included in the list of sixteen plays entered in *SR* by Edward Blount and Isaac Jaggard on 8 November 1623. F is not divided into acts and scenes, and it has 3,010 spoken lines. Eight men can play eleven principal and two minor male roles; four boys can play two principal female roles and two boys. These twelve actors speak 91% of the lines (Table 34). In addition, sixteen men are needed for thirty small speaking parts and fifty-two mutes; one boy can play three minor parts. Although O has about one-third fewer lines than F, the requirements for actors do not differ significantly in the two texts. This suggests that O is not necessarily an abridgement prepared for a small touring company.

F identifies the parts played by three actors. At 1.2.47 the stage direction reads '*Enter Gabriel*', and the prefix for his speech as a Messenger (as he is called in O) is '*Gabriel*'. This is probably Gabriel Spencer, who is named in various transactions with the Admiral's Men recorded in Henslowe's *Diary*.[3] The scene heading for 3.1 reads '*Enter Sinklo and Humfrey, with Crosse-bowes in their hands*', and throughout the scene the speech-prefixes for these Keepers (as they are called in O) are '*Sink.*' and '*Hum.*'. The plot for *2SDS* identifies '*J. Sincler*' as playing a Keeper, a Soldier, a Captain, and a Musician. In the Induction for *Shr.*, '*Sincklo*' is the prefix for a speech by one of the Players.[4] Humphrey Jeffes is a leading actor in the Admiral's Men who is mentioned frequently in Henslowe's *Diary*; the plot for *BA* identifies '*H. Jeffe*' as Muly Mahamet Xeque, and the plot for *1TC* identifies '*H. Jeffs*' as Otanes.[5]

The First Part of King Henry the Sixth (F)

Chambers ascribes *2H6* and *3H6* to 1591 and *1H6* to 1592, and he identifies the latter play with 'Harey the vi' produced by Strange's Men for Henslowe on 3 March 1592.[6]

F is the only authoritative text; it is divided into five acts, but with incomplete scene division. There are 2,652 spoken lines.

Fifteen men can play twenty-three principal and one minor male roles; two boys can play three principal female roles and a boy. These seventeen actors speak 92% of the lines (Table 35). In minor parts, thirteen men can play thirty speaking parts and thirty-one mutes. This requirement of twenty-eight adult actors is significantly higher than the average of 18.7 adults required for other Shakespeare plays.

King Richard the Third (Q1-1597 and F)

The title is entered in *SR* on 20 October 1597, and although the title page of Q1 does not name the author, it states that the play 'hath beene lately Acted by the Right honourable the Lord Chamberlaine his servants'. Meres (1598) identifies Shakespeare as author of 'Richard the 3', as do the title pages of all five subsequent quartos before F (Q2-1598, Q3-1602, Q4-1605, Q5-1612, and Q6-1622).

Q1 is not divided into acts and scenes, and there are 3,419 spoken lines. Eleven men can play sixteen principal and two minor male roles; six boys play four principal female roles and three principal boys' roles; these seventeen actors speak 95% of the lines (Table 36). In other minor parts, eight men can play twenty-seven speaking parts and ten mutes; one boy can play two small parts.

F is divided imperfectly into acts and scenes, and there are 3,721 spoken lines. The casting requirements for F are almost the same as for Q1. Eleven men can play sixteen principal and two minor male roles; six boys can play four principal female roles and three principal boys' roles. These seventeen actors speak 95% of the lines (Table 37). In other minor parts, eight men can play twenty-eight speaking parts and seventeen mutes. One boy can play two small parts.

The Comedy of Errors (F)

The earliest record of this play is for a performance at Gray's Inn on 28 December 1594; Meres (1598) mentions 'Errors' as one of Shakespeare's comedies, and it was revived at court on 28 December 1604.[7] F is the only authoritative text, and the title is included in the list of sixteen plays entered in *SR* by Edward Blount and Isaac Jaggard on 8 November 1623. F is divided into five acts numbered in Latin, but not divided into scenes; there are 1,798 spoken lines.

Eight men can play eight principal and one minor male roles; five boys play five principal female roles. These thirteen actors speak 97% of the lines (Table 38). In minor parts, five men can play four speaking parts and seven mutes.

Titus Andronicus (Q1-1594 and F)

Henslowe's *Diary* records that 'the earle of susex his men' received three pounds, eight shillings for 'titus & ondronicus the 23 of Jenewary' (1594); on 28 January and 6 February, the same company revived the play and received forty shillings at each performance. Henslowe also records that 'my Lord Admearalle men & my Lorde chamberlen men' – probably an amalgamation – received twelve shillings for a revival of this play on 5 June 1594 and seven shillings on 12 June 1594.[8] On 6 February 1594, John Danter entered the title in *SR*, and in the same year Danter printed Q1 with its title page stating that the play is 'As it was Plaide by the Right Honourable the Earle of Darbie, Earle of Pembrooke, and Earle of Sussex their Servants'. Although the title page does not identify the author, Meres (1598) attributes the play to Shakespeare.

Q1 is not divided into acts and scenes, and there are 2,416 spoken lines. Ten men can play thirteen principal male roles. Four boys play four principal female roles, and these fourteen actors speak 98% of the lines (Table 1). Thirteen men can play five small speaking parts and twenty-four mutes.[9]

F is divided into acts only, and it adds an important eighty-five-line scene (3.2); there are 2,579 spoken lines. Stage directions in F have been edited and sometimes supplemented. For example, F adds the important stage direction '*He kils him*' when Titus slays Mutius (1.1.291); as noted earlier, a speech by the Roman Lord (5.3.73–95) in Q is assigned to a Goth in F. Ten men can play eleven principal and two minor male roles; four boys play four principal female roles, and these fourteen actors speak 99% of the lines (Table 3). Thirteen men can play six small speaking parts and twenty-six mutes.

The Taming of the Shrew (F)

Henslowe notes a performance of 'the tamyinge of A shrowe' on 11 June 1594, and this possibly refers to the anonymous *The Taming of A Shrew*, printed in 1594.[10] F is the only authoritative text of *Shr.*, which is divided into acts only; there are 2,598 spoken lines. F identifies '*Sincklo*' as one of the Players in the Induction, and this is probably John Sincler, the actor also identified in minor parts for *2SDS*, *3H6*, and *2H4*.[11] Eleven men can play thirteen principal and one minor roles; three boys can play four principal female roles, and these fourteen actors speak 97% of the lines (Table 39). Seven men can play fourteen small speaking parts and six mutes. Three boys can play one small speaking part and four mutes. On 26 November 1633, Herbert notes in his office-book that *The Taming of the Shrew* was acted before the King and Queen and 'Likt'.[12]

The Two Gentlemen of Verona (F)

There is general agreement that this is one of Shakespeare's early comedies, but the only external evidence as to date is that Meres (1598) mentions 'Gentlemen of Verona'. F is the only authoritative text, and the title is included in the list of sixteen plays entered in *SR* by Edward Blount and Isaac Jaggard on 8 November 1623. The names of the characters in each scene are massed at its start, but there are no other stage directions, except *Exeunt* at the end of most scenes. Acts and scenes are divided regularly and numbered in Latin, and there are 2,234 spoken lines.

Nine actors can play ten principal and one minor male roles. Three boys play one principal female role each, and these twelve actors speak 98% of the lines (Table 40). Three men play three minor speaking roles. After the final *Exeunt*, F lists 'The names of all the Actors', but these are, in fact, all the speaking roles, including 'Out-lawes with Valentine'.

Love's Labour's Lost (Q1-1598)

Meres (1598) identifies Shakespeare as the author of 'Love labors lost', and Q1 title page states that this play 'by W. Shakespeare' was 'presented before her Highnes this last Christmas', which suggests performance at court in late 1597. It was revived at court some time between New Year's Day and Twelfth Night, 1605 and acted soon afterwards in a private performance at the Earl of Southampton's house.[13] The title is entered in *SR* on 22 January 1607. Q1 is not divided into acts and scenes; there are 2,619 spoken lines.

Nine principal actors play nine principal male roles; six boys can play five principal female roles and Moth, a page. These fifteen actors speak 99% of the lines (Table 41). Five men can play four small speaking parts and five mutes. As Greg notes, F was set from Q1 without significant change.[14]

Romeo and Juliet (Q1-1597 and Q2-1599)

Meres (1598) identifies Shakespeare as author, and Q1 title page states that the play 'hath been often (with great applause) plaid publiquely, by the right Honourable the L. of Hunsdon his Servants'; Greg notes that Shakespeare's company was known by this title only between 22 July 1596 when George Carey succeeded his father, the Lord Chamberlain, in the title and in the patronage of the players, and 17 April 1597, when he was in turn appointed to his father's office.[15] The title is entered in *SR* on 22 January 1607. Q1 is not divided into numbered acts and scenes; there are 2,218 spoken lines.

In Q1, nine men can play nine principal and three minor male roles, if the actor who plays the First Capulet Servant (58 lines) also plays the Clown (3 lines) and Peter (3 lines). Q1 assigns the 'Queen Mab' speech (35 lines) to Benvolio instead of to Mercutio; it also assigns many of Friar Laurence's early lines to Friar Francis. Three boys play three principal female roles, and the twelve actors who play principal roles speak 95% of the lines (Table 42). Seven men can play fifteen small speaking parts and six mutes. Two boys can play three small speaking parts and two mutes.

The title page of Q2 describes it as 'Newly corrected, augmented, and amended: As it hath bene sundry times publiquely acted by the right Honourable the Lord Chamberlaine his Servants'. Q2 is not divided into numbered acts and scenes; there are 3,037 spoken lines. The direction '*Enter Will Kemp*' (4.5.100) identifies this actor as Peter, the comic servant of the Capulets. Eleven men can play twelve principal and four minor parts. Three boys play three principal female roles, and the fifteen actors in principal roles speak 97% of the lines (Table 43). Thirteen men can play fourteen small speaking parts and twenty mutes; five boys can play three small speaking parts and seven mutes. Greg notes that Q3 (1609) is a reprint of Q2 and that F was set from Q3 without significant changes.[16]

King Richard the Second (Q1-1597 and F)

The title is entered in *SR* on 29 August 1597, and the title page of Q1 states that this play was 'publikely acted by the right Honourable the Lorde Chamberlaine his Servants'. Meres (1598) names Shakespeare as author, as do the title pages of Q2 (1598) and all three subsequent quartos before F (Q3-1598, Q4-1608, and Q5-1615). Greg notes that Q4 prints for the first time the scene dealing with Richard's deposition (4.1.154–318), which apparently for political reasons was cut from the text on which Q1 is based.[17] The play was revived on 7 February 1601, the day before the futile Essex rebellion, and shortly thereafter actors in the company, when questioned by the authorities, claimed the play as 'old and long out of use'. However, it was again revived at the Globe for at least two performances in June 1631.[18] Q1 is not divided into acts and scenes; there are 2,565 spoken lines. Ten men can play fifteen principal and one minor male roles; three boys play three principal female roles. These thirteen actors speak 93% of the lines (Table 44). Six men can play sixteen small speaking parts and six mutes. Three boys play one small speaking part and two mutes.

F includes the deposition scene, and Gurr observes: 'The Folio text . . . shows playhouse influences. It omits some passages (1.3.129–33, 238–41, 267–92; 3.2.29–32; and 4.1.52–9), which look like acting cuts, together with some isolated lines (2.2.77, 3.2.49 and 182, and 5.3.98), and regularises many of the stage directions and speech headings to make it a more manageable acting text.'[19] F is regularly divided into acts and scenes, but modern editors identify as 5.4 the last thirteen lines of 5.3 in F; there are 2,720 spoken lines. Ten men can play fifteen principal and one minor male roles; three boys play three principal female roles. These thirteen actors speak 94% of the lines (Table 45). Seven men can play thirteen minor parts and twenty mutes; two boys play one small speaking part and one mute. F requires a larger number of adult mutes than does Q1, but the requirements for actors in the two texts do not differ significantly.

A Midsummer Night's Dream (Q1-1600 and F)

Meres (1598) identifies Shakespeare as the author, and the title is entered in *SR* on 8 October 1600. Q1 title page states that it was 'acted by the Right honourable, the Lord Chamberlaine his servants. Written by William Shakespeare.' Q1 is not divided into acts and scenes, and it has 1,991 spoken lines. Nine actors play nine principal roles; four boys play four principal roles, and one of these boys can double as Hippolita and the Faerie who speaks with Puck in 2.1. The thirteen actors in principal roles speak 96% of the lines (Table 46). Seven men can play four small speaking parts and nine mutes; four boys can play three small speaking parts and five mutes.

Q1 was reprinted without significant variation in Q2 (1619, a piratical edition fraudulently dated 1600). F, which has 2,067 spoken lines, was printed from a copy of Q2 that had been collated with a manuscript of the play that had been used for a performance. This was probably the source of the direction '*Tawyer with a trumpet before them*', which precedes '*Enter Pyramus and Thisby, Wall, Moon-shine and Lyon*' (5.1.128).[20] Tawyer is one of the 'musicians and other necessary attendants' whom the Master of the Revels exempted from arrest 'during the time of the Revels' on 27 December 1624 (see Appendix C). F introduces two other significant differences. First, it is divided into acts but not scenes. At the end of Act 3, the lovers are asleep on stage, and here F adds the direction '*They sleepe all the Act*', which suggests a between-acts interval, probably with music. Furthermore, F substitutes Aegeus for Philostrate as master of ceremonies in Act 5. Early in the play, Theseus orders Philostrate to 'Stir up the Athenian youth to merriments' (Q1 and F, 1.1.11), but Philostrate is not named in the scene heading and speaks no lines in that scene. Greg suggests that in a performance of the F version the actor who plays Philostrate (mute in F) doubles in another part, either Oberon or one of the 'mechanicals', and that the actor playing Aegeus is therefore given Philostrates's lines in Act 5.[21] However, as the playhouse documents indicate, an actor in a large part such as Oberon (199 lines in F) probably does not double in a mute part; it seems more likely that the actor playing Philostrate doubles in a minor part such as Snug, Snout, or Starveling. In modern editions, Philostrate exits at 1.1.15; if he does so, the actor playing this part is off-stage for over three hundred lines before entering as one of the 'mechanicals' at 1.2.1.

In F, nine men play nine principal roles; four boys play four principal roles, and one of these boys can double as Hippolita and the Faerie who speaks with Puck in 2.1. The thirteen actors in principal roles speak 97% of the lines (Table 47). Six men can play three small speaking parts and eleven mutes; four boys can play three small speaking parts and five mutes.

King John (F)

Meres (1598) mentions 'King John' as one of Shakespeare's tragedies; F is the only authoritative text, and it has 2,640 spoken lines. Greg suggests that its anomalous act and scene division comes from a 'simple blunder' on the part of the printer.[22] Ten men can play twelve principal adult male roles; five boys can play Prince Arthur, Prince Henry, and four principal female roles. These fifteen actors speak 97% of the lines (Table 48); nine men can play nine small speaking parts and twenty-seven mutes.

The Merchant of Venice (Q1-1600)

Meres (1598) mentions the title, which is entered in *SR* on 22 July 1598 and 28 October 1600. Q1 title page states that the play was 'acted by the Lord Chamberlaine his Servants. Written by William Shakespeare.' Q1 is not divided into acts and scenes, and it has 2,549 spoken lines. There is some confusion in the speech-headings, especially for Solanio (sometimes misprinted 'Salanio'), Salarino, and

Salerio. Here I follow Greg's suggestion that Salarino is merely a diminutive of Salerio and thus another name for the same character.[23] Ten men can play twelve principal male roles, and three boys play three principal female roles; these thirteen actors speak 98% of the lines (Table 49). Six men can play seven small speaking parts and thirteen mutes; three boys play three mute attendants on Portia. The play was revived at court on 10 February 1605;[24] there is no significant difference in the casting requirements for Q1 and F.

The First Part of King Henry the Fourth (Q1-1598)

The title is entered in *SR* on 25 February 1598, and Meres (1598) mentions 'Henry the 4' as one of Shakespeare's tragedies. Q1 is not divided into acts and scenes, and there are 2,857 spoken lines. Eleven men can play sixteen principal male roles, and three boys play three principal female roles; these fourteen actors speak 96% of the lines (Table 50). Eight men can play fifteen minor speaking parts and six mutes. Each of four later quartos (Q2-1599, Q3-1604, Q4-1608, and Q5-1613) was set from the one before. There is no significant difference in the casting requirements for Q1 and F.

In early March 1600 'Sir John Old Castel' was acted, probably at Hunsdon House; on 20 May 1613 the King's Men were paid for 'Sir John Falstaffe' and other plays acted at court during the entertainments for Lady Elizabeth and the Prince Palatine Elector earlier that year; also on that date the company was paid for a court performance of 'The Hotspur'; on 1 January 1625, the King's Men acted 'The First Part of Sir John Falstaff' at Whitehall; in the season 1638–9 'ould Castel' was acted at the Cockpit-in-Court.[25]

The Second Part of King Henry the Fourth (Q-1600 and F)

The title is entered in *SR* on 23 August 1600, and Q title page notes that the play 'hath been sundrie times publikely acted by the right honourable the Lord Chamberlaine his servants. Written by William Shakespeare.' Examined here is a reproduction of the second issue of Q, which substitutes four leaves for the last two leaves of quire E in the first issue; Allen and Muir observe: 'E3 and E4 were cancelled and replaced by E3–6 in order to include scene 1 of Act III, which had been accidentally omitted earlier.'[26] Q is not divided into acts and scenes, and there are 2,861 spoken lines. The scene heading for 5.4 has '*Enter Sinklo and three or four officers*', and '*Sincklo*' is also named in prefixes for three speeches (nine lines) by the Beadle. Greg notes that the Hostess and Doll insult the Beadle by calling him an 'Anatomy', a 'thin man', a 'famished Correctioner', 'goodman bones' and a 'thin thing' (5.4.21–8). Greg therefore suggests that the references to the leanness of the Beadle 'proves that Shakespeare was exploiting the remarkable appearance of a particular actor and was writing the part expressly for him'.[27] Twelve actors can play twenty principal male roles; four boys play four principal female roles and the Epilogue. These sixteen actors speak 93% of the lines (Table 51). Eight men can play twenty-four minor speaking parts and twenty mutes. One boy plays Northumberland's Wife (5 lines).

F makes irregular division into acts and scenes, and there are 3,240 spoken lines. Twelve men can play twenty principal roles, and four boys can play three principal female roles, a Page, and the Epilogue. These sixteen actors speak 94% of the lines (Table 52). F prints a list of 'The Actors Names' that is, in fact, a list of thirty-six characters – plus an unspecified number of Drawers, Beadles, and Grooms – played by men and five characters played by boys: 'Northumberlands Wife, Percies Widdow, Hostesse Quickly, Doll Teare-sheete, Epilogue'. Six men can play twenty-two small speaking parts and four mutes; one boy can double as Northumberland's Wife (5 lines) and a mute Page to the King.

Much Ado about Nothing (Q-1600)

The title was entered in *SR* on 4 August and 23 August 1600; Q title page states that the play 'hath been sundrie times publikely acted by the right honourable the Lord Chamberlaine his servaunts. Written by William Shakespeare.' Q is not divided into acts and scenes, and there are 2,485 spoken lines. As Greg notes, speech-prefixes in 4.2 substitute '*Kemp*' for some, but not all, of the lines for Dogberry-Constable and '*Cowley*' for some, but not all, of the lines for Verges-Headborough. Greg concludes that 'Shakespeare was evidently writing these parts specially for these actors.'[28] Kempe, of course, was the clown with Shakespeare's company, and the author probably had him in mind when he wrote Dogberry. However, in every manuscript playbook of this period with notes in the text that identify actors, each actor's name is entered in the hand of the book-keeper, not the author. It is therefore probable that the names of Kempe and Cowley were entered by the book-keeper, perhaps at rehearsal. According to the Chamber Account, on 20 May 1613 John Heminges was paid for a performance of 'Much Adoe abowte Nothing' before Lady Elizabeth and the Prince Palatine Elector; on the same date, Heminges was paid for another court performance of 'Benedicte and Betteris'.[29]

In Q, eleven actors can play twelve principal male roles, and four boys play four principal female roles; these fifteen actors speak 97% of the lines (Table 53). Four men can play six small speaking parts and six mutes; a boy can double as the mute Wife of Leonato and a Boy (2 lines). Greg observes that F was printed from Q without material change.[30]

King Henry the Fifth (Q1-1600 and F)

The title appears as a 'staying entry' in *SR* for 4 August 1600, and Q1 title page states that the work 'hath bene sundry times playd by the Right honorable the Lord Chamberlaine his servants'; it was acted at court by 'his Majesties players' on 7 January 1605.[31] Q1 is not divided into numbered acts and scenes, and there are 1,608 spoken lines. Nine men can play eleven principal and three minor male roles, four boys play three principal females and a boy. These thirteen actors speak 90% of the lines (Table 54). Eleven men can play seventeen small speaking parts and nine mutes.

F is divided into five acts inaccurately numbered, and scenes are not numbered; there are 3,199 spoken lines. Eleven men can play eighteen principal male roles, and five boys play four principal females and a boy. These sixteen actors speak 93% of the lines (Table 55); twelve men can play twenty-two small speaking parts and twenty mutes. The most obvious differences in the two texts are that Q1 lacks the Prologue, Epilogue, Chorus, and the role of Queen Isabel (24 lines). Q1 also omits scenes 1.1, 3.1, and 4.2, and it transposes 4.4 and 4.5. Although F has about twice as many spoken lines as Q1, both texts require about the same number of actors: twenty men and four boys in Q1, twenty-three men and five boys in F. Thus it seems unlikely that Q1 is a version cut for performance in the provinces, as Greg suggests.[32] This evidence also contradicts Gary Taylor's hypothesis that Q1 is an adaptation of the play for a cast of 'nine (or possibly ten) adults and two boy actors'.[33]

Julius Caesar (F)

Thomas Platter, a German visitor, in an account of his travels notes that on 21 September 1599: 'I went with my party across the water, and in the straw-thatched house we saw the tragedy of the first Emperor Julius Caesar very pleasantly performed with approximately fifteen characters.'[34] Since there were no theatre programmes, Platter probably estimated 'fifteen characters' by counting the number of actors who appear in one of the big scenes. For example, 3.1 has sixteen characters: seven principal roles (Brutus, Cassius, Antony, Caesar, Caska, Decius, and Cinna) and nine minor parts (Soothsayer, Trebonius, Metellus, Servant to Antony, Artimidorus, Publius, Lepidus, Popillius, and Servant to Octavius). Most scholars agree that Platter refers to Shakespeare's play and to the newly erected Globe. On 20 May 1613, the King's Men received payment for a court performance of 'Caesars Tragedye'; the company acted 'the tragedie of Cesar' at St James's on 31 January 1637 and 'Ceaser' at the Cockpit-in-Court on 13 November 1638.[35] F is the only authoritative text, and the title is included in the list of sixteen plays entered in *SR* by Edward Blount and Isaac Jaggard on 8 November 1623.

The text is divided into five acts, but not into numbered scenes; there are 2,647 spoken lines. Nine actors can play fourteen principal and three minor male roles; three boys play two principal female roles and Lucius, a boy. These twelve actors speak 91% of the lines (Table 56). Eleven men can play twenty-seven small speaking parts and thirteen mutes.

As You Like It (F)

The title is listed in *SR* for 4 August 1600, probably as a 'staying entry' to prevent unauthorized publication. F is the only authoritative text, and the title is included in the list of sixteen plays entered in *SR* by Edward Blount and Isaac Jaggard on 8 November 1623. According to a letter dated 1603 – and in 1865 reportedly in the possession of the then Lady Pembroke – Shakespeare's company acted this play at

Wilton before King James on 2 December 1603.[36] F is regularly divided into acts and scenes, and there are 2,618 spoken lines. Ten men can play twelve principal male roles, and four boys play four principal female roles; these fourteen actors speak 96% of the lines (Table 57). Seven men can play nine small speaking parts and six mutes; two boys play one small speaking part each.

Twelfth Night (F)

John Manningham of the Middle Temple notes in his *Diary* a performance 'at our feast' on 2 February (Candlemas) 1602; the play was revived at court on 6 April 1618 and 2 February 1623.[37] F is the only authoritative text, and the title is included in the list of sixteen plays entered in *SR* by Edward Blount and Isaac Jaggard on 8 November 1623. F is regularly divided into acts and scenes, and there are 2,338 spoken lines. Eight actors can play nine principal male roles and three boys play three principal female roles; these eleven actors speak 98% of the lines (Table 58). Seven men can play six small speaking parts and five mutes; three boys play three mute Attendants on Olivia.

Hamlet (Q1-1603, Q2-1604, and F)

On 26 July 1602, *SR* records 'A booke called the Revenge of Hamlett Prince Denmarke as yt was latelie acted by the Lo: Chamberleyn his servantes'. Q1 title page credits Shakespeare as author and states that the play is 'As it hath beene diverse times acted by his Highnesse servants in the Cittie of London: as also in the two Universities of Cambridge and Oxford, and elsewhere'.[38] Q1 does not number acts and scenes, and there are 2,129 spoken lines; Q1 prints as one continuous scene what modern editors number as 4.1, 4.2, and 4.3. Eight actors can play ten principal and three minor male roles; three boys two principal female roles and the Boy Player-Queen. These eleven actors speak 95% of the lines (Table 59). Seven men can play eleven small speaking parts and thirteen mutes.

Q2 title page states that the play is 'Newly imprinted and enlarged to almost as much againe as it was, according to the true and Perfect Coppie', which suggests that Shakespeare, or his company, or both, intended that Q2 supersede the unauthorized Q1. Q2 does not number acts and scenes, and it has 3,680 spoken lines or, as its title page asserts, 'almost as much againe as it was'. Nine actors can play fourteen principal and one minor male roles; three boys play two principal female roles and the Boy Player-Queen. These twelve actors speak 96% of the lines (Table 60). Seven men can play twelve small speaking parts and thirteen mutes.

F numbers some early scenes, but none of the later ones, and it has 3,593 spoken lines, or about ninety fewer than Q2. Hibbard observes that the cuts and additions in F 'seem to be parts of a definite policy designed to make the play more accessible to theatre goers in general by giving it a more direct and unimpeded action, pruning away some of its verbal elaborations, and smoothing out its more abrupt transitions'.[39] Nine men can play fourteen principal and one minor male roles; three boys play two principal female roles and the Boy Player-Queen. These twelve actors speak 96% of the lines (Table 61). Nine men can play eleven small speaking parts and twenty-four mutes. The title is included in the Revels Office records, c. 1619–20, and it was acted at Hampton Court on 14 January 1637.[40]

The Merry Wives of Windsor (Q1-1602 and F)

The title is entered in *SR* for 18 January 1602, and Q1 title page states that it is 'by William Shakespeare. As it hath beene divers times Acted by the right Honorable my Lord Chamberlaines servants. Both before her Majestie, and elsewhere.' The play was acted at the Banqueting House in Whitehall on 4 November 1604 and at the Cockpit-in-Court on 15 November 1638.[41]

Q1 is not divided into acts and scenes, and there are 1,493 spoken lines; Q1 transposes scenes that are numbered 3.4. and 3.5 in modern texts, and it omits 4.1 and 5.1–4. Q1 omits Fenton from 1.4 and Pistol – as Hobgoblin – from 5.5, thereby making it possible for the same actor to play both Fenton and Pistol. Q1 omits the boys' parts of Robin and William. Ten actors can play eleven principal male roles and four boys play four principal female roles; these fourteen actors speak 97% of the lines (Table 62). Three men can play four small speaking parts and one mute; four boys can play a boy and four Fairies, one of whom has a single line.[42]

F is divided regularly into acts and scenes numbered in Latin, and there are 2,623 spoken lines. F has unusual stage directions in that each scene is headed by the names of all the characters that appear in it; the only other direction is the *exeunt* that ends most scenes. Twelve men can play twelve principal and one minor male roles. Four boys play four principal female roles, and the two boys who play Robin and William can double as two mute Fairies; these eighteen actors who play principal roles speak 99% of the lines (Table 63). Two men can play three small speaking parts, and two boys play mute Fairies.

Troilus and Cressida (Q-1609)

The title is entered in *SR* on 7 February 1603 'as yt is acted by my lo: Chamberlens Men', perhaps as a 'blocking entry' to prevent unauthorized publication. A second entry is dated 28 January 1609, and Q title page states that the play 'was acted by the Kings Majesties servants at the Globe. Written by William Shakespeare.' However, the text cited here (a second issue of Q) omits the title page reference to the Globe and includes in the front matter an unsigned Epistle describing the work as 'a new play, never stal'd with the Stage, never clapper-clawd with the palmes of the vulger and yet passing full of the palme comicall'. Greg suggests that the Epistle implies a private performance, perhaps at the Inner Temple, but he notes that there is no external evidence to support this conjecture.[43] The fourteen men required in fifteen principal parts are significantly more than the average of ten men required in principal parts for other Shakespeare plays, and this lends support to the argument that the play was written for private performance. The fourteen men and four boys in principal parts speak 98% of the lines (Table 64). Six men can play ten small speaking parts and eight mutes.

Q is not divided into acts and scenes, and there are 3,260 spoken lines. The casting requirements for Q and F differ only in that F includes a Prologue (3 lines) and the direction '*Enter common Souldiers*' (1.2.260).

All's Well that Ends Well (F)

F is the only authoritative text, and the title is included in the list of sixteen plays entered in *SR* by Edward Blount and Isaac Jaggard on 8 November 1623. F is divided into acts only, and there are 2,883 spoken lines. Chambers suggests that it was probably the book-keeper who added the letters E and G (perhaps for the actors William Ecclestone and Robert Goughe) to the speech-prefixes for a pair of male characters variously described as Lords, Captains, and Frenchmen.[44] This procedure is consistent with evidence in the King's Men prompt books in which the book-keeper identifies some, but not all, of the actors in lesser principal parts.[45] The composite roles played by E and G are the sixth and seventh largest male roles; both Ecclestone and Goughe are among the 'Principall Actors' listed in F (Illustration 3).

Eight men can play ten principal and four minor male roles, and five boys play five principal female roles; these thirteen actors speak 98% of the lines (Table 65). Eight men can play seven small speaking parts and eighteen mutes; two boys play one small speaking part and three mutes.

Measure for Measure (F)

F is the only authoritative text, and the title is included in the list of sixteen plays entered in *SR* by Edward Blount and Isaac Jaggard on 8 November 1623. The Revels Account notes that the King's Men acted this play at court on 26 December 1604.[46] The irregularities in scene division for F are rectified by modern editors; there are 2,788 spoken lines. Eight men can play nine principal male roles, and four boys play four principle roles; these twelve actors speak 96% of the lines (Table 66). Eight men can play nine small speaking parts and eleven mutes; one boy can play one small female role and a mute boy.

Othello (Q1-1622 and F)

The title is entered in *SR* for 6 October 1621, and Q1 title page states that the play 'hath beene diverse times acted at the Globe, and at the Black-Friers, by his Majesties Servants. Written by William Shakespeare.' It was performed at Whitehall on 1 November 1604, at the Globe on 30 April 1610, at court in 1612–13, at Blackfriars on 22 November 1629 and 6 May 1635, and at Hampton Court on 8 December 1636.[47] Q1 has headings for acts 2, 4, and 5, but scenes are not numbered;

there are 3,238 spoken lines. Seven actors can play nine principal and one minor male roles, and three boys play three principal female roles; these ten actors speak 97% of the lines (Table 67). Ten men can play eleven small speaking parts and eighteen mutes; two boys can play a boy and two mutes.

F is divided regularly into acts and scenes, and there are 3,572 spoken lines. Seven men can play eleven principal male roles, and three boys play three principal female roles; these ten actors speak 98% of the lines (Table 68). Nine men can play nine small speaking parts and fourteen mutes; two boys play two mutes.

King Lear (Q1-1608 and F)

The title is entered in *SR* for 26 November 1607. Q1 title page credits Shakespeare as author and states that the play was acted 'before the Kings Majestie at Whitehall upon S. Stephans night in Christmas Hollidayes. By his Majesties servants playing usually at the Gloabe on the Bancke-side.' Q1 is not divided into acts and scenes, and there are 2,907 spoken lines. Nine actors can play eleven principal male roles, and three boys play three principal female roles; these twelve actors speak 95% of the lines (Table 69). Six men can play fifteen small speaking parts and seventeen mutes.

Q2 – incorrectly dated 1608 – was printed in 1619 from a copy of Q1 in which some sheets had been corrected.[48] F is divided into acts and scenes, but it omits 4.3; there are 3,175 spoken lines. Nine men can play eleven principal male roles, and three boys play three principal female roles; these twelve actors speak 96% of the lines (Table 70). Ten men can play sixteen speaking parts and twenty-two mutes.

Macbeth (F)

F is the only authoritative text, and the title is included in the list of sixteen plays entered in *SR* by Edward Blount and Isaac Jaggard on 8 November 1623. Although Simon Forman's *Booke of Plaies* notes that he saw 'Mackbeth at the Glob, 1610 the 20 of Aprill', Chambers gives the correct year of this performance as 1611.[49] F is regularly divided into acts and scenes, and there are 2,356 spoken lines. Nine men can play twelve principal male roles, and eight boys play seven principal female roles and Macduff's Son. These seventeen actors speak 92% of the lines (Table 71). Nine men can play nineteen small speaking parts and twenty-six mutes; two boys can play three small speaking parts.

Antony and Cleopatra (F)

The title is entered in *SR* on 20 May 1608. F is the only authoritative text, and it is not divided into acts and scenes; there are 3,484 spoken lines. Twelve men can play nineteen principal male roles, and four boys play four principal female roles; these sixteen actors speak 91% of the lines (Table 72). Thirteen men can play thirty-seven small speaking roles and forty-six mutes; three boys can play twelve mutes.

Coriolanus (F)

F is the only authoritative text, and the title is included in the list of sixteen plays entered in *SR* by Edward Blount and Isaac Jaggard on 8 November 1623. F is divided into acts, but scenes are not numbered; there are 3,583 spoken lines. Eleven men can play sixteen principal male roles, and three boys play three principal female roles. These fourteen actors speak 93% of the lines (Table 73). Fourteen men can play thirty-four small speaking parts and thirty mutes; four boys can play two small speaking parts and three mutes.

Timon of Athens (F)

F is the only authoritative text, and the title is included in the list of sixteen plays entered in *SR* by Edward Blount and Isaac Jaggard on 8 November 1623. There is no division into acts and scenes, and there are 2,464 spoken lines. Ten men can play fifteen principal male roles who speak 83% of the lines; there are no principal female roles (Table 74). Eleven men can play thirty-five small speaking parts and fourteen mutes; four boys can play four small speaking parts and three mutes.

Cymbeline (F)

F is the only authoritative text, and the title is included in the list of sixteen plays entered in *SR* by Edward Blount and Isaac Jaggard on 8 November 1623. Simon Forman's *Booke of Plaies* notes that he saw 'Cimbalin, king of England' (probably at the Globe) some time between 20 and 30 April 1611; it was revived at court on 1 January 1634.[50] There is full division into acts and scenes, but this division differs at three points from that adopted by most modern editors. My table of parts follows the act and scene division in the edition of J. M. Nosworthy (Arden 1955); F has 3,604 spoken lines.

Twelve actors can play seventeen principal and one minor male roles, and four boys play four principal female roles; these sixteen actors speak 97% of the lines (Table 75). Nine men can play fifteen small speaking parts and twenty-three mutes, and three boys play one small speaking part and two mutes.

The Winter's Tale (F)

F is the only authoritative text, and the title is included in the list of sixteen plays entered in *SR* by Edward Blount and Isaac Jaggard on 8 November 1623. Simon Forman notes that he saw 'the Winters Talle at the glob 1611 the 15 of maye'; court performances are recorded for 5 November 1611, 7 April 1618, and probably in the season 1619–20. Sir Henry Herbert, Master of the Revels, grants a licence for revival on 19 August 1623; court performances are also recorded for 18 January 1624 and 16 January 1634.[51] F is regularly divided into acts and scenes, and the heading for each scene lists all the major characters who appear in that scene; there are 3,236 spoken lines. Eleven actors can play fifteen principal male roles, and five boys seven principal female roles and Mamillius, a boy; these sixteen actors speak 97% of the lines (Table 76). Seven men can play six small speaking parts and eighteen mutes; six boys play one small speaking part and twelve mutes. There is an interval of 175 lines between the Dance of Shepherds and Shepherdesses (4.4.167) and the Dance of Twelve Satyrs (4.4.342); this allows time for six men who play Shepherds and six boys who play Shepherdesses to double as the twelve Satyrs.

The Tempest (F)

F is the only authoritative text, and the title is included in the list of sixteen plays entered in *SR* by Edward Blount and Isaac Jaggard on 8 November 1623. The King's Men acted it before King James at Whitehall on 1 November 1611, and on 20 May 1613 John Heminges was paid for performances of *Temp.* and twelve other plays as part of the entertainments for Lady Elizabeth and the Prince Palatine Elector during the winter of 1612–13.[52] F is regularly divided into acts and scenes, and there are 2,204 spoken lines.

Ten men play ten principal male roles, and four boys play four principal female roles; these fourteen actors speak 99% of the lines (Table 2). Five men can play four small speaking parts and eleven mutes; four boys can play one small speaking part and six mutes.

King Henry the Eighth (F)

F is the only authoritative text, and the title is included in the list of sixteen plays entered in *SR* by Edward Blount and Isaac Jaggard on 8 November 1623. At the performance of 29 June 1613, cannons shot off to announce the entrance of King Henry (1.4.49) set fire to the roof of the first Globe playhouse, which soon burned to the ground.[53] Some scholars contend that John Fletcher collaborated with Shakespeare on this play.[54]

F is regularly divided into acts and scenes, but most modern editors divide 5.2 into two scenes; there are 3,218 spoken lines. Thirteen men can play twenty-two principal male roles, and three boys play three principal female roles; these sixteen actors speak 96% of the lines (Table 77). Seventeen men can play eighteen small speaking parts and forty-nine mutes; seven boys can play two small speaking parts and nineteen mutes.

PLAYS IN QUARTO ONLY

Pericles (Q1-1609)

The Venetian Ambassador to England, Zorzi Giustinian, paid more than twenty crowns for the admission of a party of four to a performance of *Per.* some time between 5 January 1606 and 23 November 1608 at a playhouse not identified.[55] On 20

May 1608, Edward Blount entered in *SR* 'the booke of Pericles prynce of Tyre', but this may refer to the prose narrative by George Wilkins, *The Painfull Adventures of Pericles Prince of Tyre*, which was published in 1608. Wilkins apparently knew the play, either in the text that survives or in an earlier version, because the Argument of the novel mentions 'ancient Gower the famous English Poet, by the Kings Majesties Players excellently presented'.[56] The title page of Q1 states the play was 'acted by his Majesties Servants, at the Globe on the Banck-side. By William Shakespeare.' A letter from Sir Gerrard Herbert to Sir Dudley Carleton notes a performance of 'Pirrocles, Prince of Tyre' at Whitehall in 'the kinges greate chamber' on 20 May 1619.[57]

Q1 is not divided into acts and scenes, and there are 2,254 spoken lines. Gower serves as choral commentator, and dumbshows are enacted during his speeches before 2 and 3, and during his speech in 4.4. Seven actors can play eleven principal male roles, and four boys play four principal female male roles; these eleven actors speak 90% of the lines (Table 78). Thirteen men can play twenty-nine small speaking parts and twelve mutes; three boys can play three small speaking parts and two mutes.

The Two Noble Kinsmen (Q-1634)

The title page states that the play was 'Presented at the Blackfriers by the Kings Majesties servants, with great applause: Written by the memorable Worthies of their time; Mr John Fletcher, and Mr William Shakespeare. Gent'. The title is entered in *SR* on 8 April 1634. On the basis of linguistic evidence, Cyrus Hoy assigns authorship as follows:

> Fletcher: 2.2–6; 3.3–6; 4; 5. 1a (to exit of Palamon and Knights), 2.
> Shakespeare: 1; 2.1; 3,1–2; 5.1b (from exit of Palamon and Knights to end), 3–4.[58]

Greg notes several warnings that probably originate with the prompter. For example, '2. *Hearses ready with Palamon and Arcite: the 3 Queenes, Theseus: and his Lords ready*' (1.3.68) and '*Hearses ready*' (1.4.14) anticipate the entrance of three Queens with the hearses at 1.5.1. Greg concludes that Q was probably printed from 'prompt-copy written or at least annotated by Edward Knight, book-keeper for the King's company'.[59]

Two actors are named in the text. '*T. Tucke*', (probably Thomas Tuckfeild) is identified as a mute Attendant on Theseus (5.3), and, as noted, his name is included in a list of hired men whom the Master of the Revels exempted from arrest on 27 December 1624 (see Appendix C). '*Curtis*' (probably Curtis Greville) is identified as an important Messenger (44 lines) in 4.2 and as a mute Attendant on Theseus in 5.3. Four other King's Men plays identify principal roles that Greville plays: Latinus (32 lines) in *RA* (1626), Mountayne (242 lines) in *SC* (c. 1630), Iseas (85 lines) in *Swis.* (c. 1630), and Third Merchant (44 lines) in *BAYL* (1631). There was probably a court performance of *TNK* about 1619, and Chambers suggests that the actors' names in the text may be for a revival of about 1625–6.[60]

The text is divided regularly into acts and scenes, and there are 3,123 spoken lines. Nine actors can play twelve principal and two minor male roles; six boys can play seven principal female roles. These fifteen actors speak 96% of the lines (Table 79). Eight men can play fifteen small speaking parts and eight mutes; four boys can play one small speaking part and ten mutes.

SUMMARY

Table 80 summarizes the casting requirements for the thirty-eight plays attributed wholly or in part to Shakespeare. Each of twelve plays has two early texts that differ significantly, and *Hamlet* has three such texts, so that a total of fifty-two texts of Shakespeare are studied here. On average, these texts require 9.9 men who play principal male roles – those who speak twenty-five or more lines – and 3.8 boys who play principal female roles – those who speak ten or more lines.[61] The actors in principal roles speak an average of 94.9% of the lines in these plays. Also required on average are 8.6 men who can play 32.9 minor male roles, and 1.8 boys who can play 3.5 minor parts for women and boys.

As noted, chapter 2 shows how eight Elizabethan playhouse documents – four plots from performances by Lord Strange's Men and the Lord Admiral's Men between 1590 and 1602, and four prompt books from the repertory of Shakespeare's company, the King's Men, between 1611 and 1631 – require an average of 9.9 men and 3.3 boys in principal roles who speak 95.6% of the lines; these plays also require an average of 7.9 men who can play 27.8 minor male roles, and 2.4 boys who can play 4.0 minor parts of women and boys (Table 13).

Chapter 3 describes the requirements for fifteen plays that identify actors in principal roles – seven plays acted by Shakespeare's company, the King's Men, between 1613 and 1632 and eight plays acted by other prominent London companies between 1626 and 1636. These plays require an average of 9.3 men and 3.7 boys in principal roles who speak 97.5% of the lines; these plays also require an average of 6.7 men who can play 14.8 minor male parts and 2.2 boys who can play 3.7 minor parts of women and boys (Table 30).

Thus the casting requirements for Shakespeare's plays correspond closely to the requirements for these eight playhouse documents and these fifteen pre-Restoration plays that identify actors in principal roles. This close correspondence in casting requirements for these texts indicates that the size and composition of Shakespeare's casts of characters were determined by common theatrical practice at London playhouses between 1590 and 1642.

Table 4

Parts Played by Admiral's Men Named in Six Actor Lists in Henslowe's <u>Diary</u> (H)

	(1) 1594-95	(2) 1596	<u>Fred.</u> 1597	(3) 1597	<u>BA</u> 1598	(4) 1598-99	(5) 1600	(6) 1602	<u>1TC</u> 1602
E. Alleyn	H	H	Sebastian		Muly Mahamet				Tamar Cam
J. Singer	H			H	?	H	H	H	Assinico-Clown
R. Jones	H			H	Silva / Spanish Ambas.	H	H		
T. Towne	H		Myronhamec	H	Stukeley	H	H	H	Persian Shah / Oracle / Tartar
M. Slater	H	H	Theodore						
E. Juby	H	H	King	H	Calcepius / Avero		H	H	Pitho-Satyr / Moor
T. Downton	H			H	Abdelmelec	H	H	H	Mango Cham / Tartar
J. Tunstall	H	H	Governor / Friar						
W. Bird (Bourne)				H	?	H	H	H	Colmogra / Persian Noble / Artabisus
R. Shaw				H	Irish Bishop / Gov. Tangier	H	H		
A. Jeffes				H	Young Mahamet		H	H	Linus-Satyr / Moor
H. Jeffes				H	M. Mahamet Xeque	H	H	H	Otanes
C. Massey			Thamar		Zareo / Barcelis / Span.Ambass.	H	H	H	Artaxes
S. Rowley			Heraclius		Attend. / Moor Attend.	H	H	H	Ascalon / Crim

Table 5
2 Seven Deadly Sins (c. 1590)
Principal Parts

Men

	1	2	3	4	5	6	7	8	9	10	11	12	13	14	15	16	17	18	19	20	21	22	23	24	25
#1 ?	x	-	-	-	-	-	-	-	-	-	-	-	-	-	-	-	-	-	-	-	-	-	-	-	-
Henry	-	x	-	x	-	-	-	-	-	-	-	-	-	-	-	-	-	x	-	-	-	-	-	x	-
#2 ?	-	-	-	-	-	-	-	-	-	-	-	-	-	-	-	-	-	-	-	-	-	-	-	-	-
Lidgate	-	x	x	-	-	x	-	-	x	-	-	-	-	x	-	-	-	x	-	-	-	-	x	-	x
#3 mr Brian																									
Counsailer-Lord-																									
Damasus	-	GB	GB	-	GB	-	GB	GB	GB	GB	-	-	-	-	-	-	-	-	-	-	-	-	-	-	-
Warwick	-	-	-	-	-	-	-	-	-	-	-	-	-	-	-	-	-	-	-	-	-	-	-	GB	-
#4 mr Phillipps																									
Sardinapalus	-	-	-	-	-	-	-	-	-	-	-	AP	-	-	-	-	-	-	-	-	-	-	-	-	-
#5 mr. Pope																									
Arbactus	-	-	-	-	-	-	-	-	-	-	-	TP	-	TP	-	x	TP	-	-	-	-	-	-	-	-
#6 R Burbadg																									
King Gorboduk	-	RB	-	-	-	-	-	-	-	-	-	-	-	-	-	-	-	-	-	-	-	-	-	-	-
Tereus	-	-	-	-	-	-	-	-	-	-	-	-	-	-	-	-	-	-	RB	-	x	RB	x	-	-
#7 Harry																									
ferrex	-	HC	HC	HC	-	-	-	-	-	-	-	-	-	-	-	-	-	-	-	HC	-	HC	HC	-	-
Lord																									
#8 W sly																									
Porrex	-	WS	WS	WS	x	-	x	x	WS	-	-	-	-	-	-	-	-	-	-	WS	-	WS	WS	-	-
Lord																									

Boys

	1	2	3	4	5	6	7	8	9	10	11	12	13	14	15	16	17	18	19	20	21	22	23	24	25
#1 saunder																									
Queene	-	AC	AC	-	x	-	x	AC	-	-	-	-	-	-	-	-	-	-	-	AC	-	AC	x	-	-
Progne																									
#2 Nick																									
Lady	-	-	-	-	-	-	-	NT	-	-	NT	-	-	-	-	-	-	-	-	-	-	-	-	-	-
Rodope	-	-	-	-	-	-	-	-	-	-	-	-	x	a	x	x	-	-	-	-	-	-	-	-	-
#3 R Go																									
Aspatia	-	-	-	-	-	-	-	-	-	-	RG	x	x	x	-	x	-	-	RG	-	-	-	-	-	-
Philomele	-	-	-	-	-	-	-	-	-	-	-	x	x	x	-	-	-	-	-	-	x	-	x	-	-
#4 Ned																									
Pompeia	-	-	-	-	-	-	-	-	-	-	N	x	x	x	-	x	-	-	-	-	-	-	-	-	-

a Rhodope is here erroneously assigned to Ned.

Minor Parts

Men

	1	2	3	4	5	6	7	8	9	10	11	12	13	14	15	16	17	18	19	20	21	22	23	24	25
#1 R Cowly	RC	-	-	-	-	-	-	-	-	-	-	-	-	-	-	-	-	-	-	-	-	-	-	-	-
Leutenant	-	-	-	-	-	-	-	-	-	-	-	-	-	-	-	-	-	-	-	-	-	-	-	RC	-
Soldier[Ferrex]	-	-	-	RC	x	-	-	-	-	-	-	-	-	-	-	-	-	-	-	-	-	RC	x	-	-
Lord	-	-	-	-	-	-	-	RC	-	RC	RC	-	-	-	-	-	-	-	-	-	-	-	-	-	-
Giraldus	-	-	-	-	-	-	-	-	-	-	-	-	-	RC	-	RC	RC	-	-	-	-	-	-	-	-
Captaine	-	-	-	-	-	-	-	-	-	-	-	-	-	RC	-	-	-	-	-	-	-	-	-	-	-
Musician	-	-	-	-	-	-	-	-	-	-	-	-	-	-	-	-	-	-	-	-	-	-	-	-	-

Table 5 (*cont.*)

#2 Jo Duke	JD												JD		JD		JD		JD
purceuant		JD																	
Attend.[Queen]			x											JD		x			
Soldier[Ferrex]		JD																	
will foole																			
Lord																			
#3 R Pallant	RP																		
wardere		RP																	
Attend.[Queen]		RP																	
Soldier[Porrex]			x	RP		RP	RP	RP	RP	RP				x		RP			
Dordan																			
Nicanor																			
Julio																	JS		
#4 J Sincler	y																		
Pride		JS																	
Keeper-warder			x											JS					
Soldier[Porrex]		JS			JS	JS	JS	JS											
Captaine																			
Musician																			
#5 Kit	y					y													
Sloth																			
Attend.[Queen]		CB				CB	CB												
Soldier[Ferrex]			x			CB	CB	CB	CB										
Captaine							CB												
#6 Th Goodale	y																		
Lechery		TG		TG	TG														
Counsailer–Lucius	y			TG															
Phronesius			x	TG		TG	TG		y										
Messenger												TG	TG						
Lord																			
#7 J Holland	y																		
Envy		JH																	
Attend.[Queen]	y		x																
Soldier[Porrex]		JH				JH	JH	JH											JH
Captaine	y																		
warder						V													

Boys

#8 Vincent	y																		
Gluttony																			
Musician																			
#1 T Belt	y																		
Wrath		TB															TB		
Servant																			
Panthea																			
#2 Will																			
Covetousness	y														W		W		y
Itys																	W		
Mercury	y																		y

Table 6

Frederick & Basilea (1597)

Principal Parts

Men

	P	1	2	3	4	5	6	7	8	9	10	11	12	13	14	15	16	17	18	E
#1 Mr Allen																				
Sebastian	-	-	-	EA	-	-	EA	EA	EA	EA	-	EA	-	-	-	-	EA	-	EA	-
#2 Mr Jubie																				
King	-	EJ	-	EJ	-	-	EJ	EJ	-	EJ	-	y	-	-	-	-	-	-	EJ	-
#3 Mr Martyn																				
Theodore	-	-	-	MS	-	-	MS	-	-	MS	-	MS	MS	-	MS	-	-	MS	MS	-
#4 Tho: Towne																				
Myron-hamec	-	-	-	-	TT	x	-	-	TT	TT	-	TT	-	-	-	-	TT	-	TT	-
#5 Mr Dunstann																				
Governor	-	-	JD	-	-	-	-	-	-	-	-	-	-	JD	JD	JD	-	-	JD	-
ffryer	-	-	-	-	-	JD	-	-	-	-	-	-	-	-	-	-	-	-	-	-
#6 R. Alleine																				
Prologue	RA	RA	-	-	-	-	-	-	-	-	-	-	-	-	-	-	-	-	-	-
Frederick	-	-	-	RA	-	-	RA	RA	-	RA	x	RA	-	RA	-	RA	-	-	RA	-
Epilogue	-	-	-	-	-	-	-	-	-	-	-	-	-	-	-	-	-	-	-	RA
#7 ledbeter																				
Pedro-Lord	-	-	-	RL	RL	-	RL	-	RL	RL	RL	RL	-	-	-	-	-	-	-	-
#8 Ed. Dutton																				
Philippo	-	-	-	ED	-	-	ED	ED	-	ED	-	-	-	-	-	-	-	-	-	-
#9 Charles																				
Moore-Thamar	-	-	CM	-	CM	-	x	-	-	-	-	-	CM	-	CM	-	-	-	CM	-
#10 Sam																				
Heraclius	-	-	x	-	SR	SR	SR	-	-	-	-	-	SR	-	SR	SR	-	-	SR	-

Boys

	P	1	2	3	4	5	6	7	8	9	10	11	12	13	14	15	16	17	18	E
#1 Dick																				
Basilea	-	D	-	D	-	-	D	D	-	D	x	D	-	D	-	D	-	x	D	-
#2 Will																				
Leonora	-	-	-	W	-	-	W	-	-	W	-	-	-	-	-	-	W	-	W	-
#3 Pigg																				
Andreo	-	-	-	P	-	-	P	-	-	P	-	-	P	-	P	-	-	-	-	-
#4 Griffen																				
Athanasia	-	-	G	-	-	-	-	-	-	-	-	-	-	-	-	-	-	-	-	-

Table 6 (*cont.*)

Minor Parts
Men

Part	1	2	3	4	5	6	7	8	9	10	11	12	13	14	15	16	17	18
#1 Tho:hunt	–	–	TH	–	–	–	–	–	–	–	–	–	–	–	–	–	–	–
Servant	BD	–	–	–	BD	–	–	–	–	–	–	–	–	–	–	–	–	–
Guard	–	–	–	TH	–	–	–	–	–	–	–	–	–	–	–	–	–	–
Lord	–	–	–	–	TH	–	–	TH	–	TH	–	TH	–	–	TH	–	TH	–
Messenger	–	–	–	–	–	TH	–	–	–	–	–	–	–	–	TH	–	TH	–
Soldier	–	–	–	–	TH / x	x	–	–	–	–	–	–	–	–	–	–	–	–
#2 Black Dick	–	BD	–	BD	–	–	–	–	–	–	–	–	–	–	–	–	–	–
Servant	–	–	–	–	BD	–	–	–	–	–	–	–	–	–	–	–	–	–
Guard	–	–	–	–	–	–	BD	–	–	–	BD	–	BD	–	–	BD	–	BD
Messenger	–	–	–	–	–	–	–	–	–	BD	–	–	–	–	–	BD	–	BD
Confederate	–	–	–	–	–	–	–	–	BD	–	–	–	–	–	–	–	–	–
Soldier	–	–	–	–	x	x	–	–	BD	–	–	–	BD	BD	–	BD	–	BD
#3 Attendant	–	–	–	–	–	–	–	A	–	–	–	–	–	–	–	–	–	–
Lord	–	–	–	–	–	–	–	–	–	–	–	–	–	–	–	–	–	–
#4 Attendant	–	–	–	–	–	–	–	A	–	–	–	–	–	–	–	–	–	–
Lord	–	–	–	–	–	–	–	–	–	–	–	–	–	–	–	–	–	–
#5 Attendant	–	–	–	–	–	–	–	A	–	–	–	–	–	–	–	–	–	–
Lord	–	–	–	–	–	–	–	–	–	–	–	–	–	–	–	–	–	–
#6 Gatherer	–	–	–	–	–	–	–	–	–	–	–	–	–	–	–	–	–	–
Guard	–	–	–	–	–	–	–	G	G	G	–	–	–	–	–	–	–	–
Confederate	–	–	–	–	–	–	–	G	G	–	–	–	–	G	G	–	G	–
Soldiers	–	–	–	–	–	–	–	–	–	–	–	–	–	–	–	G	–	G
#7 Gatherer	–	–	–	–	–	–	–	–	–	–	–	–	–	–	–	–	–	–
Guard	–	–	–	–	–	–	–	G	G	G	–	–	–	–	–	–	–	–
Confederate	–	–	–	–	–	–	–	G	G	–	–	–	–	–	–	–	–	–
Soldiers	–	–	–	–	–	–	–	–	–	–	–	–	–	G	–	G	–	G

Table 7

The Battle of Alcazar (1598)

Principal Parts

	1DS	1	2	2DS	3	4	5	6	3DS	7	8	9	4DS	Total Lines Q-1594
Men														
#1 mr Ed: Allen														
Muly Mahamett	EA	-	x	-	-	-	x	-	-	-	-	x	x	213
#2 ?														
Sebastian	-	-	-	-	-	-	-	y	-	y	-	-	y	196
#3 mr Rich:Allen														
Portingall-Presenter	RA	-	-	x	-	-	-	-	x	-	-	-	x	180
Governor of Lisbonne	-	-	-	-	-	RA	-	-	-	-	-	-	-	29
#4 mr Doughton														
Abdelmelec	-	TD	-	-	x	-	-	-	-	-	-	-	-	167
#5 mr Towne	-	-	-	-	-	TT	-	x	x	x	-	x	x	132
Stukeley	-	-	-	-	x	-	-	y	y	-	-	-	-	93
#6 H Jeffes														
Muly mahamet Xeque	-	HJ	-	-	x	-	-	-	-	-	-	-	-	55
#7 mr Charles														
Zareo	-	CM	-	-	x	-	-	CM	-	-	-	-	-	0
Duke of Barcelis	-	-	-	-	-	-	-	-	-	CM	-	-	-	27
Embassador of Spain	-	-	-	-	-	-	-	-	-	-	-	-	-	
#8 Antho:Jeffes														
sonne-young Mahamet	AJ	-	-	AJ	-	-	x	-	-	-	-	x	-	60
#9 mr Jubie														
Calcepis Bassa	-	EJ	-	-	x	-	-	EJ	-	x	-	x	-	41
Duke of Avero	-	-	-	-	-	-	-	-	-	-	-	-	x	9
#10 Mr Shaa														
Irish Bishop	-	-	-	-	-	RS	-	x	-	-	RS	y	-	24
Governor of Tangier	-	-	-	-	-	-	-	-	-	-	-	-	-	29
#11 mr Jones														
luis de Silva	-	-	-	-	-	-	-	RJ	-	-	-	-	-	0
Embassador of Spain	-	-	-	-	-	-	-	-	RJ	RJ	-	-	-	27
Boys														
#1 Jeames														
Ruben	-	J	-	-	x	-	-	J	-	J	-	-	-	20
Page	-	-	-	-	-	-	-	-	-	-	-	-	-	0
#2 ?														
Calipolis	-	x	-	x	-	-	x	-	-	-	-	-	-	14

Total Lines Principal Parts 1,316

Table 7 (cont.)

Minor Parts
Men

Part												Lines
#1 w. Kendall												
Abdelmenen	WK	WK	–	WK	–	–	–	–	–	–	–	0
Attendant[Bassa]	–	–	–	–	–	–	–	–	–	–	–	0
ghost	–	–	–	–	–	–	–	–	–	–	–	0
Hercules	–	–	–	–	–	y	x	y	y	–	y	23
#2 Dick Jubie												
Abdula Rais	DJ	DJ	x	–	–	DJ	–	–	–	–	–	14
Christoporo de Tavorag-	–	–	–	–	–	–	–	–	–	–	–	1
#3 Rob Tailor												
Attendant[Bassa]	RT	RT	–	RT	RT	–	RT	RT	–	–	RT	0
Fury	–	–	–	–	–	–	–	–	–	–	–	0
Jonas	–	–	–	–	–	x	x	x	–	–	–	9
#4 mr Sam												
moores attendant-	SR	–	SR	–	–	SR	–	y	–	–	SR	11
Pisano	–	–	–	–	–	–	y	y	y	y	–	0
moores embassador	–	–	–	–	–	–	–	–	–	–	–	0
Death	–	–	–	–	–	–	–	–	–	–	–	0
#5 mr hunt												
moores attendant	TH	–	TH	TH	TH	–	TH	–	–	–	–	0
moores embassador	–	–	–	–	–	–	–	–	–	–	–	0
#6 w Cartwright												
moores attendant	WC	–	WC	–	WC	–	–	WC	–	–	–	0
attendant	–	–	–	–	–	–	–	–	–	–	–	0
#7 George Somersett												
Attendant[Bassa]	GS	GS	–	GS	GS	–	–	–	–	–	–	0
Fury	–	–	–	GS	–	–	–	–	–	y	–	0
moores attendant	–	–	–	–	–	–	GS	GS	–	y	–	0
County Vinioso	–	–	–	–	–	GS	GS	–	GS	–	–	0
attendant	–	–	–	–	–	–	–	–	–	–	–	0

Boys

Part												Lines
#1 Dab												
Young brother	D	–	D	D	D	–	–	–	–	–	–	0
Ghost	–	–	–	–	–	–	–	–	–	–	–	1
#2 Parsons												
Fury	–	–	TP	TP	–	–	TP	–	–	–	TP	0
#3 mr Townes boy												
Page	TB	x	x	–	x	–	–	–	–	–	–	0
#4 mr Allens boy												
Page	AB	–	x	–	–	–	x	–	–	–	–	0
#5 Harry												
Young brother	H	–	–	–	–	–	–	–	–	–	–	0
#6 Tho. Drom												
Nemesis	–	–	TDr	TDr	–	–	–	–	–	–	–	

Total Lines Minor Parts   57= 4%
Principal Parts   1,316=96%
    1,373

Table 8

1 Tamar Cam (1602)

Principal Parts

Men

	C	1	2	3	4	C	5	6	7	8	9	C	10	11	12	13	14	15	C	16	C	17	18	19	Procession
#1 Mr. Allen																									
Tamar	-	EA	-	x	x	-	x	-	-	x	x	-	-	x	x	-	-	-	-	x	-	-	x	x	-
#2 H. Jeffs																									
Otanes	-	HJ	-	x	x	-	x	-	x	x	x	-	x	x	x	-	x	-	-	x	-	-	x	x	-
#3 Mr. Singer																									
Assinico-Clowne	-	-	-	-	JS	-	-	-	-	x	-	-	-	-	-	-	x	-	-	x	-	-	x	-	-
#4 Mr. Sam																									
Ascalon-Spirit	-	-	-	-	-	-	SR	-	-	-	-	-	-	SR	-	-	-	-	-	-	-	-	-	-	SR
Crym	-	-	-	-	-	-	-	-	x	-	-	-	-	-	-	-	x	-	-	x	-	x	x	-	-
#5 Mr. Denygten																									
Mango Cham	-	TD	-	-	x	-	-	-	-	-	-	-	-	-	-	-	-	-	-	-	-	-	-	-	-
Tartar	-	-	-	-	-	-	-	-	-	-	-	-	-	-	-	-	-	-	-	-	-	-	-	-	TD
#6 Mr. Charles																									
Artaxes	-	-	CM	-	-	-	-	-	-	-	y	-	CM	CM	CM	-	-	-	-	CM	-	CM	-	CM	-
Persian Noble	-	-	-	-	-	-	-	-	-	-	-	-	-	CM	CM	-	-	-	-	-	-	-	-	-	-
#7 Mr. Burne																									
Colmogra	-	WB	-	-	x	-	-	x	-	x	-	-	x	x	x	-	-	-	-	x	-	WB	-	-	-
Persian Noble	-	-	-	-	-	-	-	-	-	-	-	-	-	-	-	-	-	-	-	-	-	WB	-	WB	-
Artabasis	-	-	-	-	-	-	-	-	-	-	-	-	-	-	-	-	-	-	-	-	-	-	-	-	-
#8 Mr. Towne																									
Persian Shaugh	-	-	TT	-	-	-	-	-	-	-	-	-	-	TT	x	-	-	TT	-	x	-	x	-	-	TT
Oracle	-	-	-	-	-	-	-	-	-	-	-	-	-	-	-	-	-	-	-	-	-	-	-	-	-
Tartar	-	-	-	-	-	-	-	-	-	-	-	-	-	-	-	-	-	-	-	-	-	-	-	-	TT

Boys

	C	1	2	3	4	C	5	6	7	8	9	C	10	11	12	13	14	15	C	16	C	17	18	19	Procession
#1 ?																									
Tarmia	-	-	-	-	-	-	-	-	-	-	-	-	-	-	x	-	-	x	-	x	-	x	-	-	-
#2 ?																									
Palmeda	-	-	-	-	-	-	-	-	-	-	-	-	-	-	-	-	x	-	-	x	-	-	x	x	-

Minor Parts

Men

	C	1	2	3	4	C	5	6	7	8	9	C	10	11	12	13	14	15	C	16	C	17	18	19	Procession
#1 Dic Jubie	DJ	-	-	-	-	-	-	-	-	-	-	-	-	-	-	-	-	-	-	-	-	-	-	-	-
Chorus	-	-	DJ	-	-	DJ	-	x	-	-	-	-	-	-	-	-	-	-	x	-	x	-	-	-	-
Trebassus	-	-	-	-	-	-	DJ	-	-	-	-	-	-	-	-	-	-	-	-	-	-	-	-	-	-
Diaphines-Spirit	-	-	-	-	-	-	-	-	x	x	-	-	-	-	-	-	-	-	-	x	-	-	-	-	-
Trumpet	-	-	-	-	-	-	-	-	-	-	DJ	-	-	-	-	-	x	-	-	x	-	DJ	x	-	-
Attend [Shah]	-	-	-	-	-	-	-	-	-	-	-	-	-	DJ	-	-	-	-	-	-	-	DJ	-	-	-
Noble [Shah]	-	-	-	-	-	-	-	-	-	-	-	-	-	-	DJ	-	-	-	-	-	-	-	-	-	-
Messenger	-	-	-	-	-	-	-	-	-	-	-	-	-	-	DJ	-	-	-	-	-	-	-	-	-	-
Cattaian	-	-	-	-	-	-	-	-	-	-	-	-	-	-	-	-	-	-	-	-	-	-	-	-	DJ

Table 8 (*cont.*)

	1	2	3	4	5	6	7	8	9	10	11	12	13	14	15	16	17	18
#2 w. Cart																		
Noble[Mango]	WC	–	WC	WC	WC	–	WC	WC	WC	WC	WC	WC	–	WC	–	WC	–	–
Noble[Tamar]	–	–	WC	–	–	–	–	–	–	–	–	–	–	–	–	–	–	–
Noble[Colmogra]	–	–	–	–	–	–	–	–	–	–	–	–	–	–	–	–	–	–
Pledge[Tamar]	–	x	–	–	x	–	–	–	–	–	–	–	–	–	–	–	–	–
Captain	–	–	–	–	–	–	–	–	–	–	–	–	–	–	–	–	–	–
Boharian	–	–	–	–	–	–	–	–	–	–	–	–	–	–	–	–	–	–
#3 Tho. Marbeck																		
Noble[Mango]	TM	–	TM	TM	TM	TM	TM	TM	TM	–	TM	–	TM	–	TM	TM	TM	TM
Noble[Tamar]	–	–	TM	TM	–	–	–	–	–	–	–	–	–	–	–	–	–	–
Pontus-Spirit	–	–	–	TM	–	–	–	–	–	–	–	–	–	–	–	–	–	–
Noble[Colmogra]	–	–	–	–	–	–	–	–	–	–	–	–	–	–	–	–	–	–
Pledge[Persian]	–	–	–	x	x	–	–	–	–	–	–	–	–	–	–	–	–	–
Guard	–	–	–	–	–	–	–	–	–	–	–	–	–	–	–	–	–	–
Captain	–	–	–	–	–	–	–	–	–	–	–	–	–	–	–	–	–	–
Bactrian	–	–	–	–	–	–	–	–	–	–	–	–	–	–	–	–	–	–
#4 W. Parr																		
Noble[Mango]	WP	WP	WP	WP	WP	WP	WP	WP	WP	WP	WP	WP	WP	WP	–	WP	WP	WP
Scowt	–	–	–	–	–	–	–	–	x	WP	–	–	–	–	–	–	–	–
Noble[Tamar]	–	–	–	WP	–	–	x	WP	–	–	–	–	–	–	–	–	–	–
Noble[Colmogra]	–	–	–	–	–	–	–	–	WP	–	WP	–	WP	WP	WP	–	–	–
Trumpet	–	–	–	–	–	–	–	–	–	–	–	–	–	–	–	–	–	–
Guard	–	–	–	–	–	–	–	–	–	–	–	–	–	–	–	–	–	–
Attend.[Artaxes]	–	–	–	–	–	–	–	–	–	–	–	–	–	–	–	–	–	–
Boharian	–	–	–	–	–	–	–	–	–	–	–	–	–	–	–	–	–	–
#5 Parsons																		
Attend.[Mango]	TP	x	TP	TP	TP	TP	TP	TP	TP	TP	TP	TP	TP	TP	TP	TP	TP	TP
Attend.[Shah]	–	TP	TP	–	–	–	TP	–	–	–	–	–	–	–	–	–	–	–
Attend.[Tamar]	–	–	TP	TP	–	–	–	TP	TP	–	TP	TP	TP	TP	TP	–	–	–
Persian	–	–	–	–	TP	–	–	TP	–	–	–	–	–	–	–	–	–	–
Guard	–	–	–	–	–	–	–	–	–	–	–	–	–	–	–	–	–	TP
Spirit	–	–	–	–	–	–	–	–	–	–	–	–	–	–	–	–	–	–
Messenger	–	–	–	–	–	–	–	–	–	–	–	–	–	–	–	–	–	–
Nurse	–	–	–	–	–	–	–	–	–	–	–	–	–	–	–	–	–	–
Attend.[Artaxes]	–	–	–	–	–	–	–	–	–	–	–	–	–	–	–	–	–	–
Hermaphrodite	–	–	–	–	–	–	–	–	–	–	–	–	–	–	–	–	TP	TP
#6 George Somersett																		
Attend.[Mango]	GS	GS	–	GS	GS	–	GS	GS	GS	GS	GS	GS	–	GS	GS	GS	–	GS
Attend.[Shah]	–	–	GS	GS	GS	–	–	GS	GS	GS	GS	GS	–	–	–	–	–	–
Guard	–	x	–	–	x	–	–	–	–	–	–	–	–	–	–	–	–	–
Attend.[Tamar]	–	–	–	–	–	–	–	GS	–	–	–	–	–	–	–	–	–	–
Captain	–	–	–	–	–	–	–	–	–	–	–	–	–	–	–	–	–	–
Attend.[Artaxes]	–	–	–	–	–	–	–	–	–	–	–	–	GS	GS	–	GS	GS	–
Cattaian	–	–	–	–	–	–	–	–	–	–	–	–	–	–	–	–	GS	GS

Role / Character	Actor initials
#7 A. Jeffs	
Linus-Satire	AJ · · AJ
Moore	
#8 Mr. Jubie	
Pitho-Satire	EJ · · EJ
Moore	
#9 Tho. Rowley	
Nagar	TR
#10 red fast fellow	
Nagar	RF
#11 Rester	
Canniball	RE
#12 Ned Browne	NR
Canniball	NB
Crym	
#13 Gedion	
Geate	GE
#14 Gibbs	
Geate	GI

Boys

Role / Character	Actor initials
#1 Jack Grigorie	
Son of Tarmia	
Heron-Nymph	JG
Amazon	JG · · JG
#2 Denqtens little boy	
Son of Tarmia	
Thia-Nymph	DB · · DB
#3 gils his boy	
Pigmy	GB
#4 little Will Barne	
Amazon	LW
Pigmy	LW
#5 Jeames	
Hermaphrodite	J

Table 9

The Second Maiden's Tragedy (MS. 1611)

	1		2			3	4				5		
	1	2	1	2	3	1	1	2	3	4	1	2	Totals
Principal Parts													
Men													
#1 Tyrant	125	–	–	–	58	–	–	51	98	–	–	79	411
#2 Govianus	44	–	15	–	–	129	–	–	–	60	18	71	337
#3 Votarius	–	155	–	109	–	–	32	–	–	–	31	–	327
#4 Anselmus	–	74	–	51	–	–	–	–	–	–	44	–	169
#5 Helvetius	28	–	78	–	30	–	–	–	–	–	–	–	136
#6 Bellarius	–	18	–	–	–	–	16	–	–	–	42	–	76
#7 Sophonirus	20	–	–	–	33	19	–	–	–	–	–	–	72
1 Soldier	–	–	–	–	–	–	–	8	34	–	–	1	43
Boys													
#1 Wife	–	85	–	8	–	–	101	–	–	–	41	–	235
#2 Leonella	–	43	–	36	–	–	43	–	–	–	43	–	165
#3 Rich Robinson Lady	25	–	36	–	–	75	–	–	–	–	–	–	136
Lady's Spirit	–	–	–	–	–	–	–	–	–	RR 20	–	2	22

Total Lines Principal Parts 2,129

Minor Parts

Men

	1	2	1	2	3	1	1	2	3	4	1	2	Totals
#1 Mr. Gough Memphonius	2	–	–	–	1	–	–	RG 17	–	–	–	4	24
#2 1 Fellow	–	–	–	–	–	24	–	–	–	–	–	–	24
2 Soldier	–	–	–	–	–	–	–	3	12	–	–	2	17
1 Servant [Govianus]	–	–	–	–	–	–	–	–	–	–	2	–	2
#3 Servant [Lady]	–	–	1	–	–	–	–	–	–	–	–	–	1
Guard	–	–	–	–	1	–	–	–	–	–	–	–	1
2 Fellow	–	–	–	–	–	12	–	–	–	–	–	–	12
3 Soldier	–	–	–	–	–	–	–	0	2	–	–	1	3
#4 2 Servant [Govianus]	–	–	–	–	–	14	–	–	–	–	1	–	15
4 Soldier	–	–	–	–	–	–	–	1	–	–	–	–	1
#5 1 Noble-Attendant	0	–	–	–	0	–	–	0	–	–	–	0	0
#6 2 Noble-Attendant	0	–	–	–	0	–	–	1	–	–	–	0	1
#7 3 Noble-Attendant	2	–	–	–	0	–	–	0	–	–	–	0	2
#8 4 Noble-Attendant	0	–	–	–	0	–	–	0	–	–	–	0	0

Boy

	1	2	1	2	3	1	1	2	3	4	1	2	Totals
#1 Page	–	–	–	–	–	–	–	–	–	1	–	–	1
Lady's Body	–	–	–	–	–	–	–	–	–	–	–	0	0

Total Lines Minor Parts   104 = 5%

Principal Parts   2,129 = 95%

2,233

Table 10

Sir John van Olden Barnavelt (MS. 1619)

Principal Parts — Men

	Act 1			Act 2				Act 3						Act 4						Act 5			Totals
Scene	1	2	3	1	2	3	4	1	2	3	4	5	6	1	2	3	4	5	6	1	2	3	
#1 Barnavelt	66	72	22	49	–	–	17	–	–	–	44	24	105	–	102	–	105	–	–	16	160	116	790
#2 Pr. of Orange	–	111	–	–	–	–	10	–	27	–	–	–	105	–	105	–	–	38	–	–	15	32	387
#3 Leidenberch	19	4	18	40	17	–	14	1	–	–	43	–	56	–	9	–	–	–	–	–	–	–	221
#4 Jo:R: / 1 Captain[English]	JR 13	–	JR 2	JR 62	–	JR 6	–	JR 9	–	–	JR 9	–	–	JR 35	–	–	JR 40	–	–	JR 49	–	JR 29	207
#5 Servant	–	–	–	–	–	–	–	–	–	–	–	–	–	–	–	–	–	–	–	49	–	–	49
Vandort	–	8	2	–	–	–	–	–	23	35	–	–	–	8	–	–	30	–	32	32	–	2	140
#6 Modesbargen	66	1	0	12	–	–	–	–	–	–	–	–	–	39	–	–	7	–	–	–	–	–	125
Utrecht-Executioner	–	–	–	–	–	–	–	–	–	–	–	–	–	–	–	–	–	–	31	–	–	10	41
#7 Bredero	–	7	0	–	–	–	–	–	44	24	–	–	–	16	–	–	11	–	–	15	–	–	117
#8 mr Rob / 1 Captaine[Dutch]	–	RR 2	–	–	–	–	RR 1	–	RR 10	–	–	–	–	RR 2	RR 15	–	–	–	–	RR 40	RR 15	–	45
#9 Boisise	–	–	–	–	–	–	–	–	–	–	–	–	–	–	–	–	–	–	–	40	–	–	40
Provost	–	–	–	–	–	–	–	–	8	–	–	–	8	–	–	–	0	–	25	–	–	8	49
#10 Grotius	18	4	0	–	–	–	–	–	–	–	2	17	–	–	–	–	–	–	–	–	–	–	41
1 Lord	–	–	–	–	–	–	–	–	2	–	–	–	–	–	–	–	–	–	–	–	–	32	34
#11 migh / 2 Captain[English]	M 29	7	2	–	–	–	–	0	–	–	1	–	–	–	–	–	–	–	–	–	–	–	39
Soldier[English]	–	–	M 4	–	–	–	–	–	M 9	–	–	–	–	–	–	–	–	–	–	–	–	0	4
2 Captain[Dutch]	–	–	–	–	–	–	–	–	M 9	–	–	–	–	–	–	–	–	–	–	–	–	–	9
1 Huntsman	–	–	–	–	–	–	–	–	–	–	–	–	–	M 10	–	–	–	–	–	–	–	–	10

Table 10 (cont.)

																Total
#12																
Hogerbeets	3	0	–	–	–	–	–	–	13	–	–	–	–	–	–	16
1 Burger	–	6	6	–	1	–	–	–	–	–	–	18	–	–	–	31
Morier	–	–	–	–	–	–	–	–	–	–	–	–	12	–	–	12
#13																
Grave William	20	–	–	0	–	–	6	–	–	–	2	–	0	–	–	28
#14																
Rock-Giles	–	13	–	2	–	17	–	–	–	–	–	13	–	–	–	15
Barnavelt's Son	–	–	–	–	–	–	–	–	–	–	–	13	–	–	–	30
Leyden	–	–	–	–	–	–	–	–	–	–	–	–	–	23	–	23
#1																
1 Dutch Woman	–	10	–	1	–	–	–	–	–	0	–	–	–	–	–	11
Leidenberch's Boy	–	–	–	–	–	16	27	–	–	–	–	–	–	–	–	43
#2 Nick																
2 Dutch Woman	–	22	–	1	–	–	–	–	–	–	–	–	–	–	–	23
Wife																
#3										NU						
English gent'W:	–	20	–	8	–	–	–	–	–	12	8	–	20	–	–	40
#4 G. lowen	–	20	–	8	–	–	–	–	–	–	–	–	–	–	–	28
3 Dutch Woman	–	4	–	1	–	–	–	–	–	–	–	–	–	–	–	5
									GL							
Daughter	–	–	–	–	–	–	–	–	–	10	–	–	4	–	–	14

Total Lines Principal Parts 2,667

Minor Parts

Men

																Total
#1 R. T.																
Officer	0	–	RT 3	–	RT 2	RT 2	–	–	–	–	–	14	–	–	–	16
Messenger	–	–	–	RT 5	–	–	–	–	–	RT 3	–	–	–	–	–	8
Servant	–	–	–	–	–	–	RT 8	RT 2	–	–	–	–	–	–	–	5
2 Huntsman																
Harlem	–	–	–	–	TP 2	–	–	–	–	–	–	–	–	–	–	8
#2 T P Holderus	–	11	–	–	–	–	–	–	–	–	–	–	14	–	14	13
Servant	–	–	–	–	–	–	–	–	–	TP 1	–	–	0	–	–	1
Soldier[Rob.]	–	–	–	–	–	–	–	–	–	–	–	–	0	–	–	0

#3 mr Bir.
Officer
Colonel

Servant
2 Lord
#4
1 Guard
2 Burger
Soldier
#5
Lieutenant
2 Lord
Other
Attend.[Ambass.]
Soldier
#6
2 Guard
Soldier
Soldier
Other
Attend.[Ambass.]
#7
2 Captain[Dutch]
Soldier
Attend.[Ambass.]

#1 T. Holc
4 Dutch Woman

Provosts Wife

Boy

GB

TH

Total Lines Minor Parts $\frac{151}{2,667}$ = 5%

Principal Parts   2,667 = 95%

2,818

Table 11
The Honest Man's Fortune (MS. 1625)

Principal Parts

Men

Part	1			2				3			4		5			Totals
	1	2	3	1	2	3	4	1	2	3	1	2	1	2	4	
#1 Montaigne	190	-	54	-	39	-	24	35	-	39	57	21	71	-	130	660
#2 Longaville	127	-	-	30	12	17	-	-	74	-	45	35	-	-	2	342
#3 Laverdure	-	-	-	-	130	-	11	-	-	37	20	-	-	39	13	250
#4 Orleans	21	72	-	-	16	-	-	-	11	1	-	39	-	-	21	181
#5 Amiens	28	15	14	-	10	35	-	-	13	-	-	36	-	-	18	169
#6 Dubois	25	-	-	10	24	-	20	-	24	-	-	22	-	-	-	125
#7 Captaine Lapoop	-	-	-	49	-	4	-	-	24	6	-	-	-	23	6	112
#8 Maly-corne	-	-	-	16	-	30	-	-	24	7	-	-	-	20	9	106
#9 G:Ver. GV																
1 Creditor	13	-	-	-	-	-	33	-	-	-	-	-	-	-	-	46

Boys

Part	1			2				3			4		5			Totals
	1	2	3	1	2	3	4	1	2	3	1	2	1	2	4	
#1 Maddam Lamira	-	-	-	-	-	-	-	58	-	49	7	15	20	-	49	198
#2 Viramour	21	-	2	-	-	-	-	66	-	13	57	-	-	-	9	168
#3 Lady Orlean	-	39	28	-	-	-	-	31	-	0	1	33	-	-	2	134
#4 Charlotte	-	-	-	-	-	-	-	5	-	6	36	-	14	-	3	64

Total Lines Principal Parts 2,555

Minor Parts

Men

Part	1			2				3			4		5			Totals
	1	2	3	1	2	3	4	1	2	3	1	2	1	2	4	
#1																
1 Lawyer	24	-	-	-	-	-	-	-	-	-	-	-	-	-	-	24
Drawer	-	-	-	-	0	-	-	-	-	-	-	-	-	-	-	0
3 Officer	-	-	-	-	-	-	2	-	-	-	-	-	-	-	-	2
#2																
2 Lawyer	12	-	-	-	-	-	-	-	-	-	-	-	-	-	-	12
Servant	-	0	-	-	4	-	-	-	-	5	-	-	-	-	-	9
1 Officer	-	-	-	-	-	-	6	-	-	-	-	-	-	-	-	6
#3 J:Rho. JR																
2 Creditor	4	-	-	-	-	-	2	-	-	-	-	-	-	-	-	6
Drawer	-	-	-	-	0	-	-	-	-	-	-	-	-	-	-	0
Lacquey	-	-	-	-	-	-	-	-	-	-	0	-	-	-	-	0
Attendant	-	-	-	-	-	-	-	-	-	-	-	-	-	-	0	0
#4 G:Rick GR																
Servant	-	0	-	-	-	-	-	-	-	-	-	-	-	-	-	0
Drawer	-	-	-	-	0	-	-	-	-	-	-	-	-	-	-	0
2 Officer	-	-	-	-	-	-	2	-	-	-	-	-	-	-	-	2
Attendant	-	-	-	-	-	-	-	-	-	-	-	-	-	-	0	0
#5																
3 Creditor	-	-	-	-	-	-	2	-	-	-	-	-	-	-	-	2
Lacquey	-	-	-	-	-	-	-	-	-	-	0	-	-	-	-	0
Attendant	-	-	-	-	-	-	-	-	-	-	-	-	-	-	0	0

Boy

Part	1			2				3			4		5			Totals
	1	2	3	1	2	3	4	1	2	3	1	2	1	2	4	
#1 Page	-	-	-	-	-	-	-	-	-	-	0	-	-	-	-	0

Total Lines Minor Parts   63 = 2%
Principal Parts   2,555 = 98%
2,618

Table 12   III

Table 12
Believe as you List (MS. 1631)

Principal Parts

	1		2		3			4				5		
	1	2	1	2	1	2	3	1	2	3	4	1	2	Totals
Men														
#1 Mr. Taylor				JT					JT					
Antiochus	121	23	-	153	-	20	48	-	116	-	35	-	164	680
#2 Mr. Lowin			JL											
Flaminius	-	75	83	89	55	6	153	37	8	-	24	34	33	597
#3 Mr. pollard		TP												
Berecinthius	-	91	-	15	-	56	12	-	-	63	-	-	-	237
#4 Mr. Benfeild														
Amilcar	-	-	-	94	-	-	-	-	-	-	-	-	-	94
King Prusias	-	-	-	-	-	19	58	-	-	-	-	-	-	77
												RB		
Marcellus	-	-	-	-	-	-	-	-	-	-	-	88	78	166
#5 Mr.Swantton	ES													
Chrysalus	31	-	40	-	-	-	-	-	-	-	-	-	-	71
Sempronius	-	-	-	-	-	-	-	42	11	-	21	-	-	74
#6 Mr. Robinson														
Stoic	48	-	-	-	-	-	-	-	-	-	-	-	-	48
					RR									
Lentulus	-	-	-	-	36	-	-	-	-	-	-	-	-	36
Metellus	-	-	-	-	-	-	-	44	8	-	11	-	-	63
#7 J. Hony									JH					
1 Merchant	-	29	-	4	-	8	0	-	-	5	-	-	-	46
#8 wm penn												WP	WP	
2 Merchant	-	26	-	4	-	8	0	-	-	-	-	11	0	49
									WP					
Jailer	-	-	-	-	-	-	-	-	30	-	-	-	-	30
#9 Curtis												CG	CG	
3 Merchant	-	25	-	5	-	0	0	-	-	-	-	14	0	44
#10														
Hanno	-	-	-	39	-	-	-	-	-	-	-	-	-	39
#11 Rowland Dowle				RD										
1 Officer	-	-	-	0	-	-	-	-	-	-	-	-	-	0
						RD								
Philoxenus	-	-	-	-	-	6	23	-	-	-	-	-	-	29
									RD					
Other	-	-	-	-	-	-	-	-	0	-	-	-	-	0
													RD	
Servant [Marcellus]	-	-	-	-	-	-	-	-	-	-	-	-	0	0
#12 Richard Baxter														
Carthalo	-	-	-	24	-	-	-	-	-	-	-	-	-	24
					BX									
Titus	-	-	-	-	27	-	-	-	-	-	-	-	-	27
													BX	
Servant [Marcellus]	-	-	-	-	-	-	-	-	-	-	-	-	0	0
Boys														
#1														
Courtesan	-	-	-	-	-	-	-	-	105	-	-	-	-	105
#2														
Cornelia	-	-	-	-	-	-	-	-	-	-	-	77	23	100
#3														
Queene	-	-	-	-	-	7	21	-	-	-	-	-	-	28

Total Lines Principal Parts 2,636

Table 12 (*cont.*)

Minor Parts
Men

Part	1	2	3	4	5	6	7	8	9	10	11	12	13	Total
#1														
			BX	TH	TH									
Calistus	-	0	16	0	5	-	-	-	-	-	-	-	-	21
										BX				
Officer	-	-	-	-	-	-	-	-	-	5	1	-	-	6
												RD		
Attend.[Marcellus]	-	-	-	-	-	-	-	-	-	-	-	0	0	0
#2														
			PT	RD	RD	BX	BX					BX		
Demetrius	-	0	2	0	4	0	0	-	-	-	-	0	-	6
													PT	
Captain	-	-	-	-	-	-	-	-	-	-	-	-	11	11
#3														
Hasdrubal	-	-	20	-	-	-	-	-	-	-	-	-	-	20
						FB								
Attend.[Prusias]	-	-	-	-	-	0	0	-	-	-	-	-	-	0
												FB		
Attend.[Marcellus]	-	-	-	-	-	-	-	-	-	-	-	0	-	0
2 Soldier	-	-	-	-	-	-	-	-	-	-	-	-	0	0
#4														
				WM										
2 Officer	-	-	-	0	-	-	-	-	-	-	-	-	-	0
						WM								
Attend.[Prusias]	-	-	-	-	-	0	0	-	-	-	-	-	-	0
1 Soldier	-	-	-	-	-	-	-	-	-	-	-	-	0	0
#5														
				NU										
3 Officer	-	-	-	0	-	-	-	-	-	-	-	-	-	0
							NU							
Attend.[Prusias]	-	-	-	-	-	-	0	0	-	-	-	-	-	0
												NU		
Attend.[Marcellus]	-	-	-	-	-	-	-	-	-	-	-	0	-	0
3 Soldier	-	-	-	-	-	-	-	-	-	-	-	-	0	0
#6														
Syrus	9	-	5	-	-	-	-	-	-	-	-	-	-	14
				FB										
Guard	-	-	-	0	-	-	0	-	-	0	-	0	-	0
#7														
Geta	13	-	4	-	-	-	-	-	-	-	-	-	-	17
				TH										
Guard	-	-	-	0	-	-	0	-	-	0	-	0	-	0

Boys

Part	1	2	3	4	5	6	7	8	9	10	11	12	13	Total
#1														
Lady	-	-	-	-	-	0	-	-	-	-	-	-	-	0
Moor waiting woman	-	-	-	-	-	-	-	-	-	-	-	0	3	3
#2														
Boy	-	-	-	-	-	-	-	-	-	0	-	-	-	0
Servant[Cornelia]	-	-	-	-	-	-	-	-	-	-	-	-	0	0
#3														
Servant[Cornelia]	-	-	-	-	-	-	-	-	-	-	-	-	0	0

Total Lines Minor Parts 98= 4%
Principal Parts 2,636=96%
2,734

Table 13 113

Table 13
Casting Requirements for Eight Playhouse Documents, 1590-1631

	Text	Men	Principal Parts	Boys	Parts	% of lines Spoken by Principals	Men	Minor Parts	Boys	Parts	Total Men	Actors Boys
2SDS	MS. 1590	8	12	4	7	-	8	38	2	6	16	6
Fred.	MS. 1597	10	13	4	4	-	7	19	0	0	17	4
BA	MS. 1598	11	17	2	3	96 (Q-1594)	7	21	6	7	18	8
1TC	MS. 1602	8	15	2	2	-	14	58	5	9	22	7
SMT	MS. 1611	7	8	3	4	95	8	14	1	2	15	4
Barn.	MS. 1619	14	25	4	7	95	7	28	1	2	21	5
HMF	MS. 1625	9	9	4	4	96	5	17	1	1	14	5
BAYL	MS. 1631	12	23	3	3	96	7	20	3	5	19	6
Mean		9.9	15.4	3.3	4.3	95.6	7.9	26.9	2.4	4.0	17.8	5.6

Table 14

Shakespeare and his Fellow Players Named in Ten Documents, 1603-1635

	(1) Royal Patent May 1603	(2) Livery List Mar. 1604	(3) Royal Patent Mar. 1619	(4) Livery List May 1619	(5) Livery List Apr. 1621	(6) Apology Dec. 1624	(7) Livery List May 1625	(8) Royal Patent June 1625	(9) Livery List May 1629	(10) Sharer Papers 1635
Fletcher, L.	1	3	–	–	–	–	–	–	–	–
Shakespeare	2	1	–	–	–	–	–	–	–	–
Burbage, R.	3	2	2	–	–	–	–	–	–	–
Phillips	4	5	–	–	–	–	–	–	–	–
Heminges	5	4	1	1	1	–	1	1	1	–
Condell	6	3	3	2	–	2	2	2	–	–
Sly	7	6	–	–	–	–	–	–	–	–
Armin	8	7	–	–	–	–	–	–	–	–
Cowley	9	9	–	–	–	–	–	–	–	–
Lowin	–	–	4	3	3	7	15	3	2	S
Tooley	–	–	5	6	6	–	–	–	–	–
Underwood	–	–	6	5	5	–	–	–	–	–
Field, N.	–	–	7	4	–	–	–	–	–	–
Benfield	–	–	8	8	8	5	11	6	6	P
Goughe, R.	–	–	9	7	7	–	–	–	–	–
Ecclestone	–	–	10	9	9	–	–	–	–	–
Robinson, R.	–	–	11	11	11	2	6	5	4	S
Shank	–	–	12	10	10	8	8	7	5	–
Sharp	–	–	–	–	–	11	5	12	7	–
Pollard	–	–	–	–	–	4	14	13	9	P
Taylor, Jos.	–	–	–	–	12	1	10	4	3	S
Birch	–	–	–	–	–	6	4	11	–	–
Rice	–	–	–	–	4	9	12	9	–	–
Rowley, W.	–	–	–	–	–	10	–	8	–	–
Swanston	–	–	–	–	–	3	9	10	8	P
Horn	–	–	–	–	–	–	13	–	14	–
Vernon	–	–	–	–	–	–	7	–	13	–
Perkins	–	–	–	–	–	–	3	–	–	–
Smith, A.	–	–	–	–	–	–	–	–	10	–
Penn	–	–	–	–	–	–	–	–	12	–
Hobbes	–	–	–	–	–	–	–	–	11	–

P = Petitioner
S = Sharer

Table 15

The Duchess of Malfi (Q-1623)

Principal Parts

Men

Role	1.1	1.2	2.1	2.2	2.3	2.4	2.5	3.1	3.2	3.3	3.4	3.5	4.1	4.2	5.1	5.2	5.3	5.4	5.5	Totals
#1 J. Lowin — Bosola	36	40	112	24	76	–	–	68	46	96	27	–	–	21	53	169	92	29	48	824
#2 R. Burbidge(1) / J. Taylor(2) — Ferdinand	–	119	–	–	–	68	46	63	18	–	–	51	53	–	33	–	–	4	21	476
#3 W. Ostler(1) / R. Benfeild(2) — Antonio	35	121	27	35	–	30	65	18	–	33	–	–	–	24	28	23	0	–	–	448
#4 H. Cundaile(1) / R. Robinson(2) — Cardinall	3	20	–	–	–	–	–	7	–	0	–	–	–	–	111	–	–	25	35	273
#5 J. Underwood — Delio	10	15	14	13	–	25	–	14	26	–	–	–	–	–	26	30	–	12	–	185
1 Madman	–	–	–	–	–	–	–	–	–	–	–	–	–	8	–	–	–	–	–	8
#6 J. Rice — Pescara	–	–	–	–	–	–	–	–	12	–	–	–	–	–	30	14	–	7	7	70
2 Madman	–	–	–	–	–	–	–	–	–	–	–	–	–	7	–	–	–	–	–	7
#7 R. Pallant [Jr.] (2) — 1 Officer	–	–	–	–	–	–	4	–	–	–	–	–	–	–	–	–	–	–	–	4
3 Madman	–	–	–	–	–	–	–	–	–	–	–	–	–	10	–	–	–	–	–	10
Doctor	–	–	–	–	–	–	–	–	–	–	–	–	–	–	–	42	–	–	–	42
#8 — Castruchio	20	–	7	–	–	–	3	–	–	–	–	–	–	–	–	–	–	–	–	27
2 Officer	–	–	–	–	–	–	3	–	–	–	–	–	–	–	–	–	–	–	–	3
1 Pilgrim	–	–	–	–	–	–	–	–	–	–	18	–	–	–	–	–	–	–	–	18
6 Madman	–	–	–	–	–	–	–	–	–	–	–	–	–	0	–	–	–	–	–	0

Boys

Role	1.1	1.2	2.1	2.2	2.3	2.4	2.5	3.1	3.2	3.3	3.4	3.5	4.1	4.2	5.1	5.2	5.3	5.4	5.5	Totals
#1 R. Sharpe — Dutchess-Echo	–	139	33	–	–	–	–	10	117	–	–	–	0	102	65	80	10	–	–	556
#2 J. Tomson — Julia	–	0	97	–	–	–	–	36	–	–	–	–	–	–	–	9	–	–	–	142
#3 R. Pallant [Jr.] (1) — Cariola	–	3	2	–	–	–	–	21	–	–	–	–	–	30	–	–	2	–	–	58

Total Lines Principal Parts 3,151

Table 15 (*cont.*)

Minor Parts

Men

														Total
#1														
Servant [Antonio]			4								4	0		8
Servant [Julia]				8										8
Servant [Duchess]							23			23				23
#2														
T. Pollard														
Silvio	6				15									21
4 Madman								10		10				10
#3														
N. Towley														
Forobosco-Servant			9								6	4		9
Malateste					8		0			0	6			18
5 Madman														0
#4														
Roderico	2	0	2								1	7		12
3 Officer					1									1
2 Pilgrim						15	0			0				15
7 Madman														0
#5														
Grisolan	1	0	1		3					0	0	2		4
4 Officer							0			0				3
8 Madman														0
#6														
Churchman						0								0
Soldier							0							0
#7														
Churchman						0				0				0
Soldier							0							0
Executioner										1				1
#8														
Churchman						0								0
Executioner										0				0

Boys

														Total
#1														
Old Lady		3	4				0			0				7
1 Child														0
#2														
2 Child							0			0				0
#3														
3 Child							0			0				0

Total Lines Minor Parts 140 = 4%
Principal Parts 3,151 = 96%
3,291

Table 16   117

Table 16
The Roman Actor (Q-1629)

Principal Parts
Men

	1				2	3		4		5		Totals
	1	2	3	4	1	1	2	1	2	1	2	
#1 John Lowin — Domitianus Caesar	-	-	-	65	168	-	83	59	142	154	32	703
#2 Joseph Taylor — Paris	41	-	102	1	106	-	100	-	92	-	-	442
#3 Richard Sharpe — Parthenius	-	70	2	1	6	-	28	31	-	40	27	205
#4 Eyllardt Swanstone — Aretinus Clemens	-	-	45	5	29	-	11	52	3	-	-	145
#5 Curtise Grevill — Latinus	18	-	2	0	3	-	7	-	2	-	-	32
1 Tribune	-	-	-	-	-	-	-	-	-	54	29	83
#6 Thomas Pollard — Aelius Lamia	17	28	-	3	13	-	-	-	-	-	-	61
Stephanos	-	-	-	-	-	41	4	-	-	18	13	76
#7 Robert Benfield — Junius Rusticus	27	-	3	6	-	-	33	-	-	0	-	69
#8 Anthony Smith — Philargus	-	-	-	-	49	-	-	-	-	-	-	49
#9 Richard Robinson — Aesopus	12	-	3	0	23	-	-	-	8	-	-	46

Boys

	1				2	3		4		5		Totals
	1	2	3	4	1	1	2	1	2	1	2	
#1 John Tompson — Domitia	-	31	-	9	16	-	59	-	80	51	5	251
#2 John Hunnieman — Domitilla	-	-	-	1	0	41	21	46	0	-	4	113
#3 William Trigge — Julia	-	-	-	7	0	21	0	17	0	-	1	46
#4 Alexander Gough — Canis	-	-	-	4	0	30	0	3	0	-	0	37
#5 Boy-Lady	-	-	-	-	-	-	-	-	24	-	-	24

Total Lines Principal Parts 2,382

118   *Table 16*

Table 16 (*cont.*)

Minor Parts
Men

Part	1	2	3	4	5	6	7	8	9	10	11	Total
#1												
William Patrick Palphurius Sura	11	-	2	3	-	-	3	-	-	0	-	19
#2												
George Vernon												
1 Lictor	4	-	1	-	-	-	-	-	-	-	-	5
Prisoner	-	-	-	0	-	-	-	-	-	-	-	0
Hangman	-	-	-	-	-	0	-	-	-	-	-	0
2 Tribune	-	-	-	-	-	-	-	-	-	4	0	4
#3												
James Horne												
2 Lictor	4	-	1	-	-	-	-	-	-	-	-	5
Prisoner	-	-	-	0	-	-	-	-	-	-	-	0
Hangman	-	-	-	-	-	0	-	-	-	-	-	0
3 Tribune	-	-	-	-	-	-	-	-	-	3	0	3
#4												
Fulcinius	-	-	1	0	-	-	-	-	-	-	-	1
Ascletario	-	-	-	-	-	-	-	-	-	9	-	9
Sigesus	-	-	-	-	-	-	-	-	-	-	4	4
#5												
Soldier	0	-	-	-	-	-	-	-	-	-	-	0
Centurion	-	0	-	-	-	-	-	-	-	-	-	0
Prisoner	-	-	-	0	-	-	-	-	-	-	-	0
Servant	-	-	-	-	-	-	-	-	0	-	-	0
Entellus	-	-	-	-	-	-	-	-	-	-	4	4
#6												
Soldier	-	0	-	-	-	-	-	-	-	-	-	0
Captain	-	-	-	0	-	-	-	-	-	-	-	0
Guard	-	-	-	-	0	-	0	0	0	0	-	0
#7												
Soldier	-	0	-	-	-	-	-	-	-	-	-	0
Captain	-	-	-	0	-	-	-	-	-	-	-	0
Guard	-	-	-	-	0	-	0	0	0	0	-	0
#8												
Soldier	-	0	-	-	-	-	-	-	-	-	-	0
Servant	-	-	-	-	-	-	-	-	0	-	-	0

Total Lines Minor Parts 5 $\overline{4}$ = 2%
Principal Parts $\underline{2,382}$ =98%
2,436

Table 17

The Deserving Favorite (Q-1629)

Principal Parts

Men

	1					2								3					4				5				Totals
	1	2	3	4	5	1	2	3	4	5	6	7	8	1	2	3	4	5	1	2	3	4	1	2	3	4	
#1 Mr. Sharpe — Lysander	77	-	16	69	10	-	14	-	67	-	31	-	96	-	-	-	95	-	-	-	108	-	-	-	-	52	635
#2 Mr. Taylor — Duke	55	-	-	-	69	79	83	-	16	25	-	-	66	-	-	-	-	-	-	24	-	16	-	4	-	115	552
#3 Mr. Benfield — King	-	30	-	-	-	20	-	-	-	-	-	-	-	39	30	-	62	-	-	-	31	-	-	-	-	94	306
#4 Mr. Lowin — Jacomo	-	-	24	-	-	40	-	12	12	-	17	-	-	28	-	-	5	70	7	-	2	-	-	-	-	25	242
#5 Mr. Robinson — Hermite-Orsinio	-	-	-	-	-	-	-	-	-	-	-	-	-	-	-	-	43	-	-	-	17	-	-	-	3	156	219
#6 Mr. Swanstone — Count Utrante	-	11	-	-	0	-	16	-	-	-	-	-	-	4	-	13	-	-	-	-	16	-	-	-	-	8	68

Boys

	1	2	3	4	5	1	2	3	4	5	6	7	8	1	2	3	4	5	1	2	3	4	1	2	3	4	Totals
#1 John Honiman — Clarinda	-	-	5	45	64	-	64	-	62	-	-	-	-	-	22	-	83	58	25	-	24	-	-	-	-	47	499
#2 John Tomson — Cleonarda	-	-	-	-	-	-	-	-	-	-	21	38	35	-	-	83	84	-	-	117	-	1	-	69	-	-	448
#3 Edward Horton — Mariana	28	-	-	-	-	-	-	-	-	-	17	14	-	-	-	21	-	-	-	12	-	5	-	0	-	-	97

Total Lines Principal Parts 3,066

Table 17 (cont.)

Minor Parts
Men

Character									Total
#1									
<u>Mr. Smith</u>									
Jaspero	4	8	8						12
Gerard		9							17
Franciso	1								1
Priest						3		3	3
#2									
Bernardo	0	3	4	3	2	6			18
1 Huntsman					1				1
Executioner								1	1
#3									
1 Servant	8		8		3		5		16
2 Huntsman						0			0
Messenger								2	2
#4									
2 Servant	10	10							10
Guard						0		0	0
#5									
Attend.[King]	0	0		0	0				0
#6									
Attend.[King]	0	0		0					0
#7									
Attend.[King]	0	0		0	0				0
#8									
Follower[Duke]	0	0		0					0
#9									
Follower[Duke]	0	0							0
#10									
Follower[Duke]	0	0							0

Total Lines Minor Parts 81= 3%
Principal Parts 3,066=97%
3,147

Table 18   121

Table 18
The Picture (Q-1630)

Principal Parts — Men

	1		2		3						4				5			
	1	2	1	2	1	2	3	4	5	6	1	2	3	4	1	2	3	Totals
#1 Joseph Taylor / Mathias	120	-	-	79	-	-	11	-	107	-	136	-	-	61	-	-	83	597
#2 John Lowin / Eubulus	-	114	-	115	-	-	-	-	48	-	-	9	6	-	-	-	34	326
#3 Thomas Pollard / Ubaldo	-	42	-	27	16	17	-	-	-	77	-	65	-	-	22	-	11	277
#4 Eylardt Swanstone / Ricardo	-	63	-	28	16	24	-	-	-	25	-	54	-	-	31	-	7	248
#5 John Shannke / Hilario	6	-	74	-	40	10	-	-	-	-	-	24	-	-	54	-	6	214
#6 Robert Benfield / King Ladislaus	-	72	-	35	-	-	-	19	-	-	-	9	14	-	-	-	22	171
#7 William Pen / Julio Baptista	50	-	-	0	-	-	8	-	0	-	25	-	-	10	-	7	6	106
#8 Richard Sharpe / Ferdinand	-	-	-	69	-	-	-	7	-	-	-	2	3	-	-	-	11	92

Boys

	1		2		3						4				5			
	1	2	1	2	1	2	3	4	5	6	1	2	3	4	1	2	3	Totals
#1 John Hunnieman / Sophia	33	-	61	-	-	29	-	-	-	90	-	103	-	-	45	29	94	484
#2 John Tomson / Queen Honoria	-	76	-	129	-	-	-	-	84	-	34	-	17	55	-	-	19	414
#3 William Trigge / Corsica	15	-	63	-	-	13	-	-	-	-	-	5	-	-	20	-	0	116
#4 Alexander Goffe / Acanthe	-	0	-	0	-	-	8	3	9	-	-	-	0	0	-	-	0	20

Total Lines Principal Parts 3,065

Minor Parts — Men

	1		2		3						4				5			
	1	2	1	2	1	2	3	4	5	6	1	2	3	4	1	2	3	Totals
#1																		
Post	-	2	-	-	-	-	-	-	-	-	-	-	-	-	-	-	-	2
One	-	-	0	-	-	-	-	-	-	-	-	-	-	-	-	-	-	0
1 Vizard	-	-	-	-	-	-	10	-	6	-	-	-	-	-	-	-	-	16
Servant	-	-	-	3	-	-	-	0	-	-	-	-	-	3	-	-	0	4
#2																		
Servant	0	-	-	-	-	-	-	-	-	-	-	1	-	-	-	-	1	2
2 Vizard	-	-	-	-	-	-	4	-	0	-	-	-	-	-	-	-	-	4
Other	-	-	-	-	0	-	-	-	-	-	-	-	-	0	-	-	-	0
#3																		
Servant	0	-	-	-	-	-	-	-	-	-	-	1	-	-	-	-	0	1
Other	-	-	-	0	-	-	-	-	-	-	-	-	0	-	-	-	-	0
3 Vizard	-	-	-	-	-	-	0	-	0	-	-	-	-	-	-	-	-	0
#4																		
Attend.[King]	-	0	-	-	-	-	-	-	-	-	-	0	-	-	-	-	0	0
Captain	-	-	-	0	-	-	-	-	-	-	-	-	-	-	-	-	-	0
4 Vizard	-	-	-	-	-	-	0	-	0	-	-	-	-	-	-	-	-	0

Table 18 (*cont.*)

																		Totals
#5																		
Attend.[King]	-	0	-	-	-	-	-	-	-	-	-	-	0	-	-	-	0	0
Captain	-	-	-	0	-	-	-	-	-	-	-	-	-	-	-	-	-	0
Guide	-	-	-	-	1	-	-	-	-	-	-	-	-	-	-	-	-	1
#6																		
Attend.[King]	-	0	-	-	-	-	-	-	-	-	-	0	-	-	-	0		0
Servant	-	-	-	-	-	-	-	0	-	-	-	1	-	-	-	-	-	1
Other	-	-	-	0	-	-	-	-	-	-	-	-	-	-	-	-	-	0

Boys

																		Totals
#1																		
Silvia	-	0	-	0	-	-	-	-	-	-	-	-	-	-	-	-	-	0
#2																		
Boy	-	0	-	0	-	-	-	-	-	-	-	-	-	-	-	-	-	0
#3																		
Boy (lute)	-	0	-	0	-	-	-	-	-	-	-	-	-	-	-	-	-	0

Total Lines Minor Parts 31= 1%
Principal Parts 3,065=99%
3,096

Table 19
The Soddered Citizen (MS. c.1630)
Principal Parts
Men

	P	1		2		3				4			5		Totals
		1	2	1	2	1	2	3	4	1	2	3	1	2	
#1 John Lowen — Undermyne	-	56	113	114	16	64	23	-	-	-	57	-	-	163	606
#2 Thomas Pollard — Brainsicke	-	-	63	-	94	-	55	-	22	-	148	-	10	47	439
#3 Curtoys Grivell — Mountayne	-	-	107	-	-	36	-	-	-	-	-	-	-	99	242
#4 Richard Sharpe — Prologue	22	-	-	-	-	-	-	-	-	-	-	-	-	-	22
Sr. Wittworth	-	-	-	92	-	54	-	-	-	52	-	0	-	28	226
#5 Robert Benfield — Makewell	-	-	-	18	-	-	-	47	-	35	-	32	-	-	132
#6 John Honyman — Sly	-	41	-	8	-	26	3	-	-	-	-	-	-	20	98
#7 Anthony Smith — Clutch	-	-	21	-	1	-	12	-	0	-	23	-	0	5	62
#8 John Shanke — Hodge	-	-	-	-	-	-	-	-	17	-	3	-	-	5	25

Boys

	P	1		2		3				4			5		Totals
		1	2	1	2	1	2	3	4	1	2	3	1	2	
#1 Will:Trigg — Modestina	-	-	-	80	-	43	-	28	-	15	-	72	-	-	238
#2 John Thompson — Miniona	-	-	-	77	-	-	29	-	9	-	25	-	6	7	153
#3 Allex:Goffe — ffewtricks	-	40	47	-	6	-	28	-	0	-	2	-	3	3	129
#4 John:Shanks Boy — Maid[Miniona]	-	-	-	14	-	-	1	-	0	-	2	-	5	0	22

Total Lines Principal Parts 2,394

Table 20   123

Table 19 (*cont.*)

Minor Parts
Men

	1		2			3			4			5			Totals
	1	2	1	2	3	1	2	3	1	2	3	1	2	3	
#1 Mich:Underhill Shackle	–	–	5	–	0	–	0	–	0	–	8	–	0	–	13
#2 1 Creditor	–	–	–	–	–	–	6	–	–	–	–	–	–	2	8
1 Masker	–	–	–	–	–	–	–	–	–	0	–	–	–	–	0
#3 2 Creditor	–	–	–	–	–	–	2	–	–	–	–	–	–	10	12
2 Masker	–	–	–	–	–	–	–	–	–	0	–	–	–	–	0
#4 3 Creditor	–	–	–	–	–	–	1	–	–	–	–	–	–	3	4
3 Masker	–	–	–	–	–	–	–	–	–	0	–	–	–	–	0
#5 4 Creditor	–	–	–	–	–	–	3	–	–	–	–	–	–	–	3
4 Masker	–	–	–	–	–	–	–	–	–	0	–	–	–	–	0
1 Commissioner	–	–	–	–	–	–	–	–	–	–	–	–	–	19	19
#6 5 Creditor	–	–	–	–	–	–	1	–	–	–	–	–	–	–	1
5 Masker	–	–	–	–	–	–	–	–	–	0	–	–	–	–	0
2 Commissioner	–	–	–	–	–	–	–	–	–	–	–	–	–	12	12
#7 6 Creditor	–	–	–	–	–	–	1	–	–	–	–	–	–	–	1
6 Masker	–	–	–	–	–	–	–	–	–	0	–	–	–	–	0
3 Commissioner	–	–	–	–	–	–	–	–	–	–	–	–	–	2	2
#8 Servant	–	–	–	–	–	–	11	–	–	–	–	–	–	–	11
7 Masker	–	–	–	–	–	–	–	–	–	0	–	–	–	–	0
Solicitor	–	–	–	–	–	–	–	–	–	–	–	–	–	7	7
#9 1 Servant	–	–	–	–	–	–	0	–	–	4	–	0	–	4	8
#10 2 Servant	–	–	–	–	–	–	0	–	–	7	–	0	–	–	7
#11 3 Servant	–	–	–	–	–	–	0	–	–	1	–	–	–	–	1

Boys

	1		2			3			4			5			Totals
	1	2	1	2	3	1	2	3	1	2	3	1	2	3	
#1 1 Vintner Boy	–	–	–	–	0	–	–	–	–	–	–	–	–	–	0
Boy	–	–	–	–	–	–	–	–	–	–	–	0	–	–	0
#2 2 Vintner Boy	–	–	–	–	0	–	–	–	–	–	–	–	–	–	0

Total Lines Minor Parts 109 = 4%
Principal Parts <u>2,394</u> = 96%
2,503

Table 20
The Swisser (MS. 1631)

	1		2			3			4			5			Totals
	1	2	1	2	3	1	2	3	1	2	3	1	2	3	
Principal Parts **Men**															
#1 Taylor Arioldus	–	94	19	–	87	–	–	–	73	170	–	–	–	62	505
#2 Sharpe King of the Lombards	48	16	39	14	40	–	–	108	–	84	–	–	–	76	425
#3 Lowin Andrucho	86	59	84	–	–	47	25	–	–	55	–	4	–	31	391

Table 20 (*cont.*)

Part	1	2	3	4	5	6	7	8	9	10	11	12	13	14	Total
#4 Swanston — Alcidonus	-	-	48	-	-	9	61	-	-	-	59	-	61	0	238
#5 Benfield — Antharis	23	18	3	-	-	10	45	-	-	-	54	-	40	-	193
#6 Pollard — Timentes	28	-	-	29	-	32	18	-	-	-	-	5	5	-	117
#7 Smith — Asprandus	7	9	10	-	-	26	10	-	-	-	-	36	14	2	114
#8 Penn — Clephis	59	2	2	-	-	2	16	-	-	-	-	-	-	-	81
#9 Greville — Iseas	16	5	5	-	-	20	5	-	-	-	-	23	11	0	85

Boys

Part	1	2	3	4	5	6	7	8	9	10	11	12	13	14	Total
#1 Goffe — Eurinia	-	-	-	-	61	-	-	55	44	-	-	-	-	4	164
#2 Trigg — Selina	-	-	3	-	-	7	9	-	-	-	-	-	26	0	45
#3 Tompson — Panopia	-	-	7	-	-	-	-	-	-	-	-	-	-	27	34

Total Lines Principal Parts 2,392

Minor Parts
Men

Part	1	2	3	4	5	6	7	8	9	10	11	12	13	14	Total
#1 1 Soldier	2	-	-	-	-	-	-	-	-	-	-	-	-	-	2
1 Servant	-	3	-	-	-	0	0	-	-	2	-	-	-	-	5
1 Man	-	-	-	-	-	-	-	0	-	-	-	-	-	-	0
Gentleman	-	-	-	-	-	-	-	-	-	-	-	1	-	-	1
#2 2 Soldier	1	-	-	-	-	-	-	-	-	-	-	-	-	-	1
2 Servant	-	1	-	-	-	0	0	-	-	-	-	-	-	-	1
2 Man	-	-	-	-	-	-	-	0	-	-	-	-	-	-	0
#3 3 Soldier	3	-	-	-	-	-	-	-	-	-	-	-	-	-	3
Attend [King]	-	0	-	-	-	-	-	-	-	-	-	-	-	-	0
3 Man	-	-	-	-	-	-	-	0	-	-	-	-	-	-	0
#4 4 Soldier	1	-	-	-	-	-	-	-	-	-	-	-	-	-	1
Attend [King]	-	0	-	-	-	-	-	-	-	-	-	-	-	-	0
#5 Guard	0	-	-	-	-	-	0	-	-	-	-	-	-	0	0
Attend [King]	-	0	-	-	-	-	-	-	-	-	-	-	-	-	0
#6 Guard	0	-	-	-	-	-	0	-	-	-	-	-	-	0	0

Boy

Part	1	2	3	4	5	6	7	8	9	10	11	12	13	14	Total
#1 Boy	-	-	-	-	-	0	-	-	-	-	-	-	-	-	0
Gentlewoman	-	-	-	-	-	-	-	-	-	-	-	1	-	-	1

Total Lines Minor Parts   15 = 1%
Principal Parts   2,392 = 99%
2,407

Table 21   125

Table 21
The Wild Goose Chase (F-1652)

Principal Parts
Men

	1			2			3	4			5						Totals
	1	2	3	1	2	3	1	1	2	3	1	2	3	4	5	6	
#1 Mr. Joseph Taylor / Mirabell	–	55	110	140	10	48	168	20	–	72	–	65	–	11	22	34	755
#2 Mr. John Lowin / Belleur	–	28	11	25	–	62	30	–	89	32	–	51	–	–	6	27	361
#3 Mr. Thomas Pollard / Pinac	–	18	1	18	75	–	30	38	–	–	–	13	–	–	4	20	217
#4 Mr. Robert Benfield / De Gard	103	–	4	30	–	–	43	–	–	12	8	–	6	–	–	0	206
#5 Mr. Hilliard Swanston / Lugier	–	–	12	–	–	–	81	15	8	8	25	–	18	–	–	2	169
#6 Mr. Richard Robinson / La Castre	25	–	41	–	–	–	–	–	–	11	–	10	–	–	–	0	87
#7 Mr. William Penn / Nantolet	–	–	44	–	–	–	–	–	–	9	–	12	–	–	–	2	67
#8 Mr. Shanck / Servant	–	0	–	–	32	–	13	8	–	–	–	–	–	11	–	–	64
#9 Mr. John Hony-man / Young Factor	–	–	–	–	–	–	–	–	–	–	–	4	–	32	–	6	42

Boys

	1			2			3	4			5						Totals
	1	2	3	1	2	3	1	1	2	3	1	2	3	4	5	6	
#1 Sander Gough / Lillia-Bianca	–	–	27	–	75	–	85	110	11	13	–	–	6	15	–	15	357
#2 William Trigg / Rosalura	–	–	19	–	–	53	85	–	45	15	–	–	10	12	–	17	256
#3 Mr. Steph Hammerton / Oriana	45	–	10	24	–	7	23	–	–	35	–	–	–	6	–	22	172
#4 Foot Boy	11	–	–	–	–	–	–	–	–	–	–	–	–	–	–	–	11
Boy	–	–	–	–	–	–	4	–	–	–	–	–	–	–	–	–	4

Total Lines Principal Parts 2,768

Minor Parts
Men

	1			2			3	4			5						Totals
	1	2	3	1	2	3	1	1	2	3	1	2	3	4	5	6	
#1 Servant	–	0	–	–	–	–	–	3	–	–	–	–	–	–	–	–	3
Man	–	–	–	–	1	–	–	–	–	–	–	–	–	–	–	–	1
#2 1 Gentleman	–	–	–	–	–	–	3	–	4	–	–	–	–	–	–	–	7
Priest	–	–	–	–	–	–	–	0	–	–	–	–	–	–	–	–	0
1 Merchant	–	–	–	–	–	–	–	–	–	–	–	–	0	–	–	–	0
#3 2 Gentleman	–	–	–	–	–	–	1	–	3	–	–	–	–	–	–	–	4
2 Merchant	–	–	–	–	–	–	–	–	–	–	–	–	–	0	–	–	0
Servant	–	–	–	–	–	–	–	0	–	–	–	–	–	–	–	–	0

Table 21 (*cont.*)

Boys

																Totals
#1																
Petella	-	-	-	-	0	-	-	-	-	-	-	-	-	-	-	0
Mariana	-	-	-	-	-	-	0	5	-	-	-	-	-	-	-	5
#2																
Attendant [Mariana]	-	-	-	-	-	-	0	0	-	-	-	-	-	-	-	0
1 Woman	-	-	-	-	-	-	-	-	7	-	-	-	-	-	-	7
#3																
Attendant [Mariana]	-	-	-	-	-	-	0	0	-	-	-	-	-	-	-	0
2 Woman	-	-	-	-	-	-	-	-	2	-	-	-	-	-	-	2
#4																
Attendant [Mariana]	-	-	-	-	-	-	0	0	-	-	-	-	-	-	-	0
3 Woman	-	-	-	-	-	-	-	-	2	-	-	-	-	-	-	2
#5																
Attendant [Oriana]	-	-	-	-	-	-	0	-	-	-	-	-	-	-	-	0
4 Woman	-	-	-	-	-	-	-	-	2	-	-	-	-	-	-	2
#6																
Attendant [Oriana]	-	-	-	-	-	-	0	-	-	-	-	-	-	-	-	0
#7																
Attendant [Oriana]	-	-	-	-	-	-	0	-	-	-	-	-	-	-	-	0

Total Lines Minor Parts   33 = 1%
Principal Parts   2,768 = 99%
2,801

Table 22
The Wedding (Q-1629)

		1			2			3			4			5			
	1	2	3	1	2	3	1	2	3	1	2	3	1	2	E	Totals
							Principal Parts									
							Men									
#1 Michael Bowyer / Beauford	25	-	83	-	91	63	53	-	64	-	-	151	-	48	-	578
#2 William Allin / Captaine Landby	6	-	-	-	-	24	103	17	43	21	20	-	-	9	-	243
#3 William Sherlocke / Lodam	-	-	-	-	-	38	-	82	-	-	88	-	-	10	-	218
#4 Anthony Turner / Justice Landby	-	58	-	-	-	13	-	37	-	38	-	-	-	60	-	206
#5 Richard Perkins / Sir John Belfare	35	-	-	-	-	54	-	-	38	-	-	-	63	13	-	203
#6 William Robins / Rawbone	-	37	-	-	-	44	-	54	-	-	28	-	-	27	8	198
#7 John Sumpner / Marwood	22	-	47	-	29	-	-	-	-	-	-	-	-	19	-	117
#8 William Wilbraham / Isaac	34	22	-	20	-	21	-	-	1	-	-	-	12	1	-	111
#9 John Yong / Haver	-	-	-	-	-	13	-	35	-	-	21	-	-	8	-	77
#10 John Dobson / Cameleon	-	21	-	-	-	5	-	6	-	-	8	-	-	2	-	42
#11 Surgeon	-	-	-	-	-	-	9	-	-	-	-	-	-	-	-	9
Physician	-	-	-	-	-	-	-	-	-	-	-	-	29	-	-	29

Table 22 127

Table 22 (*cont.*)

Boys

#1 Edward Rogers Milisent	-	29	-	-	-	-	-	17	-	73	-	46	-	10	-	175
#2 Hugh Clarke Gratiana	-	-	-	-	-	35	29	0	-	35	-	13	-	40	-	152
#3 John Page Jane	-	6	-	-	-	1	-	49	-	-	-	-	-	26	-	82
#4 Tymothy Read Cardona	-	-	-	14	-	7	-	-	-	-	-	30	-	17	-	68

Total Lines Principal Parts 2,508

Minor Parts
Men

#1 Keeper	-	-	-	-	-	-	-	-	-	-	-	7	-	15	-	22
#2 1 Officer	-	-	-	-	-	-	-	-	-	-	-	17	-	-	-	17
#3 1 Servant	2	-	-	-	-	-	-	-	1	-	-	3	-	-	-	6
#4 2 Servant	0	-	-	-	-	-	-	-	-	-	-	0	-	-	-	0
#5 2 Officer	-	-	-	-	-	-	-	-	-	-	-	0	-	-	-	0

Total Lines Minor Parts 45 = 2%
Principal Parts 2,508 = 98%
2,553

Table 23
The Renegado (Q-1630)
Principal Parts

Men

Part (actor / role)	1.1	1.2	1.3	2.1	2.2	2.3	2.4	2.5	2.6	3.1	3.2	3.3	3.4	3.5	4.1	4.2	4.3	5.1	5.2	5.3	5.4	5.5	5.6	5.7	5.8	Totals
#1 Michael Bowier — Vitelli	61	–	64	–	6	1	64	–	19	–	23	–	57	–	82	37	–	75	–	14	20	–	–	–	–	523
#2 John Blanye — Asambeg	–	–	–	–	–	–	–	–	101	–	–	60	–	24	86	16	–	58	–	–	–	–	–	26	–	371
#3 William Reignalds — Francisco	71	–	14	–	–	–	–	13	–	25	–	29	4	24	19	45	2	7	–	–	–	–	–	–	–	253
#4 William Allen — Grimaldi	–	–	46	–	–	–	53	–	48	–	73	–	–	19	–	7	–	–	–	–	–	–	–	–	–	246
#5 Edward Shakerly — Gazet	58	–	40	–	–	–	25	–	27	44	–	23	–	–	9	–	–	–	–	–	–	–	–	–	–	226
#6 John Sumner — Mustapha	–	40	10	–	–	–	8	–	39	58	3	–	22	–	18	–	–	–	–	–	6	–	–	–	–	204
#7 William Robbins — Carazie	–	24	26	–	11	5	–	2	6	–	32	–	0	–	8	0	–	2	–	–	–	–	–	–	–	116
#8 Master	–	–	5	–	–	–	2	–	2	–	39	–	11	–	1	–	–	–	–	–	–	–	–	–	–	60
#9 Aga	–	–	–	10	–	–	3	–	–	0	3	–	6	8	–	1	11	–	–	–	–	–	–	–	–	42

Boys

Part (actor / role)	1.1	1.2	1.3	2.1	2.2	2.3	2.4	2.5	2.6	3.1	3.2	3.3	3.4	3.5	4.1	4.2	4.3	5.1	5.2	5.3	5.4	5.5	5.6	5.7	5.8	Totals
#1 Edward Rogers — Donusa	–	62	20	42	–	104	–	44	–	54	–	74	52	–	17	13	–	–	–	–	–	–	–	–	–	482
#2 Theo. Bourne — Paulina	–	–	–	–	21	–	–	–	–	19	8	–	20	30	37	–	–	–	–	–	–	–	–	–	–	135
#3 Manto	–	15	28	–	4	2	2	24	6	–	–	–	–	4	0	–	10	22	–	–	–	–	–	–	–	117

Total Lines Principal Parts 2,778

Minor Parts

Men

Character	Lines
#1	
Boteswaine	21
Jaylor	5
#2	
Capiaga	15
#3	
1 Turke	4
1 Janizarie	0
#4	
2 Turke	3
2 Janizarie	0
#5	
3 Turke	0
3 Janizarie	0
#6	
1 Saylor	0
1 Gard	1
#7	
2 Saylor	0
2 Gard	0

```
Total Lines Minor Parts      49= 2%
            Principal Parts  2,778=98%
                             ─────
                             2,827
```

Table 24

The First Part of the Fair Maid of the West (Q-1631)

Principal Parts

Men

Role	1.1	1.2	1.3	2.1	2.2	2.3	2.4	3.1	3.2	3.3	3.4	4.1	4.2	4.3	4.4	4.C	5.1	5.2	5.3	Totals
#1 Mr. Michael Bowyer — Spencer	–	57	42	–	65	–	21	–	11	–	–	5	–	–	–	–	–	32	–	233
#2 Mr. Rich. Perkins — Captain Goodlack	26	11	–	15	–	–	–	14	25	35	39	11	22	–	–	–	15	2	5	220
#3 Mr. William Robinson — Clem	62	15	–	–	–	25	–	23	23	–	–	–	8	–	–	–	–	32	24	212
#4 William Shearlock — Ruffman	44	–	43	–	61	–	–	0	7	–	–	–	22	–	–	1	–	–	3	181
#5 Mr. Will. Allen — 1 Captain	19	4	0	12	–	–	–	–	–	–	–	–	–	–	–	–	–	–	–	35
— Mullisheg	–	–	–	–	–	–	–	34	–	–	–	65	–	–	–	–	–	45	–	144
#6 Christoph. Goad — Mr. Forset	12	7	–	12	3	–	–	9	–	–	–	2	0	1	–	–	–	–	–	46
— Spanish Cap.	–	–	–	17	–	–	–	–	–	–	–	–	–	–	–	–	–	–	–	17
#7 Mr. Wilbraham — Mr. Carol	17	–	–	–	–	–	–	–	–	–	–	–	–	–	–	–	–	–	–	17
— Mayor	–	–	–	19	–	17	–	–	–	–	–	–	–	–	–	–	–	–	–	36
— Bashaw Alcade	–	–	–	–	–	–	–	–	–	–	–	8	8	2	–	–	–	–	–	18
#8 Rob. Axell — 2 Captain	8	3	0	17	–	–	–	–	–	–	–	–	–	–	–	–	–	–	–	28
— English Merchant	–	–	–	7	–	–	–	–	–	–	–	–	6	–	–	–	–	–	2	15

Boy

Role	1.1	1.2	1.3	2.1	2.2	2.3	2.4	3.1	3.2	3.3	3.4	4.1	4.2	4.3	4.4	4.C	5.1	5.2	5.3	Totals
#1 Hugh Clark — Bess Bridges	40	44	–	48	55	36	–	56	92	57	79	–	–	–	–	–	33	40	–	580

Total Lines Principal Parts 1,782

Minor Parts

Men

	Total
#1	
Mr. Anthony Turner	5
Kitching Maid	5
Bashaw Joffer	
#2	
Alderman	19
Chorus	19
#3	
1 Petitioner	0
Surgeon	19
Moore	2
1 Merchant	8
#4	
2 Petitioner	0
1 Saylor	13
Moore	0
2 Merchant	7
#5	
General	0
2 Saylor	5
Spanish Prisoner	6
#6	
3 Saylor	5
Servant	4
Attendant[Mullisheg]	0
Spanish Prisoner	0
#7	
Spanish Sailor	0
Attendant[Mullisheg]	0
#8	
Spanish Sailor	0
Attendant[Mullisheg]	0

Boys

	Total
#1	
Vintners boy-Drawer	12
#2	
Vintners boy-Drawer	17

Total Lines Minor Parts 146 = 8%
Principal Parts 1,797 = 92%
1,943

Table 25

The Second Part of the Fair Maid of the West (Q–1630)

Principal Parts

Men

		1		2		3						4							5			Totals
		1	2	1 2 3		1 2 3	C	D	1 2 3 4				1 2 3 4 5 6						1 2	3 4 5		
#1 Michael Bowyer	Spencer	7	26	–	–	–	–	–	–	–	38	94	–	37	42	–	–	60	19	27 43 –	12 29	434
#2 Joh. Somner	D. of Florence	–	–	–	–	65	0	–	27	5	–	–	–	–	–	67	–	46 23 –	62	295
#3 Will. Allen	Mullisheg	131	8	– 13	–	51	–	–	–	–	–	–	72	–	–	–	–	–	–	275
#4 Rich. Perkins	Capt. Goodlack	24	75	– 29	24	– 18	–	–	–	48	24	5	–	–	–	15	8	270
#5 William Shearlock	Ruffman	97	13	8 –	5	– 9	–	14	–	– 38	5	–	–	–	5	1	195
#6 William Robinson	Clem	24	25	–	–	– 11	–	–	4 22	27	–	–	19 25	3	160
#7 Bashaw Joffer		14	0	–	61	– 29	–	–	–	–	–	15	119
#8 Anthonie Turner	Bashaw Alcade	8	0	– 38	– 24	–	–	–	–	–	–	70
	Chorus	–	–	–	34	–	–	–	–	–	–	34
	English Merchant	–	–	–	–	33	– 14	–	5	–	2 0	–	15	69
#9 Christoph. Goad	D. of Farara	–	–	–	–	0 13	–	–	–	20	–	6	39
#10 Rob. Axall	Duke of Mantua	–	–	– 5	3	0	–	–	20	–	8	28
	Porter	–	–	–	–	–	–	–	–	–	8

Boys

| #1 Hugh Clark | Besse Bridges | 7 | 38 | – 25 | – | 102 28 | – | 0 61 | – | – | – | 11 | – | 71 4 | 50 | 397 |

Part	126	8	6	–	10	10	–	10	–	5	–	–	Total Lines Principal Parts 2,553	160
						Minor Parts								
						Men								
#1														
Messenger	–	–	–	–	17	–	–	–	–	5	–	–	–	22
#2														
Negro	–	–	–	–	10	–	–	–	0	–	2	–	–	10
Drawer	–	–	–	–	–	–	–	–	-1	–	–	–	–	2
Pedro Venturo	–	–	–	–	–	–	–	–	–	–	–	–	14	14
#3														
Attendant[Mulligheg]0	–	–	–	0	–	–	–	–	–	–	–	–	–	0
Lieutenant	–	–	–	0	–	–	–	–	–	–	–	–	–	0
Bandit	–	–	–	–	–	–	–	13	0	–	0	–	–	13
Attendant[Florence]	–	–	–	–	–	–	–	–	–	–	0	–	–	0
#4														
Attendant[Mulligheg]0	–	–	–	–	–	–	–	–	–	–	–	–	–	0
Headsman	–	–	–	–	0	–	–	–	0	–	–	–	–	0
Bandit	–	–	–	–	–	–	–	0	0	–	–	–	–	0
Attendant[Florence]	–	–	–	–	–	–	–	–	–	–	0	–	–	0
Lord	–	–	–	–	–	–	–	–	–	–	–	7	–	7
#5														
Attendant[Mulligheg]0	–	–	–	–	0	–	–	–	–	–	–	–	–	0
Captain	–	–	–	–	–	–	–	–	–	–	–	–	–	0
Bandit	–	–	–	–	–	–	–	0	0	–	–	–	–	0
Attendant[Florence]	–	–	–	–	–	–	–	–	–	–	0	–	–	0

Total Lines Minor Parts 68= 3%
Principal Parts 2,553=97%
2,621

Table 26

King John and Matilda (Q-1655)

Principal Parts
Men

	1				2					3					4			5			Totals
	1	2	3	4	1	2	3	4	5	1	2	3	4	5	1	2	3	1	2	3	
#1 M.Bowyer — King John	81	35	25	-	25	-	-	66	-	41	26	-	42	-	-	47	29	-	-	31	448
#2 M. Perkins — Fitzwater	-	95	-	-	-	-	-	73	-	-	55	47	-	11	50	-	38	-	-	-	369
#3 M. Sumner — Young Bruce	-	26	0	-	21	19	-	-	-	14	3	17	-	-	-	-	87	-	1	-	188
#4 M. Shirelock — Brand	-	-	-	-	-	-	61	-	-	-	-	-	34	-	-	-	83	-	-	-	178
#5 M. Clarke — Hubert	-	-	12	-	11	-	-	-	12	-	-	4	-	49	-	-	-	-	20	-	108
#6 M. Jackson — Chester	12	1	0	-	15	6	-	0	3	9	-	8	-	-	14	-	-	-	13	-	82
#7 M. Turner — Old Lord Bruce	-	12	-	17	-	-	-	9	-	-	10	3	-	-	-	-	-	-	17	-	68
#8 M. Goat — Oxford	18	0	-	10	-	-	-	11	4	13	-	0	-	-	2	3	-	-	6	-	67
#9 Richmond	-	2	-	17	-	6	-	0	5	-	15	13	-	-	-	-	-	-	-	-	58
#10 M. Young — Leister	-	16	-	-	-	-	-	10	-	-	13	3	-	-	-	-	-	-	3	-	45
#11 M. Allen — Pandolph	-	-	-	-	-	-	-	31	-	-	-	-	-	-	-	-	-	-	-	-	31
#12 Winchester	-	-	-	27	-	-	-	-	-	-	-	-	-	-	-	-	-	-	-	-	27
Gentleman	-	-	-	-	-	-	-	3	-	-	-	-	-	1	-	-	-	-	-	-	4
Mowbray	-	-	-	-	-	-	-	-	-	-	-	-	-	-	-	-	-	-	10	-	10

Boys

																	Total
#1 Matilda	34	–	–	–	–	–	33	–	–	–	2	2	–	34	–	15	39	0	166
#2 Lady	–	17	–	20	–	–	–	–	–	39	–	–	40	–	–	7	9	–	116
Abbess	–	–	–	–	–	–	–	–	–	–	–	–	–	–	–	7	9	15	31
#3 Queen	2	9	–	–	–	18	–	–	–	–	–	33	–	33	–	–	–	–	99
#4 Boy	–	–	–	7	–	–	–	15	–	37	–	27	–	–	–	–	–	–	49

Total Lines Principal Parts 2,144

Minor Parts

Men

#1											
Confessor									3		3
Lord	0										0
Attendant[King]			0	0	0						0
Masquer											0
#2											
Lord	0										0
Attendant[King]			0	0	0						0
Masquer											0
#3											
Lord	0										0
Attendant[King]			0	0	0						0
Masquer											0
#4											
Soldier		0	0	0							0
Guard				0							0
#5											
Soldier		0	0	0							0
Guard				0							0

Boys

#1 Lady	0	0					0
#2 Lady	0	0					0
#3 Lady	0	0					0

Total Lines Minor Parts 0

Total Lines Minor Parts   3 = 1%
Principal Parts   2,144 = 99%
2,147

Table 27
Hannibal and Scipio (Q-1637)

Principal Parts
Men

	P	1	2	3	4	5	E	Totals
#1								
William Allen								
Hannibal	-	149	120	-	128	167	-	564
#2								
Michael Bowyer								
Prologue	30	-	-	-	-	-	-	30
Scipio	-	-	52	128	133	108	-	421
Epilogue	-	-	-	-	-	-	8	8
#3								
Hugh Clerke								
Nuntius	-	38	-	-	56	-	-	94
Syphax	-	-	390	25	-	-	-	415
#4								
Theophilus Bird								
Massanissa	-	-	-	170	12	4	-	186
#5								
John Sumner								
Himulco	-	84	10	-	5	15	-	114
#6								
Richard Perkins								
Hanno	-	-	-	-	76	-	-	76
#7								
William Shurlock								
Maharball	-	62	0	-	-	-	-	62
Prusias	-	-	-	-	-	70	-	70
#8								
John Page								
Lelius	-	-	0	50	8	-	-	58
#9								
George Stutfield								
Soldier	-	13	-	-	-	-	-	13
Bostar	-	-	-	-	32	-	-	32
#10								
Anthony Turner								
Piston	-	-	31	-	-	-	-	31
Flaminius	-	-	-	-	-	0	-	0
#11								
Robert Axen								
Bomilcar	-	25	-	-	-	-	-	25
Gisgon	-	-	-	-	10	-	-	10

Boys

	P	1	2	3	4	5	E	Totals
#1								
Ezekiel Fenn								
Sophonisba	-	-	51	101	-	-	-	152
#2								
2 Lady	-	42	-	-	-	-	-	42
Attendant[Sophonisba]	-	-	0	-	-	-	-	0
#3								
Faire Lady	-	40	-	-	-	-	-	40
Attendant[Sophonisba]	-	-	0	-	-	-	-	0
Spanish Lady	-	-	-	-	12	-	-	12
#4								
1 Lady	-	10	-	-	-	-	-	10
Attendant[Sophonisba]	-	-	0	-	-	-	-	0

Total Lines Principal Parts 2,465

Table 27 137

Table 27 (*cont.*)

	Minor Parts							
			Men					
#1								
Crates	-	-	8	-	-	-	-	8
Lucius	-	-	-	-	10	-	-	10
Roman Legate	-	-	-	-	-	0	-	0
#2								
Messenger	-	-	10	0	-	-	-	10
Roman Legate	-	-	-	-	-	0	-	0
#3								
Attendant[Syphax]	-	-	0	-	-	-	-	0
Senator	-	-	-	-	0	-	-	0
Attendant[Prusias]	-	-	-	-	-	0	-	0
#4								
Attendant[Syphax]	-	-	0	-	-	-	-	0
Senator	-	-	-	-	0	-	-	0
Attendant[Prusias]	-	-	-	-	-	0	-	0
#5								
Attendant[Syphax]	-	-	0	-	-	-	-	0
Senator	-	-	-	-	0	-	-	0
Attendant[Prusias]	-	-	-	-	-	0	-	0
#6								
Soldier[Scipio]	-	-	-	0	-	-	-	0
Soldier[Hannibal]	-	-	-	-	0	-	-	0
Roman Legate	-	-	-	-	-	0	-	0
#7								
Soldier[Scipio]	-	-	-	0	-	-	-	0
Soldier[Hannibal]	-	-	-	-	0	-	-	0
#8								
Soldier[Scipio]	-	-	-	0	-	-	-	0
Soldier[Hannibal]	-	-	-	-	0	-	-	0

Total Lines Minor Parts   28 = 1%

Principal Parts   2,465 = 99%

2,493

Table 28

Holland's Leaguer (Q-1632)

Principal Parts

Men

	1-4	5+2.1	2	2/3	4-5	1	2-3/3	4+4.1/4	2	3	4	5	1	2	5/3	4	5	Totals
#1 Andrew Keyne / Trimalchio	2	91	-	-	59	-	70	23	31	29	-	23	-	-	-	72	33	433
#2 Mathew Smith / Agurtes	-	170	-	54	-	-	55	-	-	-	-	88	-	-	-	27	7	401
#3 Ellis Worth / Ardelio	135	-	-	-	-	20	-	6	10	15	-	13	-	-	40	-	-	239
#4 William Browne / Philautus	41	-	-	-	-	37	-	101	-	-	-	-	41	-	-	-	9	229
#5 Thomas Bond / Miscellanio	-	-	-	-	88	-	-	-	8	17	-	14	-	43	-	17	0	187
#6 James Sneller / Autolicus	-	65	-	22	-	-	47	-	-	2	-	4	-	-	-	27	1	168
#7 Edward May / Fidelio	81	-	47	-	-	8	-	19	-	-	-	-	10	-	-	-	-	165
#8 Richard Fowler / Snarle	95	-	-	-	-	-	-	5	-	3	-	-	21	-	10	-	29	163
#9 Henry Gradwell / Capritio	-	-	-	-	23	-	32	9	1	3	-	3	-	-	-	9	3	83
#10 Robert Huyt / Jeffery	36	-	-	-	-	-	-	-	-	-	-	-	-	-	25	-	-	61

Boys

Role (Actor)								Total Lines
#1 Richard Goodwin — Faustina	33	–	–	68	–	14	–	115
#2 Samuel Mannery — Bawd	–	81	–	–	5	1	–	87
#3 John Wright — Millescent	16	–	23	25	13	5	–	82
#4 Arthur Savill — Quartilla	–	61	–	–	–	0	–	61
#5 Robert Stratford — Triphoena	4	–	56	–	–	–	–	60
#6 Richard Fouch — Margery	3	–	8	19	–	0	–	30
#7 1 Whore	–	–	3	12	2	0	–	17
						Total Lines Principal Parts		**2,581**

Minor Parts

Men

Role	Lines
#1 Pandar / Officer	20 / 0
#2 Officer	0

Boy

Role	Lines
#1 Boy	7
2 Whore	1, 5, 1 = 7

Total Lines Minor Parts 34 = 1%
Principal Parts 2,581 = 99%
2,615

Table 29
The Tragedy of Messalina (0-1640)
Principal Parts

Column headings are grouped by act (1–5); the sub-numbers are scenes within each act (act 5 has scenes 1–4, the others 1–3). Columns below are labelled *act.scene*.

Men

Part	1.1	1.2	1.3	2.1	2.2	2.3	3.1	3.2	3.3	4.1	4.2	4.3	5.1	5.2	5.3	5.4	Totals
#1 Christopher Goad — Silius	49	38	-	-	57	89	-	-	-	57	-	0	77	-	91	0	458
#2 John Robinson — Sausellus	17	18	14	5	27	-	12	0	-	6	-	46	-	-	42	0	187
#3 Will. Hall — Mela	-	-	-	-	-	-	85	-	68	-	-	-	-	-	-	-	153
#4 Sam. Tomson — Menseter	-	-	53	-	-	-	24	-	-	9	-	10	-	-	14	0	110
#5 Narcissus	-	-	-	-	-	-	-	-	-	-	28	-	35	-	37	4	104
#6 Will Cartwright Sen. — Claudius Emperour	-	13	-	-	-	-	-	-	-	-	-	-	52	-	29	9	103
#7 Valens	32	3	-	-	-	-	13	-	-	9	-	13	-	-	14	-	84
#8 Rich. Johnson — Montanus	-	-	-	-	-	-	24	25	25	-	-	-	-	-	-	-	74
#9 Calistus	-	0	-	-	-	-	-	-	-	-	46	-	4	-	-	0	50
#10 Proculus	6	4	-	-	-	-	12	-	-	4	-	2	-	-	6	0	34
#10 1 Servant	-	-	-	14	-	-	-	-	-	-	-	-	-	-	-	-	14
#11 Pallas	-	-	-	-	-	-	-	-	-	-	14	-	10	-	4	0	28

Boys

Part	1.1	1.2	1.3	2.1	2.2	2.3	3.1	3.2	3.3	4.1	4.2	4.3	5.1	5.2	5.3	5.4	Totals
#1 John Barret — Messalina Empresse	17	32	14	104	-	-	31	10	-	5	-	0	6	-	-	61	280
#2 Tho. Jordan — Lepida	46	82	-	-	-	-	-	-	-	-	-	51	11	-	-	5	195

Minor Parts
Men

	Total Lines	Principal Parts
#3		
Mathias Morris		
1 Dame	13	0 — 13
Sylana	5 — 22 — 5 —	90
#4		
Veneria, the Bawd	63 — 20 — 63 — 0 —	83
#5		
Calphurnia	22 — 2 —	24
Ubidia	19 — 9 —	28
Total Lines Principal Parts 2,112		
#1		
Hem	6 — 1 — 20 — 5 — 0 —	12
Virgilianus–Senator		20
#2		
Stich	4 — 1 — 6 — 4 — 0 —	9
Calphurnianus–Senator		6
#3		
Evodius	9 —	9
#4		
1 Guard	0 — 1 — 0 —	1
#5		
2 Guard	0 — 2 — 0 —	2
#6		
2 Servant	1 — 0 —	1
Sulpitius	4 — 8 —	12
Headsman	0 — 0 —	0
#7		
Attendant[Claudius]	0 — 0 —	0
Soldier	0 —	0
#8		
Attendant[Claudius]	0 — 0 —	0
Soldier	0 —	0
#9		
Attendant[Claudius]	0 — 0 —	0
Soldier	0 —	0

Table 29 (cont.)

Boys

#1														
1 Fury	–	–	–	–	–	–	–	–	–	–	6	–	–	6
1 Attendant[Messalina]	–	–	–	–	0	0	–	–	–	–	–	–	–	0
1 Bachinalian	–	–	–	–	–	–	0	–	–	–	–	–	–	0
1 Courtesan	–	–	–	–	–	–	–	0	–	–	–	–	–	0
Angel	–	–	–	–	–	–	–	–	–	0	–	–	–	0
#2														
2 Dame	–	–	–	–	–	–	–	–	–	–	4	–	–	4
2 Fury	–	–	–	–	0	0	–	–	–	–	2	–	–	2
2 Attendant[Messalina]	–	–	–	–	–	–	–	–	0	–	–	–	–	0
2 Bachinalian	–	–	–	–	–	–	0	–	–	–	–	–	–	0
2 Courtesan	–	–	–	–	–	–	–	0	–	–	–	–	–	0
#3														
3 Fury	–	–	–	–	0	–	–	–	–	–	3	–	–	3
3 Attendant[Messalina]	–	–	–	–	–	0	–	–	0	–	–	–	–	0
3 Bachinalian	–	–	–	–	–	–	0	–	–	–	–	–	–	0
3 Courtesan	–	–	–	–	–	–	–	0	–	–	–	–	–	0
#4														
3 Dame	–	–	–	–	–	–	–	–	–	–	3	–	–	3
4 Fury	–	–	–	–	0	–	–	–	–	–	0	–	–	0
4 Bachinalian	–	–	–	–	–	–	0	–	–	–	–	–	–	0
#5														
5 Fury	–	–	–	–	–	–	–	–	–	–	0	–	–	0
5 Bachinalian	–	–	–	–	–	–	0	–	–	–	–	–	–	0
#6														
6 Fury	–	–	–	–	–	–	–	–	–	–	0	–	–	0
6 Bachinalian	–	–	–	–	–	–	0	–	–	–	–	–	–	0
#7														
7 Fury	–	–	–	–	–	–	–	–	–	–	0	–	–	0
7 Bachinalian	–	–	–	–	–	–	0	–	–	–	–	–	–	0
#8														
8 Fury	–	–	–	–	–	–	–	–	–	–	0	–	–	0
8 Bachinalian	–	–	–	–	–	–	0	–	–	–	–	–	–	0

Total Lines Minor Parts   90 = 4%

Principal Parts   2,112 = 96%

2,202

Table 30 143

Table 30
Casting Requirements for Fifteen London Plays, 1619-36

	Text	Principal Men Parts		Boys Parts		% of lines Spoken by Principals	Minor Men Parts		Boys Parts		Total Men	Actors Boys
						King's Men Plays						
DM	Q-1623	8	15	3	3	96	8	22	3	4	16	6
RA	Q-1629	9	11	5	5	98	8	25	0	0	17	5
DF	Q-1629	6	6	3	3	97	10	18	0	0	16	3
Pict.	Q-1630	8	8	4	4	99	6	19	3	3	14	7
SC	MS.1630	8	8	4	4	96	11	22	2	3	19	6
Swis.	MS.1631	9	9	3	3	99	6	15	1	2	15	4
WGC	F-1652	9	9	4	5	99	3	8	7	12	12	11
						Queen Henrietta's Men Plays						
Wed.	Q-1629	11	12	4	4	98	5	5	0	0	16	4
Ren.	Q-1630	9	9	3	3	98	7	13	0	0	16	3
1FMW	Q-1631	8	13	1	1	92	8	23	2	2	16	3
2FMW	Q-1631	10	13	2	2	97	5	17	0	0	15	2
KJM	Q-1655	12	14	4	5	99	5	14	3	3	17	7
Han.	Q-1637	11	18	4	8	99	8	21	0	0	19	4
						Plays of other London Companies						
HL	Q-1632	10	10	7	7	99	2	3	1	2	12	8
Mess.	O-1640	11	12	5	7	96	9	16	8	25	20	13
Mean		9.3	11.1	3.7	4.2	97.5	6.7	14.8	2.0	3.7	16.0	5.7

Table 31

The Second Part of King Henry the Sixth (Q-1594)

Principal Parts
Men

	1.1	1.2	1.3	1.4	2.1	2.2	2.3	2.4	3.1	3.2	3.3	4.1	4.2	4.3	4.4	4.5	4.6	4.7	4.8	4.9	4.10	5.1	5.2	5.3	Totals
#1 King Henry	23	–	23	–	32	–	27	12	33	9	–	–	–	–	18	–	–	–	–	13	–	26	3	–	219
#2 Humphrey	32	18	14	–	27	–	6	42	66	–	–	–	–	–	–	–	–	–	–	–	–	–	–	–	205
Cade	–	–	–	–	–	–	–	–	–	–	–	–	25	–	–	–	60	44	19	–	16	–	–	–	164
#3 Yorke	27	–	4	–	–	47	7	–	42	–	–	–	–	–	–	–	–	–	–	11	–	41	14	11	204
#4 Suffolke	20	–	11	–	2	–	28	–	37	66	–	40	–	–	–	–	–	–	–	–	–	–	–	–	204
Young Clifford	–	–	–	–	–	–	–	–	–	–	–	–	–	–	–	–	–	–	–	–	–	–	19	3	22
#5 Warwicke	8	–	–	–	–	19	–	–	–	43	–	–	–	–	–	–	–	–	–	7	–	8	12	6	103
Captain	–	–	–	–	–	–	–	–	–	–	–	23	–	–	–	–	–	–	–	–	–	–	–	–	23
#6 Cardinall	22	–	18	–	9	–	8	–	17	7	23	–	–	–	–	–	–	–	–	–	–	–	–	–	104
Lord Clifford	–	–	–	–	–	–	–	–	–	–	–	–	–	–	–	–	–	–	17	–	–	13	8	7	45
#7 Buckingham	6	–	–	–	14	–	–	–	1	–	–	–	–	–	6	–	–	–	4	17	–	4	–	–	52
#8 Salisbury	18	–	–	–	–	0	3	–	–	4	–	–	–	–	–	–	–	–	–	5	–	3	–	–	33
Lord Say	–	–	–	–	–	–	–	–	–	–	–	–	–	–	3	–	–	7	–	–	–	–	–	–	10
#9 Hume	–	19	–	3	–	–	–	–	–	–	–	–	–	–	–	–	–	–	–	–	–	–	–	–	22
Stafford	–	–	–	–	–	–	–	–	–	–	–	–	14	–	–	–	–	–	–	–	–	–	–	–	14
Eyden	–	–	–	–	–	–	–	–	–	–	–	–	–	–	–	–	–	–	–	–	20	8	–	–	28

Boys

	1.1	1.2	1.3	1.4	2.1	2.2	2.3	2.4	3.1	3.2	3.3	4.1	4.2	4.3	4.4	4.5	4.6	4.7	4.8	4.9	4.10	5.1	5.2	5.3	Totals
#1 Queene Margaret	7	–	30	–	4	–	2	–	40	46	–	–	–	–	5	–	–	–	–	–	–	–	3	3	140
#2 Dame Ellanor	–	30	–	7	5	–	1	57	–	–	–	–	–	–	–	–	–	–	–	–	–	–	–	–	100

Total Lines Principal Parts 1,647

Minor Parts
__Men__

Part	Line counts (by column, left→right)	Total
#1		
Somerset	3, 4, 2, 2, 4, 0, 0	15
Poore man	22	22
Scales	8	8
#2		
Peter	9, 11	20
One[Murderer]	1	1
1 Prisoner	1	1
Richard	6, 8, 4	18
#3		
Messenger	3	3
Bullenbrooke	17	17
Standly	3	3
2 Prisoner	2	2
Dicke	7, 7, 2	16
Edward	2, 1	3
#4		
1 Petitioner	6	6
Mayor	3	3
1 Neighbor	2	2
George	17, 2	19
1 Citizen	5	5
Soldier[Salisbury]	0	0
#5		
Beadle	2	2
Herald	0	0
Water	9	9
Robin	1, 2	3
Soldier[Salisbury]	0	0
#6		
Other[York]	0	0
Herald	2	2
Maisters Mate	1	1
Harry	2	2
Soldier[Salisbury]	0	0
#7		
2 Petitioner	8	8
2 Neighbor	1	1
Vawse	8	8
Nicke	10, 3	13
Soldier[Yorke]	0	0

Table 31 (*cont.*)

	Total
#8	
Armourer	17
Sheriffe	3
Maister	0
Will	7
Soldier[Yorke]	0
#9	
One	4
3 Neighbor	2
Sheriffe	0
Tom	4
Soldier[Yorke]	0
#10	
Other[York]	0
Brother[Mayor]	0
Servingman[Humphrey]	3
Messenger	4
Mathew Goffe	0
Soldier[Clifford]	0
#11	
Other[York]	0
Brother[Mayor]	0
Servingman[Humphrey]	0
Soldier[Stafford]	0
Messenger	6
Citizen	0
Soldier[Clifford]	0
#12	
Officer	0
Brother[Mayor]	0
Soldier[Stafford]	0
One[Say]	0
Man[Eyden]	0
Soldier[Clifford]	0
#13	
Other[King]	0
Officer	0
Soldier[Stafford]	1
Man[Eyden]	0
Soldier[Buckingham]-	0

Character	Lines
#14	
Other[King]	0
Drum[Peter]	0
1. [Murderer]	0
Clarke	3
Citizen	0
Soldier[Buckingham]	0
#15	
Other[King]	0
Drum[Armorer]	0
2. [Murderer]	1
Brother[Stafford]	0
Soldier[Buckingham]	0
Boys	
#1	
Spirit	7
1 Prentise	2
#2	
Margery Jourdaine	5
2 Prentise	1
#3	
Woman	2
3 Prentise	2

Total Lines Minor Parts 85=15%

Principal Parts 1,932=85%

1,932

Table 32

The Second Part of King Henry the Sixth (F)

Principal Parts

Men

#	Part	1.1	1.2	1.3	1.4	2.1	2.2	2.3	2.4	3.1	3.2	3.3	4.1	4.2	4.3	4.4	4.5	4.6	4.7	4.8	4.9	4.10	5.1	5.2	5.3	Totals
#1	Yorke	56	–	15	32	–	62	12	–	96	–	–	–	–	–	–	–	–	–	–	–	–	90	13	12	388
#2	King	26	–	10	–	78	–	–	–	45	70	16	–	–	–	–	–	–	–	–	32	–	32	–	–	309
#3	Duke Humfrey	59	25	22	–	70	–	14	41	70	–	–	–	–	–	–	–	–	–	–	–	–	–	–	–	301
	Cade	–	–	–	–	–	–	–	–	–	–	–	–	85	13	–	–	12	70	28	–	40	–	–	–	248
#4	Suffolke	20	–	45	13	2	–	–	–	54	99	–	62	–	–	–	–	–	–	–	–	–	–	–	–	295
	Young Clifford	–	–	–	–	–	–	–	–	–	–	–	–	–	–	–	–	–	–	–	–	–	4	42	–	46
#5	Warwicke	16	–	7	–	–	16	12	–	–	65	3	–	–	–	–	–	–	–	–	–	–	8	–	6	133
	Dicke Butcher	–	–	–	–	–	–	–	–	–	–	–	–	22	4	–	–	4	10	–	–	–	–	–	–	40
#6	Beauford	30	–	3	–	25	–	–	–	30	13	3	–	–	–	–	–	–	–	–	–	–	–	–	–	104
	Old Clifford	–	–	–	–	–	–	–	–	–	–	–	–	–	–	–	–	–	–	6	–	–	38	12	–	56
#7	Salisbury	30	–	0	–	10	5	29	–	–	1	–	–	–	–	–	–	–	–	–	–	–	14	–	8	97
	Lord Say	–	–	–	–	–	–	–	–	–	–	–	–	–	–	6	–	–	42	–	–	–	–	–	–	48
#8	Buckingham	7	–	8	9	4	–	–	–	8	–	–	–	–	–	–	–	–	–	10	3	–	16	–	–	65
	Lieutenant	–	–	–	–	–	–	–	–	–	–	–	66	–	–	–	–	–	–	–	–	–	–	–	–	66
#9	Hume	–	28	–	3	–	–	–	–	–	–	–	–	–	–	–	–	–	–	–	–	–	–	–	–	31
	Stafford	–	–	–	–	–	–	–	–	–	–	–	–	16	–	–	–	–	–	–	–	–	–	–	–	16
	Iden	–	–	–	–	–	–	–	–	–	–	–	–	–	–	–	–	–	–	–	–	42	8	–	–	50
#10	Peter	–	–	14	–	–	–	11	–	–	–	–	–	–	–	–	–	–	–	–	–	–	–	–	–	25
	Simcox	–	–	–	–	28	–	–	–	–	–	–	–	–	–	–	–	–	–	–	–	–	–	–	–	28
	Richard	–	–	–	–	–	–	–	–	–	–	–	–	–	–	–	–	–	–	–	–	–	10	6	8	24

Boys

#	Part	1.1	1.2	1.3	1.4	2.1	2.2	2.3	2.4	3.1	3.2	3.3	4.1	4.2	4.3	4.4	4.5	4.6	4.7	4.8	4.9	4.10	5.1	5.2	5.3	Totals
#1	Queene	9	–	65	10	–	–	–	–	72	129	12	–	–	–	15	–	–	–	–	0	–	6	11	–	329
#2	Elianor	–	36	7	4	–	–	2	57	–	–	–	–	–	–	–	–	–	–	–	–	–	–	–	–	106

2,805

Minor Parts
<u>Men</u>

Part	Total
#1 Bevis	
Bullingbroke	22
Follower[Cade]	16
Edward	3
#2 John Holland	
Armorer	19
Follower [Cade]	18
#3	
Somerset	19
Beadle	2
Stanley	9
Other	0
Matthew Goffe	0
#4	
2 Petitioner	6
Faulkner	0
Drum [Peter]	0
1 Murderer	5
Walter Whitmore	17
#5	
Messenger	3
One	4
Officer	0
Post	6
Clearke	3
Messenger	16
#6	
Maior	2
2 Murderer	2
Brother [Stafford]	7
Soldier	1
#7	
1 Petitioner	8
Brother [Mayor]	0
1 Neighbor	5
Commoner	0
Michael	4

Table 32 (cont.)

	Total
#8	
Guard	0
Brother [Mayor]	0
Servant [Humphrey]	3
Commoner	0
Sawyer	0
Messenger	4
#9	
Guard	0
Servant [Humphrey]	0
Vaux	11
1 Gentleman	7
Smith the Weaver	14
Attendant [King]	0
#10	
Priest-Southwell	0
2 Neighbor	4
Commoner	0
2 Gentleman	2
George	3
Messenger	8
Attendant [King]	0
#11	
Servant [York]	0
3 Neighbor	2
Master	1
Soldier [Stafford]	0
Another Messenger	5
Lord Scales	8
Army [York]	0
#12	
Priest	0
Drum [Armorer]	0
Herald	2
Attendant [King]	0
Mate	1
Soldier [Stafford]	0
1 Citizen	5
Army [York]	0

#13	
Sherife	0
Attendant [King]	0
Soldier [Stafford]	0
Citizen	0
One	0
Army [York]	0
#14	
Faulkner	0
Other	0
Officer	0
Citizen	0

Boys

#1	
Spirit	8
1 Prentice	2
#2	
Witch-Margery	6
2 Prentice	2
#3	
Wife	9

Total Lines Minor Parts   304=10%

Principal Parts   2,805=90%

3,109

Table 33

The Third Part of King Henry the Sixth (0-1595)

Principal Parts

Men

Part	1.1	1.2	1.3	1.4	2.1	2.2	2.3	2.4	2.5	2.6	3.1	3.2	3.3	4.1	4.2	4.3	4.4	4.5	4.6	4.7	4.8	5.1	5.2	5.3	5.4	5.5	5.6	5.7	Totals
#1 Warwicke	44	–	–	–	81	4	7	0	–	28	–	83	–	27	–	–	24	–	25	26	–	–	–	–	–	–	–	–	349
#2 Crookeback Richard	7	15	–	–	43	11	29	5	–	20	–	47	12	13	–	9	–	11	–	–	–	3	0	–	51	43	12	–	331
#3 Edward	5	5	–	–	29	29	4	–	–	24	–	54	47	4	9	–	24	–	17	–	17	3	19	–	30	–	–	–	325
#4 King Henrie	71	–	–	–	–	23	–	–	26	–	–	–	–	–	–	–	18	–	–	–	26	–	–	–	–	–	39	–	203
#5 Yorke	32	30	–	88	–	–	–	–	–	–	–	–	–	–	–	–	–	–	–	–	–	–	–	–	–	–	–	–	150
Oxford	–	–	–	–	–	–	–	–	–	–	–	–	19	–	–	–	–	–	–	–	–	–	–	–	–	–	–	–	38
#6 Clifford	17	–	26	48	13	–	–	8	–	29	–	–	–	–	–	–	–	–	–	–	–	–	–	–	–	–	–	–	141
King Lewis	–	–	–	–	–	–	–	–	–	–	–	–	39	–	–	–	–	–	–	–	–	–	–	–	–	–	–	–	39
#7 George-Clarence	–	–	–	–	13	–	–	–	–	5	–	–	–	9	–	–	–	–	–	–	–	20	0	0	12	1	13	5	89
#8 Northumberland	13	–	–	15	3	–	–	–	–	–	–	–	–	–	–	–	–	–	–	–	–	–	–	–	–	–	–	–	31
1 Souldier	–	–	–	–	–	–	–	–	16	–	–	–	–	–	–	–	–	–	–	–	–	–	–	–	–	–	–	–	16
Somerset	–	–	–	–	–	–	–	–	–	–	–	–	–	–	–	–	–	–	–	–	3	1	–	–	7	2	3	1	16

Boys

Part	1.1	1.2	1.3	1.4	2.1	2.2	2.3	2.4	2.5	2.6	3.1	3.2	3.3	4.1	4.2	4.3	4.4	4.5	4.6	4.7	4.8	5.1	5.2	5.3	5.4	5.5	5.6	5.7	Totals
#1 Queene Margaret	20	–	–	51	22	17	–	–	3	–	–	–	–	–	–	–	–	–	–	–	–	–	–	–	19	28	–	–	160
#2 Lady Gray-Queen Elizabeth	–	–	–	–	–	–	–	–	–	–	–	28	–	4	–	–	11	–	–	–	–	–	–	–	–	–	–	2	45
#3 Prince	2	–	–	–	5	–	–	–	3	–	–	–	–	2	–	–	–	–	–	–	–	–	–	–	10	12	–	–	34
#4 Rutland	0	–	21	–	–	–	–	–	–	–	–	–	–	–	–	–	–	–	–	–	–	–	–	–	–	–	–	–	21

Total Lines Principal Parts 1,988

Minor Parts

Men

Part	1.1	1.2	1.3	1.4	2.1	2.2	2.3	2.4	2.5	2.6	3.1	3.2	3.3	4.1	4.2	4.3	4.4	4.5	4.6	4.7	4.8	5.1	5.2	5.3	5.4	5.5	5.6	5.7	Totals
#1 Norfolke	5	–	–	–	–	–	–	–	–	–	–	–	–	–	–	–	–	–	–	–	–	–	–	–	–	–	–	–	5
Messenger	–	–	–	–	6	–	–	–	–	–	–	–	–	–	–	–	–	–	–	–	–	–	–	–	–	–	–	–	6
2 Souldier	–	–	–	–	–	–	–	–	14	–	–	–	–	–	–	–	–	–	–	–	–	–	–	–	–	–	–	–	14
Hastings	–	–	–	–	–	–	–	–	–	–	–	–	–	3	–	–	–	–	–	–	–	–	0	–	–	–	–	2	5

Role	Total
#2	
Montague	13
Huntsman	3
One	0
Messenger	2
#3	
Excester	12
Messenger(2)	3
Post	4
William Stanly-	0
Montgomery	16
Soldier[Montague]	0
#4	
Westmerland	5
Tutor	4
Messenger	6
Messenger	15
Lord Rivers	12
Soldier[Montague]	0
#5	
Sir John	2
Messenger(1)	16
Keeper	15
Penbrooke	0
Lord Mair	6
Soldier[Montague]	0
#6	
Hugh Mortimer	0
Souldier[Northumberland]	0
Keeper	0
Soldier[Edward]	0
Train[Edward]	0
Power[Edward]	0
#7	
Messenger	5
Souldier[Northumberland]	0
Dead Father	0
Soldier[Edward]	0
Train[Edward]	0
Power[Edward]	0
Nurse	0
#8	
Souldier[Northumberland]	0
Dead Son	0
Soldier[Edward]	0
Train[Edward]	0
Power[Edward]	0

Table 33 (*cont.*)

```
#9
Souldier[York]      0
Souldier[Richard]   -
Troop[Holland]      -
Soldier[Somerset]   -
#10
Souldier[York]      0
Souldier[Richard]   -
Troop[Holland]      -
Soldier[Somerset]   -
#11
Souldier[York]      0
Souldier[Richard]   -
Troop[Holland]      -
Soldier[Somerset]   -
#12
Souldier[Warwick]   -
Other[France]       -
Soldier[Montgomery] -
Soldier[Oxford]     -
Soldier[George]     -
#13
Souldier[Warwick]   -
Other[France]       -
Soldier[Montgomery] -
Soldier[Oxford]     -
Soldier[George]     -
#14
Souldier[Warwick]   -
Other[France]       -
Soldier[Montgomery] -
Soldier[Oxford]     -
Soldier[George]     -

#1
Lady Bona           -
Young Richmond-     -
Nurse               -
```

Boy

Total Lines Minor Parts   175 = 8%
Principal Parts   1,988 = 92%
   2,163

Table 34

The Third Part of King Henry the Sixth (F)

Principal Parts

Men

Part	1.1	1.2	1.3	1.4	2.1	2.2	2.3	2.4	2.5	2.6	3.1	3.2	3.3	4.1	4.2	4.3	4.4	4.5	4.6	4.7	4.8	5.1	5.2	5.3	5.4	5.5	5.6	5.7	Totals
#1 Warwick	46	–	–	–	80	8	19	0	–	78	32	–	68	93	–	28	–	–	23	–	22	34	34	–	–	–	–	–	447
#2 Edward	5	10	–	–	42	34	14	–	–	22	68	–	13	65	–	13	–	11	–	47	10	30	4	16	6	23	–	30	450
#3 Richard	7	24	–	6	66	18	15	–	25	96	–	22	0	22	–	3	20	–	14	–	4	0	13	46	9	–	–	–	406
#4 King Henry	78	–	–	–	24	–	–	60	–	25	96	–	22	–	–	–	37	22	20	–	–	–	–	–	13	46	49	–	348
#5 Plantagenet-Yorke	37	40	–	102	–	–	–	–	–	–	–	19	–	–	–	–	–	–	–	–	–	–	–	–	–	–	–	–	179
Oxford	–	–	–	–	–	–	–	–	–	–	0	2	19	–	–	–	–	1	1	–	–	2	–	8	1	–	–	–	34
#6 Clifford	22	–	28	15	46	–	–	7	–	29	–	–	–	–	–	–	–	–	–	–	–	–	–	–	–	–	–	–	147
Lewis	–	–	–	–	–	–	–	–	–	–	–	–	73	–	–	–	–	–	–	14	–	–	–	–	–	–	–	–	73
Montgomerie	–	–	–	–	–	–	–	–	–	–	–	–	–	–	–	–	–	–	–	14	–	–	–	–	–	–	–	–	14
#7 George-Clarence	–	–	–	–	11	11	–	4	–	10	–	–	–	28	1	0	–	3	22	–	4	0	6	–	–	7	–	–	117
#8 Northumberland	14	–	–	17	2	–	–	–	–	–	–	–	–	–	–	1	1	–	–	–	–	–	–	–	–	–	–	–	33
Father	–	–	–	–	–	–	–	–	27	–	–	–	–	–	–	–	1	–	–	–	12	–	4	1	–	–	–	–	27
Somerset	–	–	–	–	–	–	–	–	–	–	2	0	1	–	–	–	0	1	–	–	12	–	4	1	–	–	–	–	21

Boys

Part	1.1	1.2	1.3	1.4	2.1	2.2	2.3	2.4	2.5	2.6	3.1	3.2	3.3	4.1	4.2	4.3	4.4	4.5	4.6	4.7	4.8	5.1	5.2	5.3	5.4	5.5	5.6	5.7	Totals
#1 Queene Margaret	43	–	–	55	22	–	–	–	7	–	78	–	–	–	–	–	–	–	–	–	–	50	33	–	–	–	–	–	288
#2 Lady Gray-Queen Elizabeth	–	–	–	–	–	–	–	–	–	–	–	40	–	28	–	–	0	–	–	–	–	–	–	–	–	–	–	–	68
#3 Prince	4	–	–	–	0	0	–	–	–	3	–	6	–	–	–	–	–	–	–	–	–	13	14	–	–	–	–	–	48
#4 Rutland	–	–	28	–	–	–	–	–	–	–	–	–	–	–	–	–	–	–	–	–	–	–	–	–	–	–	–	–	28

Total Lines Principal Parts 2,728

Minor Parts

Men

Part	1.1	1.2	1.3	1.4	2.1	2.2	2.3	2.4	2.5	2.6	3.1	3.2	3.3	4.1	4.2	4.3	4.4	4.5	4.6	4.7	4.8	5.1	5.2	5.3	5.4	5.5	5.6	5.7	Totals
#1 Humfry Mountague	6	3	–	–	0	0	–	–	–	–	0	1	1	–	–	–	–	–	0	–	–	–	–	–	–	–	–	–	17
Keeper	–	–	–	–	–	–	–	–	–	–	22	–	–	–	–	–	–	–	–	–	–	–	–	–	–	–	–	–	22

Table 34 (*cont.*)

#2 Sinklo														
Exeter	14	–	–	–	–	–	22	–	3	–	–	–	3	20
Messenger	–	–	22	–	–	–	–	–	–	–	–	–	–	22
Keeper	–	–	–	S 19	–	–	–	–	–	–	–	–	–	19
#3 Gabriel														
Messenger	G 5	–	–	–	6	–	–	–	–	–	–	–	–	5
Messenger	–	–	–	–	–	–	–	–	–	–	–	–	–	6
Sonne	22	–	–	–	–	22	–	–	–	–	2	–	–	22
Nobleman	–	–	–	–	–	–	–	–	–	–	–	–	–	2
Hastings	–	–	–	–	–	–	–	12	6	2	0	–	–	20
Maior[Coventry]	–	–	–	–	–	–	–	–	–	–	–	0	–	0
Drum and Colours[Somerset]	–	–	–	–	–	–	–	–	–	–	–	0	–	0
#4														
Westmerland	13	–	–	–	–	–	–	–	–	–	–	–	–	13
Tutor	3	3	–	–	–	–	–	–	0	–	–	–	–	3
Stafford	–	–	–	–	–	–	–	–	–	–	–	–	–	0
Lieutentant	–	–	–	–	–	–	3	3	–	–	–	0	–	3
1 Messenger	–	–	–	–	–	–	–	–	0	1	1	–	–	1
Drum and Colours[Somerset]	–	–	–	–	–	–	–	–	–	0	0	–	–	0
#5														
Mortimer	2	2	–	–	–	–	–	–	–	–	–	–	–	2
Post	–	–	–	–	–	–	–	–	6	–	–	–	–	6
Rivers	–	–	–	–	–	–	–	–	9	–	–	–	–	9
Post	–	–	–	–	–	–	7	7	–	–	–	–	–	7
2 Messenger	–	–	–	–	–	–	–	–	0	1	1	–	–	1
Drum and Colours[Somerset]	–	–	–	–	–	–	–	–	–	0	0	–	–	0
#6														
Brother	0	0	–	–	–	–	–	–	–	–	–	–	–	0
Messenger	3	3	–	–	–	–	–	–	–	–	–	–	–	3
Bourbon	–	–	–	–	–	–	–	–	–	–	–	–	–	0
Post	–	–	–	–	–	–	20	–	0	–	–	–	–	20
1 Watchman	–	–	–	–	–	–	10	7	–	–	–	–	–	10
Stanley	–	–	–	–	–	–	–	–	–	–	–	–	–	0
Maior[Yorke]	–	–	–	–	–	7	–	–	–	–	–	–	–	7
#7														
Norfolke	3	–	0	–	–	–	–	–	–	–	–	–	–	3
Penbrooke	–	–	–	–	–	–	–	–	–	–	–	0	–	0
2 Watchman	–	–	–	–	–	8	–	–	–	–	–	–	–	8
Lieutenant	–	–	–	–	–	–	3	3	–	–	–	–	–	3
Somervile	–	–	–	–	–	–	–	–	–	–	5	5	–	5
Messenger	–	–	–	–	–	–	–	–	–	–	–	2	2	2
Nurse	–	–	–	–	–	–	–	–	–	0	–	–	–	0

#8
Souldier
[Warwick]   0
Body[Father]
Drum
Soldier[Montgomery]
Drum&Colours[Oxford]
Drum and Colours[Clarence]
Souldiers[Oxford]-

#9
Souldier
[Warwick]   0
Body[Son]
Soldier[Montgomery]
Drum&Colours[Oxford]
Drum and Colours[Clarence]
Souldiers[Oxford]-

#10
Souldier
[Warwick]   0
Trumpet
3 Watchman
Soldier[Montgomery]
Drum&Colours[Oxford]
Drum and Colours[Clarence]
Souldiers[Oxford]

#11
Souldier[Clifford]   0
Souldier[French]
Huntsman
Drum and Colours[Mountague]

#12
Souldier[Clifford]   0
Trumpet
Souldier[French]
Alderman
Drum and Colours[Mountague]

#13
Souldier[Clifford]   0
Drum
Souldier[French]
Alderman
Drum and Colours[Mountague]

Table 34 (*cont.*)

#14																												
Power[Edward]	-	-	-	0	-	-	-	-	-	-	-	-	-	-	-	-	-	-	-	-	-	-	-	-	-	-	-	0
Souldier[Edward]	-	-	-	-	0	-	-	-	0	-	-	-	-	-	-	-	0	0	0	-	0	0	-	-	-	-	-	0
Trumpet	-	-	-	-	-	-	-	-	-	-	-	0	-	-	-	-	-	-	-	-	-	-	-	-	-	-	-	0
Attendant[Edward]	-	-	-	-	-	-	-	-	-	-	-	-	-	-	-	-	-	-	-	-	-	-	-	-	-	-	0	0
#15																												
Power[Edward]	-	-	-	0	-	-	-	-	-	-	-	-	-	-	-	-	-	-	-	-	-	-	-	-	-	-	-	0
Souldier[Edward]	-	-	-	0	-	-	-	0	-	-	-	-	-	-	-	-	0	0	0	-	0	0	-	-	-	-	-	0
Attendant[Edward]	-	-	-	-	-	-	-	-	-	-	-	-	-	-	-	-	-	-	-	-	-	-	-	-	-	-	0	0
#16																												
Power[Edward]	-	-	-	0	-	-	-	-	-	-	-	-	-	-	-	-	-	-	-	-	-	-	-	-	-	-	-	0
Souldier[Edward]	-	-	-	-	0	-	-	-	0	-	-	-	-	-	-	-	0	0	0	-	0	0	-	-	-	-	-	0
Attendant[Edward]	-	-	-	-	-	-	-	-	-	-	-	-	-	-	-	-	-	-	-	-	-	-	-	-	-	-	0	0

<u>Boy</u>

#1																												
Bona	-	-	-	-	-	-	-	-	-	9	-	-	-	-	-	-	-	-	-	-	-	-	-	-	-	-	-	9
Young Henry[Richmond]	-	-	-	-	-	-	-	-	-	-	-	-	-	-	-	-	0	-	-	-	-	-	-	-	-	-	-	0
Nurse	-	-	-	-	-	-	-	-	-	-	-	-	-	-	-	-	-	-	-	-	-	-	-	-	-	-	0	0

Total Lines Minor Parts   282= 9%
Principal Parts <u>2,728</u>=91%
3,010

Table 35

The First Part of King Henry the Sixth (F)

Principal Parts — Men

Character	I.1	I.2	I.3	I.4	I.5	I.6	II.1	II.2	II.3	II.4	II.5	III.1	III.2	III.3	III.4	IV.1	IV.2	IV.3	IV.4	IV.5	IV.6	IV.7	V.1	V.2	V.3	V.4	V.5	Totals
#1 Talbot	–	–	–	67	32	–	20	28	33	–	–	–	56	–	–	–	74	–	–	24	41	16	–	–	–	–	–	391
#2 Gloster	25	–	44	–	–	–	–	–	–	–	–	67	–	–	–	–	–	–	–	–	–	–	34	–	–	–	18	188
#3 Plantagenet-York	–	–	–	–	–	–	–	–	–	48	37	9	–	–	–	17	–	–	–	–	–	–	–	–	27	47	–	185
#4 King	–	–	–	–	–	–	–	–	–	–	–	41	–	–	14	65	–	–	–	–	–	–	26	–	–	–	35	181
#5 Suffolk	–	–	–	–	–	–	–	–	–	11	–	–	–	–	–	–	–	–	–	–	–	–	–	–	74	–	60	145
#6 Charles-Dolphin	–	51	–	–	–	12	22	–	–	–	–	–	–	6	–	–	–	–	–	–	–	–	–	15	16	8	11	141
#7 Winchester	15	–	22	–	–	–	–	–	–	–	–	32	–	–	–	–	–	–	–	–	–	–	11	–	–	–	19	99
#8 Reignier	–	23	–	–	–	5	4	–	–	–	–	–	–	6	–	–	–	–	–	–	–	–	–	–	24	–	–	62
Mortimer	–	–	–	–	–	–	–	–	–	–	88	–	–	–	–	–	–	–	–	–	–	–	–	–	–	–	–	88
Lucy	–	–	–	–	–	–	–	–	–	–	–	–	–	–	–	–	–	27	–	–	–	31	–	–	–	–	–	58
#9 Bedford	41	–	–	–	–	–	–	–	–	–	–	–	31	–	–	–	–	–	–	–	–	–	–	–	–	–	–	72
Bassett	–	–	–	–	–	–	–	–	–	–	–	–	–	–	11	15	–	–	–	–	–	–	–	–	–	–	–	26
John Talbot	–	–	–	–	–	–	–	–	–	–	–	–	–	–	–	–	–	–	–	31	16	0	–	–	–	–	–	47
#10 Warwick	–	–	–	–	–	–	–	–	–	27	–	26	–	–	–	–	–	–	–	–	–	–	4	–	–	14	–	71
#11 Somerset	–	–	–	–	–	–	–	–	–	39	–	5	–	–	–	–	–	–	18	–	–	–	5	–	–	–	–	67
Shepheard	–	–	–	–	–	–	–	–	–	–	–	–	–	–	–	–	–	–	–	–	–	–	–	–	–	24	–	24
#12 Alanson	–	19	–	–	–	4	8	–	–	–	–	–	–	1	–	–	–	–	–	–	–	7	–	11	–	–	–	50
Captain	–	–	–	–	–	–	–	–	–	–	–	–	–	–	–	–	27	–	–	–	–	–	–	–	–	–	–	27
#13 Messenger	41	–	–	–	–	–	–	–	–	–	–	–	–	–	–	–	–	–	–	–	–	–	–	–	–	–	–	41
Burgundy	–	–	–	–	–	–	6	12	–	–	–	–	10	14	–	2	–	–	–	–	–	–	–	3	–	–	–	47
#14 Exeter	22	–	–	–	–	–	–	–	–	–	–	8	–	–	–	15	–	–	–	–	–	–	–	–	–	–	–	45
#15 Bastard	–	14	–	–	–	–	4	–	–	–	–	–	–	5	–	–	–	–	–	–	–	–	–	8	–	–	–	31
Master Gunner	–	–	–	18	–	–	–	–	–	–	–	–	–	–	–	–	–	–	–	–	–	–	–	–	–	–	–	18
Vernon	–	–	–	–	–	–	–	–	–	7	–	–	–	–	8	10	–	–	–	–	–	–	–	–	–	–	–	25

Table 35 (*cont.*)

Boys

	#1													#2									Total Lines Principal Parts
#1																							
Joane Puzel	51	8	3	12	49	32	59	16	5	29	40												255
Countess				49																			49
#2																							
Boy	4																						4
Margaret														23					23				23

Total Lines Principal Parts 2,460

Minor Parts
Men

Part														Total
#1														
Messenger	18													18
Gargrave	3		3											3
Sentinel														3
Watch						2								2
2 Messenger									20					20
#2														
Salisbury	16											4		16
Falstaff						3					2			7
Captain											2			2
Scout							5							5
#3														
Messenger	7													7
Glansdale	2													2
Sentinel			0											0
Keeper				4										4
Servant					0									0
General							0							0
#4														
Woodvile	6													6
Messenger	4													4
Captain			1			3								4
1 Servingman					5									5
Messenger								6						6
#5														
Mayor	7			10										17
Sergeant			4											4
Lawyer					4									4
Servant						0								0
Servant											16			16
#6														
1 Warder	3													3
Messenger		5												5
2 Servingman		1												1
Soldier[French]						3								3

#7
2 Warder	1	–	–	–	–	–	–	–	–	–	–	–	–	–	–	–	–	–	–	1
Messenger	–	–	–	–	9	–	–	–	–	–	–	–	–	–	–	–	–	–	–	9
Porter	–	–	–	–	–	1	–	–	–	–	–	–	–	–	–	–	–	–	–	1
3 Servingman-	–	–	–	–	–	–	10	–	–	–	–	–	–	–	–	–	–	–	–	10

#8
Soldier[English]0	0	–	0	–	4	0	0	–	0	–	–	–	–	–	–	–	–	–	–	4
Man [Gloster]	0	–	–	–	–	–	–	–	1	–	–	–	–	–	–	–	–	–	–	0
Jaylor	–	–	–	–	–	–	0	–	–	–	–	–	–	–	–	–	–	–	–	0
Soldier[York]	–	–	–	–	–	–	–	0	–	–	–	–	–	–	–	–	–	–	–	0

#9
Soldier[English]0	0	–	0	–	–	0	0	–	0	–	–	–	–	–	–	–	–	–	–	0
Man [Gloster]	0	–	–	–	–	–	–	–	1	–	–	–	–	–	–	–	–	–	–	0
Jaylor	–	–	–	–	–	–	–	–	0	–	–	–	–	–	–	–	–	–	–	0
Soldier[York]	–	–	–	–	–	–	–	0	–	–	–	–	–	–	–	–	–	–	–	0
Ambassador	–	–	–	–	–	–	–	–	–	–	–	–	0	–	–	–	–	–	–	0

#10
Soldier[English]0	0	–	0	–	–	0	0	–	0	–	–	–	–	–	–	–	–	–	–	0
Man [Gloster]	0	–	–	–	–	–	–	–	–	–	–	–	–	–	–	–	–	–	–	0
Soldier[York]	–	–	–	–	–	–	–	0	–	–	–	–	–	–	–	–	–	–	–	0
Ambassador	–	–	–	–	–	–	–	–	–	–	–	–	0	–	–	–	–	–	–	0

#11
Soldier[French] 0	0	–	0	–	–	0	–	–	–	–	0	–	–	–	–	–	–	–	–	0
Man[Winchester]	0	–	–	–	–	–	–	–	–	–	–	–	–	–	–	–	–	–	–	0
Trumpet	–	–	–	–	–	–	–	–	–	0	–	–	–	–	–	–	–	–	–	0
Army[Somerset]	–	–	–	–	–	–	–	–	–	–	–	0	–	–	–	–	–	–	–	0
Ambassador	–	–	–	–	–	–	–	–	–	–	–	–	0	–	–	–	–	–	–	0
Fiend	–	–	–	–	–	–	–	–	–	–	–	–	–	0	–	–	–	–	–	0

#12
Soldier[French] 0	0	–	0	–	–	0	–	–	–	–	0	–	–	–	–	–	–	–	–	0
Drum	0	–	–	–	–	–	–	–	–	–	–	–	–	–	–	–	–	–	–	0
Man[Winchester]	–	–	–	–	–	–	–	–	–	0	–	–	–	–	–	–	–	–	–	0
Army[Somerset]	–	–	–	–	–	–	–	–	–	–	–	0	–	–	–	–	–	–	–	0
Fiend	–	–	–	–	–	–	–	–	–	–	–	–	–	0	–	–	–	–	–	0

#13
Soldier[French] 0	0	–	0	–	–	0	–	–	–	–	0	–	–	–	–	–	–	–	–	0
Man[Winchester]	0	–	–	–	–	–	–	–	–	–	–	–	–	–	–	–	–	–	–	0
Army[Somerset]	–	–	–	–	–	–	–	–	–	–	–	0	–	–	–	–	–	–	–	0
Fiend	–	–	–	–	–	–	–	–	–	–	–	–	–	0	–	–	–	–	–	0

Total Lines Minor Parts 192= 8%
Principal Parts 2,460=92%
2,652

Table 36

King Richard the Third (Q1-1597)

Principal Parts
Men

Part	1				2				3							4					5					Totals
	1	2	3	4	1	2	3	4	1	2	3	4	5	6	7	1	2	3	4	5	1	2	3	4	5	
#1 Glocester-King	125	143	122	-	40	17	-	-	56	-	-	32	57	-	63	-	83	26	143	-	-	-	149	6	0	1,062
#2 Buckingham	-	-	12	-	11	16	-	-	56	7	-	11	34	-	143	-	27	-	27	-	10	-	-	-	-	354
#3 Clarence	22	-	-	127	-	-	-	-	-	-	-	-	-	-	-	-	-	-	-	-	-	-	8	-	-	157
#4 Hastings	10	-	4	-	3	-	-	-	6	67	-	46	-	-	-	-	-	-	-	-	-	-	5	-	-	141
#5 King Edward	-	-	-	-	63	-	-	-	-	-	-	-	-	-	-	-	-	-	-	-	-	-	-	-	-	63
Richmond	-	-	-	-	-	-	-	-	-	-	-	-	-	-	-	-	-	-	-	-	-	19	83	-	35	137
#6 Darby	-	-	8	5	2	-	-	-	-	17	-	-	12	-	-	-	-	-	21	7	-	-	-	-	8	80
Scrivener	-	-	-	-	-	-	-	-	-	-	-	-	-	14	-	-	-	-	-	-	-	-	-	-	-	14
#7 Catesby	-	-	-	-	-	-	-	-	2	8	2	2	16	2	4	13	4	-	7	-	-	-	4	-	-	64
3. Citizen	-	-	-	-	-	-	28	-	-	-	-	-	-	-	-	-	-	-	-	-	-	-	-	-	-	28
#8 Rivers	-	-	17	-	3	-	-	-	-	-	17	-	-	-	-	-	-	-	-	-	-	-	4	-	-	41
Tirrel	-	-	-	-	-	-	-	-	-	-	-	-	-	-	-	-	7	29	-	-	-	-	-	-	-	36
#9 1 Executioner	-	-	5	55	-	-	-	-	-	-	-	-	-	-	-	-	-	-	-	-	-	-	-	-	-	60
Ratliff	-	-	-	-	-	-	-	-	-	-	2	0	-	-	-	-	-	-	9	-	-	-	2	-	16	29
#10 2 Executioner	-	-	0	49	-	-	-	-	-	-	-	-	-	-	-	-	-	-	-	-	-	-	-	-	-	49
Maior	-	-	-	-	-	-	-	-	1	-	-	-	11	-	15	-	-	-	-	-	-	-	-	-	-	27
#11 Brokenbury	7	-	-	25	-	-	-	-	-	-	-	-	-	-	-	-	-	-	-	-	-	-	-	-	-	32
Cardinal	-	-	-	-	-	-	-	14	9	-	-	-	-	-	-	-	-	-	-	-	-	-	-	-	-	23

Boys

																				Total Lines Principal Parts
#1																				
Queene	–	–	7	20	–	13	–	–	–	–	24	–	–	126	–	–	–	–	–	241
#2																				
Qu. Margaret	–	51	–	–	–	–	–	–	–	–	–	–	–	89	–	–	–	–	–	210
	–	121																		
#3																				
Lady Anne	–	–	–	–	–	–	–	–	–	–	36	–	–	–	–	8	–	–	–	160
	–	116																		
#4																				
Dutchess of Yorke	–	–	–	43	–	25	–	–	–	–	12	–	–	49	–	–	–	–	–	129
#5																				
Young Yorke	–	–	–	–	–	16	22	–	–	–	–	–	–	–	–	0	–	–	–	38
Boy	–	–	–	21	–	–	–	–	–	–	–	–	–	–	–	–	–	–	–	21
#6																				
Young Prince	–	–	–	–	–	43	–	–	–	–	–	–	–	–	–	8	–	–	–	51

Total Lines Principal Parts 3,247

Minor Parts
Men

#1																				
1 Citizen	–	–	–	–	11	–	–	–	–	–	–	–	–	–	–	–	–	–	–	11
Bishop-Ely	–	–	–	–	–	–	–	5	–	–	–	–	5	–	–	–	–	–	–	5
Messenger	–	–	–	–	–	–	–	–	–	–	–	–	–	–	–	7	–	–	–	5
Henry the sixt	–	–	–	–	–	–	–	–	–	–	–	–	–	–	–	7	–	–	–	7
#2																				
Guard	0	–	–	–	–	–	–	–	–	–	–	–	–	–	–	–	–	–	–	0
Gray	–	6	–	–	–	–	–	4	–	–	–	–	–	–	–	1	–	–	–	11
Bishop	–	–	–	–	–	–	0	–	–	–	–	–	–	–	–	–	–	–	–	0
Messenger	–	–	–	–	–	–	–	–	–	–	–	–	3	–	–	–	–	–	–	3
#3																				
Guard	0	–	–	–	–	–	–	–	–	–	–	–	–	–	–	–	–	–	–	0
Dorset	–	3	4	–	–	8	–	–	–	–	2	–	–	–	–	–	–	–	–	17
Vaughan	–	–	–	–	–	–	0	–	–	–	–	–	–	–	–	2	–	–	–	2
Messenger	–	–	–	–	–	–	–	–	–	–	–	–	6	–	–	–	–	–	–	6
#4																				
Servant	1	–	–	–	–	–	–	–	–	–	–	–	–	–	–	–	–	–	–	1
2 Citizen	–	–	–	–	9	–	–	–	–	–	–	–	–	–	–	–	–	–	–	9
Priest	–	–	–	–	–	–	0	–	–	–	–	–	–	–	–	–	–	–	–	0
Messenger	–	–	–	–	–	–	–	–	–	–	–	–	2	–	–	–	–	–	–	2
Prince [son of H6]	–	–	–	–	–	–	–	–	–	–	–	–	–	–	–	6	–	–	–	6
#5																				
Servant	0	–	–	–	–	–	–	–	–	–	–	–	–	–	–	–	–	–	–	0
Bishop	–	–	–	–	–	–	0	–	–	–	–	–	–	–	–	–	–	–	–	0
Norfolk	–	–	–	–	–	–	–	–	–	–	–	–	–	–	–	11	–	–	–	11

Table 36 (*cont.*)

																						Total
#6																						
Gentleman	–	–	–	–	–	–	–	–	–	–	–	–	–	–	–	–	–	–	–	1	–	1
Messenger	–	–	–	–	–	15	–	–	–	–	–	–	–	–	–	–	–	–	–	–	–	15
Lieutenant	–	–	–	–	–	–	–	–	–	–	–	6	–	–	–	–	–	–	–	–	–	6
1 Lord	–	–	–	–	–	–	–	–	–	–	–	–	–	–	–	–	–	2	–	–	–	2
Lord	–	–	–	–	–	–	–	–	–	–	–	–	–	–	–	–	–	3	–	–	–	3
Brandon	–	–	–	–	–	–	–	–	–	–	–	–	–	–	–	–	–	–	–	–	0	0
#7																						
Gentleman	–	–	–	–	–	–	–	–	–	–	–	–	–	–	–	–	–	–	–	0	–	0
Stanley	–	–	–	3	–	–	–	–	11	–	8	–	–	–	–	–	–	–	–	–	–	14
Sir Christopher	–	–	–	–	–	–	–	–	–	–	–	–	–	–	–	–	–	–	–	8	–	8
2 Lord	–	–	–	–	–	–	–	–	–	–	–	–	–	–	–	–	–	1	–	–	–	1
Messenger	–	–	–	–	–	–	–	–	–	–	–	–	–	–	–	–	1	–	–	–	–	1
Ferris	–	–	–	–	–	–	–	–	–	–	–	–	–	–	–	–	–	–	–	–	0	0
#8																						
Pursuivant	–	–	–	3	–	–	–	–	–	–	–	–	–	–	–	–	–	–	–	3	–	3
3 Lord	–	–	–	–	–	–	–	–	–	–	1	–	–	–	–	–	–	2	–	–	–	2
Another	–	–	–	–	–	–	–	–	–	–	–	–	–	–	–	–	–	1	–	–	–	1
Blunt	–	–	–	–	–	–	–	–	–	–	–	–	–	–	–	–	5	–	–	–	–	5
Brookenbury	–	–	–	–	–	–	–	–	–	–	–	–	–	–	–	–	–	–	–	–	0	0
#1																						
Girl	–	–	–	–	8	–	–	–	–	–	–	–	–	–	–	–	–	–	–	–	–	8
Boy	–	–	–	–	–	–	–	–	Boy	–	–	6	–	–	–	–	–	–	–	–	–	6

Total Lines Minor Parts 172 = 5%
Principal Parts 3,247 = 95%
3,419

Table 37
King Richard the Third (F)
Principal Parts
Men

Part	1				2				3							4					5					Totals
	1	2	3	4	1	2	3	4	1	2	3	4	5	6	7	1	2	3	4	5	1	2	3	4	5	
#1 Richard	109	156	127	–	41	19	–	–	58	–	–	31	50	–	73	–	72	27	211	–	–	–	136	6	0	1,116
#2 Buckingham	–	–	13	–	13	24	–	–	64	7	–	11	39	–	156	–	22	–	–	–	27	–	12	–	–	388
#3 Clarence	19	–	–	139	–	–	–	–	–	–	–	–	–	–	–	–	–	–	–	–	–	–	8	–	–	166
#4 Hastings	10	–	3	–	3	1	–	–	6	71	–	48	–	–	–	–	–	–	–	–	–	–	6	–	–	149
#5 King	–	–	–	–	68	–	–	–	–	–	–	–	–	–	–	–	–	–	–	–	–	–	–	–	–	68
Richmond	–	–	–	–	–	–	–	–	–	–	–	–	–	–	–	–	–	–	–	–	–	19	87	–	33	139
#6 Derby-Stanley	–	–	8	–	5	0	–	–	13	–	–	7	–	–	11	–	3	10	13	–	–	–	20	–	8	98
Scrivener	–	–	–	–	–	–	–	–	–	–	–	–	–	14	–	–	–	–	–	–	–	–	–	–	–	14
#7 1 Murtherer	–	–	6	57	–	–	–	–	–	–	–	–	–	–	–	–	–	–	–	–	–	–	–	–	–	63
Ratcliff	–	–	–	–	–	–	–	–	–	–	2	2	0	–	–	–	–	10	4	–	–	–	15	–	–	33
#8 2 Murtherer	–	–	0	57	–	–	–	–	–	–	–	–	–	–	–	–	–	–	–	–	–	–	–	–	–	57
Lord Major	–	–	–	–	–	–	–	–	2	–	–	–	9	–	7	–	–	–	–	–	–	–	–	–	–	18
#9 Rivers	–	–	15	–	3	13	–	–	–	–	18	–	–	–	–	–	–	–	–	–	–	–	2	–	–	51
Tyrrel	–	–	–	–	–	–	–	–	–	–	–	–	–	–	–	–	7	30	–	–	–	–	–	–	–	37
#10 Catesby	–	–	–	–	–	–	–	–	5	16	–	–	0	–	2	–	1	–	9	–	–	–	2	8	–	43
3. Citizen	–	–	–	–	–	–	28	–	–	–	–	–	–	–	–	–	–	–	–	–	–	–	–	–	–	28
#11 Brakenbury	10	–	–	13	–	–	–	–	–	–	–	–	–	–	–	5	–	–	–	–	–	–	–	–	–	28
Arch-Bishop	–	–	–	–	–	–	–	9	11	–	–	–	–	–	–	–	–	–	–	–	–	–	–	–	–	20

Table 37 (*cont.*)

	Boys										Total
#1											
Queene	128	7	20	14				31	149		349
#2											
Queene Margaret	128								95		223
#3											
Lady Anne	122						41		10		173
#4											
Dutchesse of Yorke		42	28				48	55			173
#5											
Young Prince				46					10		56
#6											
Son [Clarence]		19	17								19
Yong Yorke			17	24						0	41

Total Lines Principal Parts 3,550

Minor Parts
Men

	Men										Total
#1											
1 Citizen	0		9			0					9
Messenger				15							15
Bishop-Ely					7						7
Messenger							5		5		5
Surrey									1		1
#2											
Guard	0					0					0
Halbred	0										0
Gray	8				5		1				14
Bishop	0					0					0
Messenger								3			3
Drum									0	0	0
#3											
Guard	0					0					0
Halbred	0										0
Dorset	3	4	7				2				16
Vaughan					2	2			2		4
Lovell					1	2				0	3
Messenger								7			7
Oxford									2		2
#4											
Keeper		6									6
2 Citizen			13			0					13
Priest					3						3
Messenger									10		10
Herbert									1		1
Henry 6							7		7		7

#5																				
Bishop	0																			
Norfolk																		7			7
Sheriff																	2		0		2
Colors																					0
#6																					
Gentleman	2																				2
Messenger		9																			9
Lieutenant						6															6
Train [Richard]										0				0							0
Sir Christopher												8									8
Lord																		3			3
#7																					
Gentleman	0					0															0
Other [Richard]																					0
Halbred					0				0					0			0				0
Messenger																		1			1
Train [Richard]									0												0
#8																					
Pursuivant					3																3
Halbred									0		0			0			0				0
Citizen									0												0
Other [Richard]																					0
Train [Richard]														0							0
Blunt																		2			2
														Boy						
#1																					
Daughter [Clarence]					5																5
Prince [son of H6]																		7			7

Total Lines Minor Parts $\overline{181}$ = 5%
Principal Parts $\underline{3,550}$ = 95%
3,731

Table 38
The Comedy of Errors (F)

	1		2		3		4				5	
	1	2	1	2	1	2	1	2	3	4	1	Totals

Principal Parts
Men

	1	2	1	2	1	2	1	2	3	4	1	Totals
#1 Antipholis [Syracuse]	-	55	-	83	-	85	-	-	27	6	22	278
#2 Dromio [Syracuse]	-	2	-	64	24	57	16	29	41	8	11	252
#3 Antipholis of Ephesus	-	-	-	-	56	-	53	-	-	49	75	233
#4 Dromio of Ephesus	-	33	31	-	42	-	1	-	-	34	19	160
#5 Merchant of Siracusa	109	-	-	-	-	-	-	-	-	-	34	143
#6 Duke of Ephesus	58	-	-	-	-	-	-	-	-	-	38	96
#7 Angelo-Goldsmith	-	-	-	-	3	12	36	-	-	-	38	89
#8 Balthazar	-	-	-	-	27	-	-	-	-	-	-	27
Marchant [2]	-	-	-	-	-	-	11	-	-	-	10	21

Boys

	1	2	1	2	1	2	1	2	3	4	1	Totals
#1 Adriana	-	-	25	63	2	-	-	36	-	34	75	235
#2 Luciana	-	-	30	8	-	36	-	10	-	6	7	97
#3 Abbess	-	-	-	-	-	-	-	-	-	-	74	74
#4 Curtizan	-	-	-	-	-	-	-	-	26	0	1	27
#5 Luce	-	-	-	-	11	-	-	-	-	-	-	11

Total Lines Principal Parts   1,743

Minor Parts
Men

	1	2	1	2	1	2	1	2	3	4	1	Totals
#1 Jaylor-Officer	1	-	-	-	-	-	4	-	-	10	-	15
Headsman	-	-	-	-	-	-	-	-	-	-	0	0
#2 Merchant[1]	-	15	-	-	-	-	-	-	-	-	-	15
Pinch	-	-	-	-	-	-	-	-	-	11	-	11
Messenger	-	-	-	-	-	-	-	-	-	-	14	14
#3 Attendant[Duke]	0	-	-	-	-	-	-	-	-	-	-	0
Officer	-	-	-	-	-	-	-	-	-	0	0	0
#4 Attendant[Duke]	0	-	-	-	-	-	-	-	-	-	-	0
Officer	-	-	-	-	-	-	-	-	-	0	0	0
#5 Attendant[Duke]	0	-	-	-	-	-	-	-	-	-	-	0
Officer	-	-	-	-	-	-	-	-	-	0	0	0

Total Lines Minor Parts   55= 3%
Principal Parts   1,743=97%
1,798

Table 39   169

Table 39
The Taming of the Shrew (F)

	Ind.		1		2	3		4					5		Totals
	1	2	1	2	1	1	2	1	2	3	4	5	1	2	
Principal Parts — Men															
#1 Petruchio	–	–	–	78	165	–	61	72	–	90	–	43	16	66	591
#2 Tranio	–	–	62	34	46	–	40	–	65	–	28	–	12	4	291
#3 Hortentio	–	–	26	76	15	37	–	–	25	11	–	8	–	17	215
#4 Lucentio	–	–	91	7	0	28	6	–	6	–	11	–	14	25	188
#5 Baptista	–	–	23	–	74	–	36	–	–	–	21	–	11	12	177
#6 Gremio	–	–	25	40	50	–	31	–	–	–	–	–	12	3	161
#7 Grumio	–	–	–	35	–	–	0	86	–	32	–	–	0	0	153
#8 Lord	108	31	–	–	–	–	–	–	–	–	–	–	–	–	139
Vincentio	–	–	–	–	–	–	–	–	–	–	–	9	36	2	47
#9 Biondello	–	–	6	2	–	–	36	–	8	–	28	–	17	5	102
#10 Begger-Sly	10	48	4	–	–	–	–	–	–	–	–	–	–	–	62
Pedant	–	–	–	–	–	–	–	–	14	–	19	–	15	0	48
#11 1 Servingman	2	14	2	–	–	–	–	–	–	–	–	–	–	0	18
Curtis	–	–	–	–	–	–	–	26	–	–	–	–	–	–	26
Boys															
#1 Katherina	–	–	13	–	53	–	30	3	–	45	–	23	5	51	223
#2 Bianca	–	–	0	–	16	23	1	–	7	–	–	–	0	9	56
#3 Lady	–	15	1	–	–	–	–	–	–	–	–	–	–	–	16
Widow	–	–	–	–	–	–	–	–	–	–	–	–	–	12	12

Total Lines Principal Parts 2,525

	Ind.		1		2	3		4					5		Totals
Minor Parts — Men															
#1 2 Servingman	0	14	0	–	–	–	–	–	–	–	–	–	–	0	14
Tailor	–	–	–	–	–	–	–	–	–	17	–	–	–	–	17
#2 3 Servingman	0	6	0	–	–	–	–	–	–	–	–	–	–	–	6
Phil[ip]	–	–	–	–	–	–	–	1	–	–	–	–	–	–	1
Peter	–	–	–	–	–	–	–	–	–	0	–	–	–	–	0
#3 1 Hunstman	5	–	–	–	–	–	–	–	–	–	–	–	–	–	5
Nat[hanial]	–	–	–	–	–	–	4	–	–	–	–	–	–	–	4
Attendant	–	–	–	–	–	0	–	–	–	–	–	–	0	–	0
#4 2 Huntsman	3	–	–	–	–	–	–	–	–	–	–	–	–	–	3
Jos[eph]	–	–	–	–	–	–	–	1	–	–	–	–	–	–	1
Attendant	–	–	–	–	–	0	–	–	–	–	–	–	0	–	0
#5 <u>Sincklo</u>	S														
<u>Player</u>	2	–	–	–	–	–	–	–	–	–	–	–	–	–	2
Servant	–	–	–	–	0	–	–	–	–	–	–	–	–	–	0
Attendant	–	–	–	–	–	–	0	–	–	–	–	–	–	0	0

Table 39 (*cont.*)

Part	1	2	3	4	5	6	7	8	9	10	11	12	13	14	Total
#6															
1 Player	2	–	–	–	–	–	–	–	–	–	–	–	–	–	2
Messenger	–	8	–	–	–	–	–	–	–	–	–	–	–	–	8
Nick	–	–	–	–	3	–	1	–	–	–	–	–	–	–	4
#7															
2 Player	2	–	–	–	–	–	–	–	–	–	–	–	–	–	2
Attendant	–	–	–	–	–	–	–	0	–	–	–	–	–	–	0
Haberdasher	–	–	–	–	–	–	–	–	–	–	–	1	–	–	1
Boys															
#1															
Hostes	3	–	–	–	–	–	–	–	–	–	–	–	–	–	3
Attendant[Lady]	–	0	–	–	–	–	–	–	–	–	–	–	–	–	0
#2															
Attendant[Lady]	–	0	–	–	–	–	–	–	–	–	–	–	–	–	0
Boy	–	–	–	–	0	–	–	–	–	–	–	–	–	–	0
#3															
Attendant[Lady]	–	0	–	–	–	–	–	–	–	–	–	–	–	–	0

Total Lines Minor Parts   73= 3%

Principal Parts   2,525=97%

2,598

Table 40
The Two Gentlemen of Verona (F)

Act/scene columns: 1 (scenes 1–3), 2 (scenes 1–7), 3 (scenes 1–2), 4 (scenes 1–4), 5 (scenes 1–4)

Principal Parts — Men

Part	1	2	3	1	2	3	4	5	6	7	1	2	1	2	3	4	1	2	3	4	Totals
#1 Protheus	61	–	26	–	17	–	49	–	42	–	75	39	–	32	–	31	–	16	–	40	428
#2 Valentine	43	–	–	60	–	–	108	–	–	–	77	–	22	–	–	–	–	–	–	73	383
#3 Launce	–	–	–	–	–	44	–	33	–	–	83	–	–	–	–	45	–	–	–	–	205
#4 Duke	–	–	–	–	–	–	18	–	–	–	102	39	–	–	–	–	–	18	–	19	196
#5 Speed	43	–	–	90	–	–	3	21	–	–	34	–	4	–	–	–	–	–	–	–	195
#6 Thurio	–	–	–	–	–	–	14	–	–	–	0	14	–	7	–	–	–	18	–	5	58
#7 Panthion	–	–	31	–	1	15	–	–	–	–	–	–	–	–	–	–	–	–	–	–	47
Eglamore	–	–	–	–	–	–	–	–	–	–	–	–	–	–	19	–	9	–	–	–	28
#8 Antonio	–	–	35	–	–	–	–	–	–	–	–	–	–	–	–	–	–	–	–	–	35
Host	–	–	–	–	–	–	–	–	–	–	–	–	–	20	–	–	–	–	–	–	20
#9 3. Outlaw	–	–	–	–	–	–	–	–	–	–	–	–	20	–	–	–	–	–	5	0	25

Boys

Part	1	2	3	1	2	3	4	5	6	7	1	2	1	2	3	4	1	2	3	4	Totals
#1 Julia	–	92	–	–	14	–	–	–	–	92	–	–	–	20	–	98	–	7	–	19	342
#2 Silvia	–	–	–	17	–	–	21	–	–	–	–	–	25	32	28	3	–	3	–	21	150
#3 Lucetta	–	52	–	–	–	–	–	–	–	18	–	–	–	–	–	–	–	–	–	–	70

Total Lines Principal Parts   2,182

Minor Parts — Men

Part	1	2	3	1	2	3	4	5	6	7	1	2	1	2	3	4	1	2	3	4	Totals
#1 1. Outlaw	–	–	–	–	–	–	–	–	–	–	–	–	15	–	–	–	–	–	6	1	22
#2 2. Outlaw	–	–	–	–	–	–	–	–	–	–	–	–	14	–	–	–	–	–	1	0	15
#3 Musitian	–	–	–	–	–	–	–	–	–	–	–	–	–	15	–	–	–	–	–	–	15

Total Lines Minor Parts   52= 2%

Principal Parts   2,182=98%

2,234

Table 41   171

Table 41
Love's Labour's Lost (Q1-1598)

	1.1	1.2	2.1	3.1	4.1	4.2	4.3	5.1	5.2	Totals
	1	2	1	1	1	2	3	1	2	

Principal Parts
Men

	1.1	1.2	2.1	3.1	4.1	4.2	4.3	5.1	5.2	Totals
#1 Berowne	120	-	18	49	-	-	231	-	190	608
#2 Ferdinand-King of Navar	97	-	47	-	-	-	75	-	79	298
#3 Armado-Braggart	-	81	-	52	-	-	-	38	47	218
#4 Boyet	-	-	66	-	57	-	-	-	95	218
#5 Costard-Clowne	30	12	-	35	26	12	4	7	52	178
#6 Holofernes-Pedant	-	-	-	-	-	65	-	48	18	131
#7 Nathaniel-Curat	-	-	-	-	-	75	-	12	4	91
#8 Dumaine	8	-	2	-	-	-	44	-	32	86
#9 Longavill	22	-	5	-	-	-	34	-	17	78

Boys

	1.1	1.2	2.1	3.1	4.1	4.2	4.3	5.1	5.2	Totals
#1 Princesse-Queene	-	-	65	-	49	-	-	-	171	285
#2 3. Lady-Rosaline	-	-	22	-	10	-	-	-	140	172
#3 Moth-Boy-Page	-	57	-	32	-	-	-	17	10	116
#4 2. Lady-Katherine	-	-	22	-	0	-	-	-	27	49
#5 1. Lady-Maria	-	-	18	-	5	-	-	-	23	46
#6 Wench-Jaquenetta	-	6	-	-	-	7	4	-	-	17

Total Lines Principal Parts 2,591

Minor Parts
Men

	1.1	1.2	2.1	3.1	4.1	4.2	4.3	5.1	5.2	Totals
#1 Constable-Anthony Dull	7	5	-	-	-	2	-	3	-	17
#2 Forrester	-	-	-	-	6	-	-	-	-	6
Messenger-Marcade	-	-	-	-	-	-	-	-	4	4
#3 Lord	-	-	1	-	0	-	-	-	-	1
Blackamoor	-	-	-	-	-	-	-	-	0	0
#4 Lord	-	-	0	-	0	-	-	-	-	0
Blackamoor	-	-	-	-	-	-	-	-	0	0
#5 Lord	-	-	0	-	0	-	-	-	-	0
Blackamoor	-	-	-	-	-	-	-	-	0	0

Total Lines Minor Parts 28 = 1%
Principal Parts 2,591 = 99%
2,619

Table 42

Romeo and Juliet (Q1-1597)

Principal Parts

Men

	P	1.1	1.2	1.3	1.4	1.5	2.1	2.2	2.3	2.4	2.5	2.6	3.1	3.2	3.3	3.4	3.5	4.1	4.2	4.3	4.4	4.5	5.1	5.2	5.3	Totals
#1 Romeo	–	45	27	–	25	26	2	77	24	38	–	12	31	–	66	–	24	–	–	–	–	–	50	–	49	496
#2 Friar Francis-Laurence	–	–	–	–	–	–	–	–	64	–	–	13	–	–	57	–	–	34	–	–	–	7	–	11	64	250
#3 Old Capulet	–	0	26	–	–	45	–	–	–	–	–	–	–	–	–	24	53	–	18	–	13	9	–	–	22	210
#4 Mercutio	–	–	–	–	30	–	23	–	–	78	–	–	51	–	–	–	–	–	–	–	–	–	–	–	–	182
#5 Benvolio	–	31	20	–	7	–	46	–	–	11	–	–	37	–	–	–	–	–	–	–	–	–	–	–	–	152
#6 Paris	–	–	4	–	–	–	–	–	–	–	–	–	–	–	–	9	–	21	–	–	–	5	–	–	27	66
#7 1 Servant [Cap.]	–	–	–	3	–	20	–	–	–	–	–	–	–	–	–	–	–	–	16	–	14	5	–	–	–	58
Clowne	–	–	3	–	–	–	–	–	–	–	–	–	–	–	–	–	–	–	–	–	–	–	–	–	–	3
Peter	–	–	–	–	–	–	–	–	–	–	–	–	–	–	–	–	–	–	–	–	–	3	–	–	–	3
#8 Prince	–	14	–	–	–	–	–	–	–	–	–	–	12	–	–	–	–	–	–	–	–	–	–	–	22	48
#9 Tybalt	–	0	–	–	–	17	–	–	–	–	–	–	9	–	–	–	–	–	–	–	–	–	–	–	–	26
Balthasar	–	–	–	–	–	–	–	–	–	–	–	–	–	–	–	–	–	–	–	–	–	–	7	–	6	13

Boys

	P	1.1	1.2	1.3	1.4	1.5	2.1	2.2	2.3	2.4	2.5	2.6	3.1	3.2	3.3	3.4	3.5	4.1	4.2	4.3	4.4	4.5	5.1	5.2	5.3	Totals
#1 Juliet	–	–	–	7	–	20	–	93	–	–	21	5	–	75	–	–	34	40	–	23	–	0	–	–	20	338
#2 Nurse	–	–	–	40	–	13	–	–	–	32	24	1	–	20	3	–	22	–	–	11	2	19	–	–	–	187
#3 Cap. Wife-Mother	–	0	–	15	–	–	–	–	–	–	–	–	–	–	–	9	24	–	10	–	8	3	–	–	5	74

Total Lines Principal Parts 2,106

Minor Parts
Men

#1				Total
2 Servant [Cap.]	19			19
1 Musician			6	6
Captain			10	10
#2				
1 Serv [Mont.]	2			2
Frier John		9		9
#3				
2 Servant [Mont.]	1			1
Cousin		2		2
2 Musician				2
#4				
Old Mountague	5	6	13	18
Apothecarie				6
#5				
Citizen	0			0
Masker	0			0
3 Musician		1		1
Man			8	8
#6				
Prologue	12			12
Citizen	0			0
Masker	0			0
Watch	2			2
#7				
Citizen	0			0
Masker	0			0
1 Watch			3	3

Boys

#1				Total
Mountague Wife	4			4
Page [Romeo]	3			3
Lady	0			0
#2				
Lady	0			0
Page [Paris]		4		4

Total Lines Minor Parts 112= 5%
Principal Parts 2,106=95%
2,218

Table 43
Romeo and Juliet (Q2-1599)
Principal Parts

Men

Part	1·C	1·1	1·2	1·3	1·4	1·5	2·C	2·1	2·2	2·3	2·4	2·5	2·6	3·1	3·2	3·3	3·4	3·5	4·1	4·2	4·3	4·4	4·5	5·1	5·2	5·3	Totals
#1 Romeo	–	64	26	–	34	27	–	–	2	87	25	47	–	12	36	–	72	–	–	25	–	–	–	71	–	87	615
#2 Chorus	14	–	–	–	–	–	14	–	–	–	–	–	–	–	–	–	–	–	–	–	–	–	–	–	–	–	28
Friar Lawrence	–	–	–	–	–	–	–	–	–	72	–	–	18	–	–	88	–	–	57	–	–	–	20	–	17	74	346
#3 Capulet-Father	–	3	33	–	–	56	–	–	–	–	–	–	–	3	–	–	30	61	–	14	–	33	25	–	–	10	268
#4 Mercutio	–	–	–	–	60	–	–	32	–	–	75	–	–	61	–	–	–	–	–	–	–	–	–	–	–	–	228
#5 Benvolio	–	51	20	–	34	1	–	10	–	–	11	–	–	52	–	–	–	–	–	–	–	–	–	–	–	–	179
#6 Prince Eskales	–	23	–	–	–	–	–	–	–	–	–	–	–	16	–	–	–	–	–	–	–	–	–	–	–	36	75
#7 Paris	–	–	4	–	–	–	–	–	–	–	–	–	–	–	–	–	7	–	20	–	–	–	6	–	–	32	69
#8 Old Mountague	–	28	–	–	–	–	–	–	–	–	–	–	–	0	–	–	–	–	–	–	–	–	–	–	–	10	38
#9 Tybalt	–	5	–	–	–	17	–	–	–	–	–	–	–	14	–	–	–	–	–	–	–	–	–	–	–	–	36
Man [Romeo] Balthazar	–	–	–	–	–	–	–	–	–	–	–	–	–	–	–	–	–	–	–	–	–	–	–	11	–	6	17
#10 Sampson	–	31	–	–	–	–	–	–	–	–	–	–	–	–	–	–	–	–	–	–	–	–	–	–	–	–	31
Watch	–	–	–	–	–	–	–	–	–	–	–	–	–	–	–	–	–	–	–	–	–	–	–	–	–	18	18
#11 Will Kemp: Clowne	–	–	16	–	–	–	–	–	–	–	–	–	–	–	–	–	–	–	–	–	–	–	–	–	–	–	16
Servant	–	–	–	–	–	8	–	–	–	–	–	–	–	–	–	–	–	–	–	4	–	5	–	–	–	–	17
Peter	–	–	–	–	–	–	–	–	–	–	6	–	–	–	–	–	–	–	–	–	–	–	WK 24	–	–	3	33

Boys

Part	1·C	1·1	1·2	1·3	1·4	1·5	2·C	2·1	2·2	2·3	2·4	2·5	2·6	3·1	3·2	3·3	3·4	3·5	4·1	4·2	4·3	4·4	4·5	5·1	5·2	5·3	Totals
#1 Juliet	–	–	–	7	–	115	–	–	146	–	–	44	–	–	105	–	–	48	12	–	55	–	15	–	–	24	571
#2 Nurse	–	–	–	45	–	15	–	–	–	–	2	49	–	–	35	30	–	21	–	–	–	28	24	–	–	6	255
#3 Cap. Wife-Mother	–	1	–	36	–	0	–	–	–	–	–	–	–	2	–	–	37	–	–	2	3	4	13	–	–	5	103

Total Lines Principal Parts — 2,943

Minor Parts
<u>Men</u>

Part	Lines
#1	
Gregorie	20
2 Servant	1
1 Musician	10
#2	
1 Servant	5
Petruchio	0
Apothecarie	7
Friar John	13
#3	
Abraham	5
3 Servant	2
Man [Mercutio]	0
#4	
2 Servant [Mont.]	0
2 Capulet	3
2 Musician	5
Chief Watch	2
#5	
Officer	6
Masker	0
3 Musician	1
3 Watch	3
#6	
Citizen	0
Masker	0
#7	
Citizen	0
Masker	0
#8	
Train	0
Masker	0
Man [Mercutio]	0
#9	
Train	0
Masker	0
Other [Tybalt]	0
#10	
Train	0
Masker	0
Other [Tybalt]	0

Table 43 (*cont.*)

		Boys		
#11 Guest				0
#12 Guest				0
#13 Guest				0
#1				
Mountague Wife	3	0		3
Torchbearer	0			0
Lady	0			0
Watch Boy	1		1	1
#2				
Torchbearer	0			0
Lady	0			0
Page [Paris]	7		7	7
#3 Gentlewoman				0
#4 Gentlewoman				0
#5 Gentlewoman				0

Total Lines Minor Parts $\overline{94}$ = 3%
Principal Parts 2,943 = 97%
3,037

Table 44   177

Table 44
King Richard the Second (Q1-1597)

Principal Parts — Men

Actor#	Part	1				2				3				4	5						Totals
		1	2	3	4	1	2	3	4	1	2	3	4	1	1	2	3	4	5	6	
#1	King Richard	54	-	74	39	41	-	-	-	-	147	104	-	-	64	-	-	-	95	-	618
#2	Bullingbrooke	59	-	77	-	-	-	55	-	38	-	52	-	20	-	-	53	-	-	31	385
#3	Yorke	-	-	-	-	67	39	48	-	2	-	12	-	6	-	70	27	-	-	0	271
#4	John of Gaunt	7	13	62	-	106	-	-	-	-	-	-	-	-	-	-	-	-	-	-	188
	Carleil	-	-	-	-	-	-	-	-	-	14	-	-	49	-	-	-	-	-	-	63
#5	Mowbray	83	-	52	-	-	-	-	-	-	-	-	-	-	-	-	-	-	-	-	135
	Harry Percie	-	-	-	-	-	-	21	-	-	-	8	-	5	-	-	6	-	-	5	45
#6	Northumberland	-	-	-	-	46	-	35	-	0	-	30	-	4	6	-	-	-	-	5	126
#7	Aumerle	-	-	5	14	-	-	-	-	-	12	3	-	26	-	11	13	-	-	-	84
#8	Bushie	-	-	-	4	-	32	-	-	2	-	-	-	-	-	-	-	-	-	-	38
	Gardener	-	-	-	-	-	-	-	-	-	-	-	52	-	-	-	-	-	-	-	52
	Exton	-	-	-	-	-	-	-	-	-	-	-	-	-	-	-	-	10	6	5	21
#9	Marshall	-	-	25	-	-	-	-	-	-	-	-	-	-	-	-	-	-	-	-	25
	Scroop	-	-	-	-	-	-	-	-	-	37	-	-	-	-	-	-	-	-	-	37
#10	Greene	-	-	-	5	-	26	-	-	2	-	-	-	-	-	-	-	-	-	-	33
	Fitzwater	-	-	-	-	-	-	-	-	-	-	-	-	23	-	-	-	-	-	4	27

Boys

Actor#	Part	1	2	3	4	1	2	3	4	1	2	3	4	1	1	2	3	4	5	6	Totals
#1	Queen	-	-	-	-	1	39	-	-	-	-	-	43	-	32	-	-	-	-	-	115
#2	Duch. Yorke	-	-	-	-	-	-	-	-	-	-	-	-	-	-	45	27	-	-	-	72
#3	Duch. Glocester	-	58	-	-	-	-	-	-	-	-	-	-	-	-	-	-	-	-	-	58

Total Lines Principal Parts 2,393

Minor Parts — Men

Actor#	Part	1	2	3	4	1	2	3	4	1	2	3	4	1	1	2	3	4	5	6	Totals
#1	1 Herald	-	-	6	-	-	-	-	-	-	-	-	-	-	-	-	-	-	-	-	6
	Ross	-	-	-	-	20	-	2	-	-	-	-	-	-	-	-	-	-	-	-	22
	Abbot	-	-	-	-	-	-	-	-	-	-	-	-	9	-	-	-	-	-	-	9
	Keeper	-	-	-	-	-	-	-	-	-	-	-	-	-	-	-	-	-	5	-	5
#2	2 Herald	-	-	7	-	-	-	-	-	-	-	-	-	-	-	-	-	-	-	-	7
	Bagot	-	-	-	-	-	9	-	-	-	-	-	-	12	-	-	-	-	-	-	21
	Salisbury	-	-	-	-	-	-	-	9	-	11	-	-	-	-	-	-	-	-	-	20
#3	Servingman	-	-	-	-	-	5	-	-	-	-	-	-	-	-	-	-	-	-	-	5
	Welch Captain	-	-	-	-	-	-	15	-	-	-	-	-	-	-	-	-	-	-	-	15
	Man	-	-	-	-	-	-	-	-	-	-	-	-	-	0	-	-	-	-	-	0
	Murderer	-	-	-	-	-	-	-	-	-	-	-	-	-	-	-	-	-	0	-	0
#4	Attendant [King]	0	-	0	-	-	-	-	-	-	-	-	-	-	-	-	-	-	-	-	0
	Willoughby	-	-	-	-	8	-	2	-	-	-	-	-	-	-	-	-	-	-	-	10
	Lord	-	-	-	-	-	-	-	-	-	-	-	-	5	-	-	-	-	-	-	5
	Murderer	-	-	-	-	-	-	-	-	-	-	-	-	-	-	-	-	-	0	-	0

Table 44 (*cont.*)

#5																				Totals
Attendant [King]	0	–	0	–	–	–	–	–	–	–	–	–	–	–	–	–	–	–	–	0
Barkly	–	–	–	–	–	–	8	–	–	–	–	–	–	–	–	–	–	–	–	8
Surrey	–	–	–	–	–	–	–	–	–	–	–	9	–	–	–	–	–	–	–	9
Groom	–	–	–	–	–	–	–	–	–	–	–	–	–	–	–	–	12	–	–	12
#6																				
Attendant [King]	0	–	0	–	–	–	–	–	–	–	–	–	–	–	–	–	–	–	–	0
Man	–	–	–	–	–	–	–	–	–	–	10	–	–	–	–	–	–	–	–	10
Man	–	–	–	–	–	–	–	–	–	–	–	–	–	–	–	2	–	–	–	2

Boys

#1																				Totals
Lady	–	–	–	–	–	–	–	–	–	–	6	–	0	–	–	–	–	–	–	6
#2																				
Attendant [Queen]	–	–	–	–	–	–	–	–	–	–	0	–	0	–	–	–	–	–	–	0
#3																				
Attendant [Queen]	–	–	–	–	–	–	–	–	–	–	0	–	0	–	–	–	–	–	–	0

Total Lines Minor Parts 172= 7%
Principal Parts 2,393=93%
2,565

Table 45
King Richard the Second (F)

Principal Parts
Men

	1				2				3				4	5						Totals
	1	2	3	4	1	2	3	4	1	2	3	4	1	1	2	3	4	5	6	
#1 King Richard	56	–	76	30	42	–	–	–	–	146	108	–	133	63	–	–	–	95	–	749
#2 Bullingbrooke	62	–	63	–	–	55	–	38	–	54	–	39	–	–	–	55	–	–	33	399
#3 Yorke	–	–	–	–	73	38	46	–	2	–	13	–	11	–	70	27	–	–	0	280
#4 John of Gaunt	8	16	39	–	106	–	–	–	–	–	–	–	–	–	–	–	–	–	–	169
Carlile	–	–	–	–	–	–	–	–	9	0	–	49	–	–	–	–	–	–	0	58
#5 Northumberland	–	–	–	–	52	–	36	–	0	–	30	–	13	7	–	–	–	–	5	143
#6 Mowbray	83	–	52	–	–	–	–	–	–	–	–	–	–	–	–	–	–	–	–	135
Harry Percie	–	–	–	–	–	–	22	–	0	–	8	–	5	–	–	6	–	–	5	46
#7 Aumerle	–	–	5	14	0	–	–	–	–	14	4	–	23	–	11	13	–	–	–	84
#8 Bushie	–	–	0	4	0	33	–	–	2	–	–	–	–	–	–	–	–	–	–	39
Gardener	–	–	–	–	–	–	–	–	–	–	52	–	–	–	–	–	–	–	–	52
Exton	–	–	–	–	–	–	–	–	–	–	–	–	–	–	–	–	11	6	5	22
#9 Marshall	–	–	25	–	–	–	–	–	–	–	–	–	–	–	–	–	–	–	–	25
Scroop	–	–	–	–	–	–	–	–	38	0	–	–	–	–	–	–	–	–	–	38
#10 Greene	–	–	0	5	0	23	–	–	2	–	–	–	–	–	–	–	–	–	–	30
Fitzwater	–	–	–	–	–	–	–	–	–	–	–	–	24	–	–	–	–	–	4	28

Boys

	1				2				3				4	5						Totals
	1	2	3	4	1	2	3	4	1	2	3	4	1	1	2	3	4	5	6	
#1 Queen	–	–	–	–	1	29	–	–	–	–	–	43	–	32	–	–	–	–	–	105
#2 Duch. Yorke	–	–	–	–	–	–	–	–	–	–	–	–	–	–	45	48	–	–	–	93
#3 Duch. Glocester	–	58	–	–	–	–	–	–	–	–	–	–	–	–	–	–	–	–	–	58

Total Lines Principal Parts 2,553

Table 46   179

Table 45 (*cont.*)

Minor Parts
Men

																				Total
#1																				
Bagot	-	-	0	5	0	6	-	-	-	-	-	-	12	-	-	-	-	-	-	23
Captain	-	-	-	-	-	-	-	15	-	-	-	-	-	-	-	-	-	-	-	15
Drum	-	-	-	-	-	-	-	-	-	-	0	-	-	-	-	-	-	-	-	0
Groom	-	-	-	-	-	-	-	-	-	-	-	-	-	-	-	-	-	13	-	13
#2																				
1 Herald	-	-	6	-	-	-	-	-	-	-	-	0	-	-	-	-	-	-	-	6
Ross	-	-	-	-	20	-	2	-	0	-	-	-	-	-	-	-	-	-	-	22
Soldier [King]	-	-	-	-	-	-	-	-	-	0	-	-	-	-	-	-	-	-	-	0
Colours	-	-	-	-	-	-	-	-	-	0	-	-	-	-	-	-	-	-	-	0
Keeper	-	-	-	-	-	-	-	-	-	-	-	-	-	-	-	-	-	5	-	5
#3																				
2 Herald	-	-	7	-	-	-	-	-	-	-	-	-	-	-	-	-	-	-	-	7
Servant	-	-	-	-	-	5	-	-	-	-	10	-	-	0	2	-	-	-	-	17
Abbot	-	-	-	-	-	-	-	-	-	-	-	9	-	-	-	-	-	-	-	9
Lord	-	-	-	-	-	-	-	-	-	-	-	-	-	-	-	-	-	-	0	0
#4																				
Salisbury	-	-	-	-	-	-	9	-	4	0	-	-	-	-	-	-	-	-	-	13
Surrey	-	-	-	-	-	-	-	-	-	-	12	-	-	-	-	-	-	-	-	12
Servant	-	-	-	-	-	-	-	-	-	-	-	-	-	0	0	-	-	-	-	0
#5																				
Attendant [King]	0	-	-	-	-	-	-	-	-	-	-	-	-	-	-	-	-	-	-	0
Willoughby	-	-	-	-	9	-	2	-	0	-	-	-	-	-	-	-	-	-	-	11
Attendant [Bull.]	-	-	-	-	-	-	-	-	0	-	0	-	-	-	-	-	-	-	-	0
Guard	-	-	-	-	-	-	-	-	-	-	-	0	-	-	-	-	-	-	-	0
Servant	-	-	-	-	-	-	-	-	-	-	-	-	-	0	0	-	-	-	-	0
#6																				
Attendant [King]	0	-	-	-	-	-	-	-	-	-	-	-	-	-	-	-	-	-	-	0
Barkly	-	-	-	-	-	8	-	-	-	-	-	-	-	-	-	-	-	-	-	8
Soldier [King]	-	-	-	-	-	-	-	-	0	-	-	-	-	-	-	-	-	-	-	0
Attendant [Bull.]	-	-	-	-	-	-	-	-	0	-	-	-	-	-	-	-	-	-	-	0
Officer	-	-	-	-	-	-	-	-	-	-	-	0	-	-	-	-	-	-	-	0
Lord	-	-	-	-	-	-	-	-	-	-	-	-	-	-	-	-	-	-	0	0
#7																				
Attendant [King]	0	-	-	-	-	-	-	-	-	-	-	-	-	-	-	-	-	-	-	0
Soldier [King]	-	-	-	-	-	-	-	-	0	-	-	-	-	-	-	-	-	-	-	0
Attendant [Bull.]	-	-	-	-	-	-	-	-	0	-	-	-	-	-	-	-	-	-	-	0
Officer	-	-	-	-	-	-	-	-	-	-	0	-	-	-	-	-	-	-	-	0
Servant	-	-	-	-	-	-	-	-	-	0	-	-	-	-	-	-	-	-	-	0
Lord	-	-	-	-	-	-	-	-	-	-	-	-	-	-	-	-	-	-	0	0

Boys

																				Total
#1																				
Lady	-	-	-	-	-	-	-	-	-	-	6	-	0	-	-	-	-	-	-	6
#2																				
Lady	-	-	-	-	-	-	-	-	-	-	0	-	0	-	-	-	-	-	-	0

Total Lines Minor Parts   167= 6%
Principal Parts   2,553=94%
2,720

Table 46
A Midsummer Night's Dream (Q1-1600)

	1		2		3		4		5	
	1	2	1	2	1	2	1	2	1	Totals
Principal Parts										
Men										
#1 Theseus-Duke	63	-	-	-	-	-	33	-	122	218
#2 King of Fairies-Oberon	-	-	79	8	-	63	47	-	5	202
#3 Bottom-Pyramus-Clowne	-	40	-	-	49	-	44	15	46	194

Table 46 (*cont.*)

#4 Robin Goodfellow-Pucke	–	–	35	18	10	90	3	–	36	192
#5 Lysander	53	–	–	44	–	55	10	–	8	170
#6 Demetrius	2	–	23	2	–	63	25	–	22	137
#7 Quince-Prologue	–	40	–	–	32	–	–	8	35	115
#8 Flute-Thisby	–	3	–	–	7	–	–	12	26	48
#9 Egeus	30	–	–	–	–	–	11	–	–	41

Boys

#1 Helena	43	–	34	32	–	116	4	–	0	229
#2 Hermia	58	–	–	26	–	79	3	–	0	166
#3 Queene-Tytania	–	–	72	8	33	–	22	–	4	139
#4 Hippolita-Dutchess	5	–	–	–	–	–	7	–	21	33
Fairie	–	–	24	–	–	–	–	–	–	24

Total Lines Principal Parts   1,908

Minor Parts
Men

#1 Philostrate	0	–	–	–	–	–	–	–	23	23
#2 Snugge-Lion	–	2	–	–	0	–	–	4	13	19
#3 Snout-Wall	–	1	–	–	6	–	–	0	12	19
#4 Starveling-Moonshine	–	1	–	–	3	–	–	2	6	12
#5 Other [Theseus]	0	–	–	–	–	–	–	–	–	0
Train [Oberon]	–	–	0	–	–	–	–	–	0	0
Train [Theseus]	–	–	–	–	–	–	0	–	–	0
#6 Other [Theseus]	0	–	–	–	–	–	–	–	–	0
Train [Oberon]	–	–	0	–	–	–	–	–	0	0
Train [Theseus]	–	–	–	–	–	–	0	–	–	0
#7 Other [Theseus]	0	–	–	–	–	–	–	–	–	0
Train [Oberon]	–	–	0	–	–	–	–	–	0	0
Train [Theseus]	–	–	–	–	–	–	0	–	–	0

Boys

#1 Traine [Tytania]	–	–	0	0	–	–	–	–	0	0
Peaseblossome	–	–	–	–	2	–	1	–	–	3
#2 Traine [Tytania]	–	–	0	0	–	–	–	–	0	0
Cobweb	–	–	–	–	2	–	1	–	–	3
#3 Traine [Tytania]	–	–	0	0	–	–	–	–	0	0
Mustardseede	–	–	–	–	2	–	2	–	–	4
#4 Traine [Tytania]	–	–	0	0	–	–	–	–	0	0
Moth	–	–	–	–	0	–	0	–	–	0

Total Lines Minor Parts   83= 4%
Principal Parts   1,908=96%
1,991

Table 47   181

Table 47
A Midsummer Night's Dream (F)

	1		2		3		4		5	
	1	2	1	2	1	2	1	2	1	Totals

Principal Parts
Men

	1.1	1.2	2.1	2.2	3.1	3.2	4.1	4.2	5.1	Totals
#1 Theseus-Duke	65	-	-	-	-	-	42	-	121	228
#2 Bottom-Pyramus-Clowne	-	47	-	-	62	-	45	15	50	219
#3 King of Fairies-Oberon	-	-	80	8	-	63	47	-	5	203
#4 Robin Goodfellow-Pucke	-	-	37	12	18	92	4	-	36	199
#5 Lysander	53	-	-	44	-	60	10	-	19	186
#6 Demetrius	2	-	23	2	-	64	24	-	21	136
#7 Quince-Prologue	-	47	-	-	36	-	-	9	35	127
#8 Flute-Thisby	-	4	-	-	8	-	-	11	26	49
#9 Egeus	30	-	-	-	-	-	11	-	23	64

Boys

	1.1	1.2	2.1	2.2	3.1	3.2	4.1	4.2	5.1	Totals
#1 Helena	44	-	34	32	-	116	4	-	0	230
#2 Hermia	56	-	-	26	-	79	3	-	0	164
#3 Queene-Titania	-	-	72	8	33	-	25	-	4	142
#4 Hippolita-Dutchess	5	-	-	-	-	-	7	-	22	34
Fairie	-	-	25	-	-	-	-	-	-	25

Total Lines Princpal Parts 2,006

Minor Parts
Men

	1.1	1.2	2.1	2.2	3.1	3.2	4.1	4.2	5.1	Totals
#1 Philostrate	0	-	-	-	-	-	-	-	-	0
Snout-Wall	-	1	-	-	10	-	-	0	12	23
#2 Snugge-Lion	-	2	-	-	0	-	-	4	9	15
#3 Starveling-Moonshine	-	1	-	-	3	-	-	2	7	13
#4 Tawyer										
Other [Theseus]	0	-	-	-	-	-	-	-	-	0
Train [Oberon]	-	-	0	-	-	-	-	-	0	0
Train [Theseus]	-	-	-	-	-	-	0	-	-	0
Trumpet	-	-	-	-	-	-	-	-	0	0
#5										
Other [Theseus]	0	-	-	-	-	-	-	-	-	0
Train [Oberon]	-	-	0	-	-	-	-	-	0	0
Train [Theseus]	-	-	-	-	-	-	0	-	-	0
#6										
Other [Theseus]	0	-	-	-	-	-	-	-	-	0
Train [Oberon]	-	-	0	-	-	-	-	-	0	0
Train [Theseus]	-	-	-	-	-	-	0	-	-	0

Table 47 (*cont.*)

					Boys					
#1										
Traine [Queene]	-	-	0	0	-	-	-	-	0	0
Peaseblossome	-	-	-	-	2	-	1	-	-	3
#2										
Traine [Queene]	-	-	0	0	-	-	-	-	0	0
Cobweb	-	-	-	-	2	-	1	-	-	3
#3										
Traine [Queene]	-	-	0	0	-	-	-	-	0	0
Mustardseede	-	-	-	-	2	-	2	-	-	4
#4										
Traine [Queene]	-	-	0	0	-	-	-	-	0	0
Moth	-	-	-	-	0	-	0	-	-	0

Total Lines Minor Parts 61= 3%
Principal Parts 2,006=97%
2,067

Table 48
King John (F)

	1	2	3				4			5							
	1	1	1	2	3	4	1	2	3	1	2	3	4	5	6	7	Totals
					Principal Parts												
							Men										
#1																	
Philip-Bastard	150	122	9	8	5	-	-	21	56	44	53	-	-	-	20	39	527
#2																	
King John	48	106	34	3	64	-	-	119	-	27	-	8	-	-	-	28	437
#3																	
Citizen-Hubert	-	60	-	0	8	-	42	35	25	-	-	1	-	-	31	-	202
#4																	
King of France	-	123	48	-	-	26	-	-	-	-	-	-	-	-	-	-	197
#5																	
Pandulph	-	-	71	-	-	67	-	-	-	11	14	-	-	-	-	-	163
#6																	
Salisbury	0	-	6	-	-	-	-	28	52	-	32	-	19	-	-	18	155
#7																	
Lewis Dauphin	-	28	8	-	-	18	-	-	-	-	83	-	-	17	-	-	154
#8																	
Pembroke	0	0	-	-	-	-	-	56	13	-	-	-	4	-	-	6	79
#9																	
Chattylion	17	25	-	-	-	-	-	-	-	-	-	-	-	-	-	-	42
Meloon	-	-	-	-	-	-	-	-	-	-	0	-	38	-	-	-	38
#10																	
Austria	-	24	8	-	-	-	-	-	-	-	-	-	-	-	-	-	32
Messenger	-	-	-	-	-	-	-	14	-	-	-	8	-	-	-	-	22
							Boys										
#1																	
Constance	-	49	141	-	-	74	-	-	-	-	-	-	-	-	-	-	264
#2																	
Prince Arthur	-	9	1	0	1	-	99	-	10	-	-	-	-	-	-	-	120
#3																	
Blanche	-	16	27	-	-	-	-	-	-	-	-	-	-	-	-	-	43
Prince Henry	-	-	-	-	-	-	-	-	-	-	-	-	-	-	-	29	29
#4																	
Queen Elinor	29	19	2	-	3	-	-	-	-	-	-	-	-	-	-	-	53
#5																	
Lady Faulconbridge	15	-	-	-	-	-	-	-	-	-	-	-	-	-	-	-	15

Total Lines Principal Parts 2,572

Table 48   183

Table 48 (*cont.*)

Minor Parts
Men

	1	2	3	4	5	6	7	8	9	10	11	12	13	14	15	16	Total
#1																	
Robert Faulconbridge	22	–	–	–	–	–	–	–	–	–	–	–	–	–	–	–	22
Rigot	–	–	–	–	–	–	–	–	8	–	–	–	0	–	–	0	8
#2																	
Essex	3	–	–	–	–	–	–	–	–	–	–	–	–	–	–	–	3
English Herald	–	13	–	–	–	–	–	–	–	–	–	–	–	–	–	–	13
Executioner	–	–	–	–	–	–	2	–	–	–	–	–	–	–	–	–	2
Messenger	–	–	–	–	–	–	–	–	–	–	–	–	6	–	–	–	6
#3																	
Sherriffe	0	–	–	–	–	–	–	–	–	–	–	–	–	–	–	–	0
French Herald	–	12	–	–	–	–	–	–	–	–	–	–	–	–	–	–	12
Executioner	–	–	–	–	–	–	0	–	–	–	–	–	–	–	–	–	0
Peter	–	–	–	–	–	–	–	1	–	–	–	–	–	–	–	–	1
#4																	
Gurney	1	–	–	–	–	–	–	–	–	–	–	–	–	–	–	–	1
Power [French]	–	0	–	–	–	–	–	–	–	–	–	–	–	–	–	–	0
Attendant [French]	–	–	–	–	–	0	–	–	–	–	–	–	–	–	–	–	0
Soldier [French]	–	–	–	–	–	–	–	–	–	–	0	–	–	–	–	–	0
Train [French]	–	–	–	–	–	–	–	–	–	–	–	0	–	–	–	–	0
#5																	
Trumpet [French]	–	0	–	–	–	–	–	–	–	–	–	–	–	–	–	–	0
Power [French]	–	0	–	–	–	–	–	–	–	–	–	–	–	–	–	–	0
Attendant [French]	–	–	–	–	–	0	–	–	–	–	–	–	–	–	–	–	0
Soldier [French]	–	–	–	–	–	–	–	–	–	–	0	–	–	–	–	–	0
Train [French]	–	–	–	–	–	–	–	–	–	–	–	0	–	–	–	–	0
#6																	
Power [French]	–	0	–	–	–	–	–	–	–	–	–	–	–	–	–	–	0
Attendant [French]	–	–	–	–	–	0	–	–	–	–	–	–	–	–	–	–	0
Soldier [French]	–	–	–	–	–	–	–	–	–	–	0	–	–	–	–	–	0
Train [French]	–	–	–	–	–	–	–	–	–	–	–	0	–	–	–	–	0
#7																	
Trumpet [English]	–	0	–	–	–	–	–	–	–	–	–	–	–	–	–	–	0
Power [English]	–	0	–	–	–	–	–	–	–	0	–	–	–	–	–	–	0
Lord [English]	–	–	–	–	0	–	–	0	–	–	–	–	–	–	–	–	0
Attendant [English]	–	–	–	–	–	–	–	–	–	0	–	–	–	–	–	–	0
Servant [King John]	–	–	–	–	–	–	–	–	–	–	–	–	–	–	–	0	0
#8																	
Power [English]	–	0	–	–	–	–	–	–	–	0	–	–	–	–	–	–	0
Lord [English]	–	–	–	–	0	–	–	0	–	–	–	–	–	–	–	–	0
Attendant [English]	–	–	–	–	–	–	–	–	–	0	–	–	–	–	–	–	0
Servant [King John]	–	–	–	–	–	–	–	–	–	–	–	–	–	–	–	0	0
#9																	
Power [English]	–	0	–	–	–	–	–	–	–	0	–	–	–	–	–	–	0
Lord [English]	–	–	–	–	0	–	–	0	–	–	–	–	–	–	–	–	0
Attendant [English]	–	–	–	–	–	–	–	–	0	–	–	–	–	–	–	–	0

Total Lines Minor Parts   68= 3%
Principal Parts   2,572=97%
2,640

Table 49
The Merchant of Venice (Q1-1600)
Principal Parts

Men

	1			2									3					4		5	Totals
	1	2	3	1	2	3	4	5	6	7	8	9	1	2	3	4	5	1	2	1	
#1 Shylock-Jew	-	-	126	-	-	-	-	38	-	-	-	-	56	-	16	-	-	99	-	-	335
#2 Bassanio	47	-	14	-	37	-	-	-	-	-	-	-	-	140	-	-	-	50	-	41	329
#3 Anthonio	46	-	39	-	-	-	-	-	6	-	-	-	-	-	19	-	-	66	-	12	188
#4 Lorenzo	6	-	-	-	-	-	25	-	20	-	-	-	-	5	-	12	30	-	-	76	174
#5 Gratiano	34	-	-	-	17	-	3	-	20	-	-	-	-	29	-	-	-	27	5	34	169
#6 Clowne-Launcelot	-	-	-	-	95	4	5	14	-	-	-	-	-	-	-	-	23	-	-	6	147
#7 Salaryno-Salerio	30	-	-	-	-	-	5	-	3	-	34	-	16	16	4	-	-	-	-	-	108
#8 Morochus	-	-	-	32	-	-	-	-	-	71	-	-	-	-	-	-	-	-	-	-	103
Duke	-	-	-	-	-	-	-	-	-	-	-	-	-	-	-	-	-	68	-	-	68
#9 Old Gobbo	-	-	-	-	35	-	-	-	-	-	-	-	-	-	-	-	-	-	-	-	35
Arragon	-	-	-	-	-	-	-	-	-	-	-	65	-	-	-	-	-	-	-	-	65
#10 Salanio	22	-	-	-	-	-	3	-	-	-	21	-	16	-	-	-	-	-	-	-	62

Boys

	1			2									3					4		5	Totals
	1	2	3	1	2	3	4	5	6	7	8	9	1	2	3	4	5	1	2	1	
#1 Portia	-	71	-	17	-	-	-	-	-	9	-	20	-	114	-	70	-	136	12	108	557
#2 Jessica	-	-	-	-	-	16	-	18	4	-	-	-	-	7	-	1	26	-	-	14	86
#3 Nerissa	-	36	-	0	-	-	-	-	-	-	-	6	-	5	-	2	-	5	4	25	83

Total Lines Principal Parts 2,509

Minor Parts

Men

	Lines
#1	
Servingman	4
Tuball	13
Man–Balthazar	1
#2	
Leonardo	1
Messenger	11
Man [Anthonio]	2
#3	
Serviture	0
Jaylor	0
Messenger	8
#4	
Follower [Morochus]	0
Train [Arragon]	0
Magnifico [Duke]	0
Follower [Bassanio]	0
#5	
Follower [Morochus]	0
Train [Arragon]	0
Magnifico [Duke]	0
Follower [Bassanio]	0
#6	
Follower [Morochus]	0
Train [Arragon]	0
Magnifico [Duke]	0

Boys

	Lines
#1	
Train [Portia]	0
#2	
Train [Portia]	0
#3	
Train [Portia]	0

Total Lines Minor Parts 40= 2%
Principal Parts 2,509=98%
2,549

Table 50

The First Part of King Henry the Fourth (Q1-1598)

Principal Parts

Men

	1			2				3			4				5					Totals
	1	2	3	1	2	3	4	1	2	3	1	2	3	4	1	2	3	4	5	
#1 Sir John Falstaffe	-	71	-	-	50	-	198	-	-	101	-	53	-	-	16	-	19	34	-	542
#2 Hotspur	-	-	161	-	-	62	-	101	-	-	77	-	73	-	-	39	9	16	-	538
#3 Prince of Wales	-	79	-	-	24	-	194	-	44	38	-	7	-	-	29	-	8	76	15	514
#4 King	75	-	44	-	-	-	-	-	130	-	-	-	-	-	47	-	0	17	25	338
#5 Worcester	-	-	62	-	-	-	-	16	-	-	22	-	4	-	47	34	-	-	3	188
#6 Glendower	-	-	-	-	-	-	-	77	-	-	-	-	-	-	-	-	-	-	-	77
Archbishop of York	-	-	-	-	-	-	-	-	-	-	-	-	-	34	-	-	-	-	-	34
#7 Poines	-	40	-	-	9	-	20	-	-	-	-	-	-	-	-	-	-	-	-	69
Vernon	-	-	-	-	-	-	-	-	-	-	25	-	19	-	-	20	-	-	0	64
#8 Mortimer	-	-	-	-	-	-	-	58	-	-	-	-	-	-	-	-	-	-	-	58
Douglas	-	-	-	-	-	-	-	-	-	-	12	-	4	-	-	4	15	8	-	43
#9 Westmerland	32	-	-	-	-	-	-	-	-	-	-	6	-	-	0	-	-	1	0	39
Gadshill-Ross	-	-	33	33	6	-	4	-	-	-	-	-	-	-	-	-	-	-	-	43
#10 Blunt	-	-	7	-	-	-	-	-	7	-	-	-	20	-	-	-	6	-	-	40
#11 Northumberland	-	-	33	-	-	-	-	-	-	-	-	-	-	-	0	-	-	-	-	33
Bardolph	-	-	-	-	3	-	11	-	-	9	-	3	-	-	-	-	-	-	-	26

Boys

	1			2				3			4				5					Totals
	1	2	3	1	2	3	4	1	2	3	1	2	3	4	1	2	3	4	5	
#1 Lady Percy	-	-	-	-	-	43	-	8	-	-	-	-	-	-	-	-	-	-	-	51
#2 Hostess	-	-	-	-	-	-	11	-	-	32	-	-	-	-	-	-	-	-	-	43
#3 Lady Mortimer	-	-	-	-	-	-	-	*	-	-	-	-	-	-	-	-	-	-	-	*

Total Lines Principal Parts 2,740

* Q1 notes that Lady Mortimer 'speaks in Welsh' but does not give her words.

Minor Parts

Men

	Totals
#1	
1 Carrier	16
Messenger	6
#2	
2 Carrier	15
Drawer-Francis	15
#3	
Chamberlaine	16
Sir Michael	7
#4	
John of Lancaster	8
Travailer	2
Vintner	3
#5	
Ostler	1
Sheriffe	8
Another Messenger	6
#6	
Other [King]	0
Peto	9
Power [King]	0
#7	
Other [King]	0
Servant	3
Power [King]	0
#8	
Other [King]	0
Travailer	2
Power [King]	0

Total Lines Minor Parts 117 = 4%
Principal Parts 2,740 = 96%
2,857

Table 51

The Second Part of King Henry the Fourth (Q-1600)

Principal Parts

Men

#	Role	I	I.1	I.2	I.3	II.1	II.2	II.3	II.4	III.1	III.2	IV.1	IV.2	IV.3	IV.4	IV.5	V.1	V.2	V.3	V.4	V.5	E	Totals
#1	Sir John Falstaffe	–	–	138	–	89	–	–	84	–	79	–	–	43	–	–	30	–	24	–	38	–	525
#2	Prince-Harry-King	–	–	–	–	–	84	–	35	–	–	–	–	–	–	79	–	69	–	–	26	–	293
#3	King [H4]	–	–	–	–	–	–	–	–	80	–	–	–	–	76	135	–	–	–	–	–	–	291
#4	Shallow	–	–	–	–	–	–	–	–	–	143	–	–	–	–	–	21	–	30	–	11	–	205
#5	Lord Chiefe Justice	–	–	36	–	45	–	–	–	–	–	–	–	–	–	–	–	50	–	–	7	–	138
#6	Earle Northumberland	–	87	–	–	–	–	19	–	–	–	–	–	–	–	–	–	–	–	–	–	–	106
	Westmerland	–	–	–	–	–	–	–	–	–	–	60	17	–	–	–	–	1	–	–	11	–	89
#7	Archbishop	–	–	–	10	–	–	–	–	–	–	65	28	–	–	–	–	–	–	–	–	–	103
	Pistol	–	–	–	–	–	–	–	32	–	–	–	–	–	–	–	–	–	22	–	16	–	70
#8	Rumour	40	–	–	–	–	–	–	–	–	–	–	–	–	–	–	–	–	–	–	–	–	40
	Prince John	–	–	–	–	–	–	–	–	–	–	68	22	–	–	–	–	6	–	–	1	–	97
#9	Lord Bardolfe	–	41	–	22	–	–	–	–	–	–	–	–	–	–	–	–	–	–	–	–	–	63
	Silence	–	–	–	–	–	–	–	–	–	16	–	–	–	–	–	0	–	18	–	–	–	34
#10	Mowbray-Marshal	–	–	–	5	–	–	–	–	–	–	23	8	–	–	–	–	–	–	–	–	–	36
	Poynes	–	–	–	–	–	49	–	10	–	–	–	–	–	–	–	–	–	–	–	–	–	59
	Davy	–	–	–	–	–	–	–	–	–	–	–	–	–	–	–	21	–	8	–	–	–	29
#11	Lord Hastings	–	–	–	27	–	–	–	–	–	–	10	16	–	–	–	–	–	–	–	–	–	53
	Warwike	–	–	–	–	–	–	–	–	13	–	–	–	–	18	13	–	31	–	–	–	–	75
#12	Morton	–	43	–	–	–	–	–	–	–	–	–	–	–	–	–	–	–	–	–	–	–	43
	Bardolfe	–	–	–	–	1	10	–	6	–	20	–	–	–	–	–	0	–	1	–	5	–	43

Boys

#	Role	I	I.1	I.2	I.3	II.1	II.2	II.3	II.4	III.1	III.2	IV.1	IV.2	IV.3	IV.4	IV.5	V.1	V.2	V.3	V.4	V.5	E	Totals
#1	Hostesse-Mrs.Quickly	–	–	–	–	67	–	–	65	–	–	–	–	–	–	–	–	–	–	10	–	–	142
#2	Doll Tere-sheet	–	–	–	–	–	–	–	48	–	–	–	–	–	–	–	–	–	–	10	–	–	58
#3	Page-Boy	–	–	12	–	–	2	–	13	–	–	–	–	–	–	–	2	–	0	–	0	–	29
	Kate	–	–	–	–	–	–	23	–	–	–	–	–	–	–	–	–	–	–	–	–	–	23
	Epilogue	–	–	–	–	–	–	–	–	–	–	–	–	–	–	–	–	–	–	–	–	29	29

Total Lines Principal Parts 2,673

Role	Value
#1	
Gower-Messenger	8
Other	0
Feeble	11
Clarence	21
1 Strewer	1
#2	
Servant	11
Drawer	9
Bul-calfe	10
Colevile	9
#3 Sinklo	
Porter	4
Peyto	6
Harcourt	8
Beadle	9
#4	
Travers	15
Phang	8
Francis	10
Messenger	4
2 Strewer	1
#5	
Snare	3
Will-Drawer	2
Mouldy	11
Gloucester	15
3 Strewer	2
#6	
Man [Lord]	0
Musician	0
John Blunt	0
Shadow	2
Army [John]	0
Officer	0
Train [King]	0
#7	
Man [Lord]	0
Musician	0
Surry	0
Wart	2
Army [John]	0
Officer	0
Train [King]	0

Table 51 (*cont.*)

#8
Fauconbridge
Sir John Russel
One
Army [John]
Kent
Officer
Train [King]

#1
Wife
Boy

Total Lines Minor Parts   188= 7%
Principal Parts   2,673=93%
      2,861

Table 52

The Second Part of King Henry the Fourth (F)

Principal Parts

	I	1.1	1.2	1.3	2.1	2.2	2.3	2.4	3.1	3.2	4.1	4.2	4.3	4.4	4.5	5.1	5.2	5.3	5.4	5.5	E	Totals
Men																						
#1 Falstaffe	–	–	148	–	46	–	–	111	–	95	–	–	89	–	–	27	–	33	–	33	–	582
#2 King [H4]	–	–	–	–	–	–	–	–	76	–	–	–	–	82	145	–	–	–	–	–	–	303
#3 Prince-King	–	–	–	–	–	81	–	36	–	–	–	–	–	–	84	–	69	–	–	27	–	297
#4 Shallow	–	–	–	–	–	–	–	–	–	127	–	–	–	–	–	34	–	33	–	10	–	204
#5 Chiefe Justice	–	–	77	–	35	–	–	–	–	–	–	–	–	–	–	–	50	–	–	8	–	170
#6 Northumberland	–	87	–	–	–	–	12	–	–	–	–	–	–	–	–	–	–	–	–	–	–	99
Westmerland	–	–	–	–	–	–	–	–	–	–	80	18	13	–	–	–	–	–	–	–	–	111
#7 Archbishop	–	–	–	33	–	–	–	–	–	–	80	25	–	–	–	–	–	–	–	–	–	138
Pistol	–	–	–	–	–	–	–	35	–	–	–	–	–	–	–	–	–	29	–	15	–	79
#8 Rumour	40	–	–	–	–	–	–	–	–	–	–	–	–	–	–	–	–	–	–	–	–	40
Prince John	–	–	–	–	–	–	–	–	–	–	–	69	23	–	–	–	–	–	–	21	–	113
#9 Lord Bardolfe	–	41	–	46	–	–	–	–	–	–	–	–	–	–	–	–	–	–	–	–	–	87
Silence	–	–	–	–	–	–	–	–	–	15	–	–	–	–	–	–	–	23	–	–	–	38
#10 Mowbray-Marshal	–	–	–	6	–	–	–	–	–	–	41	7	–	–	–	–	–	–	–	–	–	54
Pointz	–	–	–	–	–	58	–	11	–	–	–	–	–	–	–	–	–	–	–	–	–	69
Davy	–	–	–	–	–	–	–	–	–	–	–	–	–	–	–	27	–	10	–	–	–	37
#11 Hastings	–	–	–	28	–	–	–	–	–	–	13	14	–	–	–	–	–	–	–	–	–	55
Warwick	–	–	–	–	–	–	–	–	31	–	–	–	–	20	15	–	18	–	–	–	–	84
#12 Morton	–	78	–	–	–	–	–	–	–	–	–	–	–	–	–	–	–	–	–	–	–	78
Bardolfe	–	–	–	–	–	10	–	10	–	20	–	–	–	–	–	10	–	5	–	0	–	55
Boys																						
#1 Hostess	–	–	–	–	74	–	–	79	–	–	–	–	–	–	–	–	–	–	10	–	–	163
#2 Dol	–	–	–	–	–	–	–	69	–	–	–	–	–	–	–	–	–	–	14	–	–	83
#3 Page-Boy	–	–	25	–	2	14	–	2	–	–	–	–	–	–	–	0	–	0	–	–	–	43
#4 Lady	–	–	–	–	–	–	46	–	–	–	–	–	–	–	–	–	–	–	–	–	–	46
Epilogue	–	–	–	–	–	–	–	–	–	–	–	–	–	–	–	–	–	–	–	–	26	26
Total Lines Principal Parts																						3,054

Table 52 (*cont.*)

Minor Parts

Men

Part											Total
#1											
Travers	15	–	–	–	–	–	–	–	–	–	15
1 Drawer	–	–	10	–	–	–	–	–	–	–	10
Bull-calfe	–	–	–	13	–	–	–	–	–	–	13
Clarence	–	–	–	–	15	–	6	2	–	0	23
#2											
Porter	4	–	–	–	–	–	–	–	–	–	4
2 Drawer	–	–	11	–	–	–	–	–	–	–	11
Wart	–	–	–	2	–	–	–	–	–	–	2
Colevile	–	–	–	–	9	–	–	–	–	–	9
1 Groom	–	–	–	–	–	–	–	–	–	3	3
#3											
Servant	–	4	–	–	–	–	–	–	–	–	4
Gower-Messenger	–	6	–	–	–	–	–	–	–	–	6
Musician	–	–	–	–	–	–	–	–	–	0	0
Feeble	–	–	–	12	–	–	–	–	0	–	12
2 Groom	–	–	–	–	–	–	–	–	–	1	1
#4											
Fang	–	7	–	–	–	–	–	–	–	–	7
Peto	–	–	6	–	–	–	–	–	–	–	6
Messenger	–	–	–	–	–	4	–	–	–	0	4
Gloucester	–	–	–	–	10	4	3	–	–	–	17
#5											
Musician	–	–	0	–	–	–	–	–	–	–	0
Shadow	–	–	–	2	–	–	–	–	–	–	2
Harcourt	–	–	–	–	8	–	–	–	–	–	8
Officer	–	–	–	–	–	–	–	10	–	–	10
#6											
Snare	–	2	–	–	–	–	–	–	–	–	2
Surrey	–	–	–	0	–	–	–	–	–	–	0
Mouldie	–	–	–	12	–	–	–	–	–	–	12
Beadle	–	–	–	–	–	–	–	0	–	–	0

Boy

Part											Total
#1											
Wife [Percy]	5	–	–	–	–	–	–	–	–	–	5
Page [King]	5	–	–	0	–	–	–	–	–	–	0

Total Lines Minor Parts 186 = 6%

Principal Parts 3,054 = 94%

3,240

Table 53   193

Table 53
Much Ado about Nothing (Q-1600)

Principal Parts
Men

	1			2			3					4		5				Totals
	1	2	3	1	2	3	1	2	3	4	5	1	2	1	2	3	4	
#1 Benedick	79	-	-	76	-	72	-	10	-	-	-	48	-	21	50	-	43	399
#2 Leonato	29	10	-	34	-	45	-	4	-	-	13	66	-	108	-	-	27	336
#3 Prince-Pedro	59	-	-	59	-	58	-	43	-	-	-	12	-	60	-	7	6	304
#4 Claudio	38	-	-	27	-	35	-	30	-	-	-	57	-	53	-	12	20	272
#5 Kemp Constable-Dogberry	-	-	-	-	-	-	-	-	60	-	36	WK 44	28	-	-	-	-	168
#6 Borachio	-	-	13	4	32	-	-	-	44	-	-	-	3	19	-	-	-	115
#7 John-Bastard	2	-	34	10	15	-	-	31	-	-	-	8	-	-	-	-	-	100
#8 Messenger	25	-	-	-	-	-	-	-	-	-	-	-	-	-	-	-	-	25
Friar-Francisco	-	-	-	-	-	-	-	-	-	-	-	72	-	-	-	-	9	81
#9 Old Man-Brother-Anthonio	-	12	-	7	-	-	-	-	-	-	-	-	-	32	-	-	2	53
#10 Conrad	-	-	12	-	-	-	-	-	18	-	-	-	RC 2	0	-	-	-	32
#11 Cowley Verges-Headborough	-	-	-	-	-	-	-	-	13	-	8	-	5	2	-	-	-	28

Boys

	1			2			3					4		5				Totals
#1 Beatrice	47	-	-	101	-	8	10	-	-	16	-	50	-	-	20	-	10	262
#2 Hero	1	-	-	10	-	-	78	-	-	17	-	18	-	-	-	-	8	132
#3 Margaret	-	-	-	6	-	-	1	-	-	48	-	-	-	-	10	-	0	65
#4 Ursala	-	-	-	9	-	-	30	-	-	5	-	-	-	-	5	-	0	49

Total Lines Principal Parts 2,421

Minor Parts
Men

	1			2			3					4		5				Totals
#1 Balthazar	0	-	-	2	-	10	-	-	-	-	-	-	-	-	-	-	-	12
Sexton	-	-	-	-	-	-	-	-	-	-	-	14	0	-	-	-	-	14
Lord	-	-	-	-	-	-	-	-	-	-	-	-	-	-	3	-	-	3
Other	-	-	-	-	-	-	-	-	-	-	-	-	-	-	-	-	0	0
#2 1 Watch	-	-	-	-	-	-	-	9	-	-	-	6	0	-	-	-	-	15
Lord	-	-	-	-	-	-	-	-	-	-	-	-	-	0	-	-	-	0
Other	-	-	-	-	-	-	-	-	-	-	-	-	-	-	-	-	0	0
#3 2 Watch	-	-	-	-	-	-	-	-	12	-	-	-	2	0	-	-	-	14
Lord	-	-	-	-	-	-	-	-	-	-	-	-	-	0	-	-	-	0
Messenger	-	-	-	-	-	-	-	-	-	-	2	-	-	-	-	-	2	4
#4 Lord	-	-	-	-	-	-	-	-	-	-	-	-	-	0	-	-	-	0
Other	-	-	-	-	-	-	-	-	-	-	-	-	-	-	-	-	0	0

Boy

	1			2			3					4		5				Totals
#1 Innogen-Wife	0	-	-	0	-	-	-	-	-	-	-	-	-	-	-	-	-	0
Boy	-	-	-	-	-	2	-	-	-	-	-	-	-	-	-	-	-	2

Total Lines Minor Parts 64= 3%
Principal Parts 2,421=97%
2,485

Table 54
King Henry the Fifth (Q1-1600)
Principal Parts

Men

	1.2	2.1	2.2	2.3	2.4	3.2	3.4	3.5	3.6	3.7	4.1	4.3	4.4	4.7	4.8	5.1	5.2	Totals
#1 King Henry	89	–	77	–	–	11	–	–	39	–	65	77	9	45	43	–	94	549
#2 Flewellen	–	–	–	–	–	52	–	–	11	–	8	–	–	65	26	35	–	197
#3 Pistoll	–	31	–	4	–	19	–	–	16	–	9	–	13	1	–	21	–	114
#4 Bishop	106	–	–	–	–	–	–	–	–	–	–	–	–	–	–	–	–	106
Gower	–	–	–	–	–	21	–	–	3	–	2	–	–	15	0	3	–	44
#5 Exeter	10	–	0	–	49	–	–	–	1	–	–	25	–	–	5	–	10	100
#6 Masham	–	–	14	–	–	–	–	–	–	–	–	–	–	–	–	–	–	14
Constable	–	–	–	–	8	–	–	13	–	26	8	–	–	–	–	–	–	55
#7 King of France	–	–	–	–	12	–	–	5	–	–	–	–	–	–	–	–	15	32
2 Souldier	–	–	–	–	–	–	–	–	–	–	23	–	–	–	–	–	–	23
#8 1 Ambassador	14	–	–	–	–	–	–	–	–	–	–	–	–	–	–	–	–	14
Bourbon	–	–	–	–	0	–	–	4	–	18	6	–	4	–	–	–	–	32
#9 Nim	–	20	–	6	–	4	–	–	–	–	–	–	–	–	–	–	–	30
1 Souldier	–	–	–	–	–	–	–	–	–	–	1	–	–	6	18	–	–	25

Boys

	1.2	2.1	2.2	2.3	2.4	3.2	3.4	3.5	3.6	3.7	4.1	4.3	4.4	4.7	4.8	5.1	5.2	Totals
#1 Hostes Quickly	–	14	–	24	–	–	–	–	–	–	–	–	–	–	–	–	–	38
#2 Katherine	–	–	–	–	–	–	18	–	–	–	–	–	–	–	–	–	14	32
#3 Boy	–	4	–	5	–	12	–	–	–	–	–	–	8	–	–	–	–	29
#4 Allice-Gentlewoman	–	–	–	–	–	–	12	–	–	–	–	–	–	–	–	–	4	16

Total Lines Principal Parts 1,450

Minor Parts
Men

#1																						
Gray																						5
French Herauld						15																23
#2																						
Bardolfe	16		4														7					20
Warwick				0															0			7
#3																						
Dolphin			21	1																		22
3 Souldier							12															12
#4																						
2 Bishop	0																					0
Gloster		6			1		2							2								11
#5																						
Lord	7																					7
Cambridge		7																				7
Frenchman									8													8
#6																						
Other[French]			0															0				0
Governor				7					1													7
Orleans					14		0															15
Epinghamn							0															0
#7																						
2 Ambassador	0																					0
Other[French]		0																0				0
Messenger					3											3						4
York													2									2
#8																						
Clarence	0					0							3					0				3
Other[French]		0																				0
#9																						
Attend.[Henry]	0		0				0											0				0
Gebon					1				1													2
#10																						
Attend.[Henry]	0		0				0											0				0
Salisburie													3									3
#11																						
Attend.[Henry]	0						0															0

Total Lines Minor Parts 158=10%
Principal Parts 1,450=90%
1,608

Table 55
King Henry the Fifth (F)
Principal Parts

Men

#	Character	P	1.1	1.2	1.C	2.1	2.2	2.3	2.4	2.C	3.1	3.2	3.3	3.4	3.5	3.6	3.7	3.C	4.1	4.2	4.3	4.4	4.5	4.6	4.7	4.8	4.C	5.1	5.2	5.C	Totals
#1	King Henry	-	-	120	-	-	137	-	-	-	35	-	51	-	-	35	-	-	202	-	98	-	-	12	65	60	-	-	241	-	1,056
#2	Fluellen	-	-	-	-	-	-	-	-	-	-	2	-	-	-	43	-	-	59	-	-	-	-	-	74	40	-	48	-	-	281
#3	Bishop of Canterbury	-	84	141	-	-	-	-	-	-	-	-	-	-	-	-	-	-	-	-	-	-	-	-	-	-	-	-	-	-	225
	Gower	-	-	-	-	-	-	-	-	-	-	-	-	-	-	14	-	-	1	-	-	-	-	-	46	-	-	7	-	-	68
#4	Prologue	34	-	-	-	-	-	-	-	-	-	-	-	-	-	-	-	-	-	-	-	-	-	-	-	-	-	-	-	-	34
	Chorus	-	-	-	42	-	-	-	-	35	-	-	-	-	-	-	-	53	-	-	-	-	-	-	-	-	46	-	-	14	190
#5	Pistoll	-	-	-	-	11	-	16	-	-	-	40	-	-	-	18	-	-	13	-	-	27	-	-	-	-	-	22	-	-	147
#6	Bishop of Ely	-	20	14	-	-	-	-	-	-	-	-	-	-	-	-	-	-	-	-	-	-	-	-	-	-	-	-	-	-	34
	Dolphin	-	-	-	-	-	-	-	38	-	-	-	-	-	6	-	57	-	-	11	-	-	8	-	-	-	-	-	-	-	120
#7	Exeter	-	-	15	-	-	11	-	47	-	-	-	0	-	-	-	-	-	-	-	1	-	-	27	1	8	-	-	1	-	111
#8	Constable	-	-	-	-	-	-	-	18	-	-	-	-	-	12	-	35	-	-	31	-	-	4	-	-	-	-	-	-	-	100
	Bourgogne	-	-	-	-	-	-	-	-	-	-	-	-	-	-	-	-	-	-	-	-	-	-	-	-	-	-	-	68	-	68
#9	French King	-	-	-	-	-	-	-	28	-	-	-	-	-	40	-	-	-	-	-	-	-	-	-	-	-	-	-	28	-	96
	Orleance	-	-	-	-	-	-	-	-	-	-	-	-	-	-	-	40	-	-	4	-	-	5	-	-	-	-	-	-	-	49
#10	Bardolfe	-	-	-	-	25	-	6	-	-	-	1	-	-	-	-	-	-	-	-	-	-	-	-	-	-	-	-	-	-	32
	Williams	-	-	-	-	-	-	-	-	-	-	-	-	-	-	-	-	-	37	-	-	-	-	-	11	8	-	-	-	-	56
#11	Nym	-	-	-	-	34	-	6	-	-	-	4	-	-	-	-	-	-	-	-	-	-	-	-	-	-	-	-	-	-	44
	Mountjoy	-	-	-	-	-	-	-	-	-	-	-	-	-	-	24	-	-	-	-	13	-	-	-	0	-	-	-	-	-	37

Boys

#	Character	P	1.1	1.2	1.C	2.1	2.2	2.3	2.4	2.C	3.1	3.2	3.3	3.4	3.5	3.6	3.7	3.C	4.1	4.2	4.3	4.4	4.5	4.6	4.7	4.8	4.C	5.1	5.2	5.C	Totals
#1	Boy	-	-	-	-	8	-	4	-	-	-	30	-	-	-	-	-	-	-	-	-	38	-	-	-	-	-	-	-	-	80
#2	Katherine	-	-	-	-	-	-	-	-	-	-	-	-	35	-	-	-	-	-	-	-	-	-	-	-	-	-	-	24	-	59
#3	Quickly	-	-	-	-	15	-	24	-	-	-	-	-	-	-	-	-	-	-	-	-	-	-	-	-	-	-	-	-	-	39
#4	Gentlewoman	-	-	-	-	-	-	-	-	-	-	-	-	19	-	-	-	-	-	-	-	-	-	-	-	-	-	-	7	-	26
#5	Queen Isabel	-	-	-	-	-	-	-	-	-	-	-	-	-	-	-	-	-	-	-	-	-	-	-	-	-	-	-	24	-	24

Total Lines Principal Parts 2,976

Minor Parts
Men

Part		Value
#1		
Ambassador	–	14
Makmorrice	–	19
Messenger	–	5
Salisbury	–	9
#2		
Other [French]	–	0
Graundpree	–	18
Herald	–	14
#3		
Ambassador	–	0
Court	–	2
Beaumont	–	0
French Soldier	–	15
#4		
Cambridge	–	15
Other [French]	–	0
Erpingham	–	8
#5		
Westmerland	–	17
Governor	–	7
Bates	–	18
#6		
Scroope	–	11
Berry	–	0
Other [French]	–	0
#7		
Bedford	–	10
Messenger	–	2
Jamy	–	11
Bourbon	–	7
#8		
Britaine	–	9
Drum [English]	–	0
Ramburs	–	0
Prisoner	–	0
#9		
Gloucester	–	2
Gray	–	9
Colors [English]	–	0
Prisoner	–	0

Table 55 (*cont.*)

#10																									
Clarence	–	–	–	–	–	–	–	–	0	–	–	–	–	–	–	–	–	0	–	–	0	–	–	0	0
Traine[English]	–	–	0	–	–	0	–	–	–	0	–	–	–	–	–	–	0	–	–	0	–	–	–	–	0
Soldier[English]	–	–	–	–	0	–	0	–	–	–	–	–	–	–	–	–	–	–	–	–	–	–	–	–	0
Hoast[English]	–	–	–	–	–	–	–	–	–	–	–	–	–	–	–	–	–	–	–	–	–	–	–	–	0
#11																									
Warwick	–	–	–	–	–	–	–	–	0	–	–	–	–	–	–	–	–	0	–	–	0	–	–	1	1
Traine[English]	–	–	0	–	–	0	–	–	–	1	–	–	–	–	–	–	0	–	–	0	–	–	–	–	0
Soldier[English]	–	–	–	–	0	–	0	–	–	–	–	–	–	–	–	–	–	–	–	–	–	–	–	–	0
Hoast[English]	–	–	–	–	–	–	–	–	–	–	–	–	–	–	–	–	–	–	–	–	–	–	–	–	0
#12																									
Traine[English]	–	–	0	–	–	0	–	–	–	0	–	–	–	–	–	–	0	–	–	0	–	–	–	–	0
Soldier[English]	–	–	–	–	0	–	0	–	–	–	–	–	–	–	–	–	–	–	–	–	–	–	–	–	0

Total Lines Minor Parts 223= 7%
Principal Parts 2,976=93%
3,199

Table 56
Julius Caesar (F)
Principal Parts

	1	1 / 2	3	1	2 / 2	3 / 1	3 / 2	3	4 / 2	3 / 1	1	3	1	2	5 / 3	4	5	Totals
Men																		
#1 Brutus	–	78	–	182	3	–	80	49	–	–	37	208	34	6	18	3	40	738
#2 Cassius	–	145	97	39	–	–	44	0	–	–	9	99	49	–	31	–	–	513
#3 Antony	–	6	–	–	1	–	129	148	–	38	–	23	–	–	–	8	8	361
#4 Caesar–Ghost	–	39	–	–	74	–	39	–	–	–	–	3	–	–	–	–	–	155
#5 Caska	–	65	60	10	0	–	4	–	–	–	–	–	–	–	–	–	–	139
Messala	–	–	–	–	–	–	–	–	–	12	–	2	–	0	19	0	4	37
#6 Decius	–	0	–	13	25	–	2	–	–	–	–	–	–	–	–	–	–	40
Octavius	–	–	–	–	–	–	–	12	–	–	–	–	26	–	–	–	10	48
#7 Murellus	33	0	–	–	–	–	–	–	–	–	–	–	–	–	–	–	–	33
1 Plebeian	–	–	–	–	–	–	20	4	–	–	–	–	–	–	–	–	–	24
Lucillius	–	–	–	–	–	–	–	–	–	10	–	1	–	–	12	–	2	25
#8 Flavius	28	0	–	–	–	–	–	–	–	–	–	–	–	–	–	0	–	28
2 Plebeian	–	–	–	–	–	–	20	6	–	–	–	–	–	–	–	–	–	26
Titinius	–	–	–	–	–	–	–	–	–	0	1	–	–	–	31	–	–	32
#9 Cinna	–	–	11	4	0	–	10	–	–	–	–	–	–	–	–	–	–	25
Pindarus	–	–	–	–	–	–	–	–	–	3	–	–	–	–	15	–	–	18
Clitus	–	–	–	–	–	–	–	–	–	–	–	–	–	–	–	–	10	10
Boys																		
#1 Portia	0	–	32	62	–	–	–	–	–	–	–	–	–	–	–	–	–	94
#2 Lucius	–	–	6	17	–	–	–	–	–	–	–	11	–	–	–	–	–	34
#3 Calphurnia	–	1	26	–	–	–	–	–	–	–	–	–	–	–	–	–	–	27

Total Lines Principal Parts 2,407

Table 56 (*cont.*)

Minor Parts

Men

Minor Parts											Men
#1											
Cobler	16	—	—	—	—	—	—	—	—	—	16
Ligarius	—	—	15	0	—	—	—	—	—	—	15
3 Plebeian	—	—	—	—	15	—	6	—	—	—	21
Messenger	—	—	—	—	—	—	—	4	—	—	4
#2											
Soothsayer	3	—	—	15	1	—	—	—	—	—	19
4 Plebeian	—	—	—	—	13	7	—	—	—	—	20
Varrus	—	—	—	—	—	—	—	—	5	—	5
Volumnius	—	—	—	—	—	—	—	—	—	3	3
#3											
Trebonius	—	—	3	—	3	—	—	—	2	—	8
Claudio	—	—	—	2	—	—	—	—	—	—	2
1 Soldier	—	—	—	—	—	—	—	—	—	4	4
#4											
Carpenter	1	—	—	—	—	—	—	—	—	—	1
Metellus	—	—	9	0	8	—	—	—	—	1	17
2 Soldier	—	—	—	—	—	—	—	—	—	1	1
#5											
Servant [Antony]	—	—	—	—	16	4	—	—	—	—	20
Cinna the Poet	—	—	—	—	—	—	14	—	—	—	14
Poet	—	—	—	—	—	—	—	—	7	—	7
Dardanius	—	—	—	—	—	—	—	—	—	3	3
#6											
Commoner	0	—	—	—	—	—	—	—	—	—	0
Artemidorus	—	—	—	14	4	—	—	—	—	—	18
Army [Brutus]	—	—	—	—	—	—	—	0	0	0	0
Strato	—	—	—	—	—	—	—	—	0	7	7
#7											
Commoner	0	—	—	—	—	—	—	—	—	—	0
Servant [Caesar]	—	—	—	5	0	—	—	—	—	—	5
Lepidus	—	—	—	—	—	4	—	0	0	—	4
Army [Brutus]	—	—	—	—	—	—	—	—	0	0	0
#8											
Commoner	0	—	—	—	—	—	—	—	—	—	0
Publius	—	—	—	1	1	—	—	—	—	—	2
Army [Brutus]	—	—	—	—	—	—	—	—	3	—	0
Young Cato	—	—	—	—	—	—	—	—	5	—	8
#9											
Popillius	—	—	—	—	2	—	—	—	—	1	2
Power [Cassius]	—	—	—	—	—	—	—	—	0	—	0
Army [Octavius]	—	—	—	—	—	—	—	0	—	0	0

#10																	
Cicero	–	0	–	9	–	–	–	–	–	–	0	–	–	–	–	–	9
Power [Cassius]	–	–	–	–	–	–	–	–	–	–	0	–	–	–	–	–	0
Army [Octavius]	–	–	–	–	–	–	–	–	–	–	–	0	–	–	–	0	0
#11																	
Servant [Octavius]	–	–	–	–	5	–	–	–	–	–	–	–	–	–	–	–	5
Power [Cassius]	–	–	–	–	–	–	–	–	–	0	–	–	–	–	0	–	0
Flavius	–	–	–	–	–	–	–	–	–	–	–	–	–	0	–	–	0
Army [Octavius]	–	–	–	–	–	–	–	–	–	–	–	0	–	–	–	–	0

Total Lines Minor Parts 240 = 9%
Principal Parts 2,407 = 91%
2,647

Table 57
As You Like It (F)
Principal Parts

Men

	1			2							3					4			5				Totals
	1	**2**	**3**	**1**	**2**	**3**	**4**	**5**	**6**	**7**	**1**	**2**	**3**	**4**	**5**	**1**	**2**	**3**	**1**	**2**	**3**	**4**	
#1 Orlando	60	37	–	–	–	23	–	–	17	32	–	60	–	–	–	25	–	–	–	39	–	11	304
#2 Clowne	–	24	–	–	–	–	22	–	–	–	–	65	62	–	–	–	–	–	45	–	8	47	273
#3 Jaques	–	–	–	–	–	–	–	25	–	100	–	20	14	–	–	5	17	–	–	–	–	33	214
#4 Oliver	58	–	–	–	–	–	–	–	–	–	2	–	–	–	–	–	–	81	–	9	–	0	150
#5 Duke Senior	–	–	–	28	–	–	–	–	–	52	–	–	–	–	–	–	–	–	–	–	–	29	109
#6 Le Beau	–	50	–	–	–	–	–	–	–	–	–	–	–	–	–	–	–	–	–	–	–	–	50
Corin	–	–	–	–	–	–	27	–	–	–	–	40	–	10	–	–	–	2	–	–	–	–	79
#7 Charles	35	5	–	–	–	–	–	–	–	–	–	–	–	–	–	–	–	–	–	–	–	–	40
Silvius	–	–	–	–	–	–	19	–	–	–	–	–	–	–	29	–	–	14	–	12	–	2	76
#8 Duke Frederick	–	22	24	–	8	–	–	–	–	–	16	–	–	–	–	–	–	–	–	–	–	–	70
#9 Adam	5	–	–	–	–	54	–	–	3	2	–	–	–	–	–	–	–	–	–	–	–	–	64
#10 1 Lord[Senior]	–	–	–	39	–	–	–	–	–	3	–	–	–	–	–	–	2	–	–	–	–	–	44

Boys

	1			2							3					4			5				Totals
	1	**2**	**3**	**1**	**2**	**3**	**4**	**5**	**6**	**7**	**1**	**2**	**3**	**4**	**5**	**1**	**2**	**3**	**1**	**2**	**3**	**4**	
#1 Rosalind	–	61	54	–	–	–	25	–	–	–	–	166	–	21	139	72	–	64	–	42	–	42	686
#2 Celia	–	80	64	–	–	–	10	–	–	–	–	48	–	27	–	12	–	22	–	–	–	–	263
#3 Phebe	–	–	–	–	–	–	–	–	–	–	–	–	–	–	72	–	–	8	–	4	–	–	84
#4 Audrey	–	–	–	–	–	–	–	–	–	–	–	–	11	–	–	–	–	–	6	–	3	0	20
																						Total Lines Principal Parts	2,526

Minor Parts

Men

													Total
#1													
Attendant	0	–	–	–	–	–	–	–	–	–	–	–	0
Amyens	–	3	–	13	–	–	–	–	–	–	–	0	16
William	–	–	–	–	–	–	11	–	–	–	–	–	11
#2													
Dennis	3	–	–	–	–	–	–	–	–	–	–	–	3
Martext	–	–	–	–	5	–	–	–	–	–	–	–	5
Hymen	–	–	–	–	–	–	–	–	–	–	16	16
#3													
Attendant	0	–	–	0	–	–	–	–	0	–	–	–	0
2 Lord [Senior]–	–	2	–	–	–	–	–	–	–	–	–	–	2
Other	–	–	–	0	–	–	–	–	–	–	–	–	0
Second Brother	–	–	–	–	–	–	–	–	–	–	17	17
#4													
Attendant	0	–	–	0	–	–	–	–	0	–	–	–	0
Other	–	–	–	–	–	–	–	–	–	–	–	–	0
#5													
1 Lord [Frederick]	0	4	–	–	–	0	–	–	–	–	–	–	4
#6													
2 Lord [Frederick]	0	9	–	–	–	0	–	–	–	–	–	–	9
#7													
Lord [Frederick]	0	0	–	–	–	0	–	–	–	–	–	–	0

Boys

													Total
#1													
1 Page	–	–	–	–	–	–	–	–	–	–	6	6
#2													
2 Page	–	–	–	–	–	–	–	–	–	–	3	3

Total Lines Minor Parts 92 = 4%

Principal Parts 2,526 = 96%

2,618

Table 58
Twelfth Night (F)
Principal Parts

Men

	1.1	1.2	1.3	1.4	1.5	2.1	2.2	2.3	2.4	2.5	3.1	3.2	3.3	3.4	4.1	4.2	4.3	5.1	Totals
#1 Sir Toby	–	–	56	–	7	–	–	53	–	38	5	30	–	119	8	11	–	6	333
#2 Clowne	–	–	–	–	57	–	–	18	19	–	36	–	–	–	17	66	–	50	263
#3 Malvolio	–	10	–	–	32	–	–	18	–	96	–	–	–	40	–	43	–	18	257
#4 Duke Orsino	31	–	–	27	–	–	–	–	69	–	–	–	–	–	–	–	–	92	219
#5 Sir Andrew	–	–	46	–	5	–	–	41	–	12	5	11	–	15	–	–	–	17	152
#6 Sebastian	–	–	–	–	–	31	–	–	–	–	–	–	20	23	17	–	–	32	123
#7 Fabian	–	–	–	–	–	–	–	–	–	29	–	24	–	33	0	–	–	27	113
#8 Captain	–	32	–	–	–	–	–	–	–	–	–	–	–	–	–	–	–	–	32
Antonio	–	–	–	–	–	12	–	–	–	–	–	–	33	33	–	–	–	28	106

Boys

	1.1	1.2	1.3	1.4	1.5	2.1	2.2	2.3	2.4	2.5	3.1	3.2	3.3	3.4	4.1	4.2	4.3	5.1	Totals
#1 Viola	–	34	–	13	39	–	31	–	32	–	35	–	–	50	–	–	–	50	284
#2 Olivia	–	–	–	–	89	–	–	–	–	–	32	–	–	44	16	–	10	66	257
#3 Maria-Gentlewoman	–	–	29	–	21	–	–	34	–	16	15	–	–	27	–	5	–	–	147

Total Lines Principal Parts 2,286

Minor Parts

Men

														Total
#1														
Valentine	9		4											13
1 Officer					12				6					18
#2														
Curio	2		0			5			0					7
Servant[Olivia]					3									3
#3														
Saylor	0													0
Priest							0	8						8
#4														
Saylor	0													0
2 Officer					3				0					3
#5														
Lord[Orsino]	0		0			0								0
#6														
Lord[Orsino]	0		0			0								0
#7														
Lord[Orsino]	0		0			0								0

Boys

	Total
#1	
Attendant[Olivia]	0
#2	
Attendant[Olivia]	0
#3	
Attendant[Olivia]	0

Total Lines Minor Parts 52 = 2%
Principal Parts 2,286=98%
2.338

Table 59

Hamlet (Q1-1603)

Principal Parts

Act →	1					2				3		4			5		
Scene	1	2	3	4	5	1	2	3	4	1-3	4	5	6	7	1	2	Totals
Men																	
#1 Hamlet	-	85	-	42	83	-	219	-	152	16	72	21	-	-	76	53	819
#2 Corambis	-	2	39	-	-	36	96	14	8	-	3	-	-	-	-	-	198
Clowne	-	-	-	-	-	-	-	-	-	-	-	-	-	-	56	-	56
#3 Horatio	71	50	-	15	13	-	-	-	7	-	-	-	23	-	4	14	197
#4 King	-	34	-	-	-	-	22	11	5	2	-	32	35	30	13	9	193
#5 Leartes	-	7	15	-	-	-	-	-	-	-	-	14	-	23	9	20	88
1 Player-King-Duke	-	-	-	-	-	-	20	-	-	24	-	-	-	-	-	-	44
#6 Ghost	0	-	-	0	67	-	-	-	-	-	7	-	-	-	-	-	74
Fortenbrasse	-	-	-	-	-	-	-	-	-	-	-	-	6	-	-	11	17
#7 Marcellus	42	3	-	7	4	-	0	-	-	-	-	-	-	-	-	-	56
2 Player-Lucianus	-	-	-	-	-	-	-	-	-	6	-	-	-	-	-	-	6
#8 Gilderstone	-	-	-	-	-	-	21	5	3	-	3	-	-	-	-	-	32
Bragart	-	-	-	-	-	-	-	-	-	-	-	-	-	-	-	18	18
Boys																	
#1 Ofelia	-	-	17	-	-	24	22	-	10	-	-	-	63	-	-	-	136
#2 Queene	-	2	-	-	-	-	4	5	2	-	28	-	6	13	6	3	88
#3 Boy Player-Queene-Duchess	-	-	-	-	-	-	-	-	0	10	-	-	-	-	-	-	10

Total Lines Principal Parts 2,014

Minor Parts
<u>Men</u>

								Total
#1								
Voltemar	1		21				0	22
2 Clown				9				9
#2								
Rossencraft			9	4	9	0		22
Ambassador [England]							3	3
#3								
2 Centinel	21							21
Priest						6		6
Lord							1	1
#4								
1 Centinel	4							4
Ambassador	0		0					0
Montano		6			3			6
Prologue								3
#5								
Attendant	0							0
Soldier						0		0
Lord							0	0
Train								0
#6								
Attendant	0							0
Soldier						0		0
Lord							0	0
Train								0
#7								
Attendant	0							0
Soldier						0		0
Lord							0	0
Train								0

Total Lines Minor Parts 97 = 5%
Principal Parts 2,032 = 95%
2,129

Table 60
Hamlet (Q2-1604)
Principal Parts
Men

#	Role	1					2		3				4							5		Totals
		1	2	3	4	5	1	2	1	2	3	4	1	2	3	4	5	6	7	1	2	
#1	Hamlet	-	102	-	67	97	-	213	69	197	24	172	-	16	22	47	-	-	-	115	197	1,338
#2	Claudius-King	-	93	-	-	-	-	38	41	6	50	-	34	-	46	-	65	-	135	9	27	544
#3	Polonius	-	4	68	-	-	86	131	23	11	9	7	-	-	-	-	-	-	-	-	-	339
	Clowne	-	-	-	-	-	-	-	-	-	-	-	-	-	-	-	-	-	-	67	-	67
#4	Horatio	100	50	-	26	13	-	-	-	9	-	-	-	-	-	-	3	21	-	10	48	280
#5	Laertes	-	7	52	-	-	-	-	-	-	-	-	-	-	-	-	45	-	45	17	34	200
	1 Player-King	-	-	-	-	-	-	48	-	44	-	-	-	-	-	-	-	-	-	-	-	92
#6	Ghost	0	-	-	-	88	-	-	-	-	-	6	-	-	-	-	-	-	-	-	-	94
	Fortinbras	-	-	-	-	-	-	-	-	-	-	-	-	-	-	8	-	-	-	-	19	27
#7	Rosencrans	-	-	-	-	-	-	20	12	12	14	-	0	8	4	1	-	-	-	-	-	71
	Courtier-Ostrick	-	-	-	-	-	-	-	-	-	-	-	-	-	-	-	-	-	-	-	42	42
#8	Marcellus	44	2	-	8	6	-	-	-	-	-	-	-	-	-	-	-	-	-	-	-	60
	2 Player-Lucianus	-	-	-	-	-	-	-	-	6	-	-	-	-	-	-	-	-	-	-	-	6
#9	Barnardo	33	0	-	-	-	-	-	-	-	-	-	-	-	-	-	-	-	-	-	-	33
	Guildensterne	-	-	-	-	-	-	14	5	18	4	-	0	1	0	-	-	-	-	-	-	42

Boys

#	Role	1					2		3				4							5		Totals
		1	2	3	4	5	1	2	1	2	3	4	1	2	3	4	5	6	7	1	2	
#1	Gertradte-Queene	-	10	-	-	-	-	12	3	8	-	45	14	-	-	-	25	-	21	12	7	157
#2	Ophelia	-	-	20	-	-	28	-	33	15	-	-	-	-	-	-	30	-	-	-	-	126
#3	Boy Player-Queen	-	-	-	-	-	-	-	-	31	-	-	-	-	-	-	-	-	-	-	-	31

Total Lines Principal Parts 3,549

Minor Parts
Men

Part	Total
#1	
Voltemand	22
Prologue	3
Messenger	15
Lord	7
#2	
Francisco	9
Captain	12
Other [Clown]	14
#3	
Cornelius	0
Gentleman	13
Doctor	13
Officer	0
#4	
Reynaldo	13
Embassador	6
Saylor	4
#5	
Attendant [King]	0
Player	0
Army	0
Embassador	0
#6	
Attendant [King]	0
Player	0
Army	0
#7	
Attendant [King]	0
Player	0
Army	0
Saylor	0

Total Lines Minor Parts 131 = 4%
Principal Parts 3,549 = 96%
3,680

Table 61
Hamlet (F)
Principal Parts

#	Role	1					2		3				4							5		Totals
		1	2	3	4	5	1	2	1	2	3	4	1	2	3	4	5	6	7	1	2	
	Men																					
#1	Hamlet	–	103	–	76	149	–	227	22	148	20	141	–	–	21	–	–	–	–	130	203	1,240
#2	Claudius-King	–	95	–	–	–	–	37	39	7	50	–	32	–	45	–	67	–	113	14	30	529
#3	Polonius	–	2	68	–	–	76	149	23	13	8	9	–	–	–	–	–	–	–	–	–	348
	Clowne	–	–	–	–	–	–	–	–	–	–	–	–	–	–	–	–	–	–	71	–	71
#4	Horatio	83	51	–	22	14	–	–	–	9	–	–	–	–	–	–	12	25	–	11	50	277
#5	Laertes	–	7	52	–	–	–	–	–	–	–	–	–	–	–	–	49	–	42	18	38	206
	1 Player-King	–	–	–	–	–	–	48	–	48	–	–	–	–	–	–	–	–	–	–	–	96
#6	Rosincrane	–	–	–	–	–	–	46	12	11	14	–	–	8	5	–	–	–	–	–	–	96
	Osricke	–	–	–	–	–	–	–	–	–	–	–	–	–	–	–	–	–	–	–	36	36
#7	Ghost	0	–	–	–	87	–	–	–	–	–	6	–	–	–	–	–	–	–	–	–	93
	Fortinbras	–	–	–	–	–	–	–	–	–	–	–	–	–	–	8	–	–	–	–	21	29
#8	Marcellus	45	2	–	8	5	–	–	–	–	–	–	–	–	–	–	–	–	–	–	–	60
	Fellow-Lucianus	–	–	–	–	–	–	–	–	7	–	–	–	–	–	–	–	–	–	–	–	7
#9	Barnardo	28	0	–	–	–	–	–	–	–	–	–	–	–	–	–	–	–	–	–	–	28
	Guildensterne	–	–	–	–	–	–	26	5	21	4	–	–	1	0	–	–	–	–	–	–	57
	Boys																					
#1	Gertrude-Queene	–	10	–	–	–	–	8	3	22	–	46	11	–	–	–	18	–	21	7	9	155
#2	Ophelia	–	–	20	–	–	33	–	37	18	–	–	–	–	–	–	29	–	–	–	–	137
#3	Boy Player-Queen	–	–	–	–	–	–	–	–	26	–	–	–	–	–	–	–	–	–	–	–	26

Total Lines Principal Parts 3,491

Minor Parts
Men

	#1 col	col	col	21 col	3 col	col	11 col	col	4 col	col	12 col	Total
#1												
Voltemand	1			21								22
Player-Prologue				0	3							3
Messenger							11		4			15
Other [Clown]											12	12
#2												
Francisco	10											10
Other				0								0
Guard					0							0
Captain						1						1
Lord												0
#3												
Cornelius	0			0								0
Other					0							0
Lord												0
Servant									1			1
Priest										13		13
#4												
Reynaldo		14		14								14
Other				0	0							0
Lord					0							0
Saylor									5			5
Embassador											6	6
#5												
Lord				0	0		0					0
Army							0					0
Drum												0
#6												
One					0		0					0
Army							0					0
Colors											0	0
#7												
Attendant [King]	0			0	0					0		0
Player				0								0
Army					0							0
Attendant [Fortinbras]										0		0
#8												
Attendant [King]	0			0	0					0		0
Player				0								0
Attendant [Fortinbras]										0		0
#9												
Attendant [King]	0			0	0					0		0
Guard					0							0
Attendant [Fortinbras]										0		0

Total Lines Minor Parts 102= 4%

Principal Parts 3,491=96%

3,593

Table 62
The Merry Wives of Windsor (Q1-1602)

Principal Parts
Men

Part	1				2			3				4			5				Totals
	1	2	3	4	1	2	3	1	2	3	5	4	2	3	4	5	6	5	
#1 Syr John Falstaffe	19	-	47	-	-	91	-	-	-	28	77	-	7	-	-	30	-	34	333
#2 Ford-Brooke	-	-	-	-	16	48	-	-	15	22	23	-	18	-	10	-	-	19	171
#3 Host of the Garter	-	-	11	-	10	-	25	15	6	-	-	-	-	7	-	21	9	-	104
#4 Syr Hugh-Priest	9	10	-	-	-	-	-	29	1	8	-	-	5	-	3	9	-	26	100
#5 Maister Page	13	-	-	-	23	-	2	14	8	4	-	8	3	-	11	-	-	13	99
#6 Doctor	-	-	-	16	-	-	23	9	3	1	-	-	-	-	-	7	-	4	63
#7 Slender	34	-	-	-	-	-	0	0	2	0	-	14	-	-	0	-	-	9	59
#8 Justice Shallow	12	-	-	-	22	-	5	5	2	0	-	7	0	-	0	-	-	0	53
#9 Pistoll	3	-	20	-	8	4	-	-	-	-	-	-	-	-	-	-	-	-	35
Fenton	-	-	-	-	-	-	-	-	-	-	-	16	-	-	-	-	27	2	45
#10 Simple	-	1	-	15	-	-	-	3	-	-	-	-	-	-	12	-	-	-	31

Boys

Part	1	2	3	4	1	2	3	1	2	3	5	4	2	3	4	5	6	5	Totals
#1 Mistresse Page	3	-	-	-	39	-	-	-	-	24	-	2	17	-	23	-	-	16	124
#2 Mistresse Quickly	-	-	-	34	1	25	-	-	-	-	8	10	-	-	-	8	-	28	114
#3 Mistresse Foord	2	-	-	-	16	-	-	-	-	28	-	-	30	-	6	-	-	15	97
#4 Anne	11	-	-	-	-	-	-	-	-	-	-	9	-	-	-	-	-	1	21

Total Lines Principal Parts 1,449

Minor Parts
Men

Part	1	2	3	4	1	2	3	1	2	3	5	4	2	3	4	5	6	5	Totals
#1 Nim	3	-	15	-	5	-	-	-	-	-	-	-	-	-	-	-	-	-	23
Servant	-	-	-	-	-	-	-	-	1	-	-	1	-	-	-	-	-	-	2
#2 Bardolfe	0	-	2	-	-	3	-	-	-	-	3	-	-	3	-	4	-	-	15
#3 John Rugby	-	-	-	1	-	-	2	-	-	-	-	-	-	-	-	-	-	-	3
Servant	-	-	-	-	-	-	-	-	-	0	-	-	0	-	-	-	-	-	0

Boys

Part	1	2	3	4	1	2	3	1	2	3	5	4	2	3	4	5	6	5	Totals
#1 Boy	-	-	0	-	-	-	-	-	-	-	-	-	-	-	-	-	-	-	0
Fayrie	-	-	-	-	-	-	-	-	-	-	-	-	-	-	-	-	-	1	1
#2 Fayrie	-	-	-	-	-	-	-	-	-	-	-	-	-	-	-	-	-	0	0
#3 Fayrie	-	-	-	-	-	-	-	-	-	-	-	-	-	-	-	-	-	0	0
#4 Fayrie	-	-	-	-	-	-	-	-	-	-	-	-	-	-	-	-	-	0	0

Total Lines Minor Parts 44= 3%

Principal Parts 1,449=97%

1,493

Table 63

The Merry Wives of Windsor (F)

Principal Parts

Columns are grouped by Act (1–5) and scene. Values are line counts per scene.

Men

Part	1.1	1.2	1.3	1.4	2.1	2.2	2.3	3.1	3.2	3.3	3.4	3.5	4.1	4.2	4.3	4.4	4.5	4.6	5.1	5.2	5.3	5.4	5.5	Totals
#1 Falstoffe	17	–	45	–	–	104	–	–	–	34	–	96	–	13	–	–	30	–	24	–	–	–	61	424
#2 Master Ford	–	–	–	–	27	104	–	–	33	26	–	27	–	43	–	15	–	–	2	–	–	–	27	304
#3 Evans	66	10	–	–	–	–	42	–	–	6	–	11	32	9	–	12	8	–	–	–	–	4	20	220
#4 Master Page	22	–	–	–	25	–	–	15	9	11	8	–	–	7	–	20	–	–	–	13	–	–	23	153
#5 Slender	92	–	–	–	–	–	–	3	5	–	20	–	–	–	–	–	–	–	–	5	–	–	16	141
#6 Host	–	–	29	–	15	–	7	30	–	–	–	–	–	–	8	–	26	–	–	–	–	–	–	115
#7 Justice Shallow	51	–	–	–	16	–	13	7	11	–	3	–	–	–	–	–	–	–	–	–	–	–	23	124
#8 Doctor Caius	–	–	–	30	–	–	3	6	5	–	–	–	37	–	–	–	14	–	–	–	–	–	4	99
#9 Fenton	–	–	–	10	–	–	–	–	–	–	27	–	–	–	–	–	–	47	–	–	–	–	11	95
#10 Pistoll	6	–	25	–	13	8	–	–	–	–	–	–	–	–	–	–	–	–	–	–	–	–	8	60
#11 Simple	3	–	–	8	–	–	–	14	–	–	–	–	–	–	–	–	22	–	–	–	–	–	1	48
#12 Nym	4	–	16	–	8	–	–	–	–	–	–	–	–	–	–	–	–	–	–	–	–	–	–	28
1 Servant	–	–	–	–	–	–	–	–	–	1	–	–	–	2	–	–	–	–	–	–	–	–	–	3

Boys

Part	1.1	1.2	1.3	1.4	2.1	2.2	2.3	3.1	3.2	3.3	3.4	3.5	4.1	4.2	4.3	4.4	4.5	4.6	5.1	5.2	5.3	5.4	5.5	Totals
#1 Mistresse Page	–	–	–	–	69	12	–	–	–	53	–	–	9	66	–	14	–	–	–	14	17	–	25	279
#2 Mistris Quickly	–	–	–	86	2	70	–	–	–	–	14	17	16	–	–	–	–	–	–	13	–	–	34	252
#3 Mistresse Ford	–	–	–	–	39	–	–	–	–	60	17	–	–	62	–	–	–	–	–	–	8	–	4	190
#4 Anne Page	11	–	–	–	–	–	–	–	–	–	17	–	–	–	–	–	–	–	–	–	–	–	1	29
#5 Robin	–	–	–	–	–	1	–	–	9	3	–	–	–	–	–	–	–	–	–	–	–	–	–	13
Fairy	–	–	–	–	–	–	–	–	–	–	–	–	–	–	–	–	–	–	–	0	0	–	–	0
#6 William	–	–	–	–	–	–	–	–	–	–	–	–	12	–	–	–	–	–	–	–	–	–	–	12
Fairy	–	–	–	–	–	–	–	–	–	–	–	–	–	–	–	–	–	–	–	0	0	–	–	0

Total Lines Principal Parts: 2,589

Table 63 (*cont.*)

Minor Parts

Men

	#1													
Bardolph	5	1		4				4		4	6			24
#2 John Rugby		2			7	0								9
2 Servant						0		1	1					1

Boys

	#1													
Fairy														0
#2 Fairy														0

Total Lines Minor Parts   34 = 1%
Principal Parts   2,589 = 99%
   2,623

Table 64
Troilus and Cressida (Q-1609)

Principal Parts

Men

	Part	1.1	1.2	1.3	2.1	2.2	2.3	3.1	3.2	3.3	4.1	4.2	4.3	4.4	4.5	5.1	5.2	5.3	5.4	5.5	5.6	5.7	5.8	5.9	5.10	Totals
Troylus	#1	73	0	–	–	–	–	–	84	–	–	5	88	10	1	–	2	–	8	–	–	–	–	–	30	532
Ulisses	#2	–	–	183	85	–	78	–	–	118	–	–	31	89	26	–	27	12	8	–	–	–	–	–	–	483
Pandarus	#3	36	147	–	67	48	–	29	–	–	–	11	–	–	–	–	–	–	–	–	–	–	–	22	–	368
Thersites	#4	–	–	68	–	–	35	–	42	–	–	–	–	22	20	25	–	11	–	–	–	–	–	–	–	223
Hector	#5	0	–	74	–	–	55	–	–	77	–	5	37	–	–	10	–	4	–	–	–	–	–	–	–	210
Agamemnon	#6	–	–	54	15	–	–	–	–	33	–	3	–	–	–	11	–	–	–	–	–	5	–	–	–	176
Achilles	#7	–	–	26	–	–	8	–	71	–	–	20	22	–	–	4	5	–	8	–	–	–	–	–	–	174
Nestor	#8	–	–	88	–	–	15	–	–	2	–	25	0	–	–	14	–	–	–	–	–	1	–	–	–	145
Aeneas	#9	5	0	54	19	19	–	–	–	6	23	–	3	–	–	–	2	–	–	–	–	1	–	–	2	131
Diomedes	#10	–	–	0	–	–	4	–	2	31	–	12	6	2	3	–	3	–	–	1	–	–	–	–	–	97
Paris	#11	–	–	0	–	30	24	–	31	–	–	8	3	–	–	–	0	–	–	–	–	–	–	–	0	96
Ajax	#12	–	–	22	–	–	18	–	3	–	–	21	2	1	–	–	–	–	–	2	–	–	–	–	–	74
Patroclus	#13	–	–	3	–	–	18	–	29	–	–	7	9	–	–	–	–	–	–	–	–	–	–	–	–	66
Man[Cressid]	#14	31	–	–	–	–	–	–	–	–	–	–	–	–	–	–	–	–	–	–	–	–	–	–	–	31
Calcas		–	–	–	–	–	–	–	–	0	2	29	–	–	–	0	–	–	–	–	–	–	–	–	–	31

Boys

	Part	1.1	1.2	1.3	2.1	2.2	2.3	3.1	3.2	3.3	4.1	4.2	4.3	4.4	4.5	5.1	5.2	5.3	5.4	5.5	5.6	5.7	5.8	5.9	5.10	Totals
Cressid	#1	–	101	–	–	68	–	–	40	–	–	25	10	40	–	–	–	–	–	–	–	–	–	–	–	284
Cassandra	#2	–	–	13	–	–	21	–	–	–	–	–	–	–	–	–	–	–	–	–	–	–	–	–	–	34
Hellen	#3	–	–	–	–	27	–	–	–	–	–	–	–	–	–	–	–	–	–	–	–	–	–	–	–	27
Boy	#4	2	–	–	–	–	–	–	–	–	–	–	–	–	–	–	–	–	–	–	–	–	–	–	–	2
Andromache		–	–	–	–	–	–	–	–	–	–	–	15	–	–	–	–	–	–	–	–	–	–	–	–	15

Total Lines Principal Parts 3,199

Table 64 (*cont.*)

Minor Parts
<u>Men</u>

																			Total
#1																			
Priam	–	12	–	–	–	–	–	–	8	–	–	–	–	–	–	–	–	20
Bastard	–	–	–	–	–	–	–	–	–	–	–	–	–	3	–	–	–	3
#2																			
Man [Paris]	–	–	17	–	–	–	–	–	–	–	–	–	–	–	–	–	–	17
Deiphobus	–	–	–	–	1	–	0	–	–	–	–	–	–	–	0	–	–	1
One	–	–	–	–	–	–	–	–	–	–	1	–	–	–	–	–	–	1
#3																			
Menelaus	–	1	–	–	1	–	–	9	1	–	–	0	–	–	–	–	–	12
#4																			
Helenus	0	4	–	–	–	–	–	–	–	–	–	–	–	–	–	–	–	4
Other	0	–	0	–	–	–	–	–	–	–	–	–	–	–	–	–	–	0
Servant	–	–	–	–	–	1	–	–	–	–	–	–	–	1	–	–	–	1
Myrmidon	–	–	–	–	–	–	–	–	–	–	–	0	–	–	0	–	–	0
#5																			
Antenor	0	–	–	0	–	–	0	–	–	–	–	–	–	–	–	–	–	0
Other	0	–	0	–	–	–	–	–	–	–	–	–	–	–	–	–	–	0
Man [Troylus]	–	–	–	1	–	–	–	–	–	–	–	–	–	–	–	–	–	1
Myrmidon	–	–	–	–	–	–	–	–	–	–	–	0	–	–	0	–	–	0
#6																			
Other	0	–	–	–	–	–	–	–	–	–	–	0	–	–	–	–	–	0
One	–	–	–	–	–	–	–	–	–	–	–	–	–	–	–	–	–	0
Myrmidon	–	–	–	–	–	–	–	–	–	–	–	–	–	–	–	–	–	0
Soldier	–	–	–	–	–	–	–	–	–	–	–	–	1	–	–	–	–	1

Total Lines Minor Parts 6̄1̄ = 2%
Principal Parts 3,199 = 98%
3,260

Table 65

All's Well That Ends Well (F)

Principal Parts

Line counts by act and scene. (E = Ecclestone roles; G = Goughe roles.)

Men

Role	1.1	1.2	1.3	2.1	2.2	2.3	2.4	2.5	3.1	3.2	3.3	3.4	3.5	3.6	3.7	4.1	4.2	4.3	4.4	4.5	5.1	5.2	5.3	Totals
#1 King of France	–	69	–	32	–	98	–	30	–	–	–	–	–	–	–	–	–	–	–	–	–	–	156	385
#2 Parrolles	45	0	23	42	–	77	26	9	–	–	–	–	1	17	–	–	–	98	–	–	–	18	17	373
#3 Lord Lafew	26	0	–	32	–	87	–	30	–	–	–	–	–	–	–	–	–	–	–	48	–	18	29	270
#4 Bertram Count of Rossillion	11	7	–	34	–	27	–	40	–	–	8	–	9	36	–	–	–	34	–	–	–	–	63	269
#5 Clowne	–	–	58	–	34	–	21	–	–	18	–	–	–	–	–	–	–	–	–	29	–	17	–	177
#6 Ecclestone? 2 Lord	–	–	–	E 5	–	E 3	–	–	–	–	–	–	–	–	–	–	–	–	–	–	–	–	–	8
Frenchman	–	–	–	–	–	–	–	–	E 8	E 9	–	–	–	–	–	–	–	–	–	–	–	–	–	17
Captain	–	–	–	–	–	–	–	–	–	–	–	–	–	E 38	–	E 39	–	E 60	–	–	–	–	–	98
#7 Goughe? 1 Lord	–	G 6	G 8	–	–	–	–	–	–	25	–	–	–	–	–	–	–	–	–	–	–	–	–	39
1 Lord	–	–	–	–	–	1	–	–	–	–	–	–	–	–	–	–	–	–	–	–	–	–	–	15
Frenchman	–	–	–	–	–	–	–	–	G 3	G 14	–	–	–	–	–	–	–	–	–	–	–	–	–	17
Captain	–	–	–	–	–	–	–	–	–	–	–	–	–	G 31	–	–	–	G 65	–	–	–	–	–	96
#8 Steward	–	–	25	–	–	–	–	–	–	–	–	18	–	–	–	–	–	–	–	–	–	–	–	43
Soldier-Interpreter	–	–	–	–	–	–	–	–	–	–	–	–	–	–	–	39	–	66	–	–	–	–	–	66

Boys

Role	1.1	1.2	1.3	2.1	2.2	2.3	2.4	2.5	3.1	3.2	3.3	3.4	3.5	3.6	3.7	4.1	4.2	4.3	4.4	4.5	5.1	5.2	5.3	Totals
#1 Helena	63	–	68	40	–	–	–	20	–	32	–	10	23	–	39	–	–	–	35	–	30	–	12	451
#2 Mother-Countesse-Old Lady	40	–	109	–	33	–	–	–	–	45	26	–	–	–	–	–	–	–	–	17	–	–	14	284
#3 Diana	–	–	–	–	–	–	–	–	–	–	–	–	23	–	3	–	32	–	3	–	–	–	59	117
#4 Widow	–	–	–	–	–	–	–	–	–	–	–	–	43	–	16	–	–	–	3	–	1	–	3	66
#5 Mariana	–	–	–	–	–	–	–	–	–	–	–	–	23	–	–	–	–	–	–	–	–	–	–	23

Total Lines Principal Parts: 2,814

Table 65 (cont.)

Minor Parts

Men

Part														Total
#1														
1 Lord	1													1
1 Soldier-Interpreter-					18						18			18
Messenger-Servant-												4	4	4
Citizen			0							0				0
#2														
Duke of Florence			13	8										21
Citizen				0			0							0
Gentle Astringer								10					10	10
Gentleman									12				12	12
#3														
Attendant[King]	0			0			0		0				0	0
Drum				0					0					0
#4														
Attendant[King]	0			0			0		0				0	0
Trumpet				0			0							0
Citizen				0			0							0
#5														
Attendant[King]	0			0			0		0				0	0
Trumpet				0					0					0
Colours				0					0					0
#6														
2 Lord	1			0			0		0				0	0
Soldier [Duke]				0			0			0				0
Soldier [French]				0			0							0
#7														
3 Lord	0			0			0		0				0	0
Soldier [Duke]				0			0			0				0
Soldier [French]				0			0							0
#8														
4 Lord	1			0			0		0				0	1
Soldier [Duke]				0			0			0				0
Soldier [French]				0			0							0

Boys

Part						Total
#1						
Page	2					2
Attendant [Helen]-				0	0	0
#2						
Violenta			0			0
Attendant [Helen]-				0	0	0

Total Lines Minor Parts $\frac{69}{2,814} = 2\%$

Principal Parts $= 98\%$

$\overline{2,883}$

Table 66   219

Table 66

Measure for Measure (F)

Principal Parts
Men

	1				2				3		4						5	
	1	2	3	4	1	2	3	4	1	2	1	2	3	4	5	6	1	Totals
#1 Duke	66	–	51	–	–	–	25	–	79	110	38	84	81	–	13	–	257	804
#2 Angelo	12	–	–	–	36	84	–	117	–	–	–	–	–	26	–	–	43	318
#3 Lucio	–	53	–	62	–	15	–	–	–	92	–	–	21	–	–	–	51	294
#4 Escalus	11	–	–	–	99	–	–	–	–	30	–	–	–	17	–	–	42	199
#5 Clowne	–	18	–	–	73	–	–	–	–	14	–	30	30	–	–	–	–	165
#6 Provost	–	3	–	–	1	19	12	–	7	4	–	85	17	–	–	–	13	161
#7 Claudio	–	58	–	–	–	–	–	–	53	–	–	3	–	–	–	–	0	114
#8 Elbow	–	–	–	–	36	–	–	–	–	17	–	–	–	–	–	–	–	53
Frier Peter	–	–	–	–	–	–	–	–	–	–	–	–	–	–	1	8	30	39

Boys

	1				2				3		4						5	
	1	2	3	4	1	2	3	4	1	2	1	2	3	4	5	6	1	Totals
#1 Isabell	–	–	–	28	–	94	–	79	96	–	24	–	9	–	–	9	87	426
#2 Mariana	–	–	–	–	–	–	–	–	–	–	13	–	–	–	–	2	53	68
#3 Bawde	–	23	–	–	–	–	–	–	–	8	–	–	–	–	–	–	–	31
#4 Juliet	–	0	–	–	–	–	10	–	–	–	–	–	–	–	–	–	0	10

Total Lines Principal Parts   2,682

Minor Parts
Men

	1				2				3		4						5	
	1	2	3	4	1	2	3	4	1	2	1	2	3	4	5	6	1	Totals
#1 1 Gentleman	–	23	–	–	–	–	–	–	–	–	–	–	–	–	–	–	–	23
Justice	–	–	–	–	3	–	–	–	–	–	–	–	–	–	–	–	–	3
Barnardine	–	–	–	–	–	–	–	–	–	–	–	–	15	–	–	–	0	15
#2 2 Gentleman	–	11	–	–	–	–	–	–	–	–	–	–	–	–	–	–	–	11
Froth	–	–	–	–	11	–	–	–	–	–	–	–	–	–	–	–	–	11
Abhorson	–	–	–	–	–	–	–	–	–	–	–	8	10	–	–	–	–	18
Citizen	–	–	–	–	–	–	–	–	–	–	–	–	–	–	–	–	0	0
#3 Frier Thomas	–	–	6	–	–	–	–	–	–	–	–	–	–	–	–	–	–	6
Servant [Angelo]	–	–	–	–	0	4	–	1	–	–	–	–	–	–	–	–	–	5
Messenger	–	–	–	–	–	–	–	–	–	–	–	5	–	–	–	–	–	5
Varrius	–	–	–	–	–	–	–	–	–	–	–	–	–	–	0	–	0	0
#4 Lord [Duke]	0	–	–	–	–	–	–	–	–	–	–	–	–	–	–	–	0	0
Servant [Angelo]	–	–	–	–	0	–	–	–	–	–	–	–	–	–	–	–	–	0
#5 Lord [Duke]	0	–	–	–	–	–	–	–	–	–	–	–	–	–	–	–	0	0
Servant [Angelo]	–	–	–	–	0	–	–	–	–	–	–	–	–	–	–	–	–	0
#6 Lord [Duke]	0	–	–	–	–	–	–	–	–	–	–	–	–	–	–	–	0	0

Table 66 (*cont.*)

```
#7
Officer    -  0  -  -  0  -  -  -  -  0  -  -  -  -  -  -  -  -  0
Citizen    -  -  -  -  -  -  -  -  -  -  -  -  -  -  -  -  -  0  0
#8
Officer    -  0  -  -  0  -  -  -  -  0  -  -  -  -  -  -  -  -  0
Citizen    -  -  -  -  -  -  -  -  -  -  -  -  -  -  -  -  -  0  0
                              Boy
#1
Francisca  -  -  -  9  -  -  -  -  -  -  -  -  -  -  -  -  -  -  9
Boy        -  -  -  -  -  -  -  -  -  -  0  -  -  -  -  -  -  -  0
```

	Total Lines Minor Parts	$10\overline{6}$ = 4%
	Principal Parts	$\dfrac{2,682}{2,788}$ = 96%

Table 67
Othello (Q1-1622)

	1			2			3				4			5		Totals
	1	2	3	1	2	3	1	2	3	4	1	2	3	1	2	

Principal Parts — Men

Name	1.1	1.2	1.3	2.1	2.2	2.3	3.1	3.2	3.3	3.4	4.1	4.2	4.3	5.1	5.2	Totals
#1 Iago	110	27	74	132	-	187	5	1	214	9	126	63	-	72	12	1,032
#2 Othello	-	38	114	29	-	56	-	5	182	50	90	52	5	8	182	811
#3 Cassio	-	16	0	45	-	70	18	-	12	36	22	-	-	16	14	249
#4 Brabantio	46	24	60	-	-	-	-	-	-	-	-	-	-	-	-	130
Lodovico	-	-	-	-	-	-	-	-	-	-	25	-	2	9	39	75
#5 Roderigo	25	1	13	7	-	6	-	-	-	-	-	30	-	11	-	93
#6 Duke	-	-	66	-	-	-	-	-	-	-	-	-	-	-	-	66
Montanio	-	-	-	20	-	27	-	-	-	-	-	-	-	-	6	53
#7 Clowne	-	-	-	-	-	-	17	-	-	8	-	-	-	-	-	25
Gratiano	-	-	-	-	-	-	-	-	-	-	-	-	-	9	14	23

Boys

Name	1.1	1.2	1.3	2.1	2.2	2.3	3.1	3.2	3.3	3.4	4.1	4.2	4.3	5.1	5.2	Totals
#1 Desdemona	-	-	29	29	-	1	-	-	71	76	14	49	32	-	41	342
#2 Emillia	-	-	-	5	-	-	13	-	28	18	-	43	23	4	74	208
#3 Bianca	-	-	-	-	-	-	-	-	16	9	-	-	-	6	-	31

Total Lines Principal Parts 3,1$\overline{38}$

Minor Parts — Men

Name	1.1	1.2	1.3	2.1	2.2	2.3	3.1	3.2	3.3	3.4	4.1	4.2	4.3	5.1	5.2	Totals
#1 1 Senator	-	-	17	-	-	-	-	-	-	-	-	-	-	-	-	17
1 Gentleman	-	-	-	3	-	-	-	-	-	-	-	-	-	-	-	3
Gentleman	-	-	-	-	10	-	-	-	-	-	-	-	-	-	-	10
#2 2 Senator	-	-	5	-	-	-	-	-	-	-	-	-	-	-	-	5
2 Gentleman	-	-	-	21	-	-	-	-	-	-	-	-	-	-	-	21
Gentleman	-	-	-	-	-	0	-	1	0	-	-	-	-	-	-	1

Table 68 221

Table 67 (*cont.*)

#3	1.1	1.2	1.3	2.1	2.2	2.3	3.1	3.2	3.3	3.4	4.1	4.2	4.3	5.1	5.2	Totals
Messenger	-	-	9	-	-	-	-	-	-	-	-	-	-	-	-	9
3 Gentleman	-	-	-	17	-	-	-	-	-	-	-	-	-	-	-	17
Gentleman	-	-	-	-	-	0	-	0	0	-	-	-	-	-	-	0
#4																
Officer	-	3	1	-	-	-	-	-	-	-	-	-	-	-	0	4
Messenger	-	-	-	3	-	-	-	-	-	-	-	-	-	-	-	3
Musician	-	-	-	-	-	-	0	-	-	-	-	-	-	-	-	0
#5																
Servant [Brabantio]	0	0	-	-	-	-	-	-	-	-	-	-	-	-	-	0
Attendant [Duke]	-	-	0	-	-	-	-	-	-	-	-	-	-	-	-	0
Attendant [Lodovico]	-	-	-	-	-	-	-	-	-	-	0	-	0	-	-	0
#6																
Servant [Brabantio]	0	0	-	-	-	-	-	-	-	-	-	-	-	-	-	0
Attendant [Duke]	-	-	0	-	-	-	-	-	-	-	-	-	-	-	-	0
Musician	-	-	-	-	-	-	0	-	-	-	-	-	-	-	-	0
Attendant [Lodovico]	-	-	-	-	-	-	-	-	-	-	0	-	0	-	-	0
#7																
Attendant [Othello]	-	0	-	0	-	-	-	-	-	-	-	-	-	-	-	0
Attendant [Duke]	-	-	0	-	-	-	-	-	-	-	-	-	-	-	-	0
Attendant [Lodovico]	-	-	-	-	-	-	-	-	-	-	0	-	0	-	-	0
#8																
Attendant [Othello]	-	0	-	0	-	-	-	-	-	-	-	-	-	-	-	0
Sailor	-	-	4	-	-	-	-	-	-	-	-	-	-	-	-	4
Other [Montano]	-	-	-	-	-	0	-	-	-	-	-	-	-	-	0	0
#9																
Attendant [Othello]	-	0	-	0	-	-	-	-	-	-	-	-	-	-	-	0
Other [Montano]	-	-	-	-	-	0	-	-	-	-	-	-	-	-	0	0
#10																
Officer	-	0	0	-	-	-	-	-	-	-	-	-	-	-	-	0
Other [Montano]	-	-	-	-	-	0	-	-	-	-	-	-	-	-	0	0
Boys																
#1																
Other [Desdemona]	-	-	-	-	-	0	-	-	-	-	-	-	-	-	-	0
Boy	-	-	-	-	-	-	6	-	-	-	-	-	-	-	-	6
#2																
Other [Desdemona]	-	-	-	-	-	0	-	-	-	-	-	-	-	-	-	0

Total Lines Minor Parts 100= 3%
Principal Parts 3,138=97%
3,238

Table 68
Othello (F)

	1			2			3				4			5		
	1	2	3	1	2	3	1	2	3	4	1	2	3	1	2	Totals

Principal Parts
Men

	1.1	1.2	1.3	2.1	2.2	2.3	3.1	3.2	3.3	3.4	4.1	4.2	4.3	5.1	5.2	Totals
#1																
Iago	107	26	83	148	-	208	5	1	225	9	130	60	-	81	15	1,098
#2																
Othello	-	39	117	31	-	56	-	5	204	50	103	67	5	8	206	891
#3																
Cassio	-	16	0	52	-	84	19	-	12	38	28	-	-	18	14	281
#4																
Brabantio	46	32	66	-	-	-	-	-	-	-	-	-	-	-	-	144
Lodovico	-	-	-	-	-	-	-	-	-	-	25	-	3	9	43	80
#5																
Roderigo	43	1	14	8	-	8	-	-	-	-	-	34	-	11	-	119

Table 68 (*cont.*)

#6

Part	1	2	3	4	5	6	7	8	9	10	11	12	13	14	15	Total
Duke	-	-	65	-	-	-	-	-	-	-	-	-	-	-	-	65
Montano	-	-	-	22	-	33	-	-	-	-	-	-	-	-	7	62

#7

Part	1	2	3	4	5	6	7	8	9	10	11	12	13	14	15	Total
1 Senator	-	-	27	-	-	-	-	-	-	-	-	-	-	-	-	27
Clowne	-	-	-	-	-	-	17	-	-	12	-	-	-	-	-	29
Gratiano	-	-	-	-	-	-	-	-	-	-	-	-	-	11	18	29

Boys

Part	1	2	3	4	5	6	7	8	9	10	11	12	13	14	15	Total
#1 Desdemona	-	-	28	35	-	1	-	-	72	82	14	63	43	-	43	381
#2 Aemilia	-	-	-	3	-	-	12	-	29	19	-	48	47	5	94	257
#3 Bianca	-	-	-	-	-	-	-	-	-	17	10	-	-	7	-	34

Total Lines Principal Parts 3,497

Minor Parts
Men

Part	1	2	3	4	5	6	7	8	9	10	11	12	13	14	15	Total
#1 Torchbearer	-	0	-	-	-	-	-	-	-	-	-	-	-	-	-	0
1 Gentleman	-	-	-	12	-	1	-	1	-	-	-	-	-	-	-	14
#2 Torchbearer	-	0	-	-	-	-	-	-	-	-	-	-	-	-	-	0
2 Senator	-	-	5	-	-	-	-	-	-	-	-	-	-	-	-	5
2 Gentleman	-	-	-	8	-	0	-	0	-	-	-	-	-	-	-	8
#3 Officer	-	0	0	-	-	-	-	-	-	-	-	-	-	0	-	0
3 Gentleman	-	-	-	13	-	0	-	0	-	-	-	-	-	-	-	13
#4 Torchbearer	-	0	-	-	-	-	-	-	-	-	-	-	-	-	-	0
Messenger	-	-	9	-	-	-	-	-	-	-	-	-	-	-	-	9
Herald	-	-	-	-	12	-	-	-	-	-	-	-	-	-	-	12
#5 Servant [Brabantio]	0	-	-	-	-	-	-	-	-	-	-	-	-	-	-	0
Officer	-	3	2	-	-	-	-	-	-	-	-	-	-	0	-	5
#6 Torchbearer	-	0	-	-	-	-	-	-	-	-	-	-	-	-	-	0
Saylor	-	-	4	-	-	-	-	-	-	-	-	-	-	-	-	4
Musician	-	-	-	-	-	-	5	-	-	-	-	-	-	-	-	5
#7 Attendant [Othello]	-	0	-	0	-	0	-	-	-	-	-	-	-	-	-	0
Attendant [Lodovico]	-	-	-	-	-	-	-	-	-	0	-	0	-	-	-	0
#8 Attendant [Othello]	-	0	-	0	-	0	-	-	-	-	-	-	-	-	-	0
Musician	-	-	-	-	-	-	0	-	-	-	-	-	-	-	-	0
Attendant [Lodovico]	-	-	-	-	-	-	-	-	-	0	-	0	-	-	-	0
#9 Servant [Brabantio]	0	-	-	-	-	-	-	-	-	-	-	-	-	-	-	0
Attendant [Othello]	-	0	-	0	-	0	-	-	-	-	-	-	-	-	-	0
Attendant [Lodovico]	-	-	-	-	-	-	-	-	-	0	-	0	-	-	-	0

Boys

Part	1	2	3	4	5	6	7	8	9	10	11	12	13	14	15	Total
#1 Attendant [Desdemona]	-	0	-	-	0	-	-	-	-	-	-	-	-	-	-	0
#2 Attendant [Desdemona]	-	0	-	-	0	-	-	-	-	-	-	-	-	-	-	0

Total Lines Minor Parts 7̄5̄ = 2%
Principal Parts 3,497 = 98%
3,572

Table 69

King Lear (Q1-1608)

Principal Parts

Men

	1	2	3	4	5	1	2	3	4	1	2	3	4	5	6	7	1	2	3	4	5	6	7	1	2	3	Totals
#1 Lear	108	–	–	97	19	–	–	150	–	40	–	59	–	24	–	–	–	–	–	–	71	30	–	0	51		649
#2 Kent	41	–	–	30	2	–	91	28	–	16	–	16	–	12	–	–	24	–	–	–	–	28	–	–	21		341
#4 Gloster	21	45	–	–	–	25	14	–	–	–	19	22	–	13	31	44	–	–	–	61	–	–	2	–			297
#3 Edgar	–	9	–	–	–	1	–	21	–	–	–	56	–	35	–	27	–	–	–	101	–	11	9	72			270
#4 Bastard	3	93	–	–	–	48	1	–	–	5	–	11	–	0	–	1	–	–	–	–	–	28	–	74			264
#6 Foole	–	–	–	73	23	–	–	21	16	–	9	–	8	–	–	–	–	–	–	–	–	–	–	78			150
#7 Duke-Albany	0	–	–	8	–	–	–	–	–	–	–	–	–	37	–	–	–	–	–	–	–	14	–	78			137
#8 Duke-Cornwall	0	–	–	–	–	2	28	10	–	–	10	–	36	–	–	31	–	–	–	–	–	–	–	–			86
#9 Gentleman [Kent]	–	–	–	–	–	–	–	–	–	–	–	–	–	–	–	–	–	–	–	–	–	–	–	–			31
France	30	–	–	–	–	–	–	–	–	–	–	–	5	–	8	–	11	14	–	–	–	–	–	–			30
Steward-Oswald	–	–	4	6	–	–	23	–	–	–	–	–	–	–	–	–	–	–	–	–	–	–	–	–			71

Boys

	1	2	3	4	5	1	2	3	4	1	2	3	4	5	6	7	1	2	3	4	5	6	7	1	2	3	Totals
#1 Regan	16	–	–	–	–	21	7	54	–	–	–	–	–	17	–	–	–	31	–	–	–	11	–	14			171
#2 Gonorill	24	–	22	41	–	–	–	23	–	36	–	–	2	–	–	–	–	–	–	–	–	7	–	11			166
#3 Cordelia	41	–	–	–	–	–	–	–	–	–	–	–	–	–	–	–	–	–	–	–	22	–	0	4			89

Total Lines Principal Parts 2,752

Table 69 (*cont.*)

Minor Parts
<u>Men</u>

Character	Total
#1	
One	0
1 Servant [Cornwall]	18
Gentleman	20
Power [Regan]	6
Captain	6
#2	
Burgundie	10
2 Servant [Cornwall]	4
Old Man	11
Doctor	17
Gentleman	4
Power [Regan]	0
#3	
Curan	9
Messenger	2
Gentleman	0
Power [Regan]	0
Herald	6
#4	
Follower [Lear]	0
Knight	3
Gentleman [Albany]	15
Other [Cordelia]	0
Troup [Albany]	0
Power [France]	0
#5	
Follower [Lear]	0
Gentleman	17
Other [Cordelia]	0
Troup [Albany]	0
Power [France]	0
#6	
Follower [Lear]	0
Servant [Lear]	13
Other [Cordelia]	0
Troup [Albany]	0
Power [France]	0

Total Lines Minor Parts   155 = 5%
             Principal Parts 2,752 = 95%
                              2,907

Table 70
King Lear (F)

Principal Parts
Men

	1.1	1.2	1.3	1.4	1.5	2.1	2.2	2.3	2.4	3.1	3.2	3.3	3.4	3.5	3.6	3.7	4.1	4.2	4.3	4.4	4.5	4.6	4.7	5.1	5.2	5.3	Totals
#1 Lear	121	–	–	118	21	–	1	–	30	–	63	–	–	23	–	15	–	28	42	67	–	13	–	93	36	0	55	729
#2 Edgar	–	9	19	–	–	29	–	21	–	–	–	–	59	–	17	–	–	–	–	–	17	36	12	11	66		343
#3 Gloucester	24	50	–	–	–	30	11	–	12	–	31	–	23	–	15	36	46	–	65	–	–	9	–	3	–	–	332
#4 Kent	43	–	–	32	2	–	99	–	31	17	–	6	21	14	6	–	–	–	–	–	–	25					313
#5 Edmond-Bastard	3	109	–	–	–	63	1	–	–	–	6	–	–	–	–	0	–	1	–	–	27	–	70				294
#6 Foole	–	–	–	85	26	–	–	–	36	–	12	–	–	6	–	–	–	–	–	–	–	–	–				195
#7 Albany	1	–	–	12	–	–	–	–	–	–	–	–	–	–	–	–	19	–	–	–	10	82					124
#8 Cornwall	0	–	14	–	–	–	33	–	12	–	–	11	–	15	40	–	–	–	–	–	–	–					110
Gentleman	–	–	–	–	–	–	–	–	–	–	–	–	–	–	–	13	–	–	–	–	–	–					28
#9 France	32	–	–	–	–	–	–	–	–	–	–	–	–	–	–	–	–	–	–	–	–	–					32
Steward-Oswald	–	–	3	6	–	–	25	–	0	–	–	–	–	6	6	10	–	12	16	–	–	–					78

Boys

	1.1	1.2	1.3	1.4	1.5	2.1	2.2	2.3	2.4	3.1	3.2	3.3	3.4	3.5	3.6	3.7	4.1	4.2	4.3	4.4	4.5	4.6	4.7	5.1	5.2	5.3	Totals
#1 Regan	15	–	–	–	–	–	5	–	60	–	–	–	–	–	21	–	–	–	33	–	–	12	–	18			187
#2 Gonerill	28	–	19	67	–	–	–	–	15	–	–	–	–	–	2	31	–	–	–	–	5	–	14				181
#3 Cordelia	46	–	–	–	–	–	–	–	–	–	–	–	–	–	–	–	–	–	–	–	–	41	23	0	5		115

Total Lines Principal Parts 3,061

Minor Parts
Men

	1.1	1.2	1.3	1.4	1.5	2.1	2.2	2.3	2.4	3.1	3.2	3.3	3.4	3.5	3.6	3.7	4.1	4.2	4.3	4.4	4.5	4.6	4.7	5.1	5.2	5.3	Totals
#1 Burgundy	12	–	–	–	–	–	–	–	–	–	–	–	–	–	–	–	–	–	–	–	–	–	–	–	–	–	12
Gentleman	–	–	–	–	5	–	–	–	–	–	–	–	–	–	–	–	–	–	–	5	–	–	–	–	–	–	5
Gentleman	–	–	–	–	–	–	–	–	–	–	–	–	–	–	–	0	–	–	–	5	–	–	–	6	–	–	5
Gentleman	–	–	–	–	–	–	–	–	–	–	–	–	–	–	–	–	–	–	–	–	–	–	–	6	–	–	6
#2 Knight	–	–	14	10	–	–	–	–	–	–	–	–	–	–	–	–	–	–	–	–	–	0	–	–	–	–	14
Gentleman	–	–	–	–	–	–	–	–	–	–	–	–	–	–	–	–	–	–	–	–	–	–	–	0	–	–	10
Messenger	–	–	–	–	–	–	–	–	–	–	–	–	–	–	–	–	–	–	–	2	–	–	–	–	–	–	2
Servant [Lear]	–	–	–	–	–	–	–	–	–	–	–	–	–	–	–	–	–	–	–	1	–	–	–	–	–	–	0
Herald	–	–	–	–	–	–	–	–	–	–	–	–	–	–	–	0	–	–	–	–	–	–	–	–	–	9	9

Table 70 (*cont.*)

	Total
#3	
Gentleman	1
Old Man	11
Messenger	1
#4	
Curan	11
Messenger	17
Servant [Lear]	0
Captain	1
#5	
Attendant [Lear]	0
Attendant [Cornwall]	0
Servant [Cornwall]	6
Drum [Edmond]	0
#6	
Attendant [Lear]	0
Attendant [Cornwall]	0
Servant [Cornwall]	3
Colors [Edmond]	0
#7	
Attendant [Lear]	0
Attendant [Cornwall]	0
Soldier [Edmond]	0
#8	
Attend. [France]	0
Servant [Gloster]	0
Drum [Cordelia]	0
Drum [Albany]	0
#9	
Attend. [France]	0
Servant [Gloster]	0
Colors [Cordelia]	0
Colors [Albany]	0
#10	
Attend. [France]	0
Soldier [Cordelia]	0
Soldier [Albany]	0

Total Lines Minor Parts   114 = 4%
             Principal Parts 3,061 = 96%
                             3,175

Table 71

Macbeth (F)[3]

Principal Parts

Men

Role	1.1	1.2	1.3	1.4	1.5	1.6	1.7	2.1	2.2	2.3	2.4	3.1	3.2	3.3	3.4	3.5	3.6	4.1	4.2	4.3	5.1	5.2	5.3	5.4	5.5	5.6	5.7	5.8	Totals
#1 Macbeth	–	–	56	17	4	–	49	45	40	32	–	123	43	–	108	–	–	72	–	–	–	–	55	–	44	–	10	27	725
#2 Malcolme	–	6	–	10	–	0	–	–	–	15	–	–	–	–	–	–	–	–	–	142	–	–	–	11	–	7	2	20	213
#3 Macduff	–	–	–	–	–	0	–	–	–	39	16	–	–	–	–	–	–	–	–	88	–	–	–	3	–	2	10	19	177
#4 Rosse	–	18	16	–	–	0	–	–	–	–	28	0	–	–	5	–	–	–	19	40	–	–	–	–	–	–	–	9	135
#5 Banquo	–	–	43	2	–	0	–	25	–	11	–	21	–	5	–	–	–	–	–	–	–	–	–	–	–	–	–	–	107
#6 King	–	15	–	37	–	18	–	–	–	–	–	–	–	–	–	–	–	–	–	–	–	–	–	–	–	–	–	–	70
Doctor [Scotland]	–	–	–	–	–	–	–	–	–	–	–	–	–	–	–	–	–	–	–	–	34	–	7	–	–	–	–	–	41
#7 Lenox	–	–	–	–	–	–	–	–	–	20	–	2	–	–	6	–	33	6	–	–	–	7	–	–	–	–	–	–	74
#8 Captain	–	35	–	–	–	–	–	–	–	–	–	–	–	–	–	–	–	–	–	–	–	–	–	–	–	–	–	–	35
1 Murderer	–	–	–	–	–	–	–	–	–	–	–	8	–	10	7	–	–	–	–	–	–	–	–	–	–	–	–	–	25
#9 Porter	–	–	–	–	–	–	–	–	–	34	–	–	–	–	–	–	–	–	–	–	–	–	–	–	–	–	–	–	34
Seyward	–	–	–	–	–	–	–	–	–	–	–	–	–	–	–	–	–	–	–	–	–	–	–	10	–	2	6	11	29

Boys

Role	1.1	1.2	1.3	1.4	1.5	1.6	1.7	2.1	2.2	2.3	2.4	3.1	3.2	3.3	3.4	3.5	3.6	4.1	4.2	4.3	5.1	5.2	5.3	5.4	5.5	5.6	5.7	5.8	Totals
#1 Macbeths Wife-Lady-	–	–	–	–	72	11	43	–	50	6	–	3	18	–	40	–	–	–	–	–	20	–	–	–	–	–	–	–	263
#2 1 Witch	3	–	29	–	–	–	–	–	–	–	–	–	–	–	–	3	–	27	–	–	–	–	–	–	–	–	–	–	62
#3 Macduffes Wife-	–	–	–	–	–	–	–	–	–	–	–	–	–	–	–	–	–	–	45	–	–	–	–	–	–	–	–	–	45
#4 Hecat	–	–	–	–	–	–	–	–	–	–	–	–	–	–	–	34	–	5	–	–	–	–	–	–	–	–	–	–	39
#5 2 Witch	3	–	6	–	–	–	–	–	–	–	–	–	–	–	–	0	–	16	–	–	–	–	–	–	–	–	–	–	25
#6 3 Witch	2	–	8	–	–	–	–	–	–	–	–	–	–	–	–	0	–	16	–	–	–	–	–	–	–	–	–	–	26
#7 Son [Macduff]	–	–	–	–	–	–	–	–	–	–	–	–	–	–	–	–	–	–	21	–	–	–	–	–	–	–	–	–	21
#8 Gentlewoman	–	–	–	–	–	–	–	–	–	–	–	–	–	–	–	–	–	–	–	–	21	–	–	–	–	–	–	–	21

Total Lines Principal Parts 2,167

Table 71 (cont.)

Minor Parts
<u>Men</u>

Part																						Total
#1																						
Angus	0	13	0	–	–	–	–	–	–	–	–	–	–	–	–	–	–	–	0	–	–	22
Old Man	–	–	–	–	–	–	–	–	–	–	–	–	–	–	–	–	–	–	–	–	–	11
King [Show]	–	–	–	–	–	–	–	–	–	–	–	–	–	–	–	–	–	–	–	–	–	0
Murderer [Macd. Wife]	–	–	–	11	–	–	–	–	–	–	0	–	–	–	13	–	–	–	–	–	–	13
#2																						
2 Murderer–	–	–	–	–	6	10	–	–	–	–	0	–	–	–	–	–	–	–	–	–	–	16
King [Show]	–	–	–	–	–	–	–	–	–	–	–	–	–	–	–	–	–	–	–	–	–	0
Doctor [England]	–	–	–	–	–	–	–	–	–	–	–	–	–	5	–	–	–	–	–	–	–	5
Menteth	–	–	–	–	–	–	–	–	–	–	–	–	10	–	–	–	–	2	–	–	–	12
#3																						
Lord	–	–	–	–	–	–	–	21	–	–	–	–	–	–	–	–	–	–	–	–	–	21
Sewer	–	0	–	–	–	–	–	–	–	–	0	–	–	–	–	–	–	–	–	–	–	0
King [Show]	–	–	–	–	–	–	–	–	–	–	–	–	–	–	–	–	–	–	–	–	–	0
Cathnes	–	–	–	–	–	–	–	–	–	–	0	–	–	–	–	11	–	0	–	–	–	11
#4																						
Servant [Macbeth]	0	0	–	2	–	–	–	–	3	–	0	–	–	–	–	–	3	–	–	–	–	5
Lord	–	–	–	–	–	–	–	–	3	–	–	–	–	–	–	–	–	–	–	–	–	3
King [Show]	–	–	–	–	–	–	–	–	–	–	–	–	–	–	–	–	–	–	–	–	–	0
Messenger	–	–	–	–	–	–	–	–	–	–	0	–	–	9	–	–	–	9	–	–	–	18
#5																						
Messenger	5	–	–	–	–	–	–	–	–	–	–	–	–	–	–	–	–	–	–	–	–	5
King [Show]	–	–	–	–	–	–	–	–	–	–	–	–	–	–	–	–	–	–	–	–	–	0
Murderer [Macd. Wife]	–	–	–	–	–	–	–	–	–	–	0	–	–	–	–	–	0	–	–	–	–	0
Seyton	–	–	–	–	–	–	–	–	–	–	–	–	–	–	–	–	3	2	–	–	–	5
Thane	–	–	–	–	–	–	–	–	–	–	–	–	–	–	–	–	–	–	–	–	0	0
#6																						
Donalbaine–	0	–	–	–	–	–	5	–	–	8	0	–	–	–	–	–	–	–	–	–	–	5
3 Murderer–	–	–	–	–	–	–	–	–	–	8	–	–	–	–	–	–	–	–	–	–	–	8
King [Show]	–	–	–	–	–	–	–	–	–	–	–	–	–	–	–	–	–	–	–	–	–	0
Seyward's Son	–	–	–	–	–	–	–	–	–	–	–	–	–	–	–	–	–	–	–	7	–	7
Thane	–	–	–	–	–	–	–	–	–	–	–	–	–	–	–	–	–	–	–	–	0	0
#7																						
Att.[King]–	0	–	–	–	–	0	–	–	–	–	0	–	–	–	–	–	–	–	–	–	–	0
Torch [Fleance]	–	–	–	–	–	–	–	–	–	–	–	–	–	–	–	–	–	–	–	–	–	0
Attendant [Macbeth]	–	–	–	–	–	–	–	–	–	–	0	–	–	–	–	0	0	–	–	–	–	0
King [Show]	–	–	–	–	–	–	–	–	–	–	–	–	–	–	–	–	–	–	–	–	–	0
Soldier [Menteth]	–	–	–	–	–	–	–	–	–	–	–	–	0	–	–	0	1	–	1	–	–	1
Soldier [Macbeth]	–	–	–	–	–	–	–	–	–	–	–	–	–	1	–	–	–	1	–	–	0	0
Soldier [Malcolm]	–	–	–	–	–	–	–	–	–	–	–	–	–	–	–	–	–	–	–	–	0	0

```
#8
Att.[King]-          0
Attendant [Macbeth]
1 Apparition -                                    3
Soldier [Menteth]
Soldier [Macbeth]-
Soldier [Malcolm]-
#9
Att.[King]-          0
Attendant [Macbeth]
Servant [Macbeth]-                                2
Soldier [Menteth]
Soldier [Macbeth]-
Soldier [Malcolm]-

                    Boys

#1
Fleance -                                         3
2 Apparition -                                    5
#2
3 Apparition -

            Lines Minor Parts  -    189 =  8%
            Principal Parts    -  2,167 = 92%
                                  ───────
                                   2,356
```

Table 72
Antony and Cleopatra (F)

Principal Parts
Men

			1						2										3	
	1	2	3	4	5	1	2	3	4	5	6	7	1	2	3	4	5	6	7	8
#1 Anthony	26	63	47	-	-	-	83	25	-	-	14	28	-	20	-	25	-	-	23	-
#2 Octavius-Caesar	-	-	61	-	-	-	50	1	-	-	12	14	-	20	-	-	-	78	-	6
#3 Enobarbus	-	44	-	-	-	-	79	-	-	-	37	20	-	23	-	-	8	-	28	-
#4 Pompey	-	-	-	-	-	43	-	-	-	-	63	30	-	-	-	-	-	-	-	-
Dollabella	-	-	-	-	-	-	-	-	-	-	-	-	-	-	-	-	-	-	-	-
#5 Lepidus	-	-	-	15	-	-	25	-	7	-	4	11	-	2	-	-	-	-	-	-
Eros	-	-	-	-	-	-	-	-	-	-	-	-	-	-	-	-	16	-	-	-
#6 Menas	-	-	-	-	-	5	-	-	-	-	21	31	-	-	-	-	-	-	-	-
Scarrus	-	-	-	-	-	-	-	-	-	-	-	-	-	-	-	-	-	-	-	-
#7 Agrippa	-	-	-	-	-	-	28	-	2	-	0	0	-	12	-	-	-	4	-	-
#8 Messenger	-	-	-	-	-	-	-	-	25	-	-	-	-	15	-	-	-	-	-	-
Proculeius	-	-	-	-	-	-	-	-	-	-	-	-	-	-	-	-	-	-	-	-
#9 Alexas	-	19	0	-	17	-	-	-	0	-	-	-	-	-	3	-	-	-	-	-
#10 Ventidius	-	-	-	-	-	-	0	-	-	-	-	30	-	-	-	-	-	-	-	-
Thidius	-	-	-	-	-	-	-	-	-	-	-	-	-	-	-	-	-	-	-	-
#11 Mecenas	-	-	-	-	-	-	15	-	2	-	0	0	-	-	-	-	-	9	-	-
#12 Soothsayer	-	13	-	-	-	-	-	17	-	-	-	-	-	-	-	-	-	-	-	-
Camidius	-	-	-	-	-	-	-	-	-	-	-	-	-	-	-	-	-	-	16	-
1 Guard	-	-	-	-	-	-	-	-	-	-	-	-	-	-	-	-	-	-	-	-

Boys

	1	2	3	4	5	1	2	3	4	5	6	7	1	2	3	4	5	6	7	8
#1 Cleopatra	20	8	73	-	58	-	-	-	-	108	-	-	-	-	36	-	-	-	15	-
#2 Charmian	0	33	8	-	8	-	-	-	-	9	-	-	-	-	9	-	-	-	-	-
#3 Octavia	-	-	-	-	-	-	-	2	-	-	-	-	-	3	-	16	-	14	-	-
#4 Iras	0	11	0	-	0	-	-	-	-	0	-	-	-	-	0	-	-	-	-	-

Minor Parts
Men

	1	2	3	4	5	1	2	3	4	5	6	7	1	2	3	4	5	6	7	8
#1 Philo	18	-	-	-	-	-	-	-	-	-	-	-	-	-	-	-	-	-	-	-
Captain	-	-	-	-	-	-	-	-	-	-	0	-	-	-	-	-	-	-	-	-
Messenger	-	-	-	-	-	-	-	-	-	-	-	-	-	15	-	-	-	-	-	-
Centerie	-	-	-	-	-	-	-	-	-	-	-	-	-	-	-	-	-	-	-	-
Diomedes	-	-	-	-	-	-	-	-	-	-	-	-	-	-	-	-	-	-	-	-
#2 Messenger	-	15	-	-	-	-	-	-	-	-	-	-	-	-	-	-	-	-	-	-
Ambassador	-	-	-	-	-	-	-	-	-	-	-	-	-	-	-	-	-	-	-	-
1 Watch	-	-	-	-	-	-	-	-	-	-	-	-	-	-	-	-	-	-	-	-
Clowne	-	-	-	-	-	-	-	-	-	-	-	-	-	-	-	-	-	-	-	-

Table 72

9	10	11	12	13	1	2	3	4	5	6	7	4 8	9	10	11	12	13	14	15	5 1	2	Totals
4	-	59	-	109	-	41	-	29	11	-	8	39	-	9	-	45	-	108	23	-	-	839
-	-	-	22	-	13	-	-	-	-	10	-	-	-	-	4	-	-	-	-	54	58	403
0	15	-	-	44	-	11	-	-	-	20	-	-	17	-	-	-	-	-	-	-	-	346
-	-	-	-	-	-	-	-	-	-	-	-	-	-	-	-	-	-	-	-	-	-	136
-	-	-	5	-	-	-	-	-	-	0	-	-	-	-	-	-	-	-	-	1	42	48
-	-	-	-	-	-	-	-	-	-	-	-	-	-	-	-	-	-	-	-	-	-	64
-	-	8	-	-	-	-	-	1	9	-	2	-	-	-	-	-	-	18	-	-	-	54
-	-	-	-	-	-	-	-	-	-	-	-	-	-	-	-	-	-	-	-	0	-	57
-	20	-	-	-	-	-	-	-	-	11	0	-	1	-	7	-	-	-	-	-	-	39
-	-	-	0	-	0	-	-	-	-	1	3	-	-	-	-	-	-	-	-	0	-	50
-	-	-	-	-	-	-	-	-	-	-	-	-	-	-	-	-	-	-	-	-	-	40
-	-	-	-	-	-	-	-	-	-	-	-	-	-	-	-	-	-	-	-	1	32	33
-	-	-	-	-	-	0	-	-	-	-	-	-	-	-	-	-	-	-	-	-	-	39
-	-	-	-	-	-	-	-	-	-	-	-	-	-	-	-	-	-	-	-	-	-	30
-	-	-	2	29	-	-	-	-	-	-	-	-	-	-	-	-	-	-	-	-	-	31
-	-	-	-	-	5	-	-	-	-	-	-	-	-	-	-	-	-	-	-	3	0	34
-	-	-	-	-	-	-	-	-	-	-	-	-	-	-	-	-	-	-	-	-	-	30
-	9	-	-	-	-	-	-	-	-	-	-	-	-	-	-	-	-	-	-	-	-	25
-	-	-	-	-	-	-	-	-	-	-	-	-	-	-	-	-	-	5	0	-	20	25
-	-	8	-	45	-	2	-	10	-	-	-	5	-	-	-	1	8	-	71	-	225	693
-	-	2	-	0	-	0	-	1	-	-	-	-	-	-	-	-	4	-	5	-	19	98
-	-	-	-	-	-	-	-	-	-	-	-	-	-	-	-	-	-	-	-	-	-	35
-	-	4	-	0	-	0	-	-	-	-	-	-	-	-	-	-	0	-	0	-	7	22

Total Lines Principal Parts   3,1$\overline{71}$

9	10	11	12	13	1	2	3	4	5	6	7	8	9	10	11	12	13	14	15	1	2	Totals
-	-	-	-	-	-	-	-	-	-	-	-	-	-	-	-	-	-	-	-	-	-	18
-	-	-	-	-	-	-	-	1	-	-	-	-	-	-	-	-	-	-	-	-	-	1
-	-	-	-	-	-	-	-	-	-	-	-	-	-	-	-	-	-	-	-	-	-	15
-	-	-	-	-	-	-	-	-	-	-	-	-	13	-	-	-	-	-	-	-	-	13
-	-	-	-	-	-	-	-	-	-	-	-	-	-	-	-	-	-	15	3	-	-	18
-	-	-	-	-	-	-	-	-	-	-	-	-	-	-	-	-	-	-	-	-	-	15
-	-	-	14	2	-	-	-	-	-	-	-	-	-	-	-	-	-	-	-	-	-	16
-	-	-	-	-	-	-	-	-	-	-	-	-	5	-	-	-	-	-	-	-	-	5
-	-	-	-	-	-	-	-	-	-	-	-	-	-	-	-	-	-	-	-	-	12	12

Table 72 (*cont.*)

#3

	1	2	3	4	5	6	7	8	9	10	11	12	13	14	15	16	17	18	19	20
Mardian	–	1	–	–	6	–	–	–	–	1	–	–	–	–	–	–	–	–	–	–
Roman	–	–	–	–	–	–	–	–	–	–	11	–	–	–	–	–	–	–	–	–
Mecenas	–	–	–	–	–	–	–	–	–	–	–	–	–	–	–	–	–	–	–	–
Soldier [Caesar]	–	–	–	–	–	–	–	–	–	–	–	–	–	–	–	–	–	–	–	–
2 Watch	–	–	–	–	–	–	–	–	–	–	–	–	–	–	–	–	–	–	–	–
Counsel	–	–	–	–	–	–	–	–	–	–	–	–	–	–	–	–	–	–	–	–
Seleucus	–	–	–	–	–	–	–	–	–	–	–	–	–	–	–	–	–	–	–	–

#4

	1	2	3	4	5	6	7	8	9	10	11	12	13	14	15	16	17	18	19	20
Demetrius	4	–	–	–	–	–	–	–	–	–	–	–	–	–	–	–	–	–	–	–
Menecrates	–	–	–	–	7	–	–	–	–	–	–	–	–	–	–	–	–	–	–	–
1 Servant	–	–	–	–	–	–	–	–	–	9	–	–	–	–	–	–	–	–	–	–
Messenger	–	–	–	–	–	–	–	–	–	–	–	–	–	–	–	–	–	–	1	–
1 Soldier [Anthony]	–	–	–	–	–	–	–	–	–	–	–	–	–	–	–	–	–	–	–	–
Dercetas	–	–	–	–	–	–	–	–	–	–	–	–	–	–	–	–	–	–	–	–

#5

	1	2	3	4	5	6	7	8	9	10	11	12	13	14	15	16	17	18	19	20
Messenger	1	–	–	–	–	–	–	–	–	–	–	–	–	–	–	–	–	–	–	–
Drum	–	–	–	–	–	–	–	–	0	–	–	–	–	–	–	–	–	–	–	–
2 Servant	–	–	–	–	–	–	–	–	–	7	–	–	–	–	–	–	–	–	–	–
2 Soldier [Anthony]	–	–	–	–	–	–	–	–	–	–	–	–	–	–	–	–	–	–	–	–
Towrus	–	–	–	–	–	–	–	–	–	–	–	–	–	–	–	–	–	–	–	1
2 Guard	–	–	–	–	–	–	–	–	–	–	–	–	–	–	–	–	–	–	–	–
Servant	–	–	–	–	–	–	–	–	–	–	–	–	–	–	–	–	–	–	–	–
Counsel	–	–	–	–	–	–	–	–	–	–	–	–	–	–	–	–	–	–	–	–

#6

	1	2	3	4	5	6	7	8	9	10	11	12	13	14	15	16	17	18	19	20
Messenger	–	15	–	–	–	–	–	–	–	–	–	–	–	–	–	–	–	–	–	–
Ventigius	–	–	–	–	–	–	0	–	–	–	–	–	–	–	–	–	–	–	–	–
Trumpet	–	–	–	–	–	–	–	–	0	–	–	–	–	–	–	–	–	–	–	–
3 Soldier [Anthony]	–	–	–	–	–	–	–	–	–	–	–	–	–	–	–	–	–	–	–	–
3 Guard	–	–	–	–	–	–	–	–	–	–	–	–	–	–	–	–	–	–	–	–
Guard	–	–	–	–	–	–	–	–	–	–	–	–	–	–	–	–	–	–	–	–
Egyptian	–	–	–	–	–	–	–	–	–	–	–	–	–	–	–	–	–	–	–	–

#7

	1	2	3	4	5	6	7	8	9	10	11	12	13	14	15	16	17	18	19	20
1 Messenger	–	2	–	16	–	–	–	–	–	–	–	–	–	–	–	–	–	–	–	–
Varrius	–	–	–	–	4	–	–	–	–	–	–	–	–	–	–	–	–	–	–	–
Pacorus [body]	–	–	–	–	–	–	–	–	–	–	0	–	–	–	–	–	–	–	–	–
4 Soldier [Anthony]	–	–	–	–	–	–	–	–	–	–	–	–	–	–	–	–	–	–	–	–
4 Guard	–	–	–	–	–	–	–	–	–	–	–	–	–	–	–	–	–	–	–	–
Gallus	–	–	–	–	–	–	–	–	–	–	–	–	–	–	–	–	–	–	–	–
Soldier	–	–	–	–	–	–	–	–	–	–	–	–	–	–	–	–	–	–	13	–

#8

	1	2	3	4	5	6	7	8	9	10	11	12	13	14	15	16	17	18	19	20
2 Messenger	–	1	–	–	–	–	–	–	–	–	–	–	–	–	–	–	–	–	–	–
Army [Camidius]	–	–	–	–	–	–	–	–	–	–	–	–	–	–	–	–	–	–	–	–
Attendant [Anthony]	–	–	–	–	–	–	–	–	–	–	–	–	–	–	–	–	–	–	–	–
Other [Anthony]	–	–	–	–	–	–	–	–	–	–	–	–	–	–	–	–	–	–	–	–
Servitor [Anthony]	–	–	–	–	–	–	–	–	–	–	–	–	–	–	–	–	–	–	–	–
Army [Anthony]	–	–	–	–	–	–	–	–	–	–	–	–	–	–	–	–	–	–	–	–

#9

	1	2	3	4	5	6	7	8	9	10	11	12	13	14	15	16	17	18	19	20
Eunuch	0	–	–	–	–	–	–	–	–	–	–	–	–	–	–	–	–	–	–	–
3 Messenger	–	1	–	–	–	–	–	–	–	–	–	–	–	–	–	–	–	–	–	–
Army [Camidius]	–	–	–	–	–	–	–	–	–	–	–	–	–	–	–	–	–	–	–	–
Attendant [Anthony]	–	–	–	–	–	–	–	–	–	–	–	–	–	–	–	–	–	–	–	–
Other [Anthony]	–	–	–	–	–	–	–	–	–	–	–	–	–	–	–	–	–	–	–	–
Servitor [Anthony]	–	–	–	–	–	–	–	–	–	–	–	–	–	–	–	–	–	–	–	–
Army [Anthony]	–	–	–	–	–	–	–	–	–	–	–	–	–	–	–	–	–	–	–	–

Table 72   233

–	–	–	–	–	–	–	–	–	–	–	–	–	–	–	–	–	0	12	–	–	0	20
–	–	–	–	–	–	–	–	–	–	–	–	–	–	–	–	–	–	–	–	–	–	11
–	–	–	–	–	5	–	–	–	–	–	–	–	–	–	–	–	–	–	–	–	–	5
–	–	–	–	–	–	–	–	–	–	10	–	–	–	–	–	–	–	–	–	–	–	10
–	–	–	–	–	–	–	–	–	–	–	–	5	–	–	–	–	–	–	–	–	–	5
–	–	–	–	–	–	–	–	–	–	–	–	–	–	–	–	–	–	–	–	0	–	0
–	–	–	–	–	–	–	–	–	–	–	–	–	–	–	–	–	–	–	–	–	4	4
–	–	–	–	–	–	–	–	–	–	–	–	–	–	–	–	–	–	–	–	–	–	4
–	–	–	–	–	–	–	–	–	–	–	–	–	–	–	–	–	–	–	–	–	–	7
–	–	–	–	–	–	–	–	–	–	–	–	–	–	–	–	–	–	–	–	–	–	9
–	–	–	–	–	–	–	–	–	–	–	–	–	–	–	–	–	–	–	–	–	–	1
–	–	–	–	–	–	–	13	2	–	–	–	–	–	–	–	–	–	–	–	–	–	15
–	–	–	–	–	–	–	–	–	–	–	–	–	–	–	–	–	–	4	–	16	–	20
–	–	–	–	–	–	–	–	–	–	–	–	–	–	–	–	–	–	–	–	–	–	1
–	–	–	–	–	–	–	–	–	–	–	0	–	–	–	–	–	–	–	–	–	–	0
–	–	–	–	–	–	–	–	–	–	–	–	–	–	–	–	–	–	–	–	–	–	7
–	–	–	–	–	–	–	12	0	–	–	–	–	–	–	–	–	–	–	–	–	–	12
–	0	–	–	–	–	–	–	–	–	–	–	–	–	–	–	–	–	–	–	–	–	1
–	–	–	–	–	–	–	–	–	–	–	–	–	–	–	–	–	–	2	–	–	2	4
–	–	–	–	3	–	–	–	–	–	–	–	–	–	–	–	–	–	–	–	–	–	3
–	–	–	–	–	–	–	–	–	–	–	–	–	–	–	–	–	–	–	–	0	–	0
–	–	–	–	–	–	–	–	–	–	–	–	–	–	–	–	–	–	–	–	–	–	15
–	–	–	–	–	–	–	–	–	–	–	–	–	–	–	–	–	–	–	–	–	–	0
–	–	–	–	–	–	–	–	–	–	–	0	–	–	–	–	–	–	–	–	–	–	0
–	–	–	–	–	–	–	2	0	–	–	–	–	–	–	–	–	–	–	–	–	–	2
–	–	–	–	–	–	–	–	–	–	–	–	–	–	–	–	–	–	1	–	–	–	1
–	–	–	–	–	–	–	–	–	–	–	–	–	–	–	–	–	–	–	0	–	–	0
–	–	–	–	–	–	–	–	–	–	–	–	–	–	–	–	–	–	–	6	–	–	6
–	–	–	–	–	–	–	–	–	–	–	–	–	–	–	–	–	–	–	–	–	–	18
–	–	–	–	–	–	–	–	–	–	–	–	–	–	–	–	–	–	–	–	–	–	4
–	–	–	–	–	–	–	–	–	–	–	–	–	–	–	–	–	–	–	–	–	–	0
–	–	–	–	–	–	–	2	0	–	–	–	–	–	–	–	–	–	–	–	–	–	2
–	–	–	–	–	–	–	–	–	–	–	–	–	–	–	–	–	0	0	–	–	–	0
–	–	–	–	–	–	–	–	–	–	–	–	–	–	–	–	–	–	–	–	–	0	0
–	–	–	–	–	–	–	–	2	–	–	–	–	–	–	–	–	–	–	–	–	–	15
–	–	–	–	–	–	–	–	–	–	–	–	–	–	–	–	–	–	–	–	–	–	1
–	0	–	–	–	–	–	–	–	–	–	–	–	–	–	–	–	–	–	–	–	–	0
–	–	0	–	–	–	–	–	–	–	–	–	–	–	–	–	–	–	–	–	–	–	0
–	–	–	–	–	–	–	–	–	0	–	–	0	–	–	–	–	–	–	–	–	0	0
–	–	–	–	–	–	0	–	–	–	–	–	–	–	–	–	–	–	–	–	–	–	0
–	–	–	–	–	–	–	–	–	–	–	0	–	–	–	–	–	–	–	–	–	–	0
–	–	–	–	–	–	–	–	–	–	–	–	–	–	–	–	–	–	–	–	–	–	0
–	–	–	–	–	–	–	–	–	–	–	–	–	–	–	–	–	–	–	–	–	–	1
–	0	–	–	–	–	–	–	–	–	–	–	–	–	–	–	–	–	–	–	–	–	0
–	–	0	–	–	–	–	–	–	–	–	–	–	–	–	–	–	–	–	–	–	–	0
–	–	–	–	–	–	–	–	–	0	–	–	0	–	–	–	–	–	–	–	–	0	0
–	–	–	–	–	–	0	–	–	–	–	–	–	–	–	–	–	–	–	–	–	–	0
–	–	–	–	–	–	–	–	–	–	–	0	–	–	–	–	–	–	–	–	–	–	0

Table 72 (*cont.*)

#10
```
Eunuch           0  -  -  -  -  -  -  -  -  -  -  -  -  -  -  -  -  -  -  -  -
Army [Camidius]  -  -  -  -  -  -  -  -  -  -  -  -  -  -  -  -  -  -  -  -  -
Attendant [Anthony] -  -  -  -  -  -  -  -  -  -  -  -  -  -  -  -  -  -  -  -
Other [Anthony]  -  -  -  -  -  -  -  -  -  -  -  -  -  -  -  -  -  -  -  -  -
Servitor [Anthony] -  -  -  -  -  -  -  -  -  -  -  -  -  -  -  -  -  -  -  -
Army [Anthony]   -  -  -  -  -  -  -  -  -  -  -  -  -  -  -  -  -  -  -  -  -
```
#11
```
Train [Caesar]   -  -  0  -  -  -  -  -  -  -  -  -  -  -  -  -  -  -  -  -  -
Soldier [Menas]  -  -  -  -  -  -  -  -  -  0  -  -  -  -  -  -  -  -  -  -  -
Other [Caesar]   -  -  -  -  -  -  -  -  -  -  0  -  -  -  0  -  -  -  -  -  -
Soldier [Roman]  -  -  -  -  -  -  -  -  -  -  -  0  -  -  -  -  -  -  -  -  -
Army [Caesar]    -  -  -  -  -  -  -  -  -  -  -  -  -  -  -  -  -  -  0  -  -
Army [Mecenas]   -  -  -  -  -  -  -  -  -  -  -  -  -  -  -  -  -  -  -  -  -
```
#12
```
Rannius          -  0  -  -  -  -  -  -  -  -  -  -  -  -  -  -  -  -  -  -  -
Train [Caesar]   -  -  0  -  -  -  -  -  -  -  -  -  -  -  -  -  -  -  -  -  -
Soldier [Menas]  -  -  -  -  -  -  -  -  -  0  -  -  -  -  -  -  -  -  -  -  -
Soldier [Roman]  -  -  -  -  -  -  -  -  -  -  -  0  -  -  -  -  -  -  -  -  -
Other [Caesar]   -  -  -  -  -  -  -  -  -  -  0  -  -  -  0  -  -  -  -  -  -
Army [Caesar]    -  -  -  -  -  -  -  -  -  -  -  -  -  -  -  -  -  -  0  -  -
Army [Mecenas]   -  -  -  -  -  -  -  -  -  -  -  -  -  -  -  -  -  -  -  -  -
```
#13
```
Lucillus         -  0  -  -  -  -  -  -  -  -  -  -  -  -  -  -  -  -  -  -  -
Train [Caesar]   -  -  0  -  -  -  -  -  -  -  -  -  -  -  -  -  -  -  -  -  -
Soldier [Menas]  -  -  -  -  -  -  -  -  -  0  -  -  -  -  -  -  -  -  -  -  -
Soldier [Roman]  -  -  -  -  -  -  -  -  -  -  -  0  -  -  -  -  -  -  -  -  -
Other [Caesar]   -  -  -  -  -  -  -  -  -  -  -  -  -  -  0  -  -  -  -  -  -
Army [Caesar]    -  -  -  -  -  -  -  -  -  -  -  -  -  -  -  -  -  -  0  -  -
Army [Mecenas]   -  -  -  -  -  -  -  -  -  -  -  -  -  -  -  -  -  -  -  -  -
```

#1
```
Train [Cleo]     0  -  -  -  -  -  -  -  -  -  -  -  -  -  -  -  -  -  -  -  -
Train [Octavia]  -  -  -  -  -  -  -  -  -  -  -  -  -  -  -  -  -  0  -  -  -
Maid [Cleopatra] -  -  -  -  -  -  -  -  -  -  -  -  -  -  -  -  -  -  -  -  -
Other [Cleopatra] -  -  -  -  -  -  -  -  -  -  -  -  -  -  -  -  -  -  -  -  -
```
#2
```
Train [Cleo]     0  -  -  -  -  -  -  -  -  -  -  -  -  -  -  -  -  -  -  -  -
Train [Octavia]  -  -  -  -  -  -  -  -  -  -  -  -  -  -  -  -  -  0  -  -  -
Maid [Cleopatra] -  -  -  -  -  -  -  -  -  -  -  -  -  -  -  -  -  -  -  -  -
Other [Cleopatra] -  -  -  -  -  -  -  -  -  -  -  -  -  -  -  -  -  -  -  -  -
```
#3
```
Train [Cleo]     0  -  -  -  -  -  -  -  -  -  -  -  -  -  -  -  -  -  -  -  -
Train [Octavia]  -  -  -  -  -  -  -  -  -  -  -  -  -  -  -  -  -  0  -  -  -
Maid [Cleopatra] -  -  -  -  -  -  -  -  -  -  -  -  -  -  -  -  -  -  -  -  -
Other [Cleopatra] -  -  -  -  -  -  -  -  -  -  -  -  -  -  -  -  -  -  -  -  -
```

Table 72 235

–	–	–	–	–	–	–	–	–	–	–	–	–	–	–	–	–	–	–	–	–	–	–	–		0
0	–	–	–	–	–	–	–	–	–	–	–	–	–	–	–	–	–	–	–	–	–	–	–		0
–	0	–	–	–	–	–	–	–	–	–	–	–	–	–	–	–	–	–	–	–	–	–	–		0
–	–	–	–	–	–	–	0	–	–	–	0	–	–	–	–	–	–	0	–	0					0
–	–	–	–	–	–	0	–	–	–	–	–	–	–	–	–	–	–	–	–	–					0
–	–	–	–	–	–	–	–	–	–	–	0	–	–	–	–	–	–	–	–	–					0
–	–	–	–	–	–	–	–	–	–	–	–	–	–	–	–	–	–	–	–	0					0
–	–	–	–	–	–	–	–	–	–	–	–	–	–	–	–	–	–	–	–	–					0
–	–	–	–	–	–	–	–	–	–	–	–	–	–	–	–	–	–	–	–	–					0
–	–	–	–	–	–	–	–	–	–	–	–	–	–	–	–	–	–	–	–	0					0
0	–	–	–	–	–	–	–	–	–	–	–	–	–	0	–	–	–	–	–	–					0
–	–	–	–	0	–	–	–	–	–	–	–	–	–	–	–	–	–	–	–	–					0
–	–	–	–	–	–	–	–	–	–	–	–	–	–	–	–	–	–	–	–	–					0
–	–	–	–	–	–	–	–	–	–	–	–	–	–	–	–	–	–	–	–	0					0
–	–	–	–	–	–	–	–	–	–	–	–	–	–	–	–	–	–	–	–	–					0
–	–	–	–	–	–	–	–	–	–	–	–	–	–	–	–	–	–	–	–	–					0
–	–	–	–	–	–	0	–	–	–	–	–	–	–	–	–	–	–	–	–	–					0
0	–	–	–	–	–	–	–	–	–	–	–	–	0	–	–	–	–	–	–	–					0
–	–	–	–	0	–	–	–	–	–	–	–	–	–	–	–	–	–	–	–	–					0
–	–	–	–	–	–	–	–	–	–	–	–	–	–	–	–	–	–	–	–	–					0
–	–	–	–	–	–	–	–	–	–	–	–	–	–	–	–	–	–	–	–	0					0
–	–	–	–	–	–	–	–	–	–	–	–	–	–	–	–	–	–	–	–	–					0
–	–	–	–	–	–	–	–	–	–	–	–	–	–	–	–	–	–	–	–	–					0
–	–	–	–	–	–	–	–	–	–	–	–	–	–	–	–	–	–	–	–	–					0
0	–	–	–	–	–	–	–	–	–	–	–	–	0	–	–	–	–	–	–	–					0
–	–	–	–	0	–	–	–	–	–	–	–	–	–	–	–	–	–	–	–	–					0

Boys

–	–	–	–	–	–	–	–	–	–	–	–	–	–	–	–	–	–	–	–	–					0
–	–	–	–	–	–	–	–	–	–	–	–	–	–	–	–	–	–	–	–	–					0
–	–	–	–	–	–	–	–	–	–	–	–	–	–	–	–	–	–	0	–	–					0
–	–	–	–	–	0	–	–	–	–	–	–	–	–	–	–	–	–	–	–	–					0
–	–	–	–	–	–	–	–	–	–	–	–	–	–	–	–	–	–	–	–	–					0
–	–	–	–	–	–	–	–	–	–	–	–	–	–	–	–	–	–	–	–	–					0
–	–	–	–	–	–	–	–	–	–	–	–	–	–	–	–	–	–	0	–	–					0
–	–	–	–	–	0	–	–	–	–	–	–	–	–	–	–	–	–	–	–	–					0
–	–	–	–	–	–	–	–	–	–	–	–	–	–	–	–	–	–	–	–	–					0
–	–	–	–	–	–	–	–	–	–	–	–	–	–	–	–	–	–	–	–	–					0
–	–	–	–	–	–	–	–	–	–	–	–	–	–	–	–	–	–	0	–	–					0
–	–	–	–	–	0	–	–	–	–	–	–	–	–	–	–	–	–	–	–	–					0

Total Lines Minor Parts	317= 9%
Principal Parts	3,171=91%
	3,484

Table 73
Coriolanus (F)

Principal Parts

The scene columns are grouped by Act (1–5); within each group the numbers are the scene numbers. The final column is the row total.

Men

Role	1.1	1.2	1.3	1.4	1.5	1.6	1.7	1.8	1.9	1.10	2.1	2.2	2.3	3.1	3.2	3.3	4.1	4.2	4.3	4.4	4.5	4.6	4.7	5.1	5.2	5.3	5.4	5.5	5.6	Totals
#1 Martius-Coriolanus	75	–	–	36	17	51	–	9	44	–	–	18	22	58	141	68	51	44	–	–	–	25	62	–	14	103	–	–	34	872
#2 Menenius Agrippa	94	–	–	–	–	–	–	–	–	–	121	37	12	94	20	14	5	5	–	–	–	38	–	56	50	–	33	–	–	579
#3 Sicinius Velutus	15	–	–	–	–	–	–	–	–	–	27	8	–	51	57	52	–	15	–	–	–	11	–	37	–	–	13	–	–	286
#4 Tullus Auffidius	–	30	–	–	–	–	–	9	–	32	–	–	–	–	–	–	–	–	–	–	57	–	48	–	–	8	–	–	86	270
#5 Cominius	3	–	–	–	–	–	–	–	54	–	–	47	24	4	11	–	49	–	–	–	–	39	–	30	–	–	–	–	–	261
#6 Brutus	18	–	–	–	–	–	–	–	–	–	56	–	4	54	42	22	–	11	–	–	–	9	–	19	–	–	–	–	–	235
#7 1 Citizen	31	–	–	–	–	–	–	–	–	–	–	–	–	10	2	–	–	–	–	–	–	7	–	–	–	–	–	–	–	50
#7 1 Servingman	–	–	–	–	–	–	–	–	–	–	–	–	–	–	–	–	–	–	–	–	30	–	–	–	–	–	–	–	–	30
#7 1 Watch	–	–	–	–	–	–	–	–	–	–	–	–	–	–	–	–	–	–	–	–	–	31	–	–	–	–	–	–	–	31
#8 2 Citizen	43	–	–	–	–	–	–	–	–	–	–	–	–	16	–	–	–	–	–	–	–	2	–	–	–	–	–	–	–	61
#8 2 Servingman	–	–	–	–	–	–	–	–	–	–	–	–	–	–	–	–	–	–	–	–	32	–	–	–	–	–	–	–	–	32
#9 3 Citizen	0	–	–	–	–	–	–	–	–	–	–	–	–	49	–	–	–	4	–	–	–	–	–	–	–	–	–	–	–	53
#9 3 Servingman	–	–	–	–	–	–	–	–	–	–	–	–	–	–	–	–	–	–	–	–	47	–	–	–	–	–	–	–	–	47
#10 Titus Lartius	0	–	–	16	11	–	7	–	5	–	–	–	–	12	4	–	–	–	–	–	–	–	–	–	–	–	–	–	–	55
#11 1 Senator	7	–	–	–	–	–	–	–	–	–	–	–	13	–	–	2	–	–	–	–	–	–	–	–	–	–	–	–	–	22
#11 Roman	–	–	–	–	–	–	–	–	–	–	–	–	–	–	–	–	–	–	29	–	–	–	–	–	–	–	–	–	–	29

Boys

Role	1.1	1.2	1.3	1.4	1.5	1.6	1.7	1.8	1.9	1.10	2.1	2.2	2.3	3.1	3.2	3.3	4.1	4.2	4.3	4.4	4.5	4.6	4.7	5.1	5.2	5.3	5.4	5.5	5.6	Totals
#1 Volumnia	–	–	49	–	–	–	–	–	–	–	42	–	–	–	80	–	7	34	–	–	–	–	–	–	–	104	–	–	–	316
#2 Valeria	–	–	40	–	–	–	–	–	–	–	1	–	–	–	–	–	–	–	–	–	–	–	–	–	–	0	–	0	–	41
#3 Virgilia	–	–	24	–	–	–	–	–	–	–	3	–	–	–	–	–	1	3	–	–	–	–	–	–	–	3	–	–	–	34

Total Lines Principal Parts 3,304

Minor Parts
Men

Part	Total
#1	
Messenger	2
Drum	0
Lieutenant	1
Herald	6
Aedile	17
1 Conspiritor	8
#2	
2 Senator	4
1 Senator [Coriolus]	16
Scout	0
Messenger	11
2 Conspirator	6
#3	
2 Senator [Coriolus]	7
1 Officer	15
Citizen	4
2 Watch	11
3 Conspirator	12
#4	
Other	0
Power [Titus]	0
2 Officer	22
Voice	21
Lord	0
1 Lord	13
#5	
Other	0
Power [Titus]	0
4 Citizen	10
Lord	0
2 Lord	10
Lieutenant	10
#6	
Usher	0
Colors	0
Power [Titus]	0
5 Citizen	2
Noble	0
Lord	0
3 Lord	2

Table 73 (*cont.*)

	Total
#7	
Army [Volces]	4
6 Citizen	2
Messenger	13
Attendant [Aufidius]-	0
#8	
Army [Volces]	0
7 Citizen	2
Messenger	6
Attendant [Aufidius]-	0
#9	
Messenger	11
Patrician	2
Trumpet	0
Messenger	14
Attendant [Aufidius]-	0
#10	
1 Soldier [Roman]	8
Noble	0
Other	0
Commoner [Coriolanus]	0
#11	
2 Soldier [Roman]	2
Other	0
Commoner [Coriolanus]	0
#12	
3 Soldier [Roman]	1
Noble	1
Commoner [Coriolanus]	0
#13	
Captain [Roman]	0
Patrician	0
Drum	0
#14	
Army [Volces]	0
Colors	0
Boys	
#1	
Gentlewoman	1
Young Martius-Boy	2
#2	
Attendant[Volumnia]-	0
#3	
Attendant[Volumnia]-	0
#4	
Attendant[Volumnia]-	0

Total Lines Minor Parts 279= 7%
Principal Parts 3,304=93%
3,583

Table 74   239

Table 74
Timon of Athens (F)

Principal Parts — Men

	1		2		3						4			5				Totals
	1	2	1	2	1	2	3	4	5	6	1	2	3	1	2	3	4	
#1																		
Lord Timon	72	103	–	67	–	–	–	26	–	50	41	–	378	130	–	–	–	867
#2																		
Apemantus	51	75	–	26	–	–	–	–	–	–	–	–	99	–	–	–	–	251
#3																		
Alcibiades	2	4	–	–	–	–	–	–	80	–	–	–	–	31	–	–	40	157
#4																		
Steward	–	–	–	85	–	–	–	19	6	–	34	–	12	–	–	–	–	156
#5																		
1 Senator	0	–	36	–	–	–	–	–	35	0	–	–	–	28	3	–	25	127
Lucius	–	–	–	–	–	40	–	12	–	–	–	–	–	–	–	–	–	52
#6																		
Poet	81	–	–	–	–	–	–	–	–	–	–	–	–	30	–	–	–	111
Lucullus	–	–	–	–	33	–	–	–	–	–	–	–	–	–	–	–	–	33
#7																		
Painter	31	–	–	–	–	–	–	–	–	–	–	–	–	45	–	–	–	76
#8																		
2 Senator	0	–	–	–	–	–	–	–	11	0	–	–	–	26	1	–	24	62
Flaminius	–	–	–	1	24	–	–	3	–	–	–	–	–	–	–	–	–	28
#9																		
1 Lord	9	12	–	–	–	–	–	–	–	6	–	–	–	–	–	–	–	27
1 Stranger	–	–	–	–	–	30	–	–	–	–	–	–	–	–	–	–	–	30
#10																		
Old Athenian	29	–	–	–	–	–	–	–	–	–	–	–	–	–	–	–	–	29
Sempronius	–	–	–	–	–	–	26	–	–	–	–	–	–	–	–	–	–	26

Total Lines Principal Parts 2,032

Minor Parts — Men

	1		2		3						4			5				Totals
	1	2	1	2	1	2	3	4	5	6	1	2	3	1	2	3	4	
#1																		
2 Lord	12	7	–	–	–	–	–	–	–	4	–	–	–	–	–	–	–	23
2 Stranger	–	–	–	–	–	6	–	–	–	–	–	–	–	–	–	–	–	6
1 Bandit	–	–	–	–	–	–	–	–	–	–	–	–	11	–	–	–	–	11
Soldier	–	–	–	–	–	–	–	–	–	–	–	–	–	–	–	10	–	10
#2																		
Merchant	11	–	–	–	–	–	–	–	–	–	–	–	–	–	–	–	–	11
3 Lord	–	2	–	–	–	–	–	–	–	3	–	–	–	–	–	–	–	5
Caphis	–	–	3	17	–	–	–	–	–	–	–	–	–	–	–	–	–	20
3 Stranger	–	–	–	–	–	1	–	–	–	–	–	–	–	–	–	–	–	1
2 Bandit	–	–	–	–	–	–	–	–	–	–	–	–	7	–	–	–	–	7
#3																		
Mercer	0	–	–	–	–	–	–	–	–	–	–	–	–	–	–	–	–	0
Ventigius	–	9	–	–	–	–	–	–	–	–	–	–	–	–	–	–	–	9
Titus	–	–	–	–	–	–	–	11	–	–	–	–	–	–	–	–	–	11
1 Friend	–	–	–	–	–	–	–	–	17	–	–	–	–	–	–	–	–	17
3 Bandit	–	–	–	–	–	–	–	–	–	–	–	–	6	–	–	–	–	6
#4																		
Messenger	8	–	–	–	–	–	–	–	–	–	–	–	–	–	–	–	–	8
Flavius	–	24	–	–	–	–	–	–	–	–	–	–	–	–	–	–	–	24
Servant [Lucius]	–	–	–	–	–	–	–	18	–	–	–	–	–	–	–	–	–	18
2 Friend	–	–	–	–	–	–	–	–	–	23	–	–	–	–	–	–	–	23
Messenger	–	–	–	–	–	–	–	–	–	–	–	–	–	–	10	–	5	15

Table 74 (*cont.*)

	1	2	3	4	5	6	7	8	9	10	11	12	13	14	15	16	17	Total
#5																		
1 Servant	-	7	-	3	4	-	-	-	-	-	-	6	-	-	-	-	-	20
Hortensius	-	-	-	-	-	-	-	10	-	-	-	-	-	-	-	-	-	10
3 Friend	-	-	-	-	-	-	-	-	-	5	-	-	-	-	-	-	-	5
#6																		
Lucillius	5	-	-	-	-	-	-	-	-	-	-	-	-	-	-	-	-	5
2 Servant	-	3	-	0	-	-	-	-	-	-	-	8	-	-	-	-	-	11
1 Servant [Varro]	-	-	-	-	-	-	-	14	-	-	-	-	-	-	-	-	-	14
Attendant [Timon]	-	-	-	-	-	-	-	-	0	-	-	-	-	-	-	-	-	0
Drum	-	-	-	-	-	-	-	-	-	-	-	-	0	-	-	-	-	0
#7																		
Jeweler	12	-	-	-	-	-	-	-	-	-	-	-	-	-	-	-	-	12
Fool	-	-	-	22	-	-	-	-	-	-	-	-	-	-	-	-	-	22
Servillius	-	-	-	-	-	12	-	6	-	-	-	-	-	-	-	-	-	18
Attendant [Timon]	-	-	-	-	-	-	-	-	0	-	-	-	-	-	-	-	-	0
Fife	-	-	-	-	-	-	-	-	-	-	-	-	0	-	-	-	-	0
Power [Alcibiades]	-	-	-	-	-	-	-	-	-	-	-	-	-	-	-	-	0	0
#8																		
Attend.[Alcibiades]	0	-	-	-	-	-	-	-	0	-	-	-	-	-	-	-	-	0
Isadore	-	-	-	7	-	-	-	-	-	-	-	-	-	-	-	-	-	7
Philotus	-	-	-	-	-	-	-	6	-	-	-	-	-	-	-	-	-	6
Power [Alcibiades]	-	-	-	-	-	-	-	-	-	-	-	-	-	-	-	-	0	0
#9																		
Attend.[Alcibiades]	0	-	-	-	-	-	-	-	0	-	-	-	-	-	-	-	-	0
Varro	-	-	-	11	-	-	-	-	-	-	-	-	-	-	-	-	-	11
Creditor	-	-	-	-	-	-	-	0	-	-	-	-	-	-	-	-	-	0
Attendant [Timon]	-	-	-	-	-	-	-	-	0	-	-	-	-	-	-	-	-	0
Power [Alcibiades]	-	-	-	-	-	-	-	-	-	-	-	-	-	-	-	-	0	0
#10																		
Attend.[Alcibiades]	0	-	-	-	-	-	-	0	-	-	-	-	-	-	-	-	0	0
3 Servant	-	4	-	0	-	-	-	-	-	-	-	6	-	-	-	-	-	10
Servant	-	-	-	-	4	-	18	-	-	-	-	-	-	-	-	-	-	22
Creditor	-	-	-	-	-	-	-	0	-	-	-	-	-	-	-	-	-	0
4 Lord	-	-	-	-	-	-	-	-	3	-	-	-	-	-	-	-	-	3
#11																		
3 Senator	0	-	-	-	-	-	-	1	0	-	-	-	-	-	-	4	-	4
2 Servant [Varro]	-	-	-	-	-	-	-	7	-	-	-	-	-	-	-	-	-	7

Boys

	1	2	3	4	5	6	7	8	9	10	11	12	13	14	15	16	17	Total
#1																		
Cupid	-	6	-	-	-	-	-	-	-	-	-	-	-	-	-	-	-	6
Page	-	-	-	9	-	-	-	-	-	-	-	-	-	-	-	-	-	9
#2																		
Amazon Masquer	-	0	-	-	-	-	-	-	-	-	-	-	-	-	-	-	-	0
Phrynia	-	-	-	-	-	-	-	-	-	-	-	1	-	-	-	-	-	1
#3																		
Amazon Masquer	-	0	-	-	-	-	-	-	-	-	-	-	-	-	-	-	-	0
Timandra	-	-	-	-	-	-	-	-	-	-	-	4	-	-	-	-	-	4
#4																		
Amazon Masquer	-	0	-	-	-	-	-	-	-	-	-	-	-	-	-	-	-	0

Total Lines Minor Parts   432=17%
Principal Parts   2,032=83%
2,464

Table 75
Cymbeline (F)

Principal Parts

	Act 1							Act 2					Act 3								Act 4				Act 5					Totals
	1	2	3	4	5	6	7	1	2	3	4	5	1	2	3	4	5	6	7	8	1	2	3	4	1	2	3	4	5	
Men																														
#1 Pasthumus	29	–	–	–	52	–	–	–	–	–	133	–	–	–	–	–	–	–	–	–	–	–	–	–	33	3	85	67	33	432
#2 Iachimo	–	41	–	–	77	152	–	–	11	–	73	–	–	–	–	–	–	–	–	–	–	–	–	–	–	–	–	–	64	418
#3 Bellarius	–	–	–	–	–	–	–	–	–	–	–	–	–	–	92	–	–	30	–	–	–	110	–	26	–	3	0	–	77	338
#4 Cymbeline	21	–	–	–	–	16	–	29	–	–	–	–	–	–	–	–	29	–	–	21	–	–	–	–	–	0	0	–	174	290
#5 Clotten	–	10	–	–	–	70	–	20	–	–	–	27	24	23	–	–	82	–	–	–	–	–	–	–	–	–	–	–	–	256
1 Gaolor	–	–	–	–	–	–	–	–	–	–	–	–	–	–	–	–	–	–	–	–	–	–	–	–	–	–	–	45	–	45
#6 Pisanio	10	–	13	–	–	1	4	–	27	–	–	–	–	–	86	28	–	–	–	16	–	79	–	19	–	0	0	–	26	214
#7 1 Gent.	66	–	–	–	–	–	–	–	–	–	–	–	–	–	–	–	–	–	–	–	–	–	–	–	–	–	–	–	–	66
Guiderius	–	–	–	–	–	–	–	–	–	–	–	–	–	–	11	–	10	–	–	98	–	–	19	–	–	1	0	–	14	153
#8 Arviragus	–	–	–	–	–	–	–	–	–	–	–	–	–	–	11	–	14	–	–	79	–	–	19	–	–	1	0	–	9	133
#9 Philario	–	–	–	22	19	–	–	19	–	–	–	–	–	–	–	–	–	–	–	–	–	–	–	–	–	–	–	–	–	41
Caius Lucius	–	–	–	–	–	–	–	–	–	–	–	–	–	–	–	10	–	–	42	–	–	–	–	–	–	5	–	–	25	101
#10 1 Lord[Cloten]	12	–	7	–	–	–	–	–	6	–	–	–	–	–	–	–	–	–	–	–	–	–	–	–	–	–	–	–	–	25
Cornelius	–	–	25	–	–	–	–	–	–	–	–	–	–	–	–	–	–	–	–	–	–	–	–	–	–	–	–	48	–	73
#11 2 Lord[Cloten]	13	–	28	–	–	–	–	–	1	–	–	–	–	–	–	–	–	–	7	–	–	–	–	–	–	–	–	–	–	42
Soothsayer	–	–	–	–	–	–	–	–	–	–	–	–	–	–	–	–	–	–	7	–	–	–	–	–	–	–	–	35	–	42
#12 Frenchman	–	–	23	–	–	–	–	–	–	–	–	–	–	–	–	–	–	–	–	–	–	–	–	–	–	–	–	–	–	23
Sicillius Leonatus	–	–	–	–	–	–	–	–	–	–	–	–	–	–	–	–	–	–	–	–	–	–	–	–	–	–	33	–	–	33
Boys																														
#1 Imogen	44	–	33	–	–	11	54	–	56	–	130	–	27	30	–	–	–	–	–	86	–	–	–	–	–	–	–	34	–	580
#2 Queene	33	–	–	–	70	10	22	–	–	33	–	–	–	–	–	–	–	–	–	–	–	–	–	–	–	–	–	–	–	168
#3 Matron	–	–	–	–	–	1	8	–	–	–	–	–	–	–	–	–	–	–	–	–	–	–	12	–	–	–	–	–	–	12
#4 Lady[Queen]	–	–	–	–	–	–	–	–	–	–	–	–	–	–	–	–	–	–	–	–	–	–	–	–	–	–	1	–	–	10
Total Lines Principal Parts																														3,495

Table 75 (cont.)

Minor Parts
Men

Part	Total
#1	
Dutchman	0
Messenger	2
Captain[Britain]	4
Jupiter	21
#2	
Spaniard	0
Musician	0
1 Senator	15
Captain[Britain]	7
1 Brother	10
Guard	0
#3	
Musician	0
2 Senator	1
Lord[Britain]	7
2 Gaolor	1
Guard	0
#4	
2 Gent.	14
Attendant[Lucius]	0
Messenger	3
Captain[Roman]	11
Army[Roman]	0
Captive[Roman]	0
#5	
Attendant[Lucius]	0
Captain[Roman]	0
Army[Roman]	0
Captive[Roman]	0
2 Brother	5
#6	
Attendant[Lucius]	0
Army[Roman]	0
Captive[Roman]	0
Messenger	2
#7	
Lord[Cymbeline]	0
Tribune	2
Army[Britain]	0

#8
Lord[Cymbeline]0
Tribune   -
Army[Britain] -
#9
Lord[Cymbeline]0
Army[Britain] -

Boys

#1
Lady[Imogen]   -
#2
Lady[Queen]-
#3
Lady[Queen]-

Total Lines Minor Parts   109= 3%
Principal Parts   3,495=97%
                           3,604

Table 76
The Winter's Tale (F)

Principal Parts
Men

	1		2			3			4				5			Totals
	1	2	1	2	3	1	2	3	1	2	3	4	1	2	3	
#1																
Leontes	-	210	109	-	107	-	69	-	-	-	-	-	105	-	76	676
#2																
Camillo	23	123	-	-	-	-	-	-	-	15	-	130	-	-	2	293
#3																
Polixenes	-	128	-	-	-	-	-	-	-	38	-	94	-	-	10	270
#4																
Autolicus	-	-	-	-	-	-	-	-	-	-	57	158	-	22	-	237
#5																
Florizell	-	-	-	-	-	-	-	-	-	-	-	167	39	-	0	206
#6																
Clowne	-	-	-	-	-	-	-	33	-	-	44	77	-	33	-	187
#7																
Sheepheard	-	-	-	-	-	-	-	43	-	-	-	86	-	8	-	137
#8																
Antigonus	-	-	30	-	29	-	-	47	-	-	-	-	-	-	-	106
3 Gentleman	-	-	-	-	-	-	-	-	-	-	-	-	-	64	-	64
#9																
Lord[Leontes]	-	-	18	-	12	-	9	-	-	-	-	-	24	-	0	63
#10																
Servant[Leontes]	-	-	-	10	-	5	-	-	-	-	-	-	18	-	-	33
Time	-	-	-	-	-	-	-	-	32	-	-	-	-	-	-	32
Servant[Shepherd]	-	-	-	-	-	-	-	-	-	-	-	35	-	-	-	35
#11																
Dion	-	-	-	-	-	16	0	-	-	-	-	-	11	-	-	27
1 Gentleman	-	-	-	-	-	-	-	-	-	-	-	-	-	27	-	27

Boys

	1		2			3			4				5			Totals
	1	2	1	2	3	1	2	3	1	2	3	4	1	2	3	
#1																
Paulina	-	-	-	43	83	-	60	-	-	-	-	-	69	-	76	331
#2																
Hermione	-	67	45	-	-	-	88	-	-	-	-	-	-	-	8	208
#3																
Mamillius	-	4	18	-	-	-	-	-	-	-	-	-	-	-	-	22
Perdita	-	-	-	-	-	-	-	-	-	-	-	118	0	-	7	125
#4																
Emilia	-	-	-	16	-	-	-	-	-	-	-	-	-	-	-	16
Dorcas	-	-	-	-	-	-	-	-	-	-	-	6	-	-	-	6
#5																
Lady	-	-	9	-	-	-	-	-	-	-	-	-	-	-	-	9
Mopsa	-	-	-	-	-	-	-	-	-	-	-	15	-	-	-	15

Total Lines Principal Parts 3,125

Minor Parts
Men

	1		2			3			4				5			Totals
	1	2	1	2	3	1	2	3	1	2	3	4	1	2	3	
#1																
Archidamus	21	-	-	-	-	-	-	-	-	-	-	-	-	-	-	21
Shepherd	-	-	-	-	-	-	-	-	-	-	-	0	-	-	-	0
Satyre	-	-	-	-	-	-	-	-	-	-	-	0	-	-	-	0
#2																
Officer	-	-	-	-	-	-	23	-	-	-	-	-	-	-	-	23
Shepherd	-	-	-	-	-	-	-	-	-	-	-	0	-	-	-	0
Satyre	-	-	-	-	-	-	-	-	-	-	-	0	-	-	-	0
#3																
Gaoler	-	-	-	13	-	-	-	-	-	-	-	-	-	-	-	13
Cleomines	-	-	-	-	-	11	0	-	-	-	-	-	12	-	-	23
Shepherd	-	-	-	-	-	-	-	-	-	-	-	0	-	-	-	0
Satyre	-	-	-	-	-	-	-	-	-	-	-	0	-	-	-	0

Table 76   245

Table 76 (*cont.*)

	1	2	3	4	5	6	7	8	9	10	11	12	13	14	15	Total
#4																
Gentlemen	-	-	-	0	-	-	-	-	-	-	-	-	-	-	-	0
Shepherd	-	-	-	-	-	-	-	-	-	-	-	0	-	-	-	0
Satyre	-	-	-	-	-	-	-	-	-	-	-	0	-	-	-	0
2 Gentleman	-	-	-	-	-	-	-	-	-	-	-	-	-	16	-	16
#5																
Lord[Leontes]	-	-	0	-	0	-	0	-	-	-	-	-	-	-	0	0
Mariner	-	-	-	-	-	-	-	11	-	-	-	-	-	-	-	11
Shepherd	-	-	-	-	-	-	-	-	-	-	-	0	-	-	-	0
Satyre	-	-	-	-	-	-	-	-	-	-	-	0	-	-	-	0
#6																
Lord[Leontes]	-	-	0	-	0	-	0	-	-	-	-	-	-	-	0	0
Beare	-	-	-	-	-	-	-	0	-	-	-	-	-	-	-	0
Shepherd	-	-	-	-	-	-	-	-	-	-	-	0	-	-	-	0
Satyre	-	-	-	-	-	-	-	-	-	-	-	0	-	-	-	0
#7																
Shepherd	-	-	-	-	-	-	-	-	-	-	-	0	-	-	-	0
Satyre	-	-	-	-	-	-	-	-	-	-	-	0	-	-	-	0

Boys

	1	2	3	4	5	6	7	8	9	10	11	12	13	14	15	Total
#1																
2 Lady	-	-	4	-	-	-	-	-	-	-	-	-	-	-	-	4
Shepherdess	-	-	-	-	-	-	-	-	-	-	-	0	-	-	-	0
Satyre	-	-	-	-	-	-	-	-	-	-	-	0	-	-	-	0
#2																
Shepherdess	-	-	-	-	-	-	-	-	-	-	-	0	-	-	-	0
Satyre	-	-	-	-	-	-	-	-	-	-	-	0	-	-	-	0
#3																
Shepherdess	-	-	-	-	-	-	-	-	-	-	-	0	-	-	-	0
Satyre	-	-	-	-	-	-	-	-	-	-	-	0	-	-	-	0
#4																
Shepherdess	-	-	-	-	-	-	-	-	-	-	-	0	-	-	-	0
Satyre	-	-	-	-	-	-	-	-	-	-	-	0	-	-	-	0
#5																
Shepherdess	-	-	-	-	-	-	-	-	-	-	-	0	-	-	-	0
Satyre	-	-	-	-	-	-	-	-	-	-	-	0	-	-	-	0
#6																
Shepherdess	-	-	-	-	-	-	-	-	-	-	-	0	-	-	-	0
Satyre	-	-	-	-	-	-	-	-	-	-	-	0	-	-	-	0

Total Lines Minor Parts $11\overline{1}$ = 3%

Principal Parts $\underline{3,125}$ = 97%

$\overline{3,236}$

Table 77
King Henry the Eighth (F)

Column headers: the top digits (1, 2, 3, 4, 5) are act numbers; beneath them the scene numbers run 1 2 3 4 | 1 2 3 4 | 1 2 | 1 2 | 1 2 3 4 5. P = Prologue/pre-scene, E = Epilogue.

Principal Parts — Men

Role	P	1.1	1.2	1.3	1.4	2.1	2.2	2.3	2.4	3.1	3.2	4.1	4.2	5.1	5.2	5.3	5.4	5.5	E	Totals
#1 King Henry	-	-	77	-	19	-	32	-	96	-	61	-	-	89	13	50	-	23	-	460
#2 Cardinal Wolsey	5	42	-	43	-	32	-	35	41	231	-	-	-	-	-	-	-	-	-	429
#3 Norfolke	-	104	9	-	-	-	38	-	-	-	55	0	-	-	-	3	-	0	-	209
#4 Buckingham	-	121	-	-	-	78	-	-	-	-	-	-	-	-	-	-	-	-	-	199
3 Gentleman	-	-	-	-	-	-	-	-	-	-	-	57	-	-	-	-	-	-	-	57
#5 Prologue	32	-	-	-	-	-	-	-	-	-	-	-	-	-	-	-	-	-	-	32
Lord Chamberlain	-	-	36	28	-	26	22	-	-	19	-	-	-	-	-	9	18	-	-	158
Epilogue	-	-	-	-	-	-	-	-	-	-	-	-	-	-	-	-	-	-	14	14
#6 1 Gentleman	-	-	-	-	-	68	-	-	-	-	-	40	-	-	-	-	-	-	-	108
Archbishop Cranmer	-	-	-	-	-	-	-	-	0	-	-	-	-	19	17	43	-	57	-	136
#7 Suffolke	-	-	0	-	-	-	18	-	-	-	67	0	-	7	-	6	-	0	-	98
#8 Surveyor	-	-	61	-	-	-	-	-	-	-	-	-	-	-	-	-	-	-	-	61
Bishop Gardiner	-	-	-	-	-	-	2	-	-	-	-	0	-	42	-	48	-	-	-	92
#9 2 Gentleman	-	-	-	-	-	45	-	-	-	-	-	41	-	-	-	-	-	-	-	86
Man	-	-	-	-	-	-	-	-	-	-	-	-	-	-	-	-	38	-	-	38
#10 Surrey	-	-	-	-	-	-	-	-	-	-	81	0	-	-	2	-	-	-	-	83
#11 Lovell	-	-	0	28	4	6	-	-	-	-	0	-	-	31	-	-	-	-	-	69
Porter	-	-	-	-	-	-	-	-	-	-	-	-	-	-	-	35	-	-	-	35
#12 Cardinal Campeius	-	-	-	-	-	-	15	-	15	24	-	-	-	-	-	-	-	-	-	54
Griffith	-	-	-	-	-	-	-	-	-	-	-	-	58	-	-	-	-	-	-	58
#13 Lord Sandys	-	-	-	24	27	0	-	-	-	-	-	-	-	-	-	-	-	-	-	51
Cromwell	-	-	-	-	-	-	-	-	-	-	30	-	-	-	-	19	-	-	-	49

Boys

Role	P	1.1	1.2	1.3	1.4	2.1	2.2	2.3	2.4	3.1	3.2	4.1	4.2	5.1	5.2	5.3	5.4	5.5	E	Totals
#1 Queene	-	-	51	-	-	-	-	-	84	124	-	0	118	-	-	-	-	-	-	377
#2 Old Lady	-	-	-	-	-	-	-	51	-	-	-	-	-	17	-	-	-	-	-	68
#3 Anne Bullen	-	-	-	-	4	-	-	54	-	-	-	-	-	-	-	-	-	-	-	58

Total Lines Principal Parts   3,079

Minor Parts — Men

Role	P	1.1	1.2	1.3	1.4	2.1	2.2	2.3	2.4	3.1	3.2	4.1	4.2	5.1	5.2	5.3	5.4	5.5	E	Totals
#1 Aburgavenny	-	18	-	-	-	-	-	-	-	-	-	-	-	-	-	-	-	-	-	18
Verger	-	-	-	-	-	-	-	0	-	-	-	-	-	-	-	-	-	-	-	0
Judge	-	-	-	-	-	-	-	-	0	-	-	-	-	-	-	-	-	-	-	0
Capuchius	-	-	-	-	-	-	-	-	-	-	-	-	11	-	-	-	-	-	-	11
Keeper	-	-	-	-	-	-	-	-	-	-	-	-	-	-	-	7	-	-	-	7
Alderman	-	-	-	-	-	-	-	-	-	-	-	-	-	-	-	-	-	0	-	0
#2 Brandon	-	14	-	-	-	-	-	-	-	-	-	-	-	-	-	-	-	-	-	14
Gentleman	-	-	-	0	-	-	-	3	-	-	-	-	-	-	-	-	-	-	-	3
Verger	-	-	-	-	-	-	-	0	-	-	-	-	-	-	-	-	-	-	-	0

Table 77   247

Table 77 (*cont.*)

```
Judge             -   -  -  -  -  -  -  -  -  -  -  0  -  -  -  -  -  -  -   0
Buts              -   -  -  -  -  -  -  -  -  -  -  -  -  -  9  -  -  -  -   9
#3
Henry Guilford    -   -  -  11 -  -  -  -  -  -  -  -  -  -  -  -  -  -  -  11
Vaux              -   -  -  -  -  4  -  -  -  -  -  -  -  -  -  -  -  -  -   4
Scribe            -   -  -  -  -  -  -  3  -  -  -  -  -  -  -  -  -  -  -   3
Lord Chancellor   -   -  -  -  -  -  -  -  -  -  0  -  -  -  22 -  -  -  -  22
#4
Gentleman         -   -  -  -  0  -  -  -  -  -  -  -  -  -  -  -  -  -  -   0
Tipstaff          -   -  -  -  -  0  -  -  -  -  -  -  -  -  -  -  -  -  -   0
Scribe            -   -  -  -  -  -  -  0  -  -  -  -  -  -  -  -  -  -  -   0
Bishop of London  -   -  -  -  -  -  -  -  -  -  0  -  -  -  -  -  -  -  -   0
Messenger         -   -  -  -  -  -  -  -  -  -  -  -  4  -  -  -  -  -  -   4
#5
Servant[Cardinal] -   -  -  4  -  -  -  -  -  -  -  -  -  -  -  -  -  -  -   4
Tipstaff          -   -  -  -  -  0  -  -  -  -  -  -  -  -  -  -  -  -  -   0
Bishop of Lincolne -  -  -  -  -  -  -  8  -  -  -  -  -  -  -  -  -  -  -   8
Cique Port        -   -  -  -  -  -  -  -  -  -  0  -  -  -  -  -  -  -  -   0
Nobleman          -   -  -  -  -  -  -  -  -  -  -  -  -  -  -  -  0  -  -   0
#6
Secretary         -   1  -  -  -  -  -  -  -  -  -  -  -  -  -  -  -  -  -   1
Masker            -   -  -  -  0  -  -  -  -  -  -  -  -  -  -  -  -  -  -   0
Halbred           -   -  -  -  0  -  -  -  -  -  -  -  -  -  -  -  -  -  -   0
Bishop of Ely-    -   -  -  -  -  -  -  0  -  -  -  -  -  -  -  -  -  -  -   0
Nobleman          -   -  -  -  -  -  -  -  -  -  -  -  -  -  -  -  0  -  -   0
#7
Secretary         -   0  -  -  -  -  -  -  -  -  -  -  -  -  -  -  -  -  -   0
Commoner          -   -  -  -  -  0  -  -  -  -  -  -  -  -  -  -  -  -  -   0
Bishop of Rochester -  -  -  -  -  -  -  0  -  -  -  -  -  -  -  -  -  -  -   0
Maior of London   -   -  -  -  -  -  -  -  -  -  0  -  -  -  -  -  0  -  -   0
#8
Masker            -   -  -  -  0  -  -  -  -  -  -  -  -  -  -  -  -  -  -   0
Commoner          -   -  -  -  -  0  -  -  -  -  -  -  -  -  -  -  -  -  -   0
Bishop of St. Asaph -  -  -  -  -  -  -  0  -  -  -  -  -  -  -  -  -  -  -   0
Garter            -   -  -  -  -  -  -  -  -  -  0  -  -  -  -  -  4  -  -   4
#9
Purse Bearer -    0   -  -  -  -  -  -  0  -  -  0  -  -  -  -  -  -  -  -   0
Halbred           -   -  -  -  -  0  -  -  -  -  -  -  -  -  -  -  -  -  -   0
Nobleman          -   -  -  -  -  -  -  -  -  -  -  -  -  -  -  -  0  -  -   0
#10
Noble             -   -  0  -  -  -  -  -  -  -  -  -  -  -  -  -  -  -  -   0
Commoner          -   -  -  -  -  0  -  -  -  -  -  -  -  -  -  -  -  -  -   0
Priest            -   -  -  -  -  -  -  0  -  -  -  -  -  -  -  -  -  -  -   0
Cinque Port       -   -  -  -  -  -  -  -  -  -  0  -  -  -  -  -  -  -  -   0
Alderman          -   -  -  -  -  -  -  -  -  -  -  -  -  -  -  -  0  -  -   0
#11
Guard             -   0  -  -  -  -  -  -  -  -  -  -  -  0  -  -  -  -  -   0
Noble             -   -  0  -  -  -  -  -  -  -  -  -  -  -  -  0  0  -  -   0
Priest            -   -  -  -  -  -  -  0  -  -  -  -  -  -  -  -  -  -  -   0
Cinque Port       -   -  -  -  -  -  -  -  -  -  0  -  -  -  -  -  -  -  -   0
#12
Guard             -   0  -  -  -  -  -  -  -  -  -  -  -  0  -  -  -  -  -   0
Gentleman         -   -  -  -  0  -  -  -  -  -  -  -  -  -  -  -  -  -  -   0
Usher             -   -  -  -  -  -  -  1  -  -  -  -  -  -  -  -  -  -  -   1
Cinque Port       -   -  -  -  -  -  -  -  -  -  0  -  -  -  -  -  -  -  -   0
Denny             -   -  -  -  -  -  -  -  -  -  -  -  4  -  -  -  -  -  -   4
Nobleman          -   -  -  -  -  -  -  -  -  -  -  -  -  -  -  -  0  -  -   0
#13
Sgt-Armes-Crier   5   -  -  -  -  -  -  3  -  -  -  -  -  -  -  -  -  -  -   8
Marquesse Dorset  -   -  -  -  -  -  -  -  -  -  0  -  -  -  -  -  -  -  -   0
Nobleman          -   -  -  -  -  -  -  -  -  -  -  -  -  -  -  -  0  -  -   0
```

Table 77 (*cont.*)

```
#14
Masker          -   -   -   -  0  -   -   -   -   -   -   -   -   -   -   -   -   -        0
Gentleman[Pillar]-  -   -   -   -   -   -  0  -   -   -   -   -   -   -   -   -        0
#15
Masker          -   -   -   -  0  -   -   -   -   -   -   -   -   -   -   -   -   -        0
Gentleman[Pillar]-  -   -   -   -   -   -  0  -   -   -   -   -   -   -   -   -        0
#16
Masker          -   -   -   -  0  -   -   -   -   -   -   -   -   -   -   -   -   -        0
Noble[Sword]    -   -   -   -   -   -   -  0  -   -   -   -   -   -   -   -   -        0
#17
Masker          -   -   -   -  0  -   -   -   -   -   -   -   -   -   -   -   -   -        0
Noble[Mace]     -   -   -   -   -   -   -  0  -   -   -   -   -   -   -   -   -        0
```

Boys

```
#1
Old Duchess     -   -   -   -   -   -   -   -   -  0  -   -   -   -   -  0  -        0
Personage       -   -   -   -   -   -   -   -   -   -  0  -   -   -   -   -   -        0
Page            -   -   -   -   -   -   -   -   -   -   -  1  -   -   -   -   -        1
#2
Lady            -   -   -   -  0  -   -   -   -   -  0  -   -   -   -   -   -        0
Patience        -   -   -   -   -   -   -   -   -   -  2  -   -   -   -   -   -        2
Marchionesse Dorset -  -   -   -   -   -   -   -   -   -   -   -   -  0  -        0
#3
Lady            -   -   -   -  0  -   -   -   -   -  0  -   -   -   -   -   -        0
Attendant[Queen] -  -   -   -   -   -  0  0  -   -   -   -   -   -   -   -        0
Personage       -   -   -   -   -   -   -   -   -   -  0  -   -   -   -   -        0
Lady [Dorset]-  -   -   -   -   -   -   -   -   -   -   -   -   -  0  -        0
#4
Lady            -   -   -   -  0  -   -   -   -   -  0  -   -   -   -   -   -        0
Attendant[Queen] -  -   -   -   -   -  0  0  -   -   -   -   -   -   -   -        0
Personage       -   -   -   -   -   -   -   -   -   -  0  -   -   -   -   -        0
Lady[Dorset]    -   -   -   -   -   -   -   -   -   -   -   -   -   -  0  -        0
#5
Attendant[Queen] -  -   -   -   -   -  0  0  -   -   -   -   -   -   -   -        0
Quirrister      -   -   -   -   -   -   -   -   -  0  -   -   -   -   -   -        0
Personage       -   -   -   -   -   -   -   -   -  0  -   -   -   -   -   -        0
#6
Quirrister      -   -   -   -   -   -   -   -   -  0  -   -   -   -   -   -        0
Personage       -   -   -   -   -   -   -   -   -   -  0  -   -   -   -   -        0
#7
Quirrister      -   -   -   -   -   -   -   -   -  0  -   -   -   -   -   -        0
Personage       -   -   -   -   -   -   -   -   -  0  -   -   -   -   -   -        0
```

```
                         Total Lines Minor Parts    139̄= 4%
                                 Principal Parts   3,079=96%
                                                   ─────
                                                   3,218
```

Table 78
Pericles (Q1-1609)
Principal Parts

	Act 1					Act 2						Act 3					Act 4							Act 5				
	C	1	2	3	4	C DS	1	2	3	4	5	C DS	1	2	3	4	C	1	2	3	4 DS	5	6	C	1	2	3	Totals
Men																												
#1 Pericles	–	109	92	–	16	0	76	–	27	–	25	0	59	–	23	–	–	–	–	–	–	–	–	–	98	–	45	570
#2 Gower	42	–	–	–	–	40	–	–	–	–	–	60	–	–	–	–	52	–	–	–	54	–	24	20	–	–	18	310
#3 Simonydes	–	–	–	–	–	–	–	26	60	–	55	–	–	–	–	–	–	–	–	–	–	–	–	–	–	–	–	141
Boult	–	–	–	–	–	–	–	–	–	–	–	–	–	–	–	–	–	–	36	–	–	–	42	–	–	–	–	78
#4 Hellicanus	–	–	30	17	–	–	–	–	–	32	–	–	–	–	–	–	–	–	–	–	–	–	–	30	–	–	4	113
#5 Cleon	–	–	–	–	73	0	–	–	–	–	–	–	–	–	13	–	–	18	–	–	0	–	–	–	–	–	–	104
#6 Lord Cerymon	–	–	–	–	–	–	–	–	–	–	–	–	–	72	–	8	–	–	–	–	–	–	–	–	–	–	14	94
1 Fisherman	–	–	–	–	–	–	44	–	–	–	–	–	–	–	–	–	–	–	–	–	–	–	–	–	–	–	–	44
Pandar	–	–	–	–	–	–	–	–	–	–	–	–	–	–	–	–	–	–	25	–	–	–	3	–	–	–	–	28
#7 Antiochus	61	–	–	–	–	–	–	–	–	–	–	–	–	–	–	–	–	–	–	–	–	–	–	–	–	–	–	61
Lysimachus	–	–	–	–	–	–	–	–	–	–	–	–	–	–	–	–	–	–	–	–	–	–	45	–	45	–	–	90
Boys																												
#1 Marina	–	–	–	–	–	–	–	–	–	–	–	–	–	–	–	–	–	35	19	–	–	–	48	–	50	–	2	154
#2 Bawd	–	–	–	–	–	–	–	–	–	–	–	–	–	–	–	–	–	–	64	–	–	–	36	–	–	–	–	100
#3 Dioniza	–	–	–	–	9	–	–	–	–	–	–	–	–	–	–	–	–	34	–	30	0	–	4	–	–	–	–	77
#4 Thaisa	–	–	–	–	–	–	–	21	20	–	3	0	2	7	–	–	–	–	–	–	–	–	–	–	–	–	18	71
																												2,035

Total Lines Principal Parts

Table 78 (*cont.*)

Minor Parts
Men

Part					Total
#1					
Thaliard	7	10			17
2 Fisherman		24			24
#2					
Messenger	1	0			1
3 Fisherman		12			12
1 Gent.	13	4	1		18
#3					
Lord[Cleon]	7				7
Messenger	0				0
2 Gent	16	4	0		20
#4					
Escanes	2	0			2
Leonine	19				19
Lord[Lys]	2				2
#5					
1 Lord [H]	16	1	0		17
1 Lord[S]	2				2
Servant[Cery]	6				6
#6					
2 Lord [H]	1	2	0		3
2 Lord[S]	2				2
Servant[Cery]	0				0
#7					
3 Lord [H]	1	0			1
3 Lord[S]	2				2
Servant[Cery]	0				0
#8					
Lord[P]	0	0	0		0
1 Knight	4	1			5
1 Pirate	1				1
#9					
Lord[P]	0	0	0		0
2 Knight	2	1			3
2 Pirate	1				1
#10					
Lord[P]	0	0	0		0
3 Knight	3	1			4
3 Pirate	2				2

#11	
Follower[A]	0
4 Knight	1
1 Sayler	15
Train[P]	0
#12	
Follower[A]	0
5 Knight	3
2 Sayler	7
Train[P]	0
#13	
Follower[A]	0
6 Knight	2
Phylemon	1
Train[P]	0
#1	
Daughter	2
Bawd	0
#2	
Lichorida	9
Bawd	0
#3	
Diana	8

Boys

Total Lines Minor Parts   219=10%

Principal Parts   2,035=90%

2,254

Table 79

The Two Noble Kinsmen (Q-1634)

Principal Parts

Men

	P	1.1	1.2	1.3	1.4	1.5	2.1	2.2	2.3	2.4	2.5	2.6	3.1	3.2	3.3	3.4	3.5	3.6	4.1	4.2	4.3	5.1	5.2	5.3	5.4	E	Totals
#1 Palamon	–	–	63	–	–	–	0	163	–	62	–	29	129	–	–	33	–	76	–	–	–	–	–	–	46	–	568
#2 Arcite	–	–	47	39	–	–	0	119	–	79	–	41	104	–	–	4	–	43	–	–	–	–	4	6	–	–	507
#3 Theseus	–	63	–	–	40	–	–	–	25	–	26	–	–	–	20	–	–	17	–	62	–	50	–	38	–	–	322
#4 Pirithous	–	3	–	10	–	–	–	–	14	–	34	–	–	–	2	–	–	3	–	44	–	5	–	–	–	–	125
#5 Jailer-Keeper	–	–	26	–	–	–	20	–	24	–	–	–	–	12	–	–	–	–	33	–	2	–	–	4	–	–	119
#6 Prologue	32	–	–	–	–	–	–	–	–	–	–	–	–	–	–	–	–	–	–	–	–	–	–	–	–	–	32
Wooer	–	–	–	–	–	–	5	–	–	–	–	–	–	–	–	–	–	–	61	–	33	–	4	–	–	–	103
Epilogue	–	–	–	–	–	–	–	–	–	–	–	–	–	–	–	–	–	–	–	–	–	–	–	–	–	18	18
#7 Schoolmaster	–	–	–	–	–	–	–	–	–	–	–	–	–	–	–	–	87	–	–	–	–	–	–	–	–	–	87
Doctor	–	–	–	–	–	–	–	–	–	–	–	–	–	–	–	–	–	–	–	–	44	–	43	–	–	–	87
#8 Curtis	–	–	–	–	–	–	–	–	–	–	–	–	–	–	–	–	44	–	–	–	–	–	–	–	–	–	44
Messenger	–	–	–	–	–	–	–	–	–	–	–	–	–	–	–	–	–	–	–	–	–	–	–	–	–	–	0

Boys

	P	1.1	1.2	1.3	1.4	1.5	2.1	2.2	2.3	2.4	2.5	2.6	3.1	3.2	3.3	3.4	3.5	3.6	4.1	4.2	4.3	5.1	5.2	5.3	5.4	E	Totals
#9 Attendant [Theseus]	–	–	–	–	–	–	–	–	–	–	–	–	–	–	–	–	–	–	–	–	–	–	–	–	–	–	0
2 Countryman	–	–	–	–	–	–	–	–	21	–	–	–	–	–	–	–	–	–	28	–	–	9	–	–	–	–	30
1 Friend	–	–	–	–	–	–	28	–	–	–	–	–	–	–	–	–	–	–	–	–	–	–	–	–	–	–	28
#1 Emilia	–	22	–	56	–	–	–	27	–	–	13	47	–	–	–	–	–	2	–	69	37	40	–	89	3	–	365
#2 Jailer's Daughter	–	–	–	–	–	–	–	–	38	33	–	39	–	58	–	38	20	–	56	–	–	–	11	–	–	–	293
#3 Hipolita	–	21	–	54	–	–	–	–	6	–	–	–	–	–	–	–	14	–	–	6	–	1	9	–	–	–	111
#4 1 Queen	–	59	–	1	2	–	–	–	–	–	–	–	–	–	–	–	–	–	–	–	–	–	–	–	–	–	62
#5 2 Queen	–	35	–	2	1	–	–	–	–	–	–	–	–	–	–	–	–	–	–	–	–	–	–	–	–	–	38
#6 3 Queen	–	33	–	2	4	–	–	–	–	–	–	–	–	–	–	–	–	–	–	–	–	–	–	–	–	–	39
Woman	–	–	–	–	–	–	–	14	–	–	–	–	–	–	–	–	–	–	–	–	–	–	–	–	–	–	14

Total Lines Principal Parts 2,992

Minor Parts

Men

	P	1.1	1.2	1.3	1.4	1.5	2.1	2.2	2.3	2.4	2.5	2.6	3.1	3.2	3.3	3.4	3.5	3.6	4.1	4.2	4.3	5.1	5.2	5.3	5.4	E	Totals
#1 Countryman	–	–	–	–	–	–	–	–	11	–	–	–	–	–	–	–	4	–	–	–	–	–	–	–	–	–	15
1 Knight [Palamon]	–	–	–	–	–	–	–	–	–	–	–	–	–	–	–	–	0	–	–	–	–	–	–	7	–	–	7

#2	
Hymen	0
2 Friend	21
2 Knight [Palamon]-	5
#3	
Valerius	12
3 Countryman	23
Brother	10
3 Knight [Palamon]-	1
#4	
Herald	9
4 Countryman	16
Knight [Arcite]	0
#5	
Taborer	1
Gentleman	4
Knight [Arcite]	0
#6	
Bavian	1
Knight [Arcite]	0
Executioner	0
#7 T. Tucke	
Attendant [Theseus]	0
Messenger	1
#8	
Attendant [Theseus]	0
Messenger	4
Gard	0
Boys	
#1	
Boy	0
One	0
Nell-Wench	1
#2	
Nimph	0
Wench	0
Maid	0
#3	
Nimph	0
Wench	0
Maid	0
#4	
Nimph	0
Wench	0

Total Lines Minor Parts 131 = 4%
Principal Parts 2,992 = 96%
3,123

Table 80
Casting Requirements for Shakespeare's Plays

Title	Text	Men	Principal Parts	Boys	Parts	% of Lines Spoken by Principals	Men	Minor Parts	Boys	Parts	Total Men	Actors Boys	Total Spoken Lines
2H6	Q1-1594	9	16	2	2	85	15	79	3	6	24	5	1,932
	F	10	20	2	2	90	14	74	3	5	24	5	3,109
3H6	O-1595	8	12	4	4	92	14	71	1	3	22	5	2,163
	F	8	13	4	4	91	16	82	1	3	24	5	3,010
1H6	F	15	24	2	4	92	13	61	0	0	28	2	2,652
R3	Q1-1597	11	18	6	7	95	8	37	1	2	19	7	3,419
	F	11	18	6	7	95	8	45	1	2	19	7	3,731
Err.	F	8	9	5	5	97	5	11	0	0	13	5	1,798
Tit.	Q1-1594	10	13	4	4	98	13	29	0	0	23	4	2,416
	F	10	13	4	4	99	13	32	0	0	23	4	2,579
Shr.	F	11	14	3	4	97	7	20	3	5	18	6	2,598
TGV	F	9	11	3	3	98	3	3	0	0	12	3	2,234
LLL	Q1-1598	9	9	6	6	99	5	9	0	0	14	6	2,619
Rom.	Q1-1597	9	12	3	3	95	7	21	2	5	16	5	2,218
	Q2-1599	11	16	3	3	97	13	34	5	10	24	8	3,037
R2	Q1-1597	10	16	3	3	93	6	22	3	3	16	6	2,565
	F	10	16	3	3	94	7	33	2	2	17	5	2,720
MND	Q-1600	9	9	4	5	96	7	13	4	8	16	8	1,991
	F	9	9	4	5	97	6	14	4	8	15	8	2,067
John	F	10	12	5	6	97	9	36	0	0	19	5	2,640
MV	Q1-1600	10	12	3	3	98	6	20	3	3	16	6	2,549
1H4	Q1-1598	11	16	3	3	96	8	21	0	0	19	3	2,857
2H4	Q-1600	12	20	4	5	93	8	44	1	1	20	5	2,861
	F	12	20	4	5	94	6	26	1	2	18	5	3,240
Ado	Q-1600	11	12	4	4	97	4	12	1	2	15	5	2,485
H5	Q-1600	9	14	4	4	90	11	26	0	0	20	4	1,608
	F	11	18	5	5	93	12	42	0	0	23	5	3,199
JC	F	9	17	3	3	91	11	40	0	0	20	3	2,647

Table 80   255

Table 80 (cont'd)
Casting Requirements for Shakespeare's Plays

Title	Text	Men	Principal Parts	Boys	Parts	% of Lines Spoken by Principals	Men	Minor Parts	Boys	Parts	Total Men	Actors Boys	Total Spoken Lines
AYLI	F	10	12	4	4	96	7	15	2	2	17	6	2,618
TN	F	8	9	3	3	98	7	11	3	3	15	6	2,338
Ham.	Q1-1603	8	13	3	3	95	7	23	0	0	15	3	2,129
	Q2- 1604	9	15	3	3	96	7	25	0	0	16	3	3,680
	F	9	15	3	3	96	9	35	0	0	18	3	3,593
Wiv.	Q1-1602	10	11	4	4	97	3	5	4	5	13	8	1,493
	F	12	13	6	8	99	2	3	2	2	14	8	2,623
Tro.	Q-1609	14	15	4	5	98	6	18	0	0	20	4	3,260
AWW	F	8	14	5	5	98	8	25	2	4	16	7	2,883
MM	F	8	9	4	4	96	8	20	1	2	16	5	2,788
Oth.	Q1-1622	7	10	3	3	97	10	29	2	3	17	5	3,238
	F	7	11	3	3	98	9	23	2	2	16	5	3,572
Lear	Q1-1608	9	11	3	3	95	6	32	0	0	15	3	2,907
	F	9	11	3	3	96	10	38	0	0	19	3	3,175
Mac.	F	9	12	8	8	92	9	45	2	3	18	10	2,356
Ant.	F	12	19	4	4	91	13	83	3	12	25	7	3,484
Cor.	F	11	16	3	3	93	14	64	4	5	25	4	3,583
Tim.	F	10	15	0	0	83	11	49	4	7	21	4	2,464
Cym.	F	12	18	4	4	97	9	38	3	3	21	7	3,604
WT	F	11	15	5	8	97	7	24	6	13	18	11	3,236
Temp.	F	10	10	4	4	99	5	15	4	7	15	8	2,204
H8	F	13	22	3	3	96	17	67	7	21	30	10	3,218
Per.	Q1-1609	7	11	4	4	90	13	41	3	5	20	7	2,254
TNK	Q-1634	9	14	6	7	96	8	23	4	11	17	10	3,123
Mean		9.9	14.0	3.8	4.0	94.9	8.6	32.9	1.8	3.5	18.5	5.6	2,742.9

Table 81
The Booke of Sir Thomas More (MS. c. 1593, Original Text)

Principal Parts
Men

	1	2	3	4	5	6	7	8	9	10	11	12	13	14	15	16	17	Totals
#1																		
Moore	-	65	-	-	6	28	-	61	124	34	34	-	124	22	-	93	88	679
#2																		
Earl of Surrie	-	-	34	-	1	-	31	28	-	26	-	5	15	1	-	-	6	147
#3																		
Earl of Shrewsburie	-	23	-	12	16	-	1	-	-	28	-	5	6	1	-	-	2	94
#4																		
John Lincoln	23	-	-	16	-	2	24	-	-	-	-	-	-	-	-	-	-	65
Bishop of Rochester	-	-	-	-	-	-	-	-	-	13	-	19	-	-	-	-	-	32
#5																		
Suresbie	-	63	-	-	-	-	-	-	-	-	-	-	-	-	-	-	-	63
Inclination	-	-	-	-	-	-	-	-	46	-	-	-	-	-	-	-	-	46
#6																		
Lifter	-	55	-	-	-	-	-	-	-	-	-	-	-	-	-	-	-	55
Roper	-	-	-	-	-	-	-	3	-	14	-	22	-	-	-	11	-	50
#7																		
George Betts	13	-	-	4	-	-	-	-	-	-	-	-	-	-	-	-	-	17
1 Sheriff	-	-	-	-	-	-	38	-	-	-	-	-	-	-	-	-	7	45
1 Player-Prologue	-	-	-	-	-	-	-	24	-	-	-	-	-	-	-	-	-	24
#8																		
Lord Mayor	-	21	-	-	-	12	-	8	-	-	-	-	-	-	-	-	-	41
Catesbie	-	-	-	-	-	-	-	-	-	-	-	-	1	-	13	-	-	14
#9																		
Thomas Palmer	-	-	18	-	-	3	-	-	-	17	-	-	-	-	-	-	-	38
Lieutenant	-	-	-	-	-	-	-	-	-	-	-	0	-	1	-	17	5	23
#10																		
Sherwin	7	-	-	4	-	0	-	-	-	-	-	-	-	-	-	-	-	11
Wit	-	-	-	-	-	-	-	35	-	-	-	-	-	-	-	-	-	35
Gough	-	-	-	-	-	-	-	-	-	-	-	-	-	-	15	-	-	15

Boys

	1	2	3	4	5	6	7	8	9	10	11	12	13	14	15	16	17	Totals
#1																		
Doll	30	-	-	10	-	3	49	-	-	-	-	-	-	-	-	-	-	92
Woman	-	-	-	-	-	-	-	-	-	-	-	-	-	11	-	-	-	11
#2																		
Lady More	-	-	-	-	-	-	-	-	15	-	40	-	11	-	-	5	-	71

Total Lines Principal Parts 1,668

Minor Parts
Men

	1	2	3	4	5	6	7	8	9	10	11	12	13	14	15	16	17	Totals
#1																		
Francis de Bard	9	-	-	-	-	-	-	-	-	-	-	-	-	-	-	-	-	9
Messenger	-	-	8	-	-	-	7	-	-	-	-	-	-	-	-	-	-	15
Alderman	-	-	-	-	-	-	-	0	-	-	-	-	-	-	-	-	-	0
1 Warder	-	-	-	-	-	-	-	-	-	-	-	0	-	11	-	-	3	14
#2																		
Caveler	4	-	-	-	-	-	-	-	-	-	-	-	-	-	-	-	-	4
Randall	-	-	-	-	-	-	6	-	-	-	-	-	-	-	-	-	-	6
Alderman	-	-	-	-	-	-	-	0	-	-	-	-	-	-	-	-	-	0
2 Warder	-	-	-	-	-	-	-	-	-	-	-	0	-	9	-	-	0	9
#3																		
Williamson	7	-	-	-	0	-	2	-	-	-	-	-	-	-	-	-	-	9
Luggins	-	-	-	-	-	-	-	3	-	-	-	-	-	-	-	-	-	3
3 Warder	-	-	-	-	-	-	-	-	-	-	-	-	-	4	-	-	-	4
Porter	-	-	-	-	-	-	-	-	-	-	-	-	-	-	6	-	-	6
Officer	-	-	-	-	-	-	-	-	-	-	-	-	-	-	-	-	1	1

Table 81   257

Table 81 (*cont.*)

	1	2	3	4	5	6	7	8	9	10	11	12	13	14	Total
#4															
Recorder		4													4
Croftes				2											2
Faulkner					17										17
Brewer												7			7
Servant							0						1		1
#5															
Another		1													1
Officer				10											10
Alderman							0								0
Downes										2					2
Butler												7			7
Officer														0	0
#6															
Roger Cholmeley	10														10
Erasmus					10										10
Player						1									1
Clark									1						1
Hangman														7	7
#7															
Smart		0													0
Officer				0											0
Lord								0							0
Horsekeeper												4			4
2 Sheriff														5	5
#8															
Crew			0												0
Morris					13										13
Servant							0								0
Lord								0							0
Gentleman											3				3
#9															
Crew			0												0
Servant							0				3				3
Lord								0							0
Guard														0	0
Boys															
#1															
Harry			8												8
Lady Mayoress					3										3
#2															
Kit			7												7
More's Daughter							0		1		0		1		2
#3															
Robin			3												3
Lady Vanity					9										9
#4															
Lady							0								0
Roper's Wife									7		0			0	7

```
                                    Total Lines Minor Parts      227=12%
                                                Principal Parts  1,668=88%
                                                                 1,895
```

Transcripts of five playhouse plots

The plotte of the dead mans fortune

1 Enter the prolouge

2 Enter laertes Eschines and urganda

3 Enter pesscodde to him his father

4 Enter Tesephon allgeryus laertes wth
atendantes: Darlowe: lee: b samme: to
them allcyane and statyra

5 Enter validore & asspida at severall dores
to them the panteloun

mus
ique

  X X X X X X X X X X X X X
Enter carynus and prlior to them
6 statyra and allcyane

7 Enter urganda laertes Eschines: Exit
Eschines and enter for Bell veile

8 Enter panteloun & his man to them his
wife asspida to hir validore

Dar
lee
sam

9 Enter Tesephoun allgerius alcyane &
statyra wth attendantes to them [to th]
carynus & prelyor to them laertes &
Bell veile

10 Enter valydore & asspida cuttynge of
ruffes to them the maide

11 Enter panteloun whiles he speakes
validore passeth ore the stage disguisde
then Enter pesscode to them asspida to
them the maide wth pesscodds apparell

Musi
que

  X X X X X X X X X X
Enter carynus and prlyor = here the
12 laydes speake[s] in prysoun

13 Enter laertes & Bell veile to them the
Iayler to them the laydes

14 Enter Tesephon allgerius at severall dores
disguisd with meate to them the Iayler

15 Enter pateloun & pesscode = enter asspida
to hir validore & his man b samme to them
the panteloun & pescode wth specktakles

Musi
que

  X X X X X X X X X X X X X
Enter tesephon allgerius wth attendantes

16 Dar & tyre man & others to them Burbage
a messenger to them Euphrodore = Robart
lee & b samme

17 Enter carynus & prlyor to them urganda
wth a looking glasse acompaned with satires
plaing on ther Instruments

18 Enter carynus madde to him prelyor
[d] madde

19 Enter asspida & [valydore] pescodde to hir
Enters rose

20 Enter panteloun & pescodde

21 Enter aspida & validore diguisd like rose
wth a basket of clothes to them rose wth
a nother basket of clothes to them the
pan teloun to them [to them] pescode

Musique   X X X X X X X X X X X X X

Enter
Urganda
Alcione
Statira
Enter
Laertes
Eschinesa
Enter

22 Enter kinge Egereon allgeryus tesephon
wth lordes the [x] executioner wth[is] his
sworde & blocke & offycers wth holbreds
to them carynus & prlyor then after that
the musique plaies & ther Enters 3 an
tique faires dancynge on after a nother
the firste takes the sworde from the ex
ecutioner & sendes him a waye the other
caryes a waie the blocke & the third sends
waie[s] the offycers & unbindes allgeryus
& tesephon & as they entred so they departe

wt out
disguise

23 Enter to them urganda laertes and
Eschines leadinge there laides hand in hand

24 Enter the[n] panteloun & pescode

25 Enter validore [and asspida]

26 Enter asspida to hir rose

27 Enter the panteloun & causeth the
cheste or truncke to be broughte forth

finis

1 Transcript
British Library, MS. Add. 10449, fol. 1

The Platt of The Secound Parte of the Seven Deadlie Sinns

1 A tent being plast one the stage for Henry the sixt.he in it A sleepe to him the Leutenant A purcevaunt R Cowly Jo Duke and i wardere [J Holland] R Pallant:to them Pride.Gluttony Wrath and Covetousnes at one dore.at an other dore Envie.Sloth and Lechery.The Three put back the foure and so Exeunt

2 Henry Awaking Enter A Keeper J Sincler to him a servaunt T Belt. to him Lidgate and the Keeper. Exit then enter againe.Then Envy passeth over the stag Lidgate speakes

1DS   A senitt Dumb show
Enter King Gorboduk wth 2 Counsailers R.Burbadg mr Brian Th Goodale The Queene wth ferrex and Porrex and som attendaunts follow saunder W sly Harry J Duke Kitt Ro Pallant J Holland After Gordbeduk hath Consulted wth his Lords he brings his 2 sonns to to severall seates. They enving on on other ferrex offers to take Porrex his Corowne he draws his weapon The King Queen and Lords step between them They Thrust Them away and menasinbg [ect] ech other exit. The Queene and L (o s) Depart Hevilie. Lidgate speaks

3 Enter ferrex Crownd wth Drum and Coulers and soldiers one way.Harry.Kitt.R Cowly John duke.to them At a nother dore Porrex drum and Collors and soldie W sly.R Pallant.John Sincler.J Holland.

4 Enter [Gorb] Queene.wth 2 Counsailors.mr Brian Tho Goodale.to them ferrex and Porrex severall waies wth [his] Drums and Powers Gorboduk entreing in The midst between. Henry speaks

5   Alarum wth Excurtions After
          Lidgate speakes

6 Enter ferrex and Porrex severally Gorboduke still following them.Lucius and Damasus mr Bry T Good

7 Enter ferrex at one dore Pores at another The fight ferrex is slayn: to them Videna The Queene to hir Damasus to him Lucius

8 Enter Porrex sad wth Dordan his man.R P. w sly: to them the Queene and a Ladie Nick saunder And Lords R Cowly mr Brian to them Lucius Runing

9 Henry and Lidgat speaks Sloth Passeth over

Enter Giraldus Phronesius Aspatia Pompeia

10 Rodope R Cowly Th Goodale R Go Ned Nick

11 Enter Sardinapalus Arbactus Nicanor and Captaines marching mr Phillipps mr Pope R Pa Kit J sincler.J Holland

12 Enter A Captaine wth Aspatia and the Ladies Kitt

13   Lidgat speake
Enter Nicanor wth other Captaines R Pall. J sincler.Kitt.J Holland R Cowly.to them Arbactus.mr Pope.to him will foole J.Duke to him Rodopeie.Ned to her Sardanapalus Like a woman wth Aspatia Rodope Pompeia Will foole to them Arbactus and 3 musitions mr Pope J sincler Vincent R Cowly to them Nicanor and others R P. Kitt

14 Enter sardanapa.wth the Ladies to them A Messenger.Th Goodale to him will foole Runing   A Larum

15 Enter Arbactus pursuing Sardanapalus and the Ladies fly.After enter Sarda wth as many Jewels robes and Gold as he ca(n) cary   A larum

16 Enter Arbactus Nicanor and The other Captains in triumph.mr Pope.R Pa.Kitt J Holl R Cow.J Sinc

17 Henry speaks and Lidgate Lechery passeth over the stag

18 Enter Tereus Philomele.Julio and (ot R Burbadg Ro R Pall J s(1)

19 Enter Progne Itis and Lords saunder will J Duke w sly Hary

20 Enter Philomele and Tereus to them Julio

21 Enter Progne Panthea Itis and Lords saunder T Belt will sly Hary The Goodale to them Tereus wth Lords R Burbadge.J Duk R Cowly

2DS   A Dumb show Lidgate speakes
Enter Progne wth the Sampler to her Tereus from Hunting wth his Lords to them Philomele wth Itis hed in a dish Mercury Comes and all Vanish to him 3 Lords Th Goodale Hary w sly.

22 Henry speaks to him Leiutenant Pursevaunt and warders R Cowly J Duke J Holand Joh sincler to them Warwick mr Brian

23   Lidgate speakes to the
          Audiens and so
          Exitts

          Finis

II Transcript
Dulwich College, MS. xix

The plott of ffrederick & Basilea

P   Enter Prologue: Richard Alleine

1   Enter Frederick Kinge: Mr Jubie R Allenn To them Basilea servant Black Dick, Dick

2   Enter Governor Athanasia Morre:Mr Dunstann.Griffen Charles, To them Heraclius Servants. Tho:hunt black Dick

3   Enter Leonora, Sebastian Theodore Pedro Philippo Andreo Mr Allen well Mr Martyn Ed.Dutton ledbeter Pigg: To them King frederick Basilea Guarde. Mr Juby. R Allen Dick Tho. Hunt black Dick

4   Enter Myron-hamec, lords. Tho: Towne Tho Hunt ledbeter To them Heraclius, Thamar Sam Charles

5   Enter Governor Mr Dunstann To hym Messenger Th: Hunt To them Heraclius Sam, To them Myranhamec Goliers

6   Enter ffrederick, Basilea. R Allen Dick To them Kinge Mr. Jubie To them Messenger Black Dick To them Sebastian Heraclius Theodore Pedro Phillippo Andreo Thamar. Mr Allen Sam : Mr Martyn. leadb: Dutton Pigg To them Leonora Will.

7   Enter ffrederick Bailea R Allen : Dick To them Philippo Duttonn To her King Frederick, Mr. Jubie R Allenn:

8   Enter Myron-hamec Sebastian Pedroe lords Tho: Towne Mr. Allenn, ledbeter Attendaunts

9   Enter King Theodore ffrederick Mr. Jubie, Mr Martyn R Allenn. To them Philipo Basilea E Dutton his boye Guard Tho: Hunt[Black Dick]Gatherers To them messenger Black Dick To them Sebastian Myron-hamec leonora Pedroe Andreo Mr. Allen: Tho Towne will: Leadbeter Pigg guard gatherers.

10   Enter ffrederick Basilea To them Pedro confederates Rob : leadb : Black Dick Gatherers.

11   Enter ffrederick Guard Mr Juby R allen Th: [Tow] Hunt &c. To them Sebastian [leonora] Theodore Myranhamec Guard mr Allen.Martyn To them Pedro Basilea upon the walls. come downe Pedro Basilea. ledb. : Dick

12   Enter Theodore Andreo . Mr Martyn Pigg To hym Thamar Heraclius Sam charles.

13   Enter ffrederick, Basilea, ffryer, R. Allen : Dick Mr Dunstann

14   Enter Heraclius Thamar Andreo, Sam. Charles Pigg. To them ffryer. Mr. Dunstann, to them Theodore Martynn

15   Enter ffrederick Basilea R. Allen Dick To them ffryer Mr Dunstann, To them Heraclius Sam

16   Enter Leonora Myronhamec, Sebastian Soliers Will: Mr Towne, Mr Allen Tho Hunt black Dick

17   To the queen Theodore Martynn

18   Enter Heraclius Thamar Sam charles to hym Theodore ffryer Dunstann Martyn To them Enter King Basilea ffrederick Messenger Mr Juby R Allen Dick Black Dick . To them Sebastian leonora Myronhamec Thamar Soliers Mr Allen will Tho Towne Charles . Tho : Hunt Black Dick gatheres.

E   Epilog R Allenn Finis:/

III Transcript
British Library, MS. Add. 10449, fol. 2

The Plott of the Battell of Alcazar

	Enter a Portingall [to him] mrRich:Allen to him
sound	1 Domb shew
sennet	Enter Muly Mahamett mr Ed: Allen, his sonne Antho: Jeffes: moores attendant:
1DS	mr Sam,mr Hunt & w. Cartwright: ij Pages to attend the moore mr Allens boy, mr Townes boy : to them 2 young brethren : Dab: & Harry: : to them Abdel(m)enen w Kendall: exeunt.
sound	Enter Aldelmelec : mr Doughton:
1	Calcepius bassa mr Jubie: Zareo mr Charles attendats wth (th)e Bassa: w.
sound	Kendall: Ro : Tailor & George (e) them Muly mahamet Xeque Abdula Rais & Ruben. H Jeffes, dick Jubie & Jeames :
sound	exeunt
sound	Enter in a Charriott Muly (M)ahamett &
sennett	Calipolis: on each side ( ) page (e) moores attendant Pisano mr Hunt & w.
2	Cartwright and young Mahamet Anthony Jeffes : exit mr Sam manet the rest: to
A)laru	them mr Sam a gaine exeunt
d)	E(n)ter the Presenter : to him
	2 domb shew
t)	En(te)r above Nemesis, Tho: Dro(m) to
2DS	them 3 ghosts w. kendall Dab (&) ines 3 t)o them (l)ying behind the Curt(a)
)brand &	Furies : Parsons : George &(l)or one
)Chopping	wth a whipp : a nother with a (b)lody tor
)knife :	(h):& the 3d with a Chop(p)kni(fe):exeunt

3sound Ch)airs bx)es for Pre(s)ents	Enter Abdelmelec, mahamet (X)ue, Zare(o) Calcepius Bassa [Adb] Abd(u R)ais : & Ruben : Attendants : mr Hunt (& G)eorge & young sonne Dab : exeunt
4	Enter Diego Lopis : Governor of Lisbo(n)e mr Rich : Allen : Stukeley : Jonas Hercules : & an Irish Bishopp mr Towne : Ro : Tailor : w Kendall & mr Shaa : exeunt
5) raw) flesh	Enter Mully Mahamet, Calipolis : young mahamet & 2 moores w. Cartwright & mr Hunt ex ( ) muly mahamet manet the rest : to them muly mahamet a gains wth raw flesh exeunt manet muly (:) exit
s u d) nett 6	Enter [2 Pages] Sebastian : a Page Jeames (:) Duke of Barecelis : mr Charles Duke of Avero : mr Jubie luis de Silva : mr Jones County Vinioso George : Christoporo de Tavora : Dick Jubie to them : 2 : moores : embassadors mr Sam mr Hunt & 2. Pages : exit moores : manet the rest : to them Stukeley Jonas, Hercules, & Irish Bishopp exeunt
3DS 3 violls of blood & a sheeps gather	Enter the Presenter : to [them] him 3 domb shew Enter Nemesis above : Tho: Drom (to) her 3 Furies bringin(g) in the(Scales : George Somersett (m P)ars(and Robin Tailo ( ) to them (3) div(mr Sam: H Jeffes (them 3 ghosts (:) w. (the Furies [Fech](& Carrie him out (Fech in Stukeley (bring in the Moo(r
sound 7	Enter: 2 bringin(g y Tor (ch) [mr Hunt] : W. Kend(all enter at one doore : Seba( ) D(e) of Avero : Stukeley : Pa(g) mes Jonas : & Hercules [th] to ( )t anothe(r) dore Embassadors of Spain(n r) Jones mr Charles : attendants Ge(o ge &) w Cartwright : exeun( ) manet Stu(kel)ey & Duke of Av(e) exeunt
8	Enter Governor ( ) Tan(ge)r (:) & A Captains mr Sha(a H) J(eff e)xeunt
sound 9	Enter at one d(o) w drom & cullors: (Duke of A(Hercules(att anoth(mr Shaa(m(r) Sam(them mu(l po) is

	an their (th) moores o(n)e on (n)ding young m(a)hame(t, & w C)right : & George : exeu(n)t

so(u)d
4DS
2 tap(
 	
Dead mens
heads
& bon(es)
banquett
blood
	Enter the Presenter : to him :
	      Domb shew
	E (n)er s (a)nquett br(ou ht) in by
	mr Hunt & W. Cartwri(g) the (
	banquett enter Sebastian : Muly
	mahamet Duke of Avero : & Stukeley
	to them De(a)th : & (3) F(ur) : mr
	Sam Ro: Tailor (G &) Parson(s
	one wth blood to Dy(li)ghts :
	(w)th Dead mens head(s) in dishes : an
	(o (t)h Dead mens bon( ) to the
	k da)ll[D] (.. (..)
	    )Furie (w (..) Jub
	                       exeunt

	Ma(att(e d mr [Joe Enter(Seba((wt & (t the(

IV Transcript
British Library, MS. Add. 10449, fol. 3

The plott of the First parte of *Tamar Cam*

C	Enter Chorus Dick Jubie
Sound Sennett 1 Sound flourish	Enter Mango Cham, 3 noblemen: Mr. Denygten 1 w. Cart. 2 & Tho. Marbeck & W. Parr. attendants: Parsons & George: To them Otanes: Tamar: & Colmogra: H. Jeffs: Mr. Allen & Mr. Burne. exit Mango & nobles: manet the rest Exit Tamor & Otanes manet Colmogra Exit.
2	Enter the Persian shaugh: Artaxes: Trebassus: Mr. Towne, Mr. Charles & Dick Jubie attendants: To them a Scowt: W. Parr: Exeunt.
Alarum: 3	Enter Tamor Cam: Otanes: Parsons Tho: Marbeck: & W. Cart: Exeunt.
Alarum. 4	Enter Assinico & a Persian : Mr. Singer & Parsons: To them Colmolgra Exeunt. manet Colmogra: To him Tamor Cam Otanes: 3 nobles: W. Cart: Tho:

Sound.

Marbeck: & W. Parr: Exit Colmogra To them Colmogra & Mango: guard George: parsons Exeunt, manet Colmogra: Exit

14

C

Enter Chorus Dick Jubie: Exit.

15

Thunder.

Enter Otanes: to him a spiritt: Parsons: To him another Spirritt: Pontus: Tho Marbeck:
To him another Diaphines: Dick Jubie.

5

To him another: Ascalon : Mr Sam : Exit Spirritts: To him Tamor Cam: Exit Tamor.
To him Spirritts againe: Exeunt.

Sound
6

Enter Colmogra: & 3 noblemen : W. Cart: Tho: Marbeck & W. Parr. To them Mango

---

7

Enter Otanes: to him Spirritts: Ascalon To him Diaphinies: Exeunt.

Sound.
8

Enter Colmogra: To him 3 nobles & a Drum: To them Assinico Drunk: To them Tamor Cam: Otanes: & guard: & George Parsons: To them Diaphines: Dick Jubie: Exeunt. manet clowne. Exit.

Sound
Alarm

9

Enter Tamor Cam : Otanes: attendants: W. Cart: W. Parr: & Tho. Marbeck: Parsons & George: To them a Trumpet. Dick Jubie:Exeunt.

C

Enter Chorus: exit.

10

Enter Colmogra: To him Otanes & Mr. Charles a pledge for Tamor: W.Cart: for the Persian Tho:Marbeck

---

Sound

11

Wind
horne

Enter at one dore Tamor Cam: Otanes: a Trompett: W. Parr: Attendaunts: Parsons: To him at another dore: the Persian Mr. Towne attendants Mr. Charles: Dick Jubie Exeunt. manet Tamor: Otanes & Persian: To them Colmogra like a post: Exit Colmogra: To Otanes enter Ascalon: Mr. Sam exeunt

---

Sound

12
Drum a
far of

Sound.

Sound.

Enter Colmogra: & 3 nobles: W.Cart: Tho: Marbeck & W. Parr: to them a Messinger: Tho. Parsons: To them an other Messinger: Dick Jubie. To them Tamor Cam: King of Persia: Tarmia his daughter Otanes: noblemen: Mr. Charles: Dick Jubie: Guard George & Parsons. Exeunt Otanes & nobles wth the 3 Rebbells: To them Otanes: wth a head. To them Mr. Charles wth an other head To them Dick Jubie wth an other head. Exeunt. manet Otanes. Exit.

13

Enter Captaine & guarde. George & Parsons: & W. Parr: Exeunt.

Enter Clowne, Ascalon & Diaphines: To them Otanes & Palmeda

Enter Tamia & Guard: Thom. Marbeck, Parsons: W. Parr & George: To her the orracle speakes Mr. Towne. Exeunt.

Enter Chorus

C

[Enter Otanes & Palmeda: Jack Jones to them] [2 spirits: Exeunt.]

Enter Cam : Otanes: attendants: W. Cart : & W. Parr : To them Tarmia the nurss Tho. Parsons wth children. Tho. Marbck: & George: To them Otanes & Palmida: & 2. spirritts: Exeunt. manet Tamor & Assinico: To them Palmida. Exeunt. manet Palmida. To herr Tamor Cam: To them Tarmia: To them guard: Tho. Marbeck: W. Parr: Parsons: To them the 2. spirritts : To them the Persian attendants: Mr. Charles: Parsons: George & soldiers: To them Colmogra: To them Tarmia & her 2 sonns: Jock grigerie & Mr. Denygtens little boy. Exeunt.

16

C

17

Enter Chorus

18

Enter Persian: Tarmia, nobles: Mr. Charles : Dick Jubie : & Mr. Bourne.

Enter Tamor Cam ; Otanes : & Palmeda To them Pitho & linus 2 Satires : & 2 nymphes, Heron, and Thia: Mr. Jubie, A. Jeffs. Jack Grigorie & the other little boy. To them Captaines: Tho. Marbeck: & W. Cartwright: To them Ascalon & Diaphines: to them Palmida: Exeunt.

19

Enter Attaxes: & Artabisus: Mr. Charles: Mr. Boone: attendants: George W. Parr: & Parsons: Drom and Cullers: To them Captaine Tho Marbeck: To them Tamor Cam: & Palmida & Otanes:

1. Enter the Tartars: Mr. Towne, Mr. Denygten.
2. Enter the Geates: Gedion & Gibbs.
3. Enter the Amozins: Jack Grigorie & little Will.
4. Enter the Nagars: Tho:Rowley: and the red fast fellow
5. Enter the ollive cullord moores: A. Jeffs Mr. Jubie
6. Enter Canniballs: Rester: old Browne.
7. Enter Hermophrodites: Jeames, Parsons.
8. Enter the people of Bohare: W. Parr: W. Cart.

9. Enter Pigmies: gils his boy & little will Barne.

10. Enter the Crymms: Mr. Sam. Ned Browne.

11. Enter Cattaians: Dick Jubie and George.

12. Enter the Bactrians: [W.Parr]: Th. Marbeck

FINIS

v Transcript
Plot in George Steevens's 'Variorum'
Shakespeare (1803)

Seven manuscript playbooks that identify actors in minor roles

Each of the seven manuscripts described here carries names or initials that identify one or more actors who play minor parts, and none of these characters speaks more than a few lines. This evidence is consistent with evidence about casting for minor roles in the eight playhouse documents discussed in chapter 2. In these texts, minor roles are usually described by function rather than by name: Messenger, Servant, Soldier, Guard, Fellow, and Captain. These parts are usually assigned to less experienced actors, probably hired men or playhouse attendants who joined the cast late in the rehearsal period.

1. *The Booke of Sir Thomas Moore* (A. Munday, H. Chettle [?], and others, c. 1590) British Library, MS. Harley 7368

The original text (S) is apparently in the hand of Anthony Munday, but Henry Chettle probably shared authorship with him. Five distinct hands appear in additions:
(A) Chettle, (B) Heywood, (C) an anonymous reviser, (D) Shakespeare (?), and (E) Dekker. In revision V, hand C adds a marginal note: '*Mess. T. Goodal*' opposite '*Enter a Messenger to moore*' (13a). Thomas Goodale is also identified in four small parts in the plot for *2SDS*, probably performed by an amalgamation of Lord Strange's Men and the Admiral's Men at the Theatre about 1590. My Table 81 describes the casting requirements for the original text (S), and it shows how ten men can play thirteen principal and six minor male roles. Two boys can play three principal female roles, and these twelve actors in principal roles speak 88% of the lines. These casting requirements are consistent with the average requirements for Shakespeare's plays (see Table 80). In other words, before Munday, or Chettle, or both, wrote the original text, they first drafted a plot with a cast of characters that was similar in size and composition to the casts of characters for Shakespeare's early plays. For example, in *2H6* (Q1-1594) nine men can play eleven principal and five minor male roles and two boys play two principal female roles; these eleven actors in principal roles speak 85% of the lines (Table 31). I cite the edition of W. W. Greg, *The Book of Sir Thomas More* (*MSR* 1911; repr. with a supplement by Harold Jenkins, 1961). Also see Scott McMillin, *The Elizabethan Theatre and the Book of Sir Thomas More* (Ithaca 1987); Peter W. M. Blayney, '*The Booke of Sir Thomas Moore* Re-examined', *SP* 69 (1972), 167–91; John Jowett, 'Henry Chettle and the Original Text of *Sir Thomas More*', in *Shakespeare and Sir Thomas More: Essays on the Play and its Shakespearian Interest*, ed. T. H. Howard-Hill (Cambridge 1989), pp. 131–49. S. Schoenbaum, *William Shakespeare: A Documentary Life* (Oxford 1975) offers a careful appraisal of the evidence that Shakespeare possibly wrote the revision in hand D (pp. 157–8).

2. *John of Bordeaux* or *The Second Part of Friar Bacon* (1590–1600) Alnwick Castle

This anonymous and untitled play is called *John of Bordeaux* after one of the leading characters. A theatrical reviser, probably the book-keeper, adds the name of John Holland in three places to identify him in two minor parts: a mute Messenger, '*John Holland with a letter*' (5b), and twice as a mute assistant to Vandermast: '*[E]nter john holland*' (7b) and '*Enter John Holland vandermast*' (12a). As we have seen, John Holland plays five small parts within the plot for *2SDS*, and he plays a rebel in *2H6*. I cite the edition of W. L. Renwick, *MSR* 1935 (1936); also see Scott McMillin, 'Casting for Pembroke's Men: The *Henry VI* Quartos and *The Taming of A Shrew*', *SQ* 23 (1972), 141–59.

3. *Richard II* or *Thomas of Woodstock* (c. 1592–5), British Library, MS. Egerton 1994[8]

This anonymous and untitled play dramatizes various events of Richard's reign between 1382 and 1397, and some scholars have seen it as a possible source for Shakespeare's *R2*. Although there are verbal correspondences between the two plays, it cannot be determined whether or not *Woodstock* preceded *R2*. The book-keeper adds three actors' names to the text, but these give no evidence about the possible date of performance or about the acting company: '*G[ ]ad*' (Grad?) is added before a speech-prefix for '*Mayre*' (162a); '*George*' is added above '*Enter a servant*' (172b); '*Toby*' is substituted for a speech-prefix, '*Ser[vant]*' (178b). Microfilm courtesy of the British Library. See W. B. Long, '"A bed/for woodstock": A Warning for the Unwary', *MRDE* 2 (1985), 91–118.

4. *The Two Noble Ladies* (1619–23) British Library, MS. Egerton1994[11]

This anonymous play was acted at the Red Bull by the Players of the Revels some time between 1619 and 1623. The text is prepared for performance by the book-keeper, who adds notes to identify five actors in small parts and to specify that a stage-keeper plays a Guard and a Soldier: '*Anth:Gibs:*' are apparently two actors who play soldiers (227a); '*guard Tay: Stage K:*' apparently refers to two guards (228b); '*Ent Anth Brew:*' appears opposite '*Enter Lord of Babilon with his sword drawn*'. The Lord speaks a total of nine lines (232a); '*Tay. Gib: Stage K.*' are added apparently for soldiers (233a); '*Ent Spirit Geo Stut*' appears at the foot of 234b, thus anticipating his entrance on the next page; '*Anth: Gibs:*' appears opposite '*Enter 2 Souldiers dragging Justina bound*', and '*Bond Sutf.*' appears opposite '*The Tritons dragge them in sounding their trumpets*' (235b); '*Tay:Gibs*' are added apparently for soldiers (236b). Thomas Bond is identified as Miscellanio in *HL* in 1631 (Table 28), and he was a leading actor with Prince Charles's (II) Men at Salisbury Court (Nungezer, p. 51). George Stutfield is identified as Bostar and a Soldier in *Han.* in 1635 (Table 27), and he was a leading actor with Queen Henrietta's Men (Nungezer, p. 342). Anthony Brew and H. Gibson played other minor parts in the 1630s (Nungezer, pp. 57 and 152). Microfilm courtesy of the British Library.

5. *The Captives or the Lost Recovered* (Heywood, 1624) British Library, MS. Egerton 1994[3]

Sir Henry Herbert, Master of the Revels, records a licence on 3 September 1624: 'For the Cockpit Company; a new play, called *The Captive or the Lost Recovered* written by Heyward' (*Herbert*, p. 29). The text, in Heywood's autograph, has been prepared for performance by the book-keeper, who identifies small parts played by three actors and stage-keepers: after '*Enter An abbot withhis Covent off frfyars, amongst them Fryar Jhon, and ffryar Ritchard*' is added '*Chaire*' to the left and '*Jack:Gibsen*' to the right (54a); '*Gib:Stage:Taylor*' is inserted three lines before '*A tumult with in and suddein noyse enter att one door godffrey with Contry Fewllows ffor theire reskewe*' to which is added '*[Gi]bs: Cont: fellowes*' (61b); after '*Enter Thomas Ashburne the yonger brother to Jhon a Merchant wth one off his factors*' is added '*Fact: Gibson*' (69a); after '*Enter The Abbot the baker ffryar Richard prisoner and guarded Etc*' is added '*stagekeepers as a guard*' (70a). As noted, H. Gibson is identified in other minor parts in the 1630s (Nungezer, p. 152). Microfilm courtesy of the British Library.

6. *Edmond Ironside* (1590–1600, revival 1632) British Library, MS. Egerton 1994[5]

This anonymous play was probably written in the late sixteenth century and revived by Prince Charles's (II) Men about 1632. The stage reviser adds names or initials to identify four men in minor parts: '*m: Grad: Stutf:*' play two Pledges (104b); '*H. Gibs:*' plays a '*messenger runinge*' (105b) and '*a Messenger*' (107a); '*mr gradell*' plays a '*Herrold*', and '*may*' plays '*1 Balife*' (107a); Henry Gradwell, Edward May, and George Stutfield, were Prince Charles's (II) Men in 1632; H. Gibson was probably a hired man with that company (Nungezer, pp. 159, 249, 340, 152). Microfilm courtesy of the British Library.

7. *The Wasp* or *Subject's Precedent* (c. 1635) Alnwick Castle

This anonymous manuscript – bound with, but not otherwise related to, *John of Bordeaux* – was prepared for performance by a book-keeper whose warnings in the left margin identify six actors in minor parts: '*Jordan*' anticipates by ten lines '*Enter Capt. Jordan*' (7a); '*Barot*' anticipates by fourteen lines '*Enter serv.*' (10b); '*Morris*' and '*Noble*' anticipate by thirty lines '*enter . . . officers*' (13a); '*Barrot*' anticipates '*Messenger*' (15a); '*Ambris*' anticipates by nine lines '*Enter . . . Lords*' (19b). I cite the edition of J. W. Lever, *MSR* 1974 (1976). Thomas Jordan and John Barret, who appear as thirteenth and fifteenth in the list of the King's Revels company in Norwich on 10 March 1635 (*JCS* 1, p. 286) are also named in the cast list for *Mess.* about 1635 (Table 27), where they are identified in female roles, as is Mathias Morris. Ellis Bedowe is twenty-first in the Norwich list of 1635, and Ambrose Matchit was probably the boy who played 'filius'; nothing further is known of Noble. See J. W. Lever, '*The Wasp*: A Trial Flight', in *The Elizabethan Theatre IV*, ed. G. R. Hibbard (Toronto 1974), pp. 74–5.

Order of the Master of the Revels protecting musicians and 'necessary attendants' from arrest, 27 December 1624

Theise are to Certefie you That Edward Knight, William Pattrick, William Chambers, Ambrose Byland, Henry Wilson, Jeffery Collins, William Sanders, Nicholas Underhill, Henry Clay, George Vernon, Roberte Pallant [Jr], Thomas Tuckfeild, Robert Clarke, [George Rickner *deleted*] John Rhodes, William Mago, Anthony Knight [*marginal insert* Edward Ashborne, William Carver, Allexander Bollard, William Toyer, William Gascoyne] are all imployed by the Kinges Majesties servantes in theire quallity of Playinge as Musitions and other necessary attendantes, And are att all tymes and howers to bee readie with theire best endeavours to doe his Majesties service (dureinge the tyme of the Revells) in Which tyme they nor any of them are to bee arested, or deteyned under arest, imprisoned, Press'd for Souldiers, or any other molestation Whereby they may bee hindered from doeing his Majesties service. Without leave firste had and obteyned of the Lord Chamberlyne of his Majesties most honourable household, or of the Maister of his Majesties Revells. And if any shall presume to interrupt or deteyne them or any of them after notice hereof given by this my Certificate, hee is to aunswere itt att his utmost perill. Given att his Majesties Office of the Revells under my hand and Seale the xxviith day of December, 1624.

H. Herbert

To all Mayors, Sheriffes, Justices of the Peace, Bayleiffes, Constables, knight Marshalls men, and all other his Mojesties Officers to whom it may or shall assperteyne.

(British Library MS Add. 19256, p. 44, as cited by *JCS* 1, pp. 15–16)

My text identifies eleven of the twenty-two men named in this document: Edward Knight is the book-keeper for *BAYL*, *SC*, and *HMF*; William Patrick, Nicholas Underhill, and William Mago play minor parts in *BAYL*; John Rhodes and George Rickner play minor parts in *HMF*; Thomas Tuckfeild plays a minor part in *TNK*; William Gascoyne, a stage-keeper, opens a trap door in *BAYL*; William Tawyer is named 'with a trumpet' in a stage direction for *MND*. Two men are identified in lesser principal parts: George Vernon plays 1 Creditor (46 lines) in *HMF*, and Robert Pallant, Jr plays a Doctor (42 lines) and an Officer (4 lines) in *DM* (1623 cast).

Notes

1 Introduction

1 T. W. Baldwin, *Shakespere's Five-Act Structure* (Urbana 1947), contends that Shakespeare wrote his plays to conform with a five-act structure derived from classical drama. However, other scholars have shown this hypothesis to be inadequate and misleading, primarily because act and scene division is not found in any of Shakespeare's plays published in his lifetime. Although some plays in F are divided into acts and scenes, this division is not applied consistently; division was not assigned to all of Shakespeare's plays until Nicholas Rowe's edition of 1709. For other studies of this problem, see W. T. Jewkes, *Act-division in Elizabethan and Jacobean Plays 1583–1616* (Hamden, Conn. 1958); Henry Snuggs, *Shakespeare and Five Acts* (Washington 1960); Emrys Jones, *Scenic Form in Shakespeare* (Oxford 1971); Mark Rose, *Shakespearean Design* (Cambridge, Mass. 1972).

2 Chambers observes: 'The shares were often subdivided, so that some members of the company were full sharers, others half sharers or three-quarter sharers.' He adds in a note: 'The number of players named in Jacobean patents varies from 7 to 14, but this gives us little direct guidance as to the number of sharers' (*ES* 1, pp. 354, and 354 n. 3). Also see S. P. Cerasano, 'The "Business" of Shareholding, the Fortune Playhouses, and Francis Grace's Will', *MRDE* 2 (1985), 231–51.

3 Baldwin, *Organization*, pp. 229–83.

4 *Ibid.*, p. 187.

5 *Ibid.*

6 Bevington, p. 6.

7 *Ibid.*, p. 269.

8 *Ibid.*, p. 103.

9 As cited by Bevington, p. 103.

10 *Ibid.*, p. 205.

11 *Ibid.*, p. 207.

12 *Ibid.*, p. 221.

13 *Ibid.*, p. 236.

14 *Ibid.*, p. 257.

15 Ringler, pp. 112–13.

16 Sprague, p. 35.

17 Ringler, p. 113.

18 *Ibid.*, p. 125.

19 *JCS* 1, p. 80.

20 *Herbert*, p. 31.

21 Cerasano notes that not all the available players with the Admiral's Men acted in every

play for that company, 'The "Business" of Shareholding', p. 235.

22 Ringler, p. 126.

23 *Ibid.*, p. 132.

24 The financial arrangements between Henslowe and the Admiral's Men were probably similar to those described in articles of agreement between Philip Henslowe and Jacob Meade, as one party, and Lady Elizabeth's Men represented by Nathan Field, as the other party, about 1613. These state that for three years Henslowe and Meade will 'fynde and provide a sufficient howse or howses for the saide Company to play in . . . and duringe the saide tearme disburse and lay out all suche some or somes of monny [to provide] the said Company wth playinge apparrell towarde the settinge out of their new plays . . . and lay out . . . somes of monny . . . to be paide for any play which they shall buy or condition or agree for [provided that] the saide Company shall truly repay the saide Philipp and Jacob', *Papers*, pp. 23–4; also see Neil Carson, *A Companion to Henslowe's Diary* (Cambridge 1988), *passim*.

25 *Diary*, p. 85.

26 *Ibid.*, p. 100.

27 As cited in *Documents* I, p. 5. Facsimiles of recto and verso are reproduced in *Documents* I, between pp. 4 and 5.

28 *Papers*, p. 49.

29 *Diary*, p. 126.

30 *Ibid.*, p. 167.

31 *Papers*, p. 57.

32 *Diary*, p. 181.

33 *Ibid.*, p. 182.

34 *Papers*, p. 84.

35 *Documents* I, p. 96.

36 *Papers*, p. 73.

37 *Documents* I, p. 176–81; also see W. W. Greg, *Two Elizabethan Stage Abridgements* (Oxford 1923).

38 Fol. 262, as cited in *Documents* II.

39 Fol. 264, as cited in *Documents* II.

40 As cited by Chambers *WS* I, p. 106 n. 4.

41 *Papers*, p. 124.

42 *JCS* II, p. 688.

43 *Diary*, pp. 268–9.

44 *Diary*, p. 92.

45 *Ibid.*

46 *Ibid.*, p. 94.

47 *Documents* I, p. 19; also see Bernard Beckerman, 'Theatrical Plots and Elizabethan Stage Practice', in *Shakespeare and Dramatic Tradition: Essays in Honor of S. F. Johnson*, ed. W. R. Elton and W. B. Long (Newark, Del. 1989), pp. 109–24.

48 *Documents* I, p. 123.

49 *Ibid.*, p. 146.

50 *Ibid.*, p. 161.

51 *The Battell of Alcazar* (1594); also see W. W. Greg, *Two Elizabethan Stage Abridgements*.

52 *Herbert*, p. 19.

53 *Ibid.*, p. 20.

54 *Ibid.*, pp. 17–18.
55 *JCS* II, p. 688.
56 *Ibid.*
57 *Ibid.*
58 See T. J. King, 'The Versatility of Shakespeare's Actors', in *Shakespeare and Dramatic Tradition*, pp. 144–50.
59 *JCS* II, p. 602.
60 *Ibid.*, pp. 476–7. Robert Pallant, Jr. was baptized on 28 September 1605, and Bentley suggests that Pallant played Cariola (58 lines) in the earlier cast of *DM* (c. 1614) when he was about nine and the Doctor (42 lines) in a revival (1623) when he was about eighteen. On 27 December 1624, the Master of the Revels lists him as a hired man with the King's Men (see Appendix C); *JCS* II, p. 520.

Alexander Goughe was baptized on 7 August 1614; he played Caenis, a concubine (37 lines), in *RA*, licensed on 11 October 1626; he played Acanthe (20 lines) in *Pict.*, licensed on 8 June 1629; he played Fewtricks, a boy (129 lines), in *SC* (1630?); he played Eurinia (164 lines) in *Swis.* (1631); he played Lillia-Bianca (357 lines) in a 1632 revival of *WGC*; on 17 May 1636, Goughe is named on a list of hired men for the King's Men, *JCS* II, p. 447.
61 *Diary*, p. 21.
62 *WS* II, p. 342.
63 Contemporary allusions indicate that Burbage plays at least four other leading Shakespeare roles: King Richard III, Hamlet, King Lear, and Othello; Nungezer, p. 70.
64 For example, Stephen Booth, 'Doubling in Shakespeare's Plays', in *Shakespeare: The Theatrical Dimension*, ed. Philip C. Maguire and David A. Samuelson (New York 1979), pp. 103–31, revives the idea that since Cordelia and the Fool are never on stage at the same time, it is possible for the same boy actor to play both parts. If this were done, Booth contends, then Lear's line 'And my poor fool is hang'd' takes on 'extra dimension in a play notable for irreverence of definitions and ideational boundaries' (p. 103). Booth is careful to note that his speculations are just that (p. 109) and that his essay 'does not pretend to add to our knowledge of Renaissance stage practices' (p. 127). Nevertheless, he apparently overlooks some historical evidence. The Fool was first played by Robert Armin, who had probably joined the Lord Chamberlain's Men as an adult in 1599 (*ES* II, p. 300); Armin was undoubtedly an adult when his daughter Elizanna was baptized on 11 May 1603 (Nungezer, p. 18) and when *Lear* was performed at court on 26 December 1606 (*WS* I, p. 468). Furthermore, in the extant plays that identify actors in principal roles, there is no example of an adult actor playing a principal female role, nor is there an example of a boy playing a principal adult male role. Thus while it is possible for the same actor to play Cordelia and the Fool, such doubling would be contrary to usual casting procedures for Shakespeare's company. Sprague notes that Armin's age 'makes it most unlikely that he played Cordelia as well [as the Fool]', *Doubling of Parts*, p. 34.
65 Eugene M. Waith (ed.), *Titus Andronicus* (Oxford 1984) includes a chart showing a possible doubling scheme for a company of at least twenty-seven actors, including boys, p. 217.
66 Folio, p. 203.
67 One should keep in mind Greg's caveat about determining the probable source of printer's copy for playbooks: 'We enter . . . a misty mid region of Weir, a land of shadowy shapes and melting outlines, where not even the most patient inquiry and the most penetrating analysis can hope to arrive at any but tentative and proximate conclusions'

Folio, p. 105. A careful re-appraisal of bibliographical and textual studies that attempt to identify the possible sources of printer's copy is offered by Paul Werstine, 'Narratives About Printed Shakespearean Texts: "Foul Papers" and "Bad" Quartos', *SQ* 41 (1990), 65–86.

2 Eight playhouse documents

1 *The Dead Man's Fortune* (1590) lists 'Burbage' as an actor, but the part he plays is uncertain. The other actors listed are 'Darlowe', 'Robert Lee', and 'b samme', who apparently play minor parts; a 'tire-man' plays an attendant. See *Documents* I, p. 94–101, and Appendix A, Transcript I. Two other plots from Elizabethan playhouses survive, but only in fragments and neither provides adequate evidence for the study of casting: *2 Fortune's Tennis* (1597–98) and *Troilus and Cressida* (1599); see *Documents* I, pp. 130–8).

2 *The Battell of Alcazar* (1594).

3 *ES* II, p. 126.

4 See Greg on 'Actors' Names', *Folio*, pp. 114–20.

5 *Documents* I, p. 38.

6 *Diary*, p. xxxix.

7 S. P. Cerasano, 'The "Business" of Shareholding, the Fortune Playhouses, and Francis Grace's Will', *MRDE* 2 (1985), 235; also see S. P. Cerasano, 'Anthony Jeffes, Player and Brewer', *N&Q* 31 (1984), 220–5.

8 *Diary*, p. 8.

9 *Diary*, p. 50.

10 *Diary*, p. 84.

11 *Diary*, p. 87.

12 *Diary*, p. 136.

13 *Diary*, p. 198.

14 Andrew Gurr, *The Shakespearean Stage*, 2nd ed. (Cambridge 1980), p. 36.

15 As cited by D. T. Starnes and E. W. Talbert, *Classical Myth and Legend in Renaissance Dictionaries* (Chapel Hill 1955), p. 219.

16 *Documents* I, p. 123.

17 *Diary*, p. 241.

18 *ES* III, p. 459.

19 *Diary*, pp. 16–19.

20 *Documents* I, pp. 146–7.

21 See W. W. Greg, *Two Elizabethan Stage Abridgements* (Oxford 1923), p. 113.

22 *Documents* I, pp. 160–1.

23 See Anne Lancashire (ed.), *The Second Maiden's Tragedy* (Manchester 1978), p. 18; also see Eric Rasmussen, 'Shakespeare's Hand in *The Second Maiden's Tragedy*', *SQ* 40 (1989), 1–26.

24 *JCS* II, p. 550.

25 *JCS* III, p. 415.

26 See F. P. Wilson, 'Ralph Crane, Scrivener to the King's Players', *Library*, 4th ser., 7 (1926), 194–215; T. H. Howard-Hill, *Ralph Crane and Some Shakespeare First Folio Comedies* (Charlottesville 1972).

27 T. H. Howard-Hill (ed.), *Sir John van Olden Barnavelt* (Oxford 1980), p. iv. Also see T. H. Howard-Hill, 'Buc and the Censorship of *Sir John van Olden Barnavelt* in 1619', *RES* n.s. 39 (1988), 39–63.

28 T. H. Howard-Hill, 'Crane's 1619 "Promptbook" of *Barnavelt* and Theatrical Processes', *MP* 86 (1988), 146–70.

29 *JCS* II, p. 547.

30 *JCS* II, p. 551.

31 *ES* III, p. 227.

32 As cited by *Herbert*, p. 30.

33 *ES* III, p. 227.

34 J. Gerritsen (ed.), *The Honest Man's Fortune* (Djakarta 1952), pp. xxviii–xxix.

35 *JCS* II, p. 611.

36 As cited by *Herbert*, p. 19.

37 C. J. Sisson (ed.), *Believe as you List* (Oxford 1927), p. xix.

38 *MSC* II, p. 350.

39 *JCS* II, p. 688.

40 *JCS* II, p. 476, 451, 425, 362.

41 *JCS* II, p. 474.

42 *JCS* II, p. 354.

43 Sisson, p. xxxiii and D. Bradley, 'The Ignorant Elizabethan Author and Massinger's *Believe as you List*', *Sidney Studies in English* 2 (1976–7), 98–125, contend that in *BAYL* several parts are each played by more than one actor. However, neither scholar takes into account the evidence about casting in the playhouse plots, where only one actor is assigned to any one part.

3 Fifteen plays that identify actors in principal roles

1 *ES* II, p. 208.

2 *ES* II, p. 211.

3 *WS* II, p. 75.

4 *JCS* I, p. 7.

5 *JCS* I, p. 8.

6 *JCS* I, p. 14.

7 *MSC* II, pp. 325–6.

8 *JCS* I, p. 17.

9 *MSC* II, p. 350.

10 The petitioners, Benfield, Pollard, and Swanston, assert that although they have 'a long time and with much patience expected to be admitted Sharers in ye playhouses of the Globe and Blackfriers' they have been disappointed. As sharers in the acting company – but not in the playhouses – they get only the receipts at the outer doors and half the receipts from the galleries and boxes, and from this sum they must pay the wages of hired men and boys, the cost of lights, music, and other theatre expenses. However, the housekeepers get half the takings from the galleries and boxes at the Globe and Blackfriars and all the receipts from the tiring house door at the Globe; see *MSC* II, pp. 362–5.

11 *ES* III, p. 511.

12 *JCS* II, p. 520.

13 *Herbert*, p. 31.

14 *JCS* I, p. 18.

15 *MSC* II, pp. 325–6.

16 *Ibid.*

17 *JCS* III, p. 115.

18 *JCS* I, p. 24.

19 *Herbert*, p. 32.
20 *JCS* I, p. 24.
21 *JCS* III, p. 165.
22 John Henry Pyle Pafford (ed.), *The Soddered Citizen* (Oxford 1926), p. viii; J. Gerritsen (ed.) *The Honest Man's Fortune*, p. 50.
23 *MSC* II, p. 350.
24 *Documents* I, p. 361.
25 *MSC* II, p. 350.
26 *JCS* II, p. 451.
27 *JCS* III, p. 429.
28 *MSC* II, p. 350.
29 *JCS* I, p. 247.
30 *Ibid.*
31 *JCS* II, p. 688.
32 *JCS* I, p. 247.
33 *Ibid.*
34 *Ibid.*
35 *JCS* V, p. 1,164.
36 *JCS* II, p. 688.
37 *Herbert*, p. 28.
38 *JCS* II, p. 688.
39 *JCS* IV, pp. 568–70.
40 *JCS* II, p. 688.
41 *JCS* IV, p. 570.
42 *JCS* II, p. 688.
43 *JCS* III, p. 233.
44 *JCS* II, p. 688.
45 *JCS* I, p. 247.
46 *Ibid.*
47 *JCS* II, p. 688.
48 *Herbert*, p. 45.
49 *JCS* II, p. 688.
50 *JCS* V, p. 1,003.
51 *JCS* II, p. 688.
52 Bentley, *Profession*, p. 282.
53 *JCS* II, p. 688.
54 *Ibid.*
55 *JCS* , p. 247.
56 *JCS* II, p. 688.
57 *Herbert*, p. 32.
58 *JCS* II, p. 476.

4 Thirty-eight plays by Shakespeare

1 *WS* I, pp. 243–74.
2 See William Montgomery, 'The Original Staging of *The First Part of the Contention* (1594)', *ShS* 41 (1989), 13–22; also see Scott McMillin, 'Casting for Pembroke's Men: The *Henry VI* Quartos and *The Taming of A Shrew*', *SQ* 23 (1972), 141–59.

3 Nungezer, pp. 336–7.

4 *Ibid.*, pp. 326–7.

5 *Ibid.*, pp. 204–5; also see S. P. Cerasano, 'Anthony Jeffes, Player and Brewer', *N&Q* 31 (1984), 220–5.

6 *WS* I, p. 292.

7 *WS* II, pp. 319–331.

8 *Diary*, pp. 21–2.

9 In both Q1 and F, the supernumeraries who play the followers of Saturninus and Bassanius have the direction '*Exit Soldiers*' (1.1.55), and these actors can therefore double as '*others as many as can be*' with Titus on his triumphal entrance (1.1.69).

10 The relation of *A Shrew* to *Shr.* has long been a matter of scholarly controversy, with three principal theories advanced: 1. that *A Shrew* was the main source for *Shr.*; 2. that both texts were derived from a now lost play, the *Ur-Shrew*; 3. that *A Shrew* is a pirated version of *Shr.* Richard Hosley provides convincing arguments to refute the first two theories and to support the third. He shows how in *Shr.* Shakespeare uses a wide variety of sources and how the anonymous author or authors of *A Shrew* deliberately altered the text of *Shr.* See Hosley, 'Sources and Analogues of *The Taming of the Shrew*', *HLQ* 27 (1964), 289–308.

11 Nungezer, pp. 326–7.

12 *Herbert*, p. 53.

13 *WS* II, pp. 331-2.

14 *Folio*, p. 223.

15 *Folio*, p. 225.

16 *Folio*, pp. 231–2.

17 *Folio*, p. 236.

18 *WS* II, pp. 325, 348.

19 *King Richard the Second*, ed. Andrew Gurr (Cambrige 1984), p. 176.

20 An actor with a trumpet is also specified in the plot for *1 Tamar Cam*, scene 9: 'To them a Trumpet Dick Jubie'; this plot identifies Jubie in seven other small parts.

21 *Folio*, p. 243.

22 *Folio*, p. 250.

23 *Folio*, p. 258.

24 *WS* II, p. 332.

25 *WS* II, pp. 322, 343, 347, 353.

26 *Shakespeare's Plays in Quarto* (Berkeley 1981), p. xxiii.

27 *Folio*, p. 266.

28 *Folio*, p. 279.

29 *WS* II, p. 347.

30 *Folio*, p. 279.

31 *WS* II, p. 331. G. P. Jones, '"Henry V": The Chorus and the Audience', *ShS* 31 (1978), 93–104, offers strong arguments that the Chorus, found only in F, reflects an unrecorded performance of *H5* at the Royal Cockpit.

32 *Folio*, p. 282.

33 *Henry V*, ed. Gary Taylor (Oxford 1982), p. 22.

34 As translated by Ernest Schanzer, 'Thomas Platter's Observations on the English Stage', *N&Q* 201 (1956), 466.

35 *WS* II, pp. 322, 343, 353.

36 *WS* II, p. 329.

37 *WS* II, pp. 327–8, 346.

38 Alan H. Nelson observes: 'In view of the many prohibitions at Cambridge, including the privy council letter of 29 July 1593 and various payments to companies in lieu of performance, it may be questioned whether the lord chamberlain's players would have been permitted to play even though they did visit Cambridge in 1594–5; the claim of the [Q1] title page . . . may be a printer's groundless boast', *Cambridge*, ed. Alan H. Nelson, Records of Early English Drama (Toronto 1989), II, p. 985.

39 *Hamlet*, ed. G. R. Hibbard (Oxford 1987), p. 126.

40 *WS* II, pp. 346, 353.

41 *WS* II, 331, 353.

42 Gerald D. Johnson, '*The Merry Wives of Windsor*, Q1: Provincial Touring and Adapted Texts', *SQ* 38 (1987), 154–65, offers a 'Hypothetical Casting Pattern for Fourteen Actors'. However, in addition to these fourteen actors Johnson includes four boys for the last scene in Q. This brings his total to eighteen actors, or close to the thirteen men and eight boys that I suggest in Table 62.

43 *Folio*, p. 340.

44 *WS* I, p. 450.

45 For example, *Barn.* identifies 'migh' as the actor who plays 2 English Captain (39 lines); he also plays an English Soldier (4 lines), 2 Dutch Captain (9 lines), and 1 Huntsman (1 line); see Table 10.

46 *WS* I, p. 453.

47 *WS* II, pp. 331, 336, 343, 348, 352, 353.

48 *W&T*, p. 529. Also see Steven Urkowitz, *Shakespeare's Revision of* King Lear (Princeton 1980) and *The Division of the Kingdoms: Shakespeare's Two Versions of* King Lear, ed. Gary Taylor and Michael Warren (Oxford 1983).

49 *WS* II, p. 337.

50 *WS* II, pp. 338–9, 352.

51 *WS* II, pp. 340, 346–7, 352.

52 *WS* II, pp. 342–3.

53 *ES* II, p. 419.

54 Cyrus Hoy, 'The Shares of Fletcher and his Collaborators in the Beaumont and Fletcher Canon VII', *SB* 15 (1962), 76, assigns authorship as follows:

> Fletcher: 1.3–4; 3.1; 5.2–4.
> Shakespeare: 1.1–2; 2.3–4; 3.2a (to exit of King); 5.1.
> Fletcher and Shakespeare: 2.1–2; 3.2b (from exit of King to end); 4.1–2.

However, R. A. Foakes reviews the arguments for joint authorship – based mainly on studies of spelling and style – and notes that although the case 'seems to be a strong one . . . most of the evidence is suspect on one ground or another'. He concludes that Fletcher's share, if any, is 'considerably less than the usual division ascribed to him', *King Henry the Eighth* (Arden 1957), p. xxv.

55 *WS* II, p. 335.

56 *WS* I, pp. 520–2.

57 *WS* II, p. 346.

58 Cyrus Hoy, 'Shares of Fletcher and his Collaborators in the Beaumont and Fletcher Canon (VII)' *SB* 15 (1962), 71.

59 *Folio*, p. 98, note A.

60 *WS* I, p. 530.

61 As Table 80 indicates, in at least four of Shakespeare's plays the requirements for principal actors differ significantly from the average of about ten men and four boys in principal roles. For each of these variations I suggest an explanation that lacks positive proof: 1. *1H6* requires fifteen men in principal male roles, and this variation may be the result of multiple authorship, which is suggested by *W&T* (p. 217); 2. *Tro.* requires fourteen men in principal male roles, but this play may have been written for private performance, as Greg suggests (*Folio*, p. 340); 3. *H8* requires thirteen men in principal male roles, and Cyrus Hoy suggests this play was written by Shakespeare in collaboration with Fletcher (*SB* 15 (1962), 76); 4. *Tim.* has no principal female roles, and the ten men in principal male roles speak only 83% of the lines, considerably less than the average of 95% spoken by actors in principal roles in the other Shakespeare plays. This irregularity may be caused by a hand other than Shakespeare, perhaps Middleton, who is suggested as part author of *Tim.* by *W&T* (p. 501).

Index of persons

Index of plays

Index of subjects